Volume II **Crime and Insanity in England**

Daniel M'Naghten in Bethlem, about 1855

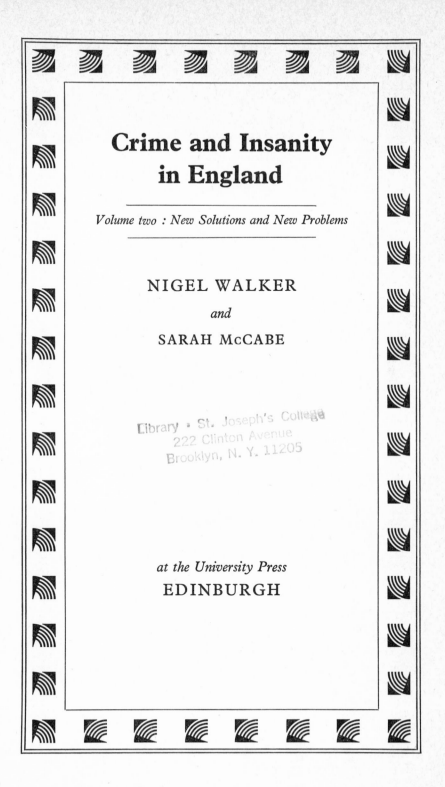

Crime and Insanity
in England

Volume two : New Solutions and New Problems

NIGEL WALKER

and

SARAH McCABE

at the University Press
EDINBURGH

© Nigel Walker and Sarah McCabe 1973

EDINBURGH UNIVERSITY PRESS
22 George Square, Edinburgh

ISBN 0 85224 228 X

North America
Aldine · Atherton Inc.
529 South Wabash Avenue, Chicago

Library of Congress
Catalog Card Number 68-19882

Printed in Great Britain by
T. and A. Constable Ltd, Edinburgh

Preface

This volume is concerned with what might be called 'the utilitarian revolution' in the trial and disposal of the disordered offender, as a result of which the defence of insanity and the kindred legal devices with which Volume I is concerned have receded into numerical insignificance.

Revolutions usually begin some time before they are noticed, and the utilitarian revolution has been no exception. Consequently, although most of this volume consists of a description of the working of Part V of the Mental Health Act, 1959 in the sixties, we make no apology for going back to its origins in the administrative difficulties of the prisons in the nineteenth century. Our story begins with the provision of a special wing for criminal lunatics in Bethlem, which eventually develops into the Special Hospitals as we know them today. The next chapter (chapter 2) is concerned with the transfer of prisoners to these and other establishments, beginning in the nineteenth century but ending with a survey of those transferred in a twelvemonth in 1966–7. At no time, however, has this system of transfers relieved the gaols of all disordered inmates; and chapter 3 is therefore concerned with the prison service's efforts to cope with certain residual problems. In chapter 4 we show how the prisons' efforts to rid themselves of some of their problems led to legislation which–by a series of rather muddled developments–culminated in the 1959 Act.

Those who find history boring may prefer to begin at chapter 5, which describes the way in which the criminal courts have applied the Act. This is followed by a chapter which describes our one-year cohort of hospital order cases, collected in the middle of the nineteen-sixties. The next two chapters, 7 and 8, follow this cohort into hospital and in many cases out of it and back again to hospital or prison as the case may be. Finally, there are two chapters–one of them unrepentantly historical–dealing with that special sub-group of offender-patients which the collusion of psychiatrists and lawyers has endowed with a pseudo-diagnostic label, 'psychopathic disorder'.

There are one or two aspects of the system which we have not been able to study with sufficient thoroughness to enable us to describe them in this book. One is the guardianship order, which was–and still is–too uncommon to allow of safe generalisations. Another is the process by which an offender is recognised as disordered by police, courts, probation officers, prison doctors or other agents of the system. A third is the situations in which offenders who are recognised as disordered are disposed of without prosecution; but we have felt able to make a few observations on this subject in Appendix A. The main theme of both volumes, however, is the detention and treatment of the offender who is officially recognised as mentally disordered, and the problems which he poses not only for the traditional moralist but also for the utilitarian reformer.

Nigel Walker
Sarah McCabe
Oxford, January 1972

Contents

Tables and Figures

The Frontispiece and Figure 1 are reproduced by kind permission
of the Archivist, Bethlem Royal Hospital.

Acknowledgments

So many people have helped in the collection of our data and the writing of this book—whether by advising us on method, suggesting sources and interpretations or commenting on draft chapters—that it would take several pages to do justice to their contributions. In many cases their assistance with specific problems has been acknowledged in footnotes; and all we can do here is record our gratitude to: Miss Patricia Allderidge, Archivist of Bethlem Royal Hospital; Dr J.A.Baldwin, Director of the Oxford Record Linkage Study; Mr Norman Bishop, now at the Kriminal-vårdstyrelsen, Stockholm; Mr P.Burgess, now Lecturer at Dundee University; Mr R.A.Carr-Hill, now Lecturer at Sussex University; Mr D.J. Cowperthwaite, of the Scottish Home and Health Department; Professor A.R.N.Cross, of All Souls College, Oxford; Mr P.Duncan-Jones, Research Fellow of Nuffield College, Oxford; Dr Mary Ellis, of Feltham Borstal; Dr W.Gray, Medical Superintendent and Governor of Grendon Prison; Dr J.Gunn, of the Institute of Psychiatry, University of London; Dr K.Hope, Lecturer in Methods of Social Research and Fellow of Nuffield College, Oxford; Miss Christine Kennedy, Librarian of Nuffield College, and her staff; Professor V. Kudriavtzev, of the All-Union Institute for the Study of the Causes of Crime etc., Moscow; Mrs Judy Lay, of the Chilton Computer Laboratory; Dr F.J.Letemendia of the Ashurst Clinic, Oxford; Dr J.McDougall, Medical Superintendent, Moss Side Hospital; Dr W.Ll.Parry-Jones, of the Oxford University Department of Psychiatry; Mrs Frances Partridge; Mr C.Payne, Senior Research Officer of the Nuffield College Research Services Unit; Mr P.J.Pope, of the Institute of Psychiatry, University of London; Dr H.R.Rollin, of Horton Hospital; Dr Rosemary Rue, Senior Administrative Medical Officer, Oxford Regional Hospital Board; Dr S.Spencer, of the Warneford Hospital, Oxford; Dr T.G.Tennent, Director of the Special Hospitals Research Unit; Dr C. Treves-Brown, of the Special Hospitals Research Unit; Dr A.Walk, Librarian of the Royal College of Psychiatrists; Miss Anita Warneford, St Anne's College, Oxford.

Government Departments and other agencies: The Home Office, and especially its Research Unit, Statistical Division, Criminal Divisions, Prison Department and Prison Medical Service; The Department of Health and Social Security, including its Central Offices at Blackpool and Newcastle; The Criminal Record Office, Scotland Yard; The Ethical Committee of the British Medical Association.

Psychiatric Advisers: Dr P. G. McGrath, Physician Superintendent, Broadmoor Hospital; Dr Ian Skottowe, formerly Consultant at the Warneford Hospital, Oxford.

Research Assistants at various times: Miss Barbara Allen, Mrs Margaret Cameron, Miss Sheila Cohen, Mrs Kate Cooper, Miss Sarah Hanger, Mrs Constance Rollett, Mrs Alexandra Seddon and Miss Joan Watson.

Secretaries: Miss Jenny Butler, Nuffield College, Oxford; Mrs Gill Ashworth, Mrs Nancy Bartrum, Miss Jan Chapman and Miss Katherine Smyth (formerly or now at the Penal Research Unit, Oxford).

Finally, we have not overlooked the contributions of all the police forces and hospital staffs who so conscientiously completed our dossiers and questionnaires (see pp. 114 and 115).

Some short passages in this book have already appeared in articles in *Medicine, Science and the Law,* the CIBA Foundation's *Symposium on Mentally Abnormal Offenders* (1968) and the Proceedings of the Cambridge Institute of Criminology's Cropwood Conference on *Psychopathic Offenders* (1968), to all of which we should like to make due acknowledgment.

Note on Terms

To save cumbersome phrases, especially in the chapters
dealing with the Oxford survey, we have used the term

'the Act' or 'the 1959 Act' to mean the Mental Health Act, 1959;

'admissions' to mean admissions to psychiatric hospitals, or persons so
admitted;

'current offence' to mean the offence leading to the hospital order,
guardianship order or prison sentence which brought the offender
into one of our samples;

'depressive' to include 'manic-depressive';

'disorder' to mean mental disorder as defined in Section 4 of the 1959 Act
(see pp. 82-5);

'hospitals' or 'psychiatric hospitals' to mean hospitals for the mentally ill
or subnormal;

juveniles' to mean persons under the age of 17;

'men' and 'women' to include juveniles (but very few of our subjects were
juveniles);

'NS' to indicate that there is a high probability that a difference is due to
chance (i.e. that $p > 0.05$, see 'p' below).

'offender-patient' to mean any person who has become a patient in a
psychiatric hospital as a result of a decision of a criminal court;

'our' to mean 'from the Oxford sample of hospital or guardianship orders'
(see pp. 113-15);

'p' to mean the probability that a difference is due to nothing more than
chance;

'psychopath' to include any patient whose predominant disorder was said
to be one of personality, however described.

The real names of offender-patients are not used unless they
have already been disclosed in the Press or in a law report.

Chapter 1. **From Bedlam to Broadmoor**

In chapters 2 and 3 of volume I there were brief references to the custody and care of the insane offender before the Industrial Revolution. This chapter is concerned with subsequent developments, and especially the establishment of special institutions for what came to be known as 'the criminal lunatic'.[1]

This was a nineteenth-century achievement. In the preceding century the natural repository for the lunatic who had committed a felony–and indeed for some who had not, but were obviously dangerous–was the local gaol or house of correction, where he was accepted as an unavoidable nuisance. John Howard summed up the evils of the situation

> . . . in some few gaols are confined idiots and lunatics. These serve
> for sport to idle visitants at assizes, and other times of general resort.
> Many of the bridewells are crowded and offensive, because the rooms
> which were designed for prisoners are occupied by the insane. Where
> these are not kept separate they disturb and terrify other prisoners. No
> care is taken of them, although it is probable that by medicines, and
> proper regimen, some of them might be restored to their senses, and
> to usefulness in life.[2]

Sometimes two inconvenient minorities were combined, the lunatics being put into the women's room. Even the first attempt to legislate for the segregation of certain classes of prisoners, in the Act of 1784,[3] was completely silent on the subject of the insane, although it aimed at separating men from women, felons from misdemeanants, witnesses from accused, and the convicted from the unconvicted.

It is true that by the second half of the eighteenth century there was an extensive system of private madhouses; but these were profit-making establishments, and accepted only paying patients, although an exception might occasionally be made if a parish with no other way of disposing of a pauper lunatic were willing to pay for his keep. A few asylums had been provided by private subscription–for example, at York–but these too were unwilling to take criminal lunatics without payment.[4]

Many a pauper lunatic went to the workhouses, some of which were probably no worse than the asylums proper; and indeed it would have been difficult to be worse than the ill-famed York Asylum. An example was St Peter's workhouse at Bristol, founded in 1696, which from its early days had separate wards for the insane, and by the end of the century was known as St Peter's Hospital. But workhouses, too, only rarely received

B

criminal lunatics. The same was true of St Luke's Hospital for Lunaticks in London (see volume I, p. 71) and the Tukes' Retreat near York, founded in 1792 as a rival to the York Asylum, which by this time was an open scandal.

Bethlem

Finally, there was Bethlem. Originally a priory, this had been used for the confinement of the acutely insane since late in the fourteenth century. At first it seems to have been a monastic house under the supervision of the City of London; but the day-to-day management was probably left to a janitor. Like most mediaeval jailors the janitors seem to have run the establishment for their profit, for in 1403 the excesses of a janitor called Peter led to an 'inquisition'—the first of several which were to probe into the scandals of Bedlam until the middle of the nineteenth century. At this time the place seems to have held only six insane inmates, together with the usual psychiatric equipment of the day—six chains of iron, with six locks, four pairs of manacles of iron and two pairs of stocks. In the next century, with the dissolution of the monasteries, the management was transferred to the City of London. A 'court' of governors was appointed, which was also made responsible for that newly created institution, the original Bridewell; and in their hands it remained until Bethlem was taken over by the National Health Service in 1948.[5]

By 1676 the capacity of the place was between fifty and sixty; but in that year the need for more spacious buildings caused it to move to Moorfields, where it was said in the eighteenth century to be able to hold about 250. It seems to have been used on occasion, and in a rather unofficial way, by the Crown or the courts as a place of safe custody for lunatics. In 1630, for example, Charles I's Privy Council decided to write to the Justices of the Peace of the City of Westminster about the disturbance caused by three mentally disordered persons:

> Whereas there are certaine persons who run up and downe the streets and doe much harme, being either distracted or els counterfeites, and therefore not to be suffered to have their liberties to range, as now they doe; of which persons one is called King Robert, another Doctor Owen, and the third Mistris Vaughan: we doe hereby will and require you to see them all sent to Bedlam, there to be kept, ordered and looked unto, to which purpose wee sende you herewith a warrant directed to the Master and Matrone of Bedlame, for the receiving of them.[6]

We have also seen how in the late eighteenth century an Old Bailey judge recommended Mary Cavenhau to the Governors of Bedlam 'as a proper object of that charity' when she was on trial for larceny (volume I, p. 65), and how the Home Secretary sent Margaret Nicholson to the same place—with questionable authority—after the Privy Council had cross-examined her about her attack on George III (volume I, p. 185). It was therefore natural that when the legislation resulting from Hadfield's case saddled Whitehall with the responsibility for disposing of persons acquitted by reason of insanity, or found insane on arraignment, it should turn to Bethlem. Hadfield himself went back to Newgate immediately after his trial, but was escorted to Bethlem a few months later by the Newgate 'Keeper'. Two years later, he and another inmate, John Dunlop, escaped, and Hadfield seems to have got as far as Dover before being re-taken and returned, for security's sake, to Newgate. (The steward of Bethlem was formally censured by the governors for going in immediate pursuit of him without reporting and obtaining permission, but the minute of censure was later obliterated, although it is still legible.)

Hadfield's case was exceptional, however, and for the most part the ordinary criminal lunatics continued to lie in gaol. The evils of this—to which John Howard had drawn attention a generation earlier—were begin-ning to make an impression. In 1806 Sir George Onesiphorus Paul, the admirer of Bentham who had done so much to improve his own county's house of correction, wrote a long letter to the Secretary of State about the condition of criminal and pauper lunatics. This led to the appointment of a Select Committee by the House of Commons, which made an attempt to ascertain the size of the problem by means of a survey, although they had to admit that the returns were very incomplete (some counties simply denied that they had any criminal or pauper lunatics). The Committee were impressed by such cases as those of Aaron Bywater, confined in the county gaol of Montgomery after being acquitted of murder by reason of insanity: three months later, although the gaoler had been ordered to keep a close watch on him, he managed to murder another prisoner. They agreed with Sir George that 'to confine such persons in a common gaol is equally destructive of all possibility of the recovery of the insane and of the security and comfort of the other prisoners'. Although the principal result of their report was the County Asylums Act of 1808 (48 Geo. III. c. 96), they also recommended the building of a separate establishment for criminal lunatics, to serve the whole country from somewhere in or near London, and under regulations made by the Home Secretary.

The Act of 1808 was silent on the subject of a criminal lunatic asylum: but silence did not mean inaction. The Bethlem governors wanted to re-build on a new site at St George's Fields in Lambeth, which the City of London were willing to exchange for the Moorfields land. Some of the cost of the new building they could meet out of their own funds, and some they obtained in the form of contributions from various public bodies and private individuals; but most of it was to be met by grants from Parliament. While this was afoot, an Under-Secretary of State wrote to the governors' clerk, enquiring whether it seemed practicable to them to set aside part of the land for an additional building for criminal lunatics. The governors were apprehensive lest this should bring them, like ordin-ary county asylums, under the powers of inspection and control which the 1808 Act had conferred on magistrates[7]; but on being reassured by the Law Officers of the Crown they entered into negotiations, and agreement was finally reached in 1814. The Government would pay for the building, provided that the cost did not exceed £19,800 (it did, by a handsome margin of £5,344, but the Government were hardly in a position to back out, especially as the site had been provided free). It was to hold 45 male and 15 female criminal lunatics, whose maintenance at a fixed sum the Government would pay, as well as—a grim piece of foresight—their funeral expenses.

The complement of 60 was regarded as based on a generous estimate.

Bethlem itself held at that time only about 20 men and a dozen women whom it seemed necessary to move; and it was not intended that the new building should hold all the criminal lunatics in the country—only those who could not be safely left to the county asylums. Whitehall can hardly be blamed for failing at this early stage to foresee the rapid increase in this group which would take place in the next few decades as a result of the abolition of hanging for most felonies, the abandonment of transportation and the lowering of mortality in the asylums.

Into the new wing went all the famous criminal lunatics of the day. Aaron Bywater (see p. 3) was transferred there as soon as it opened. Margaret Nicholson, who had been sent to Bethlem in her middle forties, was still there in her eighties.[8] Hadfield, who had been kept in Newgate since his escape from the old Bethlem, was transferred to the new building as soon as it opened: he did not die until 1841, when the surgeons were at last able to examine the internal damage caused by the wound on his forehead which Erskine had displayed to the jury (it was considerable, said the autopsy report). Later admissions included Edward Oxford, who seemed perfectly sane to the staff of Bethlem, and Daniel M'Naghten, who was still deluded ten years later. Sometimes, too, a convict under sentence of transportation or penal servitude would be received from the hulks (where sentences of transportation of seven years or less were usually spent) or from the penitentiaries. Austere as Bethlem was, it must have seemed a haven[9] in comparison with the crowded 'tween-decks of 'Bellerophon' or 'Retribution', and by the eighteen-fifties the Resident Physician said openly that many a convict feigned madness in the hope of a transfer. The end of transportation to eastern Australia resulted in a small spate of such transfers in 1853.

The eighteen-fifties saw considerable improvements in the regime and the standard of care. The Monro dynasty, which had ruled Bethlem for four generations, came to an end at last with another scandal in 1852, and Dr Hood from Colney Hatch was appointed Resident Physician—the first resident physician the place had ever had! It is probably significant that nearly all the case-records of patients who were in Bethlem at that time—even of those who had been there many years—were written after he took over. Regular purging was abolished, and mechanical restraint—already uncommon, if we may believe the last of the Monros—was abolished. In 1859 Hood even secured the Home Office's permission to take some of the female inmates of the special wing for walks outside the grounds. He was a strong administrator, quick to get rid, whenever possible, of transferred convicts, whose behaviour was much more troublesome and objectionable to other patients than that of Her Majesty's Pleasure patients.

Even in Monro's day, however, it was by no means unheard of for an inmate of the criminal lunatics' wing to be set free. It is true that transferred prisoners who, like Dalmas or Townley, were found to be sane were usually returned to the penitentiary, the gaol or the hulk (see volume 1, pp. 205 ff.). Edward Oxford, though regarded as sane, was not released during his time at Bethlem, presumably for fear that he molested the Queen again, although in 1868, some years after his transfer to Broadmoor, he was allowed to emigrate.[10] Nevertheless, there was a steady trickle of discharges. James Gorham, a labourer who had been sentenced in 1844 to ten years penal servitude for housebreaking and transferred from Pentonville to Bethlem a year later, was being reported as 'sane' to the Home Office four years later. Eventually the Home Office enquired 'whether in the opinion of the Medical Officers any danger is to be apprehended from (his) release' and, on being reassured, consented to his being discharged and 'sent home to his friends' before the end of his sentence.[11] Eliza Huntsman, acquitted at the age of 20 of the murder of her child by reason of insanity, was discharged into the care of her mother six years later,[11] although some years afterward Hood was to tell the Capital Punishment Commission that it was advisable to detain infanticidal women until they had passed child-bearing age![12]

The majority of criminal lunatics however, did not go to Bethlem. The Home Office, which was responsible for disposing of persons detained at His Majesty's Pleasure under the 1800 Act, used first to ask the visiting justices of the gaol where the lunatic was in custody whether there was a county asylum to which they could send him; and Bethlem was requested to take only those who were considered most dangerous. The first complete—or ostensibly complete—national survey, published in 1837,[13] showed a total of 178 criminal lunatics, of whom only 55 were in Bethlem. Of the rest, 48 were distributed in handfuls amongst 17 county asylums (Maidstone held the largest group, numbering 16) and 35 were in private licensed houses. The remaining 40 were scattered in ones and twos through the local gaols.

Nevertheless, by 1830 the Metropolitan Commissioners in Lunacy were complaining of the insufficiency of room for criminal lunatics in Bethlem, and in 1836, at the request of the Home Office, an extension was begun to provide another 30 places. This failed to keep pace with increasing numbers, however, and in 1849 the Home Department were compelled to subsidise the building of a special wing for the less dangerous sort of criminal lunatics at Fisherton House, a provincial licensed house (as private madhouses were now called) near Salisbury.

Even so, all was far from well. On the one hand county asylums and private licensed houses were being forced to take more and more criminal lunatics, some of whom were undoubtedly dangerous. By 1856 there were 596 criminal lunatics, of whom 22 were still in gaols, and less than a quarter of the remainder in Bethlem and Fisherton House. On the other hand, the idea of 'moral management', so energetically preached by Willis in the eighteenth century, was at last beginning to prevail, and superintendents such as Connolly were doing away with mechanical restraints. Just as today's hospital order cases are a nuisance in 'open door' hospitals, the nineteenth century criminal lunatics were unwanted patients in the county asylum or private establishment. Several took advantage of reduced security to commit further crimes of violence. Patients who had not committed crimes resented being forced to associate with them, and their relatives and doctors shared this resentment, although Bucknill, that level-headed asylum doctor, pointed out that many a patient who was not officially a criminal lunatic had broken the law before being committed.

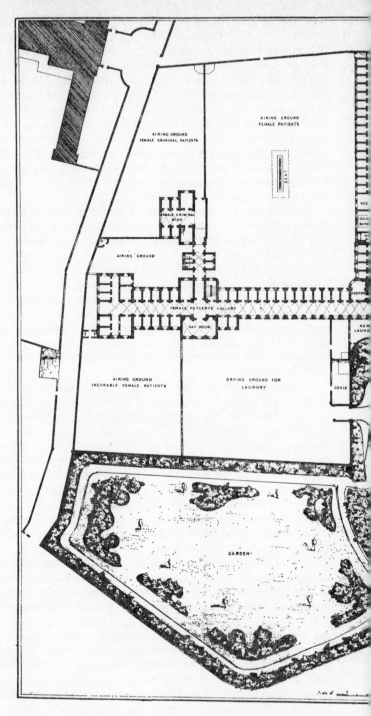

FIGURE 1. Bethlem about 1840 (From the Bethlem Archives)

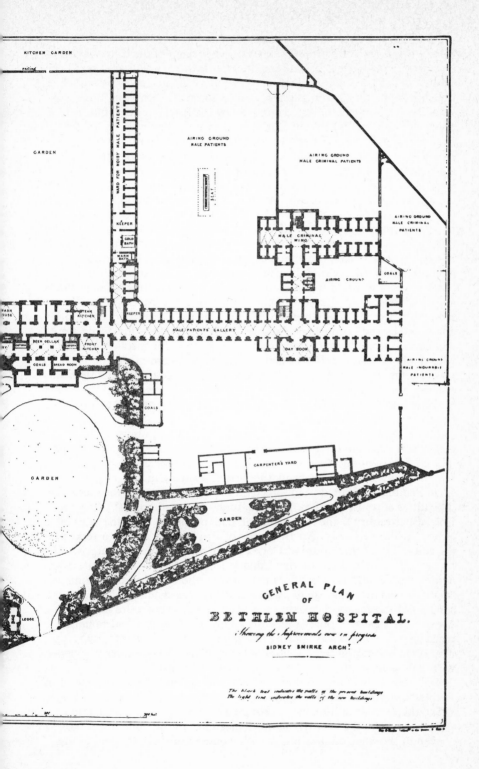

GENERAL PLAN
OF
BETHLEM HOSPITAL.
Shewing the Improvements now in progress
SIDNEY SMIRKE ARCH.T

The black tint indicates the walls of the present buildings
The light tint indicates the walls of the new buildings

A State Asylum

Meanwhile a new influence was at work, in the shape of the Commissioners in Lunacy. Since 1774 private madhouses in the London area had been subject to licensing and inspection by a body which came to be known as 'the Metropolitan Commissioners'. In its original form this body consisted of five physicians elected annually by the Royal College, but in 1828 they were replaced by a body of fifteen members, appointed by the Home Secretary, of whom only five were physicians (the majority were members of Parliament, notably Gordon and Ashley, who, as members of Select Committees, had helped to bring about these and other reforms). The responsibilities of the new Metropolitan Commissioners were extended to include not only private madhouses but also all 'subscription hospitals' for the insane, with the exception of Bethlem. (Bethlem's success in protecting itself from inspection and control through successive measures of reform has already been remarked upon–see p. 3 n. 7.) In 1842 some of the Commissioners, of whom Ashley was again one, successfully introduced a Bill to enlarge their jurisdiction so that for an experimental period of three years it would include provincial as well as metropolitan asylums and madhouses. At the end of the three years the Metropolitan Commissioners were formally replaced by the Lunacy Commissioners, a body appointed by the Lord Chancellor, with a permanent full-time inspectorate and central secretariat. In addition to the powers of inspection which the Metropolitan Commissioners had acquired they were given the right to visit the insane in whatever institution they were confined. Bethlem was still exempt from these inspections; but a special clause allowed the Home Secretary or the Lord Chancellor to order a special visitation to any institution–including Bethlem.

It was the Commissioners who revived the 1807 committee's idea of a completely separate establishment for criminal lunatics: a State Asylum. The climate of opinion was now much more favourable to such a proposal, for analogous developments in the prison system, in the shape of the State Penitentiaries, had been forced on the Government by the increasing difficulties of transportation. By 1852, under the prodding of Ashley (now Lord Shaftesbury), the Government had begun to take the idea of a State Asylum seriously. An Inspector of Prisons was asked to report on the suitability of the House of Correction at Brixton for the purpose. His report was favourable, but the Lunacy Commissioners set higher standards. They found the corridors too narrow, the cells and day-rooms too small, the heating inadequate, water-closets non-existent and the site too small, with no means of making the place sufficiently secure and private. Meanwhile a private purchaser with an eye for business had bought the place for £8,450, and was offering to sell it to the Government for £12,930. The offer was not accepted, although negotiations were later re-opened with a view to acquiring it for use as a convict prison.

The idea of a State Asylum was not without its opponents. Hood of Bethlem published his objections in 1854:

Would it be fair or humane to shut up a lady or a gentleman who may . . . have committed a very trivial misdemeanour, in the same ward, or even in the same establishment with women or men belonging to the lowest classes of society, who may have committed revolting and nameless offences?

Other objections were that a concentration of criminal lunatics would cause the asylum to assume the character of a prison rather than of a curative hospital; that it would make it necessary for relatives and friends of some patients to travel great distances to visit them; and that it would be very much more expensive than leaving them in Bethlem and the county asylums:

There is a feeling, I am aware, abroad, that lunatic asylums should be built in the style of palaces, and surrounded with beautiful and attractive scenery; it has even been suggested by the Medical Superintendent of an asylum in Scotland that such places as Bethlem should be planted with trees, have a fountain, a portion of ground prepared as a bowling green and should be stocked with sheep, hares, a monkey and other domestic animals. It is however obvious that where the security and safe custody of a dangerous criminal lunatic is an object, pleasant and umbrageous avenues would afford opportunities for concealment and escape . . .[14]

Nevertheless, two years later the Lunacy Commissioners were able to make the triumphant announcement that it had been resolved by the Government to provide a new State Asylum at once, for the accommodation of 600 criminal lunatics, and that 'active measures' were now being taken for the selection of a suitable site.

The choice of site, on the summit of a Berkshire ridge, was in accordance with the fashionable belief in the therapeutic powers of country air. As for the design, security was clearly of the first importance, and the task was given to Sir Joshua Jebb, the former military engineer who had been responsible for the architecture of Pentonville. Convicts from nearby Woking provided some of the labour, living on the site. The result was Broadmoor, much of whose original structure still stands today.

The original members of the Asylum's Council of Supervision included not only its designer, Jebb, but also Hood of Bethlem. The latter had evidently decided by 1860 that continued opposition to the establishment of a Criminal Lunatic Asylum (which was by then a foregone conclusion) would be unwise. He had written a letter to the Lunacy Commissioners arguing that the classification of criminal lunatics in Bethlem had proved impossible, and that there was much that could be done for them only in a State Lunatic Asylum – for instance the provision of greater opportunities for employment and healthy exercise.

The patients began to arrive in 1863. Since the buildings – and in particular the boundary walls – were by no means complete, it was thought safer to make a start with women, some 90 of whom were collected from Bethlem, Fisherton House and various asylums and prisons. Early in the following year, over 200 men were transferred from Bethlem and Fisherton House. By the end of the eighteen-sixties fully two thirds of all the country's criminal lunatics were in Broadmoor.

This was the high-water mark, however. It had never been intended to relieve the county asylums of all the criminal lunatics, many of whom were not dangerous, even by the standards of the day. In any case, the behaviour of Broadmoor's first inmates soon led to complications. Even the women chosen as the first arrivals were not above escaping; one did so within a few weeks, and another not long afterwards. When the first men began to arrive in 1864 the boundary walls were still too low, and several of them escaped. One man and one woman were never traced. All but one of these early escapers were transferred convicts, whose criminal sophistication caused as much trouble in the new asylum as it had in Bethlem; and for most of the seventies and eighties the Directors of Convict Prisons had to make other arrangements at Woking and Dartmoor for housing this category. As for 'prisoners' proper—that is, persons committed or sentenced to ordinary gaols—they were not accepted at Broadmoor until the Directors of Convict Prisons became responsible for the local gaols in 1877. For a brief period, as we shall see, part of Parkhurst Prison had to be approved as a Criminal Lunatic Asylum.

Eventually, in 1912, the Lunacy Commissioners were able to open Rampton, near Retford, to receive dangerous criminal lunatics whose homes were in the north of England. Two years later, when the final version of the Mental Deficiency Bill (see chapter 3) had at last become law, they were on the point of opening Moss Side, near Liverpool, for dangerous defectives, but were forced by the outbreak of war to hand it over to the army for mentally disordered soldiers. During the war it was found possible to provide for 90 dangerous female defectives at Farmfield in Surrey; but something more secure was thought necessary, and in 1918 the Prison Commissioners lent Warwick Prison for this purpose for five years, although in the event the Board of Control (as the Lunacy Commissioners were now called) were allowed to use it, in spite of its many defects, until 1932.

One effect of the 1914–18 war had been an unexpected number of empty beds in county asylums and even in Broadmoor and Rampton. It seemed possible to do without Moss Side after all. Broadmoor and Rampton unloaded their less dangerous cases onto the county asylums; Rampton's insane patients were transferred to Broadmoor; and Rampton was handed over to the Board to become the principal state institution for dangerous defectives, with Warwick and Farmfield taking care of most of the dangerous female defectives. Moss Side became a hospital for epileptics under the Ministry of Pensions. During the twenties, however, numbers began to rise again, especially as a result of the epidemics of *encephalitis lethargica*, colloquially called 'sleepy sickness'. This is a virus disorder, in which an acute stage of delirium, alternating with somnolence, is often followed by chronic symptoms of brain damage, and especially Parkinsonian trembling. In children, however, the after-effects are apt to take the form of restless, aggressive and destructive behaviour, which is beyond ordinary control. In this country the epidemic swelled the numbers of young defectives who had to be cared for in institutions; the statutory definition of mental deficiency had to be amended (see p. 211); and Rampton had to provide two new houses and a school for dangerous young defectives, fully 40 per cent of whom were cases of sleepy sickness. By 1933 Rampton had reached the limits of its expansion, and in the end

Moss Side had to be reclaimed and put to the use for which it had originally been intended.

The Special Hospitals

The domestic history of Broadmoor has already been written by Ralph Partridge,[15] who dealt with its development up to 1952. Rampton and Moss Side still await their chroniclers; but we have space to deal only with the Special Hospitals' roles within the system. Broadmoor remained the responsibility of a Council of Supervision, appointed by the Home Secretary, until 1948. The Minister of Health and the Home Secretary had agreed in 1937 that it should become the responsibility of the Board of Control, as Rampton and Moss Side were, and the Criminal Justice Act of 1948 eventually gave effect to this decision, although the fate of individual Broadmoor patients[16] remained the Home Secretary's responsibility. Broadmoor continued, however, to differ from the other two establishments in one important respect. They were not, and had never been, criminal lunatic asylums in the strict sense, and while many of their inmates were criminal lunatics others were simply dangerous patients, inmates who had been committed to them without prosecution either direct or by transfer from other hospitals which did not feel it safe to keep them. Broadmoor, on the other hand, received only criminal lunatics. It was not until the Mental Health Act of 1959 placed all three 'Special Hospitals', as it called them, under the direct management of the Ministry of Health that they were on exactly the same footing. Since then, all three have received Her Majesty's Pleasure cases, transferred prisoners (whether sentenced or not), offender-patients committed by criminal courts (usually but not always under restriction orders), and non-offenders under compulsory treatment who are transferred from other psychiatric hospitals because of their dangerous or criminal propensities.

Broadmoor specialises in mentally ill or psychopathic patients whose intelligence is average or higher: in the mid-sixties 58 per cent of its admissions were of the schizophrenic type, 29 per cent 'personality disorders', and only 6 per cent depressives. Its average number of occupied beds over the same period was 777, a reduction on immediately preceding years. Since the bed occupancy at this time was more or less stable, however, its admissions can be used as a rough measure of its 'turnover': they represented about 17 per cent of its occupied beds. Of those who left it during this period, 17 per cent were discharged direct to freedom (subject in most cases to certain requirements, as we shall see later (p. 199); but the majority—57 per cent—were transferred to ordinary National Health Service hospitals, in most cases with a view to discharge after their behaviour in less secure institutions had been observed over a substantial period. (The remainder were transferred to one of the other Special Hospitals, died, were repatriated or—in a few cases—returned to prison to complete a sentence.)[17]

Rampton and Moss Side specialise in patients with some degree of subnormality or brain damage. The principles on which it is decided to allocate a given patient to one or other seem to be a mixture of security considerations (Rampton providing a somewhat higher degree of protection against escapes),[18] the patient's geographical origin and no doubt the

availability of vacancies at the date in question. Rampton is the largest of
the Special Hospitals, with an average number of 972 occupied beds over
the years 1964–6 but a rather lower turnover[19] of 11 per cent. It seems
to discharge a slightly higher percentage of 'leavers' direct to freedom (21
per cent) but fully 60 per cent are transferred to ordinary N.H.S. hospitals,
and very few indeed are returned to prison. Moss Side, with an average
of only 377 occupied beds over the same period, is the smallest of the
Special Hospitals. It had a turnover,[19] however, of 16 per cent–closer to
Broadmoor's than to Rampton's, and fully 35 per cent of its leavers were
discharged to ordinary N.H.S. hospitals. These differences between it and
Rampton can probably be explained by a tendency to allocate to it somewhat less dangerous cases.

It should be emphasised that at no time in the history of the Special
Hospitals–from Bethlem onward–has there been any statutory category
of patient which was *bound* to be sent to one or any of them. Her Majesty's
Pleasure patients, transferred prisoners and offenders committed by
criminal courts under the 1913, 1948 and 1959 Acts have gone and
still go to the ordinary mental hospitals which are now under the authority of the Regional Hospital Boards. Nor does it seem possible to define
in non-statutory terms the sorts of patient who should and should not
be sent to a Special Hospital, as a Working Party found when they tried
to do so in 1961.[20] The best they could do was to lay down the principle
that

> . . . *a patient should be accepted for admission to a special hospital only
> after all the other possibilities have been carefully examined and have been
> considered unsuitable.* We regard this as important for three main
> reasons–first, because it is wrong in principle to place more
> restrictions on the liberty of the individual than are necessary;
> secondly because it is plainly wasteful to provide elaborate security
> precautions . . . for patients for whom they are not really necessary.
> Thirdly, and even more important . . . the fact that a patient is known to
> have been in a special hospital may complicate his long-term
> rehabilitation and make it more difficult for him to be absorbed
> successfully into the community.

The same Working Party, however, made two important recommendations. The spread of the 'open door' policy, the reduction of the number
of locked wards and relaxation of control over patients' behaviour had
greatly reduced the willingness of ordinary hospitals to accept patients
who seemed likely to be dangerous or troublesome to the public, the staff
or their fellow-patients. Many of these patients were of the kind which is
loosely labelled 'psychopathic' (a diagnosis which is discussed in chapters
9 and 10). Although the management of these patients in conditions of
relaxed security clearly called for special skill and experience, only a few
of the country's ordinary hospitals had made a serious attempt to meet
this need. One was Belmont Hospital, where in 1947 an Industrial
Neurosis Unit had been opened for patients with records of chronic unemployment. Under the direction of Dr Maxwell Jones its clientele had
gradually widened to include patients referred by criminal courts, who
eventually accounted for nearly a third of its intake. The unit was officially

renamed the Social Rehabilitation Unit in 1954, but the whole hospital was later named the Henderson Hospital in memory of the Scots psychiatrist who popularised the concept of psychopathy in Britain (see p. 215), and it is under this name that it has become internationally known for its attempts to treat personality disorders in both sexes with the minimum of security.[21]

One or two institutions for mental defectives had set aside special wings for those with anti-social personalities. The best-known of these was the unit at Balderton Hospital in Nottinghamshire, where from 1958 to 1961 adolescent male psychopaths of rather low intelligence were treated, some by the methods evolved by Maxwell Jones at the Henderson Hospital, others under a more orthodox and authoritarian regime. The Balderton Psychopathic Unit came to an end when the consultant in charge, Dr Michael Craft, took up another post in North Wales, where he established on a remote mountainside a unit for adult male psychopaths.[22]

Neither the Henderson nor Balderton Hospital, however, was able to cater for more than a fraction of the patients whose personality disorders seemed to call for special regimes. The Special Hospitals were under increasing pressure to take patients who between the wars would either have been sent to prison or readily accepted in the locked wards of ordinary hospitals.

In this situation both the British Medical Association and the Royal Medico-Psychological Association suggested to the Working Party that there ought to be a number of special centres for patients who presented special difficulty because of their aggressive, anti-social or criminal tendencies, and who also presented special problems of diagnosis, treatment and management. Clearly the majority of these patients would consist of those labelled as 'psychopaths', but the centres were not intended to be limited to this category. The Working Party agreed, with the difference that whereas the associations had stressed the diagnostic function of the proposed centres, and had not envisaged more than short-term treatment in them, the Working Party realised that in practice they would have to provide long-term treatment for some patients.[23] They should be located near the remand centres which the Prison Commissioners were planning to provide, and should be within reasonable reach of a teaching hospital or university. At most, one would be needed for each hospital region, but a start should be made with one or two.

As the Working Party intended, the responsibility for setting up the centres was placed on Regional Hospital Boards, and so far only one new centre has been created: the Northgate Clinic in the North West Metropolitan Region, which was opened in 1968 under Dr Brian O'Connell, formerly a Broadmoor consultant. The official view seems to have been summed up by the Secretary of State for the Social Services (Mr Crossman) when he said in reply to a Parliamentary question on the subject that 'special facilities on a substantial scale can be developed only as medical knowledge increases'.[24]

Another proposal of the 1961 Working Party was that each Regional Hospital Board's ordinary hospitals should include some secure units, although not necessarily with the same degree of security as that provided by Broadmoor or Rampton. Clearly, although the report did not say so, the Working Party felt that the open door policy had become too whole-sale. Again, the response to this recommendation has not been either rapid or spectacular: only the Oxford Regional Hospital Board has so far pro-duced a proposal on these lines.

Finally, the Working Party proposed that patients in the Special Hos-pitals should be regrouped so as to separate those whose intelligence was normal or near normal and whose predominant feature was psychopathic behaviour. This proposal underlined, in effect, the need for a fourth Special Hospital, which was already pressing. Broadmoor's obsolete buildings were seriously overcrowded, and the numbers of patients who would have to be accommodated in strict security seemed likely to get larger rather than smaller. A fourth Special Hospital would not merely relieve overcrowding in the long run but would also provide the temporary accommodation which would enable Broadmoor to be rebuilt. It took most of the sixties, however, to sort out all the considerations involved – including the choice of a site – and it was not until some time after the Ministry of Health had been criticised for the delay by the Estimates Committee of the House of Commons[25] that a decision was announced. A fourth Special Hospital for 410 males would be built on the Moss Side estate, thus enabling a start to be made on the rebuilding of Broadmoor.

Since security is the essential feature which distinguishes the Special Hospitals, it is bound to be in the forefront of the minds not only of the Press and Parliament but also of the staff. So far as staff are concerned, however, there is clearly a conflict between this consideration and their desire to give the patient treatment. As another Working Party[26] put it in 1967

> Too much freedom for the patients would be dangerous to the public but excessive restriction on the movement and association of patients would not only impede treatment but could also increase the threat to security by producing boredom and tension among the patients. The public must be provided with strong protection against the most serious risks and with adequate protection against lesser risks. But to make security the overriding aim would, in our view, be incompatible with the therapeutic function of the hospitals.

The Working Party analysed the escapes of recent years, making two important distinctions. One was between escapers who had been selected for outside work, and escaped while on it, and those who had not been so selected: the latter seemed to be a better index of failure in security. The other distinction was between patients who were 'seriously dangerous' – that is, who might be expected to make unprovoked attacks if not quickly recaptured – and those who were only 'potentially dangerous' – that is, who 'if they remained at large might, in some circumstances, cause physical harm (including sexual assault) to a member of the public'.

A comparison of the male escape-rates from Special Hospitals with escape-rates from the security prisons at Birmingham and Durham during the three years 1964–6[27] showed that from Broadmoor and Rampton they were lower, but from Moss Side much higher, than from the prisons.[28] Although Moss Side's rate was high, however, it received patients who were regarded as less dangerous than those who go to Rampton or Broad-moor, and none of those who escaped were in the 'seriously dangerous' category – that is, likely to make an unprovoked attack. At the other ex-treme, escapers from Broadmoor, though rare, were more often than not 'seriously dangerous', and have in the last twenty years been responsible for one murder (of a child), an indecent assault and another incident involving serious physical and emotional harm. In contrast the escapes of mentally normal prisoners, such as Blake the spy, are usually accomplished without violence to staff or members of the public.

It was fairly reassuring, however, to note how soon the escapers were recaptured. Out of 189 escapers of both sexes during the twelve years from 1955–66, the great majority were retaken in a matter of hours, and within a few miles of the hospital. The Moss Side statistics were less reassuring: 13 of their male escapers were at large for more than a week. It is possible that after escaping these received assistance from friends or relatives, who are sometimes misguided enough to send hacksaw blades and other imple-ments to Special Hospital patients; but the Working Party discounted rumours that the escapes themselves were planned with the assistance of professional criminals. Nevertheless, one of the sequels to the Working Party's report was a number of improvements in the security of Moss Side.

Notes

1. The term 'criminal lunatic' was used by the Select Committee of 1807 to refer to persons who were in custody as a result either of an acquittal by reason of insanity or of a finding that they were insane on arraignment: that is, what came to be known later as 'Her Majesty's Pleasure patients'. At that time there was no third category of persons found insane and transferred to an asylum on the authority of the Secretary of State while serving a sentence of transportation, imprisonment or penal servitude; but when this category was created and enlarged by the Acts of 1816, 1840 and 1853 the term 'criminal lunatic' was used so as to include them too.

    The first statutory definition of the term 'criminal lunatic' (in the 1860 Act) included not only Her Majesty's Pleasure patients but also 'any person whom a Secretary of State or the Admiralty has in pursuance of an Act of Parliament directed to be removed to an asylum or other place for the reception of such persons': a defini-tion which not only had a touch of circularity but also included unsentenced prisoners. In 1938 the Home Office decided to replace the term 'criminal lunatic asylum' and 'criminal lunatic' with 'Broadmoor' and 'Broadmoor patient' respectively, partly because the older phrase caused distress to such patients and their relatives, but partly also because of the somewhat belated reflection that some of them were not convicted crimiuals. The Criminal Justice Bill of 1938 – which eventually reached the statute-book in 1948 – amended the earlier statutes accordingly. It was of course realised that 'Broadmoor patients' was also something of a misnomer, since

many of them went to other mental hospitals. However that may
be, like all euphemisms it had a short life: the significance of
'Broadmoor' was too well known, and the Percy Commission,
whose proposals were in any case intended to minimise the distinctions between such patients and other patients, recommended the
abolition of the term. This was done in the 1959 Act, which
deliberately refrained from replacing it with any substitute. As a
result, the most precise terms that can now be used are 'Special
Hospital patients', 'Part V patients', 'restriction order patients',
'hospital order patients', 'Section 72 patients' and so on, as the
case may be.

2. John Howard, *The State of the Prisons* (Warrington, 1777).

3. 24 Geo. III. c. 54.

4. Even at the end of the nineteenth century there were cases in
which insane prisoners were discharged to the workhouse because
the county asylum could not or would not take them.

5. By that date Bridewell had of course ceased to exist as a penal
establishment, but had become a reformatory school in 1860 and
later an ordinary school called 'King Edward's School'.

6. Acts of the Privy Council, 1630.

7. They argued that if a magistrate had the power to close the establishment this would set him above the Crown, since Bethlem
operated under a Royal Charter obliging it to care for the insane:
an argument which seems to have carried enough weight to protect
them from State control throughout the reforms of the nineteenth
century.

8. See *Sketches in Bedlam* by a 'constant observer' (London, 1823).

9. Amongst convicts in the eighteen-fifties, Bethlem was known as
the' Golden Bank' (meaning perhaps 'the heavenly shore'?).

10. See Ralph Partridge, *Broadmoor: A History of Criminal Lunacy and
its Problems* (London, 1953), 10; and see n. 15 *infra*.

11. From the Bethlem Sub-Committee Minutes.

12. Minutes of Evidence, answer 2826.

13. Return of two addresses of the Honourable the House of Commons
5 July 1836 and 12 May 1837 (Parliamentary Papers XLIV).

14. William Charles Hood, *Suggestion for the Future Provisions for
Criminal Lunatics* (London, 1854).

15. In *Broadmoor* (op. cit., n. 10). The author was a close friend of
Lytton Strachey and his brother James Strachey; and the latter
(who was one of Freud's translators) gave him an interest in
abnormal psychology. We are indebted to his widow, Mrs Frances
Partridge, for this information.

16. See note 1.

17. Sources: Ministry of Health Statistical Report Series no. 4 (HMSO,
1969): Second Report from the Estimates Committee (1967–8)
on the Special Hospitals and the State Hospitals (HMSO, 1968).

18. See the Report of the Estimates Committee, loc. cit.

19.   Again measured by admissions.

20.   In a report called 'Special Hospitals', published by the Ministry
      of Health (HMSO, 1961). The chairman was Mr D. Emery of the
      Ministry.

21.   For a brief account of the work of the Henderson Hospital, see the
      article by one of Maxwell Jones's successors, F. H. Taylor, in M.
      Craft (ed.) *Psychopathic Disorders* (Oxford, 1966); and for a
      longer account of its early days see R. N. Rapoport, *Community as
      Doctor* (London, 1960).

22.   See the articles by M. Craft in *Psychopathic Disorders* and in
      A. V. S. de Reuck and R. Porter (edd.) *The Mentally Abnormal
      Offender* (London, 1968).

23.   It also thought that the centres should have a third function:
      research.

24.   Hansard Commons, for 7 July 1969, cols. 937-8.

25.   See the Second Report from the Estimates Committee (Session
      1967–8) on 'The Special Hospitals' (HMSO, 1968).

26.   This report is annexed to the Second Report of the Estimates
      Committee, loc. cit. *supra* (n. 25).

27.   These were the three years before the Mountbatten Report.

28.   The crude figures were: Broadmoor and Rampton, 3 men from an
      average population of 1,300; Birmingham and Durham, 6 men
      from an average population of 1,600; Moss Side, 11 men from an
      average population of 290. These figures exclude some escapes
      from outside working parties, since these are not a fair index of
      security.

C

Chapter 2. **From Prison to Hospital**

If the previous chapter has given the impression that the criminal lunatics'
wing of Bethlem, the county asylums and the Special Hospitals relieved
the prisons of the problem of the disordered offender, nothing could be
further from the reality we are trying to describe. At best they enabled the
prison system to get rid of its more spectacular or troublesome cases; and
there were periods, as we shall see, when they did not even do that.

From the Middle Ages onward the security of prisons has made them
the most convenient place for the dangerously insane. Even when a few
asylums were compelled to accept lunatics who had been convicted of
serious violence, the prisons were still relied upon in the worst cases. Hadfield, who was homicidal at intervals, and once escaped from Bethlem, was
subsequently kept in Newgate for a year or two. Indeed, the 1814 Committee on Madhouses mentioned men who seemed to have been committed to Kendal gaol and Exeter House of Correction simply as places
of safe custody, and without having been charged with any crime. Even
the creation of Special Hospitals for the dangerously disordered offender
has not completely eliminated the occasional case in which a disordered
offender who has shown himself able to escape from one of these hospitals
has subsequently been kept in prison. One such offender was Straffen,
whose story is described in volume 1 (pp. 116-17); another was Frank
Mitchell, a subnormal gangster who escaped from Rampton in 1957 and
Broadmoor in 1958, committing crimes of violence for which he was subsequently sentenced to life imprisonment. Although both men could have
been transferred from prison back to hospital, neither was.[1]

Prisons function, however, not only as repositories of last resort. They
are also human reservoirs from which comes the pressure of numbers
that leads to changes in the system. It was this pressure of numbers which
from time to time stimulated legislation permitting the transfer to asylums
of men and women whom the courts had committed to prison–an important interference with the rigour of the law. This is the subject of the first
section of this chapter. Later we shall see how the volume of insane
prisoners committed for trial or sentence compelled the Prison Commissioners to initiate a procedure which can fairly be called the forerunner
of the present-day hospital order.

A more recently developed function is that of providing care and treatment as well as diagnosis for prisoners who seem to be disordered, but not
severely enough to justify transfer to hospital. This will be the subject of

the following chapter. It would be tempting to link it logically to the most recent development of all: the application of psychotherapeutic techniques to the inmates of certain prisons and borstals regardless of their normality or abnormality; but as we shall see this was probably an independent phenomenon.

Yet another function of the prison system is to provide the diagnostic facilities on which criminal courts rely in the great majority of cases in which the mental state of the accused is suspect. The importance of the prison medical officer in the detection of disorder amongst offenders has already been mentioned at several points in volume 1; and it is even more striking when we are faced with the growing stream of remands for medical examination with which the twentieth-century prisons have to deal. This will be the subject of the final section of the next chapter.

Taking these developments in turn, let us begin with the effort to rid the prisons of the severely disordered inmate.

The Insane Prisoner

Although it was the intention of the Act of 1800 that felons found insane on arraignment or acquitted by reason of insanity should be committed to asylums or madhouses, the prisons and gaols continued to hold more than a few unfortunate lunatics and idiots. In the first place, there was the diminishing group of insane offenders who had been committed to prison before the passing of the Act. A second group consisted of those who were awaiting trial. Sometimes their wait could be a long one: John Frith, who threw a stone at George III in 1790, and was found unfit to try, was kept for two years in Newgate before being acquitted on the grounds of insanity and released to private custody.[2] A third group consisted of prisoners whose mental abnormality had either not been made an issue at their trial or had been insufficiently spectacular to exempt them from ordinary punishment. Offenders who were charged with mere misdemeanours for which the maximum penalty was a term of imprisonment had little, if anything, to gain by being found insane. Those dealt with summarily could not hope to raise the issue at all, even if they had wanted to. Finally, there has always been the prisoner whose mental illness does not manifest itself until some time after he has begun to serve his sentence.

The first legislation, in 1816,[3] is attributed by the Webbs[4] to the activities of James Nield, High Sheriff of Buckinghamshire, who in the first few years of the nineteenth century emulated Howard's attack on the state of the prisons. He may well have prepared the ground, but the more immediate stimulus appears to have been the state of Newgate. In 1810 a resolution of the City of London had deplored the keeping of lunatics there, and in 1814 renewed complaints by the aldermen led to an investigation of the gaol's administration by a Select Committee of the House of Commons. One result of its recommendations was an Act which allowed the Home Secretary, acting on a certificate of insanity by two physicians or surgeons, to transfer any *sentenced* prisoner to an asylum 'or other proper receptacle for insane persons'.[3] So far as Newgate and the other London gaols were concerned, the obvious 'receptacle' was Bethlem. In the provinces, it was intended that the county asylums which justices were now supposed to provide under the 1808 Act would receive the certified prisoners, although by 1816 only three county asylums had been built, and only six more came into being over the next decade.

It was probably the scarcity of places in the asylums as much as the slackness of the gaols which prevented the legislation of 1816 from working as it was meant to. However that may be, when the Home Secretary (Lord John Russell) appointed Inspectors of Prisons in 1835, he asked them to pay particular attention to the subject of criminal lunatics in their first inspection. Their first report[5] was chiefly concerned with the perennial scandal of Newgate, where the sane and the insane were still mixed together, and where Macmurdo the surgeon had 'complained of insane prisoners being placed in the Infirmary until he was tired of saying more about it'.[5] A lengthy general section of the report, however, was devoted to the subject of insane prisoners, both there and elsewhere. They found that while the justices of most counties had made use of their powers to transfer prisoners to those new establishments, the county asylums, several local gaols still held insane prisoners who had been there for very long periods. One, in Pembroke gaol, had been there twenty-four years.

The report drew attention to a number of difficulties, and made sensible proposals for remedying them, although only a few were eventually implemented in the Home Secretary's legislation of 1840. First, there was the prisoner who was committed for trial and discovered to be insane, but who could not be transferred until he had been found so by a jury. Second, the prisoner who had been committed on summary conviction by the justices (who, then as now, had no power to return a special verdict). It was doubtful whether he could be transferred at all, since it was said that summary commitment was not a sentence within the meaning of the statute of 1828. Lord John Russell's Bill made it possible to transfer almost any category of prisoner: not only those sentenced to imprisonment or transportation but also those under sentence of death (with the consequences described in volume I, chapter 13), as well as those imprisoned as a result of a summary conviction, or under a charge or in custody because of their inability to find bail for their good behaviour. The only categories not included were convicts in the penitentiaries (an oversight that was remedied a couple of years later)[6] and civil prisoners, who were not made transferable until the passing of the 1959 Act. The Bill made no attempt, however, to remedy two features of the law which the inspectors considered unfortunate. One was the justices' inability to return a special verdict: a defect which survives today. The other was less clearly discussed by the inspectors. They thought that the Home Secretary should have 'additional powers' to deal with a prisoner who had been 'wrongly convicted as a sane man'. As they rightly pointed out, prolonged observation in prison was a better test than the impressions of a justice or jury; but exactly what powers they wanted the Home Secretary to have they did not explain. They may have had in mind a power to alter the verdict, of a kind which eventually was given to the newly created Court of Criminal Appeal in 1907. At all events, the Act of 1840[7] did nothing about either of these points. The Home Secretary probably reasoned that his power to transfer such prisoners to asylums would put the matter right in practice if not in law.

A contrasting problem was that presented by prisoners who had been pronounced insane by a court but who turned out not to be. Some of them had feigned madness, some had merely been under the influence of prolonged use of 'stimulants', and were restored to normality simply by depriving them of 'ardent spirits'. The court's verdict had declared them too dangerous to be restored to society ('except perhaps in special cases') but at the same time to subject them to correction after they had been found not responsible for their acts would be both morally and legally wrong. Sometimes their sanity was a matter of dispute between the asylum and the prison. If they were returned to an ordinary prison, regulations had to be relaxed in their favour, which was 'mischievous as an example to others'. The inspectors proposed that Millbank, the first of the State Penitentiaries, should receive such cases, although the county or parish should continue to bear the cost.

The dangers of setting criminal lunatics at large were certainly emphasised, in the year following the publication of the inspectors' report, by the tiny insurrection in Kent which was led by the self-styled 'Sir William Courtenay'.[8] This extraordinary man was the son of a Cornish innkeeper and of a mother who herself died insane in middle age. Their son, a handsome man of enormous physical strength, became a clerk in a Truro firm of wine merchants, of which he managed to purchase the ownership seven years later when his employers decided to retire. Soon after this, however, at the age of thirty, he began to show signs of depression and eccentricity, and was treated for insanity by bleeding and blistering. A few years later, in 1832, he disappeared to London, where he called himself Squire Thompson, and in the autumn of that year turned up in Canterbury, with long black hair and beard, under the title of 'Count Rothschild'. He seems to have had an astonishing capacity not only for impressing people with his claims but also for inducing them to part with money, on which he lived extravagantly. Nor do the citizens of Canterbury seem to have lost faith in him when he suddenly decided that he was Sir William Courtenay, heir to the earldom of Devon. (The choice was a clever one, for the rightful heir had fled to France under suspicion of sodomy, and was unlikely to confront him.) Incredibly, he was invited by some Tories to stand as a candidate in the reformed Parliamentary election of 1832, and his popularity was such that he secured nearly 400 of the 2,000 votes cast.

He founded a radical weekly journal in Canterbury, and in his role as champion of the poor tried to assist in the defence of some fishermen accused of smuggling. His evidence was so palpably false, however, that he was convicted of perjury, and sentenced to three months' imprisonment followed by seven years' transportation. While he was in Maidstone gaol, his wife and relatives turned up to identify him, and confirmed the prison surgeon's opinion that he was of unsound mind. In October 1833, therefore, he was transferred to the county asylum by warrant of the Home Secretary. Even then he did not forfeit the confidence of some of his followers, for ten months later George Francis, a prosperous but gullible farmer, was asking whether 'Sir William' was fit to be released.

Strictly speaking, the Act seemed to require that he should either remain in the asylum until the end of his sentence, or, if he was certified as of sound mind again, be returned to the Maidstone gaol, to be transported or put to work in the hulks (where the shorter sentences of transportation were spent at this time). But his wife and father, as well as his friends, were anxious for his release, and made persistent requests to be allowed to care for him in Cornwall. Although it was now four years later, he was still insane in the view of the asylum superintendent, so that there was no question of returning him to Maidstone, and the idea of releasing him to someone's guardianship must have seemed attractive. The Home Secretary was approached, and the Gordian knot was cut by a pardon from the new Queen. 'Sir William' still refused, however, to acknowledge his real identity, and the only guardian he would accept was the credulous farmer Francis. Rather than leave him in the asylum his family consented to this arrangement.

Within a few weeks he was stirring up the farm labourers of East Kent, already provoked by the new Poor Laws. Now proclaiming himself a reincarnation of Christ, he assembled a small band of about two dozen followers, and marched them around the hinterland of Whitstable Bay in an effort to recruit more. When the High Constable of Boughton-under-Blean and his brother came with a warrant to arrest him he shot the brother down and finished him off with his sword. A company of troops had to be turned out, and in a brief mêlée in Bossenden Wood 'Sir William' and some of his followers were killed, the remainder being later imprisoned or transported. Lord John Russell had to defend himself in Parliament for allowing 'Courtenay' to be released, but argued that the real blame lay with the credulous folk of Kent! A Select Committee was appointed and reported in July 1838, but its report was factual and made no recommendations: nor did the Home Secretary's Bill of 1840 deal with the release of prisoners such as 'Courtenay'. Indeed, beyond making it possible to transfer almost every category of prisoner except the debtor, it did nothing to improve either the prisoner's chances of transfer or the procedure for arranging it. There was still too much scope for inertia on the part of prison doctors and justices, and for resistance on the part of asylums.

Under the Prison Commission

As for Grey's Act of 1864,[9] it merely ensured that the certifying doctors must be on the medical register (which had not existed in 1840), and that –to avoid a repetition of *l'affaire* Townley (see volume I, p. 207)–only justices responsible for the gaol in question could initiate any transfers. The 1884 Act[10] was largely concerned with the financial responsibility for 'criminal lunatics'[11] now that the central Government had become responsible for local gaols as well as convict prisons, although, as we have seen (volume I, p. 209), it had important consequences for prisoners under sentence of death. The financial question was whether criminal lunatics from local prisons should be treated as 'pauper lunatics', and so be maintained by the local ratepayers, or be paid for by the Prison Commissioners; and the Act placed the burden (with certain exceptions) on the Commissioners.

Many insane prisoners, however, were serving such short sentences that it was hardly possible to complete the necessary procedure before they became due for release; in such cases the procedure was to arrange for a justice of the peace (usually a member of the prison's Visiting Committee) to order the prisoner's detention as a pauper lunatic from the day of his release. When mental defectives were legally distinguished from lunatics by the Act of 1913[12] a similar but distinct procedure was introduced for transferring them to institutions, either during sentence or on release.

By the turn of the century the system seemed to have settled down. Considerable numbers of prisoners were being recognised as insane and transferred to asylums while awaiting trial or sentence: in 1900 the number was well over 300. Once a prisoner had been sentenced, however, his chances of being transferred varied with the nature of his sentence. If he was fortunate enough to be serving a mere sentence of imprisonment—which would normally be of two years or less—in a local gaol, and was 'certifiable', he could expect early removal to a county asylum or, if there were no room there, to a workhouse. Of the 130 men, women and children to whom this happened in 1900, 43 per cent were transferred within a month of entering prison (some in less than a week), and 85 per cent in less than four months.

The convict prisons provided a grim contrast to this encouraging picture. From Parkhurst, where (as we shall see in the following chapter) male prisoners whose sanity was suspect were now concentrated, only five were transferred during the year, having served periods of 6 years, 5 years, 16 months, 15 months, and 3 months. Thirteen others had been certified during the year, but not yet transferred, perhaps because there was difficulty in finding vacancies for men whose offences for the most part consisted of serious violence. (From Aylesbury, where weak-minded women prisoners were now concentrated, two were transferred, one after serving a month, the other after serving eleven months.) It is true that, according to the records, most of these convicts had only recently been recognised as disordered. Even today a prisoner may not develop recognisable symptoms of disorder until some time after he has been sentenced. It would be unfair to argue that by today's standards most of these convicts should have been 'certified' much earlier in their sentence. Nevertheless, even by Victorian standards it is difficult to explain away the case of the twenty-eight-year-old seaman, sentenced to life imprisonment in 1888 for manslaughter on the high seas, who began to show symptoms of insanity about six years later but was not certified (as suffering from 'secondary dementia') until 1900, and was still in Parkhurst at the end of the year.

By the turn of the century, however, it was mental deficiency which was the main preoccupation of alienists, psychologists, educationalists, eugenicists and administrators. For some decades this form of disorder had been distinguished from mental illness by doctors, if not by lawyers. The Idiots Act of 1886 had allowed local authorities to provide special asylums for this type of disorder, although the Lunacy Act of 1890 included 'idiots' as well as 'persons of unsound mind' within its scope, and made no distinction when it came to the procedure for certification. Rising statistics of feeble-mindedness provided fodder for the alarmist and ammunition for the eugenicist, although in all probability they reflected nothing more than a heightened sensitivity to the phenomenon, coupled perhaps with the increasing degree of competence and social adaptation which urban life demanded. The Radnor Commission on the Care of the Feeble-minded was appointed in 1904 and reported in 1908: some of its recommendations are discussed in chapter 4.

Feeble-mindedness was also a windfall for criminologists, who found it a more precise and plausible concept than Morel's 'degeneracy' or Lombroso's 'atavism'. The first Binet-Simon intelligence tests were published in 1905 and an American version was in use within a few years. The initial failure to distinguish between educational attainment and innate intelligence led to astounding over-estimates of the prevalence of feeble-mindedness amongst offenders: the Psychopathic Laboratory of the Chicago Municipal Court reported that 85 per cent of their female and young male offenders were 'distinctly feeble-minded'. Other estimates were less startling, but still very high. Amidst all this enthusiasm the English prison doctors kept their heads, although they may have erred in the other direction. Smalley estimated in 1904 that not more than 1·77 per cent of all prisoners received in that year were feeble-minded, a much lower estimate than some of those which were being bandied about in evidence to the Royal Commission and in the national Press. In the full-ness of time Dr Sullivan of Holloway made an expedition to Paris in 1911 to see what the Binet-Simon method was all about, and it may have been as a result of his visit that intelligence testing was introduced in Borstals just after the First World War.

The origins and scope of the Mental Deficiency Act of 1913 are described in chapter 4. From the point of view of prison administration it was important chiefly because of a minor provision (in s. 9) which allowed mentally defective as well as insane prisoners to be transferred to institutions, thus lightening the prisons' burden to such an extent that Park-hurst ceased to specialise in the weak-minded. Nevertheless, this advance created new difficulties. The local authorities who were responsible for providing–and paying for–the new institutions were not anxious to add to their responsibilities a lot of troublesome inmates of penal establish-ments. Medical Officers of Health would sometimes refuse to accept prisoners who had been certified as defective, and, while the law appeared to give them no right to review such certificates, it was difficult for the Prison Commissioners to make them honour their obligations. In 1923, for example, two sisters of 19 and 17 years of age, with mental ages below 8 and several convictions for theft, were certified as feeble-minded by a prison medical officer 'of great experience and a specialist of wide reputa-tion'. They were, said the Prison Commissioners' report, 'of the type that become prison habitués and spend their time in committing petty offences and propagating their kind'. But the local M.O.H.–no doubt out of loyalty to his ratepayers–refused to certify them, and they had to be released.

By the end of the twenties, however, the Prison Commissioners had ceased to complain of this particular difficulty, possibly because the wider definition of mental defect in the 1927 Act (see p. 62) made quibbling more difficult for Medical Officers of Health, possibly also because the new Medical Commissioner, Norwood East, was more interested in types of disorder for which the prisons could hope to provide positive treatment. From this period until just before the passing of the Mental Health Act the transfer of prisoners seems to have proceeded without any major problem. In 1957, however, there occurred a prosecution which, although by a side-wind, had important and lasting implications for prison medical officers and other doctors who were called in to certify prisoners for transfer. A man called Head was convicted of having carnal knowledge of a domestic servant although (as he had been warned) she was a mental defective who had been 'placed out on licence' from an institution. When her history and status were examined, however, it was found that she had been transferred to the institution by an order of the Home Secretary which was based on inadequate certificates by two doctors. They were inadequate because, while she was described in them as a moral defective, neither of them showed that she 'required care, supervision and control for the protection of others' (which was essential if she was to be so classified), and none of the facts adduced supported the allegation that she was a moral defective. (In fact her behaviour at the institution had been so violent that she had to be removed to a Special Hospital: but that occurred after her certification.) The prosecution had to concede that the Home Secretary's order was invalid, with the result that the man's conviction was quashed on appeal. The importance of the case,[13] however, lay not in the fate of the accused but in the effect which it had upon Home Office practice. Nowadays every certificate that a prisoner (or inmate of a senior or junior detention centre, remand home or borstal) is so disordered as to warrant transfer is scrutinised by the Home Office's legal adviser if the disorder is classified as subnormality, severe subnormality or psychopathic disorder.[14]

Transfers under the Mental Health Act

The Mental Health Act, whose origins and operation are described in chapters 4 and 5, not only tidied up the procedure for transferring disordered prisoners, but was also an attempt to ensure that so far as sentenced prisoners were concerned the criteria approximated to those which courts were required to apply to the making of hospital orders. Not less than two doctors—of whom at least one must be on the local list of psychiatrically qualified or experienced doctors—must report that the prisoner is suffering from one of the four statutory subdivisions of mental disorder,[15] and that this is of a nature or degree which warrants[16] detention in hospital for medical treatment.[17]

In addition the Home Secretary, like the court, is required to be of the opinion that to put the offender in a mental hospital is 'expedient', having regard to 'all the circumstances'. Unlike the courts, however, he is also expressly required to have regard to 'the public interest'—a phrase which seems to have a wider meaning than 'the protection of the public'.[18] If all these requirements are satisfied, the Home Secretary may issue a warrant for his removal to a specified hospital.[19]

Although our main field-work was concerned with hospital order cases, we decided to supplement it by collecting information about a one-year sample of cases in which this power was used. With the help of the Home

Office's Statistical Division we were able to do so for the twelve months from April 1966 to March 1967, and the sample consisted of 131 men and 4 women.

Of this one-year cohort, 90 per cent were serving custodial sentences: that is, sentences of imprisonment or, in a handful of cases, borstal training. In such cases the Home Office has a choice. They may transfer the prisoner without any restriction on his discharge, and it is usual to do this when his 'earliest date of release' (or 'e.d.r.')[20] is less than a month or so off. Eight of the cohort had been transferred in this way, having only short periods still to serve, varying from part of a day to five weeks. The legal status of patients transferred without restrictions on their discharge is that of hospital order cases. Consequently, while the hospital can discharge them at any time, or reclassify them as 'informal' (i.e. voluntary), it can also detain them for a twelve-month, at the end of which it must either let them go, justify further detention or reclassify them as informal (see p. 64). In the event, all but one of our eight transferred prisoners stayed on in hospital voluntarily.

The exception illustrates an interesting point. He was a forty-year-old schizophrenic, serving four years for arson, and with an impressive criminal record which included grievous bodily harm and robbery with violence. (He also assaulted prison officers on two occasions.) At the date of his transfer he was still sixteen months from the end of his sentence; but having apparently lost no remission he would–as an ordinary prisoner –have been released only a month later. No doubt for this reason he was transferred (to an ordinary London hospital) without a restriction on discharge, although he could have been made subject to such a restriction until the expiry of his sentence sixteen months later. Consequently, when he absconded from hospital and succeeded in avoiding recapture for the necessary twenty-eight days[21] he became a free man in law as well as in fact (but was imprisoned in the following year for burglary). If the court which sentenced him to four years had instead made him subject to a hospital order it could–and might well–have added a restriction order *without limit of time* (see p. 91), which would have meant not only that the Home Office had a veto on discharge but also that he would have been liable to recapture for however long he managed to abscond.

More often, the Home Office exercises its right (under s. 74) to direct that the prisoner shall be subject to the special restrictions on discharge which a higher court can impose in the case of certain hospital orders (see pp. 89-97). The practical effect is that he must not be given leave of absence, or transferred to another hospital, without the Home Office's consent; that he cannot gain his freedom by absconding (see p. 165); and that if he recovers before the expiration of his sentence[22] the Home Office can insist on his return to prison (or whatever other type of custodial institution he had been sentenced to). In the comparatively few cases in which he does recover before the expiry of his sentence the Home Office does insist on return to prison, unless his earliest date of release is past or near; but in a few cases they have instead arranged for a conditional discharge (see p. 199).

Late Transfers. Since the transferred prisoner is liable to be detained for a year or perhaps longer (see p. 164), even if the Home Office has not attached a restriction on his discharge, to use the power of transfer towards the end of his sentence could conceivably be criticised as a doubtful method of extending his detention. Nor is it a complete answer to point out that it has been so used—and with less effective safeguards than under the 1959 Act (see p. 26)—ever since transfer became possible; or that in most cases the prisoner is said to consent to transfer. A sounder answer would be that in order to be eligible for transfer prisoners must be suffering from a mental disorder of a nature or degree which warrants their detention in hospital for medical treatment, and thus must be persons who should, if at liberty, be compulsorily admitted in any case. It is true that if at liberty some of them would no doubt succeed in avoiding compulsory admission, so that to this extent transfer from prison towards the end of a sentence ensures detention in hospital for some who would not otherwise have gone to hospital—or at least not so quickly. But this objection savours of the sportsman's argument that the quarry should have a chance of escape, and seems quite inappropriate when one is concerned with a person who, 'in the interests of his own health or safety or for the protection of other persons' (see p. 70) should be in hospital.

Nevertheless, we paid particular attention to cases in which the prisoner was transferred not long before the end of his sentence. Most had simply been serving rather short sentences, of a few weeks or months, so that by the time the doctors had decided that they should be in hospital and found vacancies for them their e.d.rs. were not far off. In three cases, however, the explanation was more complex. One had been serving a 15-month sentence for armed robbery. At the time of trial two doctors agreed that he was not mentally ill enough for a hospital order, although the year before he had been an informal patient in two hospitals. After six months of his sentence, however, they decided that he was sufficiently schizophrenic to justify a transfer; but it took four months to find a vacancy, since his last hospital objected to his behaviour there (but eventually accepted him). Another, a fifty-year-old schizophrenic with a long but trivial record of theft and fraud, had been transferred early in his sentence to a large London hospital (which had accepted thirteen of our cohort), but had absconded from there—as did several other transferred prisoners. He was recaptured, returned to prison and later transferred again to the same hospital.

There were three cases, however, in which the explanation was not so reassuring. One was that of a thirty-year-old man with a long record of thefts and assaults, who was transferred to Broadmoor after serving nearly the whole of a 7-year sentence for robbery with violence. He had no known history of psychiatric treatment before his current sentence, but had been recognised as in need of it at least four years before his transfer, for he had been under psychotherapy and chemotherapy in Wormwood Scrubs since 1962. Having lost all but five months of his remission he was still there in 1966. In that year his condition seems to have worsened, and a medical officer reported that he seemed completely unfit to face the world unaided when released, and had sufficient insight to appreciate

this. After two Regional Hospital Boards had refused to find a place for
him he was accepted by Broadmoor, but transferred two years later to an
ordinary mental hospital.

There were also two 'lifers' who had been transferred after serving no
less than nine years. One turned out to be a paranoid immigrant who at
the age of 31 had killed a fellow-countryman in a brawl. The medical
officer's notes on his state of mind said that his responsibility had probably
been diminished at the time of his crime, but whether or not a defence
of diminished responsibility was considered he was convicted of non-
capital murder. It may well have been difficult at that stage of his illness
–especially in view of his different cultural background–to tell how disordered he was, and his paranoid schizophrenia may have developed very
slowly, although he also seems to have been violent while in prison. He
received psychotherapy and electro-convulsion therapy in Wormwood
Scrubs before it was decided to transfer him.

In the case of the other lifer his disorder must have been recognisable
long before he killed his mother with a chopper at the age of 40, for he had
already spent periods in mental hospitals. His defence of diminished
responsibility had been successful, but he too had received a life sentence,
perhaps because at that date a hospital order was not a possibility. He
had done his time at Wandsworth and then Wormwood Scrubs, where he
received psychotherapeutic treatment before being transferred to an ordinary hospital. By this time he was described as a schizophrenic who had
deteriorated to the condition of a 'vegetable'.

With these exceptions, however, the intervals between the beginning of
the sentence and the transfer were on the whole reassuringly short, especially when the difficulties of finding hospital vacancies for troublesome and
sometimes violent men are concerned. The distribution is shown below:

Months spent in prison	%	% (cumulative)
under 1	11	11
1–3	39	50
4–8	26	76
9–11	10	86
12–17	2	88
18–24	5	93
25–48	4	97
49–59	–	97
60 or more	3	100 (N = 135)

The exact periods varied from a couple of days in the case of a young
depressive labourer to nine years in the cases just described. As the table
shows, however, half were transferred within four months, and three-
quarters within nine months.

What light do these periods throw on the efficiency with which the
system of transfer operated? On the whole, when one remembers that the
prison medical officer must not only notice–or be told of–the signs of disorder or a previous medical history, but also find a hospital vacancy for
the prisoner before he can be transferred, the figures are fairly reassuring.
In most of the cases which were not transferred for a year or more the

nature of their diagnoses was such that their symptoms may not have
become clear until they had served part of their sentence. It is true that
a few psychopathic prisoners were not transferred until they had been
in prison for a year or more; but it is notoriously difficult to find hospital
vacancies for such prisoners. In contrast it is reassuring to find that all
but one of those who were classified as subnormal were transferred within
a few months.[23]

Nevertheless, we thought it advisable to look for any association between
length of sentence and time served before transfer. At least some degree
of association was of course to be expected, since however efficient the
system the longer a person spends in any sort of institution–whether it is
a prison, a hospital, a military barracks or a hotel–the more likely he is to
manifest symptoms of disorder, physical or mental. But a strong association between length of sentence and time served before transfer would
have suggested dilatoriness. Once again, the result[24] was reassuring. For
sentences of two years or less the association was negligible. For sentences
of three to five years there was a slight tendency for transfers to take place
when the prisoner had served between a tenth and a fifth of his sentence;
but this was a fairly low fraction. There was no real evidence of any deliberate policy of waiting until the end of his sentence was in sight before
transferring him.

Unsentenced Prisoners. Thirteen, or 10 per cent, of our cohort had been
transferred before trial or sentence (under s. 73). The status of such cases
is inevitably even more complicated than that of sentenced prisoners. If
at the time of transfer they are awaiting trial or sentence at a higher court
(whether because they have been committed to that court by a summary
court or have been remanded by the higher court itself) the transfer
direction lapses when, and only when, they are either finally disposed of
by the court–for example with a hospital order or a prison sentence–or
their disorder is found no longer to need treatment and they are returned
to normal custody by direction of the Home Secretary (s. 76). It is worth
noting, by the way, that this is one of the rare types of situation in which
a higher court can make a hospital order without convicting the accused
(the others being those in which the accused is found unfit for trial or
not guilty by reason of insanity), and it is the only situation in which
they can make a hospital order in his absence. If on the other hand the
prisoner is merely awaiting another appearance in a magistrates' court (or
is a civil prisoner or alien detained under the Aliens Order) the transfer
direction either expires with the period of remand (unless of course this
is renewed) or is replaced by a hospital or guardianship order or by a
custodial sentence. But if the court's final disposal does not involve one
of these measures, he remains liable to be kept in hospital as if he had been
compulsorily admitted for treatment under civil procedure.[25] If he is a
civil prisoner it expires when his liability to be kept in prison expires; but
he too can be treated as if he had been compulsorily admitted under civil
procedure (s. 78).

Another difference between the sentenced and the unsentenced prisoner
is that whereas the former can be transferred with a diagnosis which falls
under the statutory heading of mental illness, subnormality, severe

subnormality or psychopathic disorder (see pp. 68-9), the unsentenced prisoner's diagnosis must be classifiable as mental illness or *severe* subnormality. This is not the only situation in which this distinction is drawn: others are discussed on pp. 142 and 165. The reason in this case is that non-severe subnormality and psychopathic disorder are not regarded as conditions which make transfer so urgent as to justify the indefinite postponement of trial or sentence.

Two-thirds of our thirteen unsentenced prisoners were schizophrenics in an acute stage of the disorder, so hallucinated or withdrawn that it was impossible to communicate normally with them. Of the rest, one was in a 'toxic confusional state' from abuse of heroin, cocaine and possibly other drugs (he had been twelve years in a mental hospital in the U.S.A., and a year in a British mental hospital, but was given two months' imprisonment by the magistrates when fit for trial a few weeks later). Another, charged with murder, was suffering from 'epileptic psychosis'. He was transferred to Broadmoor, and eventually committed to the same place indefinitely under a hospital order.

All but two of these thirteen offenders were eventually brought to trial, most of them within a few weeks, and all within four months. Of those who were not, one was a paranoid schizophrenic who had been charged with wilful damage to a window and remanded in custody. He was quickly transferred to a mental hospital, and so was not present in court at the appointed date. The clerk simply entered 'no appearance' in the court register, and treated the case as closed. The result was that his transfer direction ceased to have effect when the period of remand expired, and he simply became liable to detention in hospital as if he had been admitted compulsorily for treatment under the non-criminal provisions of the Act (see p. 70 and s. 77 of the Act). The other offender was a schizophrenic woman: she had been charged with stealing, but before her trial a direction was given for her transfer from prison to an ordinary mental hospital. Before the transfer took place, however, she was brought before the magistrates again, who remanded her for two weeks on bail on condition that she remain at the hospital, thus invalidating the transfer direction (which can apply only to a person in lawful custody, and not to persons remanded on bail). When she was brought back to court she was made the subject of an ordinary hospital order.

It is more normal, however, for the case to be disposed of by a sentence of the court. If the patient responds so well to treatment that his psychiatrist considers he no longer needs it, he is returned to prison and dealt with by the court in the ordinary way. Thus two of our thirteen cases received ordinary sentences. One was the heroin addict, who pleaded guilty to obtaining drugs by false pretences, and was simply given two months' imprisonment. The other was a paranoid schizophrenic, who had assaulted a policeman and was fined £25 but detained in lieu of payment until the court rose at the end of the day—a good example of a sentence designed to achieve nothing more than a declaration of the court's disapproval. Two more cases had been committed for trial by higher courts, but were there found unfit for trial: an outcome which underlines the suggestion that magistrates' courts should be allowed to find the accused unfit for trial (see p. 239 of volume 1 and p. 107 of this volume).

At least, however, a finding of unfitness to plead restores the accused to a mental hospital, and this is what happened, in one way or another, to all but the two cases already mentioned. Most of the rest were made subject to 'psychiatric probation orders', that is, probation with a requirement that they accept treatment–in these cases as informal in-patients–at the hospital to which they had been transferred. (For an account of psychiatric probation orders see pp. 64-7.) One of these–a man who had made a serious attack on a neighbour–was remarkable for the fact that he had been considered dangerous enough to be accepted by Broadmoor, yet was eventually placed in a hospital near his home (and no doubt beside the same neighbour). Since his status was informal he was presumably free to walk out of the hospital, the only sanction being recall to court for breach of his probation order–a sanction which is very rarely applied in such cases. One man–the psychotic (or hysterical) epileptic–who had been transferred to Broadmoor, was simply committed to that hospital three months later by Assizes, with a restriction order.

One case was so complicated that it deserves a fuller description. It involved a depressive, amphetamine-addicted diabetic, charged with receiving stolen prescription forms. As the prison medical officer said in his letter to us,

His case, as you will see, makes rather interesting reading in that he was initially committed to [this prison] on the 13th June and no medical report was requested. A voluntary one was sent on the 21st June requesting a further remand so that we could make arrangements to have him admitted to hospital for both physical and mental treatment. This was done and he subsequently reappeared at the Magistrates' Court with a recommendation for treatment under Section 4 of the Criminal Justice Act, 1948 [i.e. a psychiatric probation order]. He was further remanded to the . . . . Sessions and returned here. By the 6th July his diabetes was so obviously out of control and his state of mind so disturbed that we managed to have him admitted to . . . . Hospital in an attempt to stabilize him. He was then returned to us on the 11th July, with the following note from the consultant: 'In view of the problem of his drug dependency he has been transferred back to prison on account of his lack of co-operation.' At this stage he was so depressed and suicidal that arrangements were made to transfer him under Section 73.

He seems, however, to have recovered sufficiently by the following January to abscond successfully from the London hospital mentioned earlier, and to have incurred three more convictions in rapid succession, one of them for possessing dangerous drugs.

A third category must be briefly mentioned, although it is so rare that no instance of it appeared in our cohort. For the first time the 1959 legislation brought civil prisoners within the transfer powers, so that debtors, recalcitrant wife-maintainers and people imprisoned for contempt of court[26] can now be compulsorily transferred to mental hospitals. Their position resembles that of sentenced prisoners, for the transfer direction has effect

TABLE 1. Men and women transferred from prisons or borstals to mental hospitals between 1 April 1966 and 31 March 1967

		totals
Transferred before trial or sentence (under s. 73) and eventually		
a. committed to hospital as unfit to plead	2	
b. detained in hospital under Part VI	2	
c. disposed of by court with hospital order or psychiatric probation order	7	
d. disposed of by court with ordinary sentence (fine or imprisonment)	2	
		13
Transferred during sentence (under s. 72) *without restriction on discharge, and eventually*		
e. regraded as informal patient	6	
f. discharged from hospital	1	
g. absconded successfully	1	
		8
Transferred during sentence (under s. 72) *with restriction on discharge (under s. 74) and eventually*		
h. regraded as informal patient	8	
i. discharged from hospital before end of sentence	19	
j. discharged from hospital at end of sentence	10	
k. detained in hospital after end of sentence (under s. 60) and later discharged	19	
l. returned to prison	26	
m. absconded successfully		
before end of sentence	1	
after end of sentence	4	
n. repatriated or deported	3	
o. died	1	
p. still in hospital at the end of 1969	23	
		114
		135

until the end of the full period for which they are liable to be detained; they can but do not have to be subject to restrictions on their discharge,[27] and they are in the same position, whether or not a transfer direction has been imposed, as patients admitted compulsorily for treatment.

Table 1 summarises the fates of our 135 transferred prisoners. What it does not of course show are the cases in which medical opinion was in favour of a transfer but for one reason or another this did not take place. It is widely believed—even in the prison service—that this happens frequently, and especially in the case of 'psychopaths'. Yet figures which we were given by the Home Office suggested that the frequency of that particular problem has been exaggerated. The numbers were in fact so small that only a period of several years could safely be taken as representative. In the four years 1967–70, out of 443 cases in which the transfer of a *sentenced*[28] prisoner was initially recommended, there were only 27–an average of less than 7 a year–in which it did not eventually take place. In 5 cases it had been impossible to find a hospital vacancy; in 3 others the medical report had not been considered adequate to justify transfer, and in 13 cases the report had been withdrawn by the doctors, no doubt after being queried by the Home Office.[29] Thus a transfer recommendation by the doctors had a 94 per cent chance of success. Where the diagnosis was psychopathic disorder, however, the chances of success were lower–about 85 per cent–although it could not be said that this was due to any particular reason, such as the greater difficulty of securing hospital vacancies. It must be admitted, of course, that these figures could not, in the nature of things, reflect the cases which prison medical officers *would have* recommended for transfer if they had been more optimistic about the chances of success; but it is impossible to say whether the number of these is large or small.

Finally, there is the exceptional case in which, although all the necessary conditions of transfer are fulfilled, a dangerous prisoner is regarded as so serious an escape-risk that the interests of the public are allowed priority over his need for treatment in a hospital, and transfer is refused. This does not of course mean that he receives no treatment: as we shall see in the next chapter the prison service makes serious efforts to provide psychiatric treatment for its charges. Nor can it be confidently argued that the prisoner is necessarily worse off than he would have been in the strict security of a Special Hospital.

In contrast to hospital order cases, of which only about one in ten go to Special Hospitals, one in four of our transferred prisoners did so. Of the 103 who went to ordinary hospitals, fully a quarter (29) absconded during their first six months there, some of them several times. It was noticeable that all the absconders had criminal records, compared with only 83 per cent of the non-absconders ($p < 0.025$);[30] but this was the only sign of an association between criminal sophistication and absconding.[31]

Psychiatric Aspects. It is time, however, to turn from the legal and administrative aspects of such transfers to other points of interest. For instance, the sex-ratio of our sample, at 4:131, was surprisingly close to the sex-ratio for the daily average prison population, which in 1966 was 1:35. We had expected a somewhat higher proportion of females, since female prisoners are often said to be more likely to be disordered than their male counterparts. Indeed, it has been officially stated that 'more than half' of all women in custody receive some form of psychiatric treatment during their sentence, the corresponding fraction for men being somewhat less than a fifth.[32] Either the hospital wing at Holloway is coping with cases which, had they been male, would have been transferred, or else the mental disorders to which women prisoners seem so prone are on the whole of a milder or more quickly treatable sort. A contributing factor may be the comparative shortness of most women's sentences.

Equally striking, when one recalls the large numbers of subnormal prisoners with which the service had been burdened in earlier decades, was the small percentage (10 per cent) of transferred prisoners who fell into this category, although another 17 per cent were classified as psychopathic,

D

and would in some cases at least have been included among the 'defectives' as 'moral imbeciles' in the days before the Mental Health Act (see pp. 211 and 212). Even so, 10 per cent is markedly less than the 38 per cent of our hospital order sample which were diagnosed as subnormal.

In comparison with the other transferred prisoners this small group of subnormals was young: the oldest was 34, and half were under 23. The careers of subnormal offenders will be discussed more fully when we come to our hospital order cases in chapter 6. It is sufficient here to say that if a subnormal is going to fall foul of the law he is likely to do so fairly soon after leaving the shelter of home or school. It was fairly consistent with this that our older subnormals had long records of appearances in criminal courts: the two thirty-four-year-olds had 19 and 20 respectively, chiefly for theft and other dishonesties. Half of the group were known to have been patients in mental hospitals, and as always this should be regarded as a minimum estimate.

It was to a large extent the scarcity of subnormals which made the percentage of schizophrenics amongst our transferred prisoners (61 per cent) seem so large, especially in comparison with the 41 per cent of our hospital order sample which fell into this diagnostic group (see p. 140). When the subnormals were deducted roughly two-thirds of the remainder was schizophrenic in both samples.

Slightly less than half of our transferred schizophrenics had no known history of previous psychiatric treatment outside prison. As a group, however, they were practically indistinguishable from those with psychiatric histories. They were slightly younger, containing three youths under 20 (yet also containing the oldest schizophrenic in the sample, aged 65); but it was possible to match the great majority age for age with the other group. They had slightly fewer previous convictions, but a formidable number none the less (a mean of 7·1 per prisoner compared with 8·3). One schizophrenic with a previous psychiatric history had 28 previous appearances in a criminal court; but one of those with no such history had 26!

As for the 13 depressives, their numbers were too small to make comparisons with the schizophrenics reliable. It was noticeable, however, that at least two-thirds had previous psychiatric histories; and that they averaged no less than 13·1 previous appearances in criminal courts. But they owed this high average to two men, one with 54 the other with 40 previous appearances, mostly for being 'drunk and disorderly'; and if these were excluded the average would be 6·9–not very different from the schizophrenics.

The only female depressive was a rather dangerous woman. She had a long record of petty thefts, but at the age of 26 had tried to kill her father, using insecticide in his drink and then gas. She received a 5-year sentence, and when released at her e.d.r. became a voluntary patient in an ordinary mental hospital, but left it a week later. Within a matter of weeks she had tried to kill her niece, using sleeping-pills in a drink and then gas. This time she received a 10-year sentence, but was rapidly transferred to Broadmoor, where schizophrenia as well as depression was diagnosed. Her sentence will expire in the mid-seventies, after which she will no longer be subject to a formal restriction on discharge, so that her continued detention will be a matter for the hospital, but subject to her right of appeal to the local Mental Health Review Tribunal.

The 22 'psychopaths'—whose diagnostic label will be discussed fully in a separate chapter—not surprisingly averaged more court appearances (9·7) than any other diagnostic group (if we disregard the two depressive drinkers), although next to the subnormals they were the youngest group. Two-thirds of those transferred went to Broadmoor or Rampton. The seven who were accepted by ordinary hospitals were kept in locked wards, with two exceptions. One of these exceptions was the only psychopathic absconder, and as his record seemed to consist entirely of theft, fraud or 'being a suspected person' he seemed relatively harmless.

The remaining diagnoses included the oldest prisoner in the cohort, a seventy-four-year-old pensioner who was serving a short sentence for his thirty-sixth conviction for larceny (to say nothing of ten others, mostly for vagrancy). He was transferred to a local hospital, where he was re-classified as an informal patient about seven months later, and eventually left.

Of our whole cohort rather more than half were known to have pre-viously been in mental hospitals or in the psychiatric prison at Grendon. We also asked for information about any psychiatric treatment which they had received during their current sentences, and noted that those with previous psychiatric histories were only slightly more likely (41 per cent) to have received treatment while in prison than those without (36 per cent): a difference which was not large enough for significance.[33]

We shall have a little more to say about this cohort at various junctures in the rest of this book. For the moment it is time to consider the residual psychiatric problems of the prison service.

Notes

1. Mitchell eventually escaped from a working party at Dartmoor in 1966, but was murdered by the gang which helped him to do so.
2. See the article 'A Chapter in the History of Criminal Lunacy in England' by D. Nicolson in (1877) 23, *Journal of Mental Science*, 165 ff. Although Nicolson cites no source for this information and we have been unable to discover any, we have no reason to doubt it; so that page 224 in volume 1 of this book should be amended accordingly.
3. 56 Geo. III. c. 117, later consolidated into 9 Geo. IV. c. 40 (the Act of 1828).
4. S. & B. Webb, *English Prisons under Local Government* (London, 1922), 70.
5. 'Report of the Inspectors appointed under the provisions of the Act 5 & 6 Will. IV. c. 38 to visit the different prisons of Great Britain' (1836) Parliamentary Papers, XXXV.
6. See 5 & 6 Vict. c. 29 and 6 & 7 Vict. c. 26.
7. 3 & 4 Vict. c. 54.
8. His story has been told in full by P. G. Rogers in *The Battle of*

Bossenden Wood (Oxford, 1961) from which most of our abridged account is taken.

9.   27 & 28 Vict. c. 29.

10. 47 & 48 Vict. c. 64.

11. See chapter 1 note 1.

12. 3 & 4 Geo v. c. 28.

13. R. v. Head (1957) 41 Cr. App. R. 249 and (for the House of Lords Judgement) (1958) 42 Cr. App. R. 98.

14. We are indebted to the Home Office for this information.

15. See pp. 68-9.

16. See pp. 85-6.

17. A phrase which is given a very wide meaning by the Act: see p. 223.

18. 'The protection of the public' is one of the considerations which the court must have in mind when deciding whether to make a restriction order (see pp. 89-99), so that 'the public interest', though it may *include* this, must mean something different.

19. I.e., a National Health Service hospital, or one of the Special Hospitals or one of certain local authority establishments, but *not* a mental nursing home: see ss. 72, 147.

20. This date, known as the 'e.d.r.' is the date on which he is due for release when allowance is made for any remission which he has not forfeited for breaches of discipline. He has no absolute right to this remission (see Morris v. Winter [1930] 1 K.B. 243), and s. 75 of the 1959 Act allows the Home Secretary to place a restriction on his discharge before the *expiration* of his sentence: that is, to disregard any remission. But in practice his e.d.r. determines not only the decision whether to impose any restriction when transferring him, but also the decision whether it is worth transferring him back to prison if he recovers while a restriction is still in force.

21   See p. 165.

22. But see note 20.

23. The exception was a subnormal borstal boy who was not transferred for nine months: but he was at Feltham, which specialises in mildly disordered cases (see p. 42).

24. We plotted a scatter-diagram, in which one parameter was length of sentence, the other the fraction of the sentence served before transfer.

25. See s. 77 and pp. 163-4. It is worth nothing that the section provides for the patient's return to prison if (improbably) he recovers, but only in cases where he has been committed for trial by a higher court. This has caused inconvenience in at least one case, in which the diagnosis of mental illness appeared to have been mistaken, and the patient was so disruptive that the hospital wanted him to return to prison, but had to be told that they had to wait until he appeared in the magistrates' court again.

26. Unless they are committed *sine die*, in which case the agreement of the court is sought to their release so that they can be compul-

sorily admitted to hospital under Part IV of the Act (see p. 70).

27. The same is true of a person detained under the Aliens Order.

28. Unsentenced prisoners were not included; and in view of the complications surrounding their transfer–among which is shortage of time–this was understandable.

29. The remaining reasons were miscellaneous.

30. Excluding, of course, those who went to Special Hospitals, and also excluding the immigrant lifer already mentioned, whose clean record may simply have been due to lack of information about his previous career.

31. There seemed to be no significant association between number of previous convictions and *number* of abscondings, nor between diagnosis and absconding.

32. See the Home Office's 'People in Prison' (Cmnd. 4214, HMSO, 1969), 34 .We noted, however, that only one of our four women was said to have received treatment in prison.

33. The difference was no greater if the subnormals, none of whom were said to have received treatment in prison, were excluded.

Chapter 3. **The Prisons' Residual Problems**

The transformation of prisoners into patients has never done more than relieve the gaols of the obviously disordered. They have always had to cope with the residual problem of the prisoner whose degree of disorder, though marked enough to interfere with discipline and communication, is not sufficient to satisfy the psychiatric criteria of the day. It is true that these criteria have gradually been widened to include cases which would previously have been rejected; but this process has been paralleled by an increasing readiness to recognise mild disorder in prisoners who would formerly have been regarded as normal, so that there probably always will be a residual problem.

We saw in the previous chapter that the first report of the Inspectors of Prisons recommended the use of Millbank, the first of the State Penitentiaries, to cope with this problem. That grim establishment, however, had enough troubles of its own. Some were architectural, some spiritual. Built on marshy ground where the Tate Gallery now stands, some of its walls were cracking and leaning outwards at a visible angle. More important, it was harassed by disease and rioting amongst the prisoners, to say nothing of 'jars and jealousies' between governor and chaplain. In those days the chaplain was at least as powerful as the medical officer is today, and it was to avoid these top-level conflicts that in 1836–the year of the Inspectors' Report–the retiring governor was actually replaced by the chaplain. The Reverend Daniel Nihill was a fanatical believer in the separate system, which confined men, women and children to individual cells to meditate on their sins; but after a few years of his regime the medical officer managed to persuade his committee that this was the main cause of the increasing numbers of insane prisoners, and Nihill was forced to adopt a more relaxed, if equally religious, approach.[1]

All things considered, it must have been obvious that Millbank was not the right 'receptacle' for borderline cases of mental disorder. As a result, nothing much was done to meet the inspectors' point during the eighteen-forties. It is true that one of the hulks was set aside for 'invalid prisoners', on the assumption that seaside air would be healthier than the stench and damp of the penitentiaries, and these invalids included some insane and 'weak-minded' offenders. The standard of care, however, can be judged from what an inspection of this hulk disclosed in 1847:

. . . a violent lunatic confined in what is not inaptly termed the cage. This cage is situated at the head of the ship on the lower deck, is of

irregular shape . . . and scarcely of sufficient height to admit of a man
to stand upright. The front is secured by open iron bars, and . . .
the inmate is exposed to the full view of the patients. This place has
been resorted to for unmanageable insane prisoners and also on some
occasions for prisoners under punishment, as in the case of T. V. kept
in it for two months. Taking into consideration the violence manifested
by the prisoner G. W. and the intolerable nuisance he was both day and
night to the patients in the hospital and invalid ship for three months,
the medical officer ought to have taken proper steps for his removal
three months before.

It was not until the end of transportation seemed imminent in the early
fifties that a slightly more constructive step was taken. New convict prisons
had to be opened in a hurry to cope with the backwash of untransported
convicts. Among these was Dartmoor, originally built for Frenchmen
during the Napoleonic wars, and now uninhabited and dilapidated.
Hastily renovated by convict labour it began in 1852 to receive the first
invalid prisoners. It was soon decided to make it the receptacle for 'weak-
minded' men–a category which seems to have included 'dull intellect, . . .
despondency, eccentricity'; and there were also a few who were frankly
insane, as well as more than a few epileptics.

At first the medical officers were enthusiastic. Not even the desolation
of the moors, nor the rain-soaked, chilly weather daunted them, and they
reported improvement even amongst phthisics, who were notoriously supposed to deteriorate in such a climate. The invalids were put to light work,
and morale seemed high. All might have been well had it not been for the
weak-minded prisoners. They became excited and unmanageable; were
occasionally violent, and generally interfered with the smooth running of
the place. In 1856, when there were 'upwards of 80' of them, the medical
officer recommended that they be segregated from the others, and put
under officers with experience in managing the insane, helped by a few
normally behaved prisoners in each gang. In the following year something
of the sort seems to have been done. The weak-minded were segregated
in a special ward next to the infirmary. A 'distinct class of officer' was
selected to cope with them and they were subject to 'a qualified system of
discipline more adapted to their state of comparative mental incapacity'.

Even so, all does not seem to have gone well. As so often, it is not easy
to make out from the annual reports of medical officers and governors
exactly what was wrong. All that was said was that the 'accommodation
was deficient', which may have meant that it was not large enough to hold
all the weak-minded, or not secure enough, or both. However that may
be, there was a widespread reorganisation of the convict prisons in 1863.
Parkhurst–until then a boys' prison–became the female prison; the boys
went to Dartmoor; and the weak-minded were at long last concentrated
in Millbank. Broadmoor was on the point of being opened (see chapter
1), and no doubt it was hoped that this would make it possible to get rid
of many more of these troublesome and dangerous convicts, especially if
they were more accessible to visiting experts than they had been at Dartmoor. Certainly Millbank seems to have been regarded chiefly as a sort of
observation centre so far as disordered convicts were concerned. Men in

this category were put into a special part of the prison (women, being less numerous, had no special accommodation, but were simply put in a cell with two other females of known sanity!). A close watch was kept on them, for the prison staff—including the doctors—were well aware that some convicts were capable of feigning insanity in order to be sent to 'the Farm', as Broadmoor was now called in convict slang. So determinedly sceptical were the doctors that in the case of 'T.W.', who in their view was feigning, but so skilfully that months of observation failed to expose him, they eventually conceded that he was genuinely insane—but added that it was because he had made himself so by feigning. At first those unfortunates who were diagnosed as malingerers or simply weak-minded remained in Millbank, but in 1869, when female convicts were moved from Parkhurst to Woking, a part of the former was set aside for invalid males, and at least some of the weak-minded went there.

Even where the certifiable convict was concerned, the opening of Broadmoor did not provide the complete and lasting solution which had been hoped for. Within a short time it had just over 150 insane convicts, and there were others still in prison for whom it had no room. Insane convicts were regarded as far more troublesome and cunning than the ordinary 'Her Majesty's Pleasure' lunatics, who were not usually sophisticated criminals; but there was not room to segregate all of them. Their attempts to escape were more frequent, and in 1873 no fewer than four got clean away, two of them for good. One, William Bisgrove, was a murderer, whose conduct for the last eighteen months had been so good that he had been allowed to exercise outside the walls under the escort of an attendant. One July day he asked his attendant some question about a rabbit burrow which they were passing on their walk. The attendant bent to look at it, and Bisgrove hit him with a stone and tried to strangle him. After a struggle the patient ran off into the woods, and was never seen or heard of again.[2]

These escapes caused considerable public alarm, and in 1874 the Commissioners in Lunacy put a stop to the transfer of any more male (but not female) convicts to Broadmoor. Part of nearby Woking Prison had been designed as a hospital, and to this the insane men were now sent to spend the rest of their sentence. Although the transfer of men to Broadmoor was cautiously resumed in 1886, the use of Woking was decided upon at the time not as a temporary expedient but as part of a permanent reorganisation by the Directors of Convict Prisons, who took the view that

> . . . there is good ground for anticipating that a propensity to sham insanity, or that deliberate abandonment of self-control which resembles, or may actually develope into insanity, will be checked by the knowledge that it will not lead to a transfer to the comforts and comparative freedom of 'The Farm'. . .

Those who had not recovered by their day of release were transferred at the last moment to Broadmoor (usually via Millbank!) so that they could correctly be sent to the asylum of the county where their offence had been committed, there to be maintained by the ratepayer instead of the taxpayer.

Until 1877 these expedients were used only for convicts, that is, the felons sentenced to penal servitude in the State prisons. Prisoners in local gaols were the responsibility of the justices, whose duty it was to have them transferred to county asylums if their mental state justified this and the asylum would accept them. The inmates of the local gaols were serving relatively short sentences, whose expiry must often have solved the problem, at least for the justices. When the Prison Commissioners took over the responsibility for all gaols in 1877 they had no place for all the insane and weak-minded inmates, and they merely continued the practice of transferring as many as possible to the county asylums, although perhaps rather more conscientiously than the justices had done.

By the mid eighteen-eighties, however, the prisons were becoming restive about the numbers of obviously insane men and women who were being dumped on them by the courts, usually by means of sentences which were too short to enable them to be found places in asylums. These prisoners had to be looked after with special care, for suicide or violence was an ever-present risk. Staff were instructed that they must not be left alone, but placed in rooms together, and kept under constant surveillance by warders or hired attendants. Nor were the courts unaware of what they were doing. 'The prison authorities', complains the Commissioners' report of 1884, 'are placed in a position of especial difficulty when the medical officers report a person to be insane but the magistrates decline to give the certificate necessary for his removal to a lunatic asylum, and it is a question whether in such cases a prisoner should not be simply discharged.' This solution was both legally and administratively attractive: if the accused was insane he did not deserve imprisonment, and by discharging him the magistrates would both see that justice was done and relieve the prisons of a burden. It did not of course face the real problem, or the possibility that the lunatic, if he could not be sent to an asylum, would at least be better off in prison than in the streets.

Nor were the insane the only problem, for courts were committing the seriously ill and the dying. It was not until 1889, however, after renewed complaints from the Medical Inspector of the prisons, that the Home Office summoned up the courage to lecture magistrates on their duty, with the far-reaching results that will be described in the next chapter (see p. 59).

At the time, however, it provided only a slight relief for the prisons. The official prevalence of insanity amongst prisoners did decline slightly over the next decade, but there remained the problem of the weak-minded. This could no longer be treated as a minor nuisance, for the Penal Servitude Commission[3] of 1879 had pointed out that they 'form a large proportion of the habitual criminal class and are notorious for the repeated commission of petty thefts and other comparatively trivial offences'. They were a hindrance to staff who were trying to enforce discipline, an irritation to other prisoners, and victims of those who were ready to take advantage of them. The Commission said firmly that they ought to be completely segregated in a distinct wing of some prison, instead of being divided between Millbank, Woking, Parkhurst and other establishments. No attention seems to have been paid to this recommendation at the time, but it was renewed by the medical officers who gave evidence to the

Gladstone Committee of 1894–5. The Directors acted with belated speed, and in the following year Parkhurst was designated as the prison for all weak-minded men whose sentences were long enough to make transfer worth while.

Ten years later, in 1906, the problem of finding places for certifiable but dangerous prisoners was again acute (Broadmoor was full); and Parkhurst had to become not merely the prison for weak-minded males[4] but also an officially approved Criminal Lunatic Asylum, using for the purpose a specially adapted wing. The Commissioners in Lunacy, though sufficiently satisfied with the adaptations to approve the building, were critical of the cramped space for exercise and the prison-like atmosphere, and it was recognised that the arrangement was to last only until Rampton opened, which–as we saw in chapter 1–it did in 1912.

Although the opening of Rampton and the passing of the Mental Deficiency Act in the following year relieved the prisons of a considerable part of the problem, we have seen in the previous chapter that they were not able to rid themselves of as many defectives as they would have liked. Parkhurst had ceased to be a repository for the weak-minded, and when it once more became necessary–in the mid twenties–to designate special units for them parts of Birmingham, Liverpool, Lincoln and Wormwood Scrubs Prisons were used for this purpose.

It was especially difficult to find institutional places for certifiable males in the borstal age-group (16-21), and many had to wait so long that in 1920 a special borstal was reserved for them. This was Feltham, a large 'industrial school' building on the outskirts of London. At first it operated both as a reception centre where boys were picked out and retained; but it was not long before this function was performed instead by Wandsworth and later Wormwood Scrubs. Feltham continued, however, to receive the mentally handicapped, along with the less tough of the normal borstal boys. After the 1939–45 war the retarded boys were supplemented by growing numbers of boys suffering from mild mental illness and personality disorders, who eventually replaced the normal inmates. The full-time medical officer was joined by one part-time psychotherapist (and later by two more) and eventually by a full-time psychiatrist. The borstal's capacity is now about 320, although it sometimes holds more than that number. Most male borstal trainees who seem likely to be candidates for transfer to a mental hospital go to Feltham for observation and examination, and all seven of the borstal youths in our sample of transferred prisoners had come from this establishment. The great majority of Feltham youths, however, are not transferred, but spend the whole of their sentence there.

Nevertheless, with the exception of some borstal boys, by the end of the nineteen-twenties the prison system had more or less rid itself of the responsibility for the unmanageably insane or defective offender, and its medical officers were able to give more of their attention to disorders that seemed likely to respond to treatment. The nineteen-twenties saw the birth of the psychoanalytic movement in British psychiatry, with Sir William Brown, Ernest Jones and Edward Glover as its *accoucheurs*. It was not a popular infant, and there were Herods in the medical profession who would have gladly stifled it, especially when it began to be taken up by the laymen. In the prison service the pioneers of the psychoanalytic approach were Drs Hamblin Smith and Grace Pailthorpe in Birmingham Prison's observation unit, both of whom published books on the psychology of the criminal.[5]

Treatment in Prison

The first prison unit for psychotherapeutic treatment, however, was not created until the Dove-Wilson Committee on Persistent Offenders reported in 1932. Although the medical evidence to the Committee had been scientifically cautious on the subject, the members were on the whole sufficiently impressed to recommend the experimental appointment of a medical officer to try out the method. Norwood East, who had recently become the Medical Commissioner, appointed Dr Hubert of St Thomas's Hospital as 'psychotherapist' to Wormwood Scrubs, where a good deal of mental observation was already carried out. A good idea of the types of case which he treated, and his approach to them, can be got from the report which East and Hubert published in 1939.

The East-Hubert report on the Psychological Treatment of Crime[6] had a good deal to say about the psychotherapeutic approach in general, to which the experienced Norwood East was by no means wholly favourable ('. . . in this field enthusiasm not uncommonly outruns discretion, and it would be a great misfortune if the psychiatric approach to crime became discredited by irresponsible exponents unaware, perhaps, of the complexity of the problems involved'). Its most important recommendation, however, was the creation of a special institution, which was to fulfil several functions:

First, as a clinic and hospital, where cases could be investigated and,
if necessary, treated by psychotherapy and other means, and their
disposal decided upon. This would serve also as a centre for
criminological research . . .

Second, as an institution in which selected cases could live under special
conditions of training and treatment. Many cases who proved unsuitable
for, and unmodified by, the re-educative and rehabilitative influences
of the modern prison system would be allocated to this section . . .

Third, as a colony in which a further type of offender would live, who
had proved himself quite unable to adapt himself to ordinary social
conditions but for whom reformative measures, however specialised,
seemed useless and the severity and hardship of ordinary prison life
inappropriate.

Fourth, as an observation and treatment centre for Borstal lads who
because of mental abnormality appeared unsuitable for, or had failed
to respond to, ordinary Borstal training and for various reasons were
considered unfit for early licence.

Although the report was welcomed not only by the prison service but also by the medical profession, it is doubtful whether either the authors or anyone else at the time realised quite how mixed a bag they were trying to bring home with this blunderbuss. Leaving aside the Borstal inmates, who were a separate category merely by virtue of their age, the institution was to fulfil at least four distinct functions – investigation, short-term treatment, long-term training and simple care and custody of the incorrigible. The idea of combining these in a single establishment has little to recommend it except economy. It is true that for the unfortunate prison service economy has always had to be an important consideration; the Treasury, Parliament and the Press have always grudged expenditure on the care of malefactors. Moreover, economy means counting not only money but also medical officers and other highly trained staff. A single institution with several 'wings' allows psychiatrists to devote part of their time to different categories of patient in a way which would be impossible if each category were accommodated in different parts of England.

To do East and Hubert justice, they were planning at a time when enormous psychiatric institutions comprising units for different types of patient were standard; and they cannot be blamed for thinking along similar lines. From this point of view it may have been fortunate that the war put their plan on the shelf for a whole decade. In 1947 the Commissioners admitted that 'no progress' had been possible with the acquisition of land and buildings for the purpose, and went on to outline a more modest aim for the institution, at least in its initial stages. It might cater for prisoners who did not need 'full security'; this would exclude most of the psychopaths who were the bulk of the problem in prisons and Borstals, but would offer better prospects of cure for those amenable to psychotherapy. The optimism of Hubert was still alive: 'the restorative effects of psychotherapy in suitable cases is known', wrote East's successor, Dr Methven. When plans for the new institution were finally approved, however, it was clear that whatever categories of prisoners were now in the minds of the Commissioners, security *was* an important consideration. The site chosen[7] adjoined the open prison at Springhill in Buckinghamshire; but the new buildings were surrounded by a high wall, and the buildings themselves were also designed with an eye to security. The architecture may well have been a concession to local alarm, which was considerable.

The new prison, called Grendon after the nearby village, was opened in 1962. The first batch of prisoners came from the unit at Wormwood Scrubs, with their psychotherapist, Dr H.P.Tollington. Instead of a governor the institution had–as East and Hubert proposed–a Medical Superintendent, with considerable experience as a prison medical officer, Dr W.J.Gray. It was not the first time that an English prison had been governed by a doctor, for Maidstone had been governed by Dr Mathieson a generation before. Mathieson, however, was a Governor, appointed not because he was a doctor but because he had shown his capacity for management, whereas it was clear that Grendon was to be the responsibility of a psychiatrically experienced doctor. He was assisted, however, by a lay Deputy Governor, and the 'discipline staff' were uniformed prison officers, although many were trained hospital officers, and most had volunteered for duty in the new establishment. The professional staff consisted of psychiatrists, psychologists, a psychiatric social worker and a welfare officer; and the ratio of professional staff to inmates was extremely high, even by the standards of European or American psychiatric prisons.

The main wings of the prison were of course for adult males: that is men aged 21 or older, although after a few months a small 'boys' wing was opened for 'young prisoners' (i.e. males under 21 serving prison sentences) and Borstal trainees, who might be of any age from 15 to 20, but were usually at the older end of this age-range.

Although part of the prison was designed as a women's wing, it has never operated as such. The admission of women seemed likely to add to the already numerous problems, psychological and administrative, with which the main prison had to cope; and although the hospital wing at Holloway was agreed by all concerned to be most unsatisfactory, it has continued to cope with the female counterparts of the men who go to Grendon. The wing intended for women at Grendon eventually became a second 'boys' wing, deliberately run on more authoritarian lines than the original wing for boys, in order to compare results.

The choice of prisoners for treatment at Grendon was originally the responsibility of the Director of Prison Medical Services, to whom prison medical officers would refer cases which they considered suitable. Since the division of prisons into four regions in 1969, the choice has for the most part been the task of regional Principal Medical Officers, although lifers and other long-term prisoners are still the responsibility of the director. The Medical Superintendent of Grendon is consulted about cases which seem to present special problems of treatment or security, and in every case about the date of transfer, since the stage of sentence at which this takes place may be of great importance. On the whole it is considered better to arrange matters so that a prisoner can be discharged direct to freedom, but about one in every eleven is returned from Grendon to an ordinary prison or Borstal. Re-transfers for disciplinary reasons, which were at first quite frequent and happened with such speed that they were known as 'the Ghost Train', have become less frequent as the staff's skill has increased.

So far as treatment is concerned, the main emphasis is on psychotherapy, in *tête-à-tête* sessions and groups, although chemotherapy, behaviour therapy and other techniques are employed in selected cases. From the start a determined effort was made to make the prison a 'therapeutic milieu', in particular by involving uniformed staff in the process, so that they would understand what the psychiatrists and psychologists were attempting and reinforce it. Most of the prison officers, who had volunteered for duty at Grendon, were very ready to fulfil this function, and responded enthusiastically. Group counselling (see pp. 46 ff.) with basic grade officers in charge, was launched within a few months, and did a great deal to break down the communication-gap which separates custodians from inmates in the ordinary penal establishment. Never in any British prison can relations between prisoners and staff have been so relaxed and informal.

By 1970 several developments had either taken place or been approved. One was the use of the open prison which adjoins Grendon as a place to which selected prisoners could graduate without severing their contacts with psychiatrists and other staff 'inside'. Another was the establishment of hostels in nearby towns, where suitable patients could spend the final part of their sentence going out to work under everyday conditions, though the opening of the first hostel was delayed by various difficulties. The psychiatric social worker, Mrs Millar-Smith, was running an informal club in central London, where ex-patients could meet each other and members of the staff.

An interesting phenomenon, however, was the volley of criticism from psychiatrists and criminologists, which began almost as soon as the new prison opened, and indeed came sometimes from long-distance snipers who had not even entered it. Some of the criticisms were shrewd, some merely ill-informed; but their most interesting aspect was the extent to which they appeared to be ideological. Many critics seemed to assume that a prison–or at least a secure prison–could not be a therapeutic establishment (an assumption which was turned into a slogan by some of the more intellectual prisoners, who would heckle staff with the question 'Is this a prison or a hospital?'). Some critics seemed to hold this as a self-evident proposition; others based it, more empirically, on their acquaintance with the English prison system. Both kinds appeared to take it for granted that the more closely the establishment resembled an ordinary mental hospital the more successful it would be, although the success of the latter–as we shall see in later chapters–is by no means spectacular.

Another criticism–that the system is highly selective, so that Grendon receives no more than a fraction of the prisoners who need a psychiatric regime–begs almost as many questions. As we suggested at the beginning of this chapter, as soon as the needs of any category of disorder are recognised and catered for, this will of itself create a penumbra of border-line cases; and if these were catered for the penumbra would be widened rather than abolished. This is not to deny that there may be many inmates of ordinary prisons who are as disordered as some of those in Grendon, or, by the same token, that more places for such prisoners are needed in Grendon and the psychiatric units of other prisons. It is equally possible, however, that this approach has been carried as far as–or even beyond– the point at which it is profitable (whether profit is reckoned in terms of post-release behaviour or in terms of humane treatment during sentence); and that instead of concentrating scarce and expensive resources on selected prisoners it would be more effective to aim at the diffusion of a psychiatric or psychological enlightenment throughout the regimes of ordinary prisons.

Group Counselling

As an object-lesson however in what can go wrong with an approach of this kind it seems worth while to give a brief account of the rise and fall of 'group counselling', without which this chapter would in any case be incomplete. One of the most important developments of the last few decades has been the way in which psychiatric, or more precisely psychotherapeutic, techniques have been applied to problems which do not necessarily involve mental disorder. A striking example is social casework, in which the concept of psychoanalysis, and some techniques derived from it, are applied to the 'moral management' of rebellious children, irresponsible parents, helpless octogenarians and delinquents of all ages. More closely connected with penal systems, however, is the development known as 'group counselling'.

This can be traced to California, probably the most psychoanalytically-minded area in the world, where group psychotherapy was popularised in the nineteen-forties by practitioners such as Corsini, Moreno and Helen Jennings.[8] By the end of the 1939–45 war those responsible for the State Penitentiaries, and especially San Quentin, were looking for psychiatrists and psychologists to form groups of long-term prisoners for psychotherapy. Qualified psychotherapists, however, were already in demand for other work, with higher pay and prestige, and few were willing to spend much time in the penitentiaries.

The climate was thus favourable for the formation of groups which did not rely on the presence of a trained psychotherapist. By 1944 the Reception-Guidance Center at San Quentin Prison (which was the rough equivalent of an allocation wing in an English prison) was providing educational and vocational classes for newly received prisoners, and the teachers in charge were soon made aware of the new inmates' desire to use the classes as an opportunity to discuss their personal problems and difficulties. Some of the teachers already had experience of what is known as 'counseling'[9] in schools and colleges, and they soon found themselves playing the role of counsellors in San Quentin. This created a demand for groups of this sort among inmates of other prisons who had passed through the Reception-Guidance Center; but although the demand had the support of prison psychiatrists and psychologists, the necessary money to pay for more trained staff was not forthcoming. In 1954, therefore, Folsom prison was persuaded to experiment with groups which were in the charge not of teachers or psychotherapists but of 'correctional officers' (i.e., uniformed prison staff). The experiment was largely the result of the efforts of Norman Fenton, who wrote the first manuals of instruction for the 'group counselors'.

In the English prison system personal communication – whether between the inmates themselves or between staff and inmates – had normally been regarded as pernicious. The Quakers had justified solitary confinement as positively beneficial. Our nineteenth-century prison governors knew better, for they saw the ill-effects of the separate system every day, but they substituted a negative justification: that it prevented unsophisticated prisoners from being contaminated by habitual criminals. When the separate system in its turn was abandoned, the 'rule of silence' remained, and was enforced – in prison workshops for example – until the middle of this century. As for conversation between inmates and staff, this too was seen as dangerous, leading to lax discipline, favouritism, blackmail and corruption.

The Borstals were the first establishments in the prison system to explore the beneficial possibilities of increased staff-prisoner communication, followed by the prisons where long sentences were served. It was not until the middle of the nineteen-fifties that the change of attitude towards communication in English custodial establishments can really be said to have penetrated to local prisons. It is an indication of the caution with which it was received that it began in a small local prison in the provinces, and was called the 'Norwich experiment'. The features of this experiment, as they were described in the Prison Commissioners' annual report for 1956, do not sound very startling nowadays. They were: 'dining in association for all convicted prisoners; increasing labour hours from 26 to 35 hours a week without increasing staff; and an attempt to improve the officer-prisoner relationship by allocating groups of prisoners to specific officers'. In the work-shops, officers were encouraged to move about, instead of sitting on raised platforms (which were removed), and not only to allow more conversation between prisoners but also 'to have no qualms about having a helpful conversation' with prisoners themselves. As the governor said in his first report on this innovation, 'It is obviously taking time for this change in outlook to sink in amongst prisoners. Occasionally one enters a workshop to find an officer talking to a prisoner openly and amicably, only for the prisoner to give a quick warning look to the officer and then resume his work with excessive vigour.'

The governor's report, however, was so encouraging that governors of other small provincial 'locals' were sent to see Norwich prison, with the result that in the following year Shrewsbury, Swansea and Oxford followed suit. What had been referred to as 'the Norwich experiment' was now called 'the Norwich system'; and in 1958 and 1959 six more establishments, some of them large prisons, adopted the system. Unfortunately, the overcrowding and staffing difficulties of the sixties have meant that some features of the system have rather withered away, especially in large, hard-pressed locals. For example, it has not been easy to ensure that the same officers are in charge of the same prisoners for long periods, since frequent transfers of both officers and staff have been necessary. Again, the idea of increasing the part of the evening during which men in the same wing can associate freely depends on having enough officers on duty to deal with any trouble; in some prisons there are not enough officers after 5.30 p.m. to make this possible. Finally, even if the official attitude to fraternisation between officers and inmates is relaxed, there seem to be natural limits to the willingness of officers and prisoners to be on friendly terms. What can be said is that nowadays it is these natural limits rather than official ones which are operative.

Group counselling, however, went a step further than the mere encouragement of informal relations between officers and prisoners. It was introduced to the British penal system by Norman Bishop, while Governor of Pollington Borstal in the late nineteen-fifties. Bishop had been influenced not only by Fenton's book but also by training conferences at the Tavistock Institute and by Dr Maxwell Jones's methods at the Henderson Hospital for personality disorders (see p. 12); and he shared the belief of innovators such as Homer Lane, A. S. Neill and David Wills that inmates should share with staff the responsibility for decisions governing their lives. From Pollington, the innovation spread to many other Borstals and eventually to prisons for medium and long sentences: in the early sixties it was in operation in eight Borstals and nine prisons. For obvious reasons no serious attempt was made to introduce it in local prisons or detention centres with their high turnover of short-term inmates. Some Borstal governors, too, were opposed to it; and one of the principles on which the English prison system is based is the governor's almost viceregal power to shape the regime of his establishment.

While Bishop intended group counselling to focus on inmates' personal problems, the essence of the technique, as it was practised in English Borstals and prisons, was that the meetings involved both staff and inmates, although staff were also encouraged to hold additional meetings of their own in order to discuss some of the emotional and disciplinary problems which the primary groups created for them. (Some groups were in charge of outsiders who did not belong to the institution; but outsiders, whether psychiatrists, psychologists or laymen, suffer from the handicap of being slightly out of touch with the day-to-day events of the establishment.) Discussions were intended to concentrate on the running of the institution or on the inmates' careers: some groups even discussed whether its members were ready for release. Conversation was free of the threat of official retaliation, even for the most provocative remarks; but there were one or two rules to which most groups paid lip service, even if they often broke them. One was that members should treat what was said as confidential: a rule which was bound to be broken, with much resulting recrimination. Another was that groups should not discuss identifiable inmates or officers who were not present: a rule designed to reassure the more paranoid or insecure non-participants, and impossible to observe without sabotaging many profitable arguments. Intelligent group counsellors soon learned to modify these principles, but with varying success.

Group counselling–as distinct from group psychotherapy–is a technique which has been developed very largely in penal institutions and other establishments for the treatment of anti-social behaviour,[10] even if it has now been adopted or adapted by other institutions where staff-inmate relations are a problem. Whether it is possible or fair to measure its usefulness by the conduct of inmates after they have left the institution is a controversial issue, and certainly there is no clear evidence that it reduces recidivism. Many administrators would prefer to justify it by the more modest claim that it reduces tensions and misconduct within the institution, and so enables it to function more smoothly and apply other forms of treatment more effectively. Not all psychiatrists or psychologists, however, would support even this claim. The therapist who participates fully in group sessions runs some risk of exhibiting his own weaknesses, and so of forfeiting the prestige on which some treatment is undoubtedly based. Moreover, it seems likely that there are some types of patient who not only do not benefit from the rough-and-tumble of group discussion, but even deteriorate under it. It is quite possible that, like the psycho-analytic techniques from which it is descended, group counselling has been over-extended and so misapplied. But its beneficial effects on relationships between staff and inmates in notoriously tense penal establishments can hardly be denied.

The heyday of group counselling was the period immediately after the Prison Commissioners gave it their official blessing in their Circular Instruction no. 62 of 1962. Within a couple of years, the enthusiasm of headquarters–always subject to quick changes of temperature–had cooled a little. Group counselling might be good for prisoners, but it could upset staff, especially those who preferred the traditional, formal relationship between themselves and prisoners. Governors–who have to be sensitive

E

to climatic fluctuations at headquarters–sensed that the idea was no longer quite as fashionable as it had been, and only those who were themselves real enthusiasts persisted with it. Elsewhere, the innovation was allowed to peter out, usually through the inevitable promotion or transfer of trained counsellors.

Is it fair, however, to let the psychological approach to prison regimes be judged by the fate of group counselling? It is arguable that this particular importation failed to take root properly for reasons which were special to it. May it not have been too exotic, too stylised and too dependent on an expertise which is not easily learned? Certainly its very close resemblance to psychotherapy could not help but alarm and antagonise the more authoritarian governors and senior officers. What is clear is that if 'moral management' is to become the guiding principle not only of a few special institutions modelled on mental hospitals but of the prison service as a whole it will have to be introduced more skilfully–or more resolutely–than group counselling.

Diagnosis

The last function of the prison system which falls to be dealt with in these chapters is that of ensuring the recognition of disorder, at least in cases in which recognition could conceivably make a difference to the way in which the prisoner is being treated. Until the eighteen-sixties–when prison doctors were at last required to inspect every prisoner regularly (see vol. I, pp. 226-8)–the recognition of disorder depended largely on fortuitous circumstances. The prisoner might have relatives who could draw attention to his mental state–as 'Courtenay' and Townley did. Or his behaviour might be sufficiently violent or bizarre to impress even the ignorant prison staff. The regulations for local gaols of 1843 required the governor to call the attention of the chaplain and the medical officer without delay to 'any prisoner whose state of mind or body requires their attention'.

The chaplain was a more important functionary in the prisons of those days than he is now, and the regulations gave him considerable responsibilities. It was for him to 'pay particular attention to the state of mind of every prisoner'; and if he observed that it was being 'injuriously affected by the discipline or treatment', to report this to the governor, surgeon and visiting justices. The medical officer was not required to bother about every prisoner, but merely to report to the governor when discipline or treatment appeared to be injuriously affecting a prisoner's mind or body. He could however do what the chaplain could not, and give the governor 'such directions as he may think proper'; so that the inspector of 1847 could fairly place the blame for G.W.'s treatment on the medical officer of the hulk (see p. 39). Prison doctors were also required to call the chaplain's attention to any prisoner whose state of mind appeared to require his special care. In defence of this rather awkward division of responsibility it must be recalled that the clergy of those days were often better equipped, both by education and experience, to deal with disorders of the mind than were doctors, whose training was almost entirely in physical medicine.

By the eighteen-sixties, however, mental disorder had clearly become the responsibility of the prison medical officer. Not only was there now a register for the medical profession; psychological medicine was now a respectable speciality, and there was even an Association of Medical Officers of Asylums. The work and legislation of Shaftesbury and his colleagues had sensitised the minds of legislators and the educated public to the subject of insanity. The reciprocal interaction of demand and supply was inflating the statistics year by year. Courts were beginning to ask on their own initiative for advice about offenders' states of mind. At that time all they could do when they wanted time for investigation was to adjourn proceedings; it was not until the 1948 Act that special forms of remand were created for the purpose.[11]

Even so, it is surprising how early the London courts, and especially the stipendiary magistrates, seem to have developed the practice of remanding in custody prisoners whose mental state was suspect, so that they could be put under observation. Exactly when this began we have not been able to establish. Certainly it was in full swing by 1888, for the Prison Commissioners' report for that year refers to 401 prisoners of 'doubtful sanity' who were expressly remanded to Holloway for observation. Holloway–which by now had enlarged its hospital wing–had replaced Clerkenwell Gaol as a remand prison in 1886, but even in 1883 there are references in Prison Commissioners' reports to as many as 621 prisoners committed 'under suspicion of insanity'. This suggests that the practice had originated at Clerkenwell, which from the middle of the century had served as a remand prison for the busy Quarter Sessions of Middlesex. If so, it probably began at some date after 1861, for in that year it was visited by the indefatigable Mayhew and his collaborator Binney, and their comprehensive report–while mentioning two cases of 'insanity'–makes no reference to prisoners remanded for this purpose.[12]

Whatever the origins of the practice, the Prison Commissioners at first complained that their establishments were 'not a proper place for persons such as these', and that many of them had been reported as insane to the magistrates, who nevertheless had failed to commit them to asylums. It was not long, however, before the Commissioners became resigned to this new responsibility. During the last decade or so of the century, they had to defend themselves against the accusation that the high incidence of insanity in their prisons was the result of excessively strict treatment; so that it was to their advantage to be able to say that the great majority of insane patients were in this condition when received. Prison medical officers were asked to give their explanation of each case of insanity which they recorded, and the result was summed up by the Medical Inspector:

> Among the probable causes . . . are mentioned business worries, drinking, injury to the head, sunstroke, attending revival meetings, ill-usage, epilepsy, grief, over-work, speculations on the stock exchange, domestic trouble, fear of 'Jack the Ripper', privation and irregular life; but imprisonment is not suggested as the cause of the insanity in a single instance.[13]

Since the doctors were either wholly or partly in the employment of the Commissioners, and must have felt some responsibility for the well-being of their charges, it is hardly surprising that they did not blame prison conditions. Nevertheless, the defence based on this rather shaky evidence was probably a reasonable one. Confinement, however harsh, does not cause subnormality, delirium tremens, or general paralysis of the insane, to name three of the disorders which were commonly recognised. It could have precipitated depressions, and prison staff were on the alert to prevent suicides, although not always successfully; and it may well have played a part in exacerbating paranoid or aggressive temperaments. Yet although the prison system of the late nineteenth century was grim and repressive, the Medical Inspector was probably right in claiming that nearly all insane prisoners were insane, or becoming so, before reception. One obvious question, however, was why these unfortunates were not being dealt with under the civil law, and committed to the asylums. At least part of the answer, he thought, lay in the dangers of certification from the point of view of the doctors, some of whom had suffered from litigation by aggrieved patients who claimed that they had been improperly detained. Among these unlucky alienists appears the son of Forbes Winslow, who was hired by a Mr Weldon to take the latter's wife into his private asylum at Hammersmith. Mrs Weldon, who was probably manic, and certainly eccentric, eluded him and then sued him for libel, assault, wrongful arrest, false imprisonment and trespass, successfully.[14] There is no doubt that by this time, in the eighteen-seventies and eighties, the man in the street was on the side of the patient, and certification was unpopular as well as legally dangerous. Some protection against litigious patients, if not against unpopularity, was conferred on doctors by legislation in 1889,[15] and it may be that a greater readiness to certify members of the outside population contributed to the decline in the prevalence of detected insanity amongst prisoners which the Commissioners reported.

The use of prisons, however, as places of psychiatric examination continued to grow in popularity. When the first annual statistics on the subject were published, just after the First World War, it could be seen that some 1,600 prisoners were being received for 'mental observation'. By this time the practice had spread to the large provincial cities; in 1919, for example, a special unit was established under Dr Hamblin Smith at Birmingham Prison in order to meet the demand of the local justices for diagnostic facilities.

It was of course possible to arrange psychiatric examination in some cases without keeping the accused in custody. The establishment of the first out-patient psychiatric clinics for adults in the nineteen-thirties encouraged courts in London to adjourn and grant bail to some offenders, on their undertaking to attend a clinic for examination. Norwood East, now the head of the prison medical service but no less sceptical of the new psychotherapeutic movement, disapproved of this practice, pointing out that round-the-clock observation in a prison hospital was more likely to be effective.[16] Nevertheless, the practice was popular enough to demand recognition, and when the Criminal Justice Bill of 1938 reached the statute-book—ten years later—it conferred on summary courts an express power to remand an offender either on bail or in custody for enquiries into his physical and mental condition. The power was limited to offences carrying imprisonment; but the court could exercise it without convicting

TABLE 2. Remands to prisons for psychiatric examination

Year	Remands for psychiatric examination	Year	Remands for psychiatric examination
1920	1611	1946	4588
1921	1738	1947	5090[a]
1922	1836	1948	5190
1923	1842	1949	5007
1924	1866	1950	5009
1925	2013	1951	5210
1926	2285	1952	5179
1927	2248	1953	5218
1928	2203	1954	4851
1929	2268	1955	4860
1930	2528	1956	4735
1931	2396	1957	5464
1932	2704	1958	5832
1933	2731	1959	5733
1934	2596	1960	5825
1935	2703	1961	6366
1936	2596	1962	7015
1937	2777	1963	7881
1938	2779	1964	7782
1939	no figures published	1965	9555
1940		1966	10,919
1941		1967	11,061
1942	3695	1968	11,846
1943	4166	1969	13,452
1944	4603	1970	13,680
1945	4418		

Source: Annual Reports of the Prison Commissioners or (from 1963) Prison Department.

[a] The figures for 1947 and later years include certain minor, not numerous, categories of prisoner not included in earlier figures.

the offender, so long as it was satisfied that he had acted as charged. At the same time the Act was careful to make it clear that summary courts which had been using their old power of adjournment in order to allow enquiries between conviction and sentence had not been acting improperly.[17] Higher courts did not, apparently, need a similar indemnity.

By this time remands to prisons for 'mental observation' had reached a level of about 5,000 a year. The 1948 Act had little, if any, effect upon their volume, which remained remarkably stable through most of the nineteen-fifties, in spite of fluctuations in crime and prison 'receptions'. Not until 1957 did the numbers begin to rise again, probably because of the publication of the Percy Report (see p. 68) rather than the passing of the Homicide Act. The rise was not yet spectacular; but with the coming into operation of the Mental Health Act it began in earnest, and continued almost without a break until by 1970 it had reached 13,680, more than two and a half times the level of the nineteen-fifties (see table 2).

In order to see the increase in perspective, however, we must relate it to the 'population at risk', so as to see the extent to which, if one had been a member of this population, one's chances of being remanded for psychiatric examination increased. Strictly speaking, this population at risk should be defined as 'all persons whom the courts could have remanded in this way and whose mental condition could have justified this step'; but since we have no means of knowing how many people would have satisfied the second half of this definition we have no hope of estimating this population. The best we can do is to exclude several categories whose members are most unlikely to be remanded in this way, and assume that among the rest the percentage whose mental condition would have justified a psychiatric remand, though unknowable, is roughly constant. We can therefore exclude juveniles, persons not eventually convicted and most but by no means all non-indictable offenders.[18]

When the population at risk is calculated in this way for certain selected years[19] in the period 1920–70 it is possible to estimate roughly by how much the probability of a psychiatric remand to prison has *increased*, although it would be too risky to use it to estimate the *magnitude* of that probability at any given date. Taking 1922[19] as our base, the probability seems to have increased as follows:

$$
\begin{array}{ll}
1922 & p \\
1937 & p \times 1\text{·}66 \\
1951 & p \times 2\text{·}26 \\
1961 & p \times 2\text{·}24 \\
1970 & p \times 2\text{·}80 \\
\end{array}
$$

In other words, the calculation confirms that–as the crude figures in table 2 suggest–the probability remained more or less static during the fifties; but shows that the increases between 1922 and 1951, and during the sixties, were less spectacular than table 2 suggests.

More interesting still is the outcome of all these psychiatric remands. In 1970, for example, out of 13,680 such remands, only 1,267 resulted in hospital or guardianship orders, although a further 466 led to psychiatric probation orders (see p. 65). What happened to the remaining 11,900 or so offenders?[20]

Our best information on this subject comes from a valuable study by Dr R. F. Sparks of diagnostic remands in two London courts presided over by five stipendiary magistrates.[21] The 494 cases which they remanded in custody[22] in 1961 represented 2·7 per cent of all the cases heard by them. The remanded males were examined at Brixton by one of the four prison medical officers; the females at Holloway by one of two medical officers. Forty per cent were diagnosed as normal; and the higher the percentage of his cases which a magistrate remanded the higher the percentage which were found normal. The remaining 60 per cent consisted of 24 per cent (104) who were dealt with by hospital order, psychiatric probation order or compulsory admission to hospital or discharge (see pp. 70-1), another 1 per cent for whom probation officers were able to arrange psychiatric treatment informally, and 35 per cent (153) who were disposed of by ordinary measures (i.e. imprisonment, fine, probation or discharge). Many of these seem to have been diagnosed as suffering from rather ill-defined disturbances of personality, for which the prison medical officers may well have felt unable to recommend treatment with much optimism. For it was observed that in 90 per cent of the cases in which treatment was definitely recommended the courts acted accordingly. The great majority of cases dealt with by ordinary measures were those in which the doctors had made no definite recommendation for treatment; some were cases in which the offender himself refused his consent to the necessary probation order; and only a few were cases in which for some unknown reason the magistrate did not take the medical advice. Even when ordinary measures were used, however, it was noticeable that they consisted very largely of discharges or ordinary probation orders: less than one in four cases were fined or imprisoned, a much lower fraction than was observed in the case of un-remanded offenders in these courts. In other words, if the prison medical officer found some degree of abnormality his diagnosis was likely at the very least to induce the court to use a discharge or probation order instead of a penalty, and if he made a definite recommendation for treatment this was very likely to be followed.

Although Dr Sparks' study was confined to London, he chose two of the busiest courts and two of the busiest remand prisons for it; and the results reinforce what has been said in volume 1 (chapters 5 and 14) about the influence wielded by the prison medical officer over the decisions of the court. The picture sometimes painted, in which clear medical advice in favour of psychiatric treatment is disregarded by sceptical lawyers, will not fit these facts, although it may be true of the occasional recorder, bench of provincial magistrates, or even – as we shall show – Queen's Bench judges. On the basis of Sparks' observations – which are the best we have on this subject – we must infer, without being too precise about the actual per-centages, that

1. a very substantial percentage of cases remanded for psychiatric diagnosis is reported as normal by prison medical officers;
2. another substantial fraction is diagnosed as cases of ill-defined personality disorders for which prison medical officers are unable to recommend psychiatric treatment with honest optimism.

This does not mean, of course, that none of these cases should have been remanded for investigation. It would have been much more alarming if no such cases had been found in the sample, for this would have suggested that the courts were not remanding enough of their offenders. Neverthe-less, as Dr Sparks himself points out, those of his magistrates who re-manded the highest percentages appear to have achieved little more than an increase in the percentage of their remands which come back with a diagnosis of normality. In other words, this pair of courts seems at the very least to have reached the upper limit of profitable remanding, *given the existing standards of diagnosis and treatment*. This is, of course, an im-portant qualification. A different group of doctors might have yielded lower percentages of 'normality': even amongst his six medical officers Dr Sparks noticed differences. Again, had there been better facilities for the in-patient treatment of 'personality disorders' there might have been a higher percentage of definite recommendations for such treatment. Moreover, there may well have been plenty of scope in other areas of England and Wales for useful increases in the percentage of remanded cases. With these reservations, however, it is important to realise that these London courts were probably within sight of the upper limit of profitable remanding, and that this upper limit will rise only if there are marked changes in diagnostic criteria or in facilities for effective treatment.

Notes

1. See A. Griffiths, *Memorials of Millbank* (London, 1875; new edition 1884), from which most of the information in this chapter about Millbank is taken. Griffiths was a Deputy Governor there in the eighties, and his comments illustrate vividly the harshness of the outlook of even senior staff at that time.

2. R. Partridge, *Broadmoor* (London, 1953), 78-9.

3. See the Report of the Penal Servitude Commissioners (Parliamentary Papers 1878-9, vol. XXXVII-XXXVIII, p. xlii).

4. Weak-minded women now went to Aylesbury.

5. M. Hamblin Smith, *The Psychology of the Criminal* (London, 1922); G. W. Pailthorpe, *Studies in the Psychology of Delinquency* (HMSO, 1932). Most of Dr Pailthorpe's research was in fact done at Holloway, under the auspices of the Medical Research Council.

6. W. N. East and W. H. de B. Hubert, Report on the *Psychological Treatment of Crime* (HMSO, 1939).

7. It had originally been intended to site it in a London suburb, but there had been so much delay that to save time it was decided to build on what was already Crown land. The prison's distance from London is one of its serious problems, for it makes it difficult to recruit good staff and to involve prisoners' relatives in their treatment.

8. All of whom were strongly influenced by Alfred Adler, to whom group psychotherapy owes much of its original inspiration: see N. Walker, *A Short History of Psychotherapy* (London, 1957) ch. IX.

9. A technique developed by Carl Roger: see Walker, loc. cit., ch. IV.

10. Such as hospital units for behaviour disorders.

11. The 1848 Act, which regularised summary proceedings before justices and thus in effect created the 'magistrates' court', expressly gave them power to adjourn (11 & 12 Vict. c. 43, s. 16). A century later the Criminal Justice Act of 1948 (s. 26) gave them express powers to remand offenders for investigation of their physical or mental condition.

12. See H. Mayhew and J. Binney, *The Criminal Prisons of London and Scenes of Prison Life* (London, 1862).

13. Medical Inspector's Report for 1889-90, in the annual Report of the Prison Commissioners and Directors of Convict Prisons.

14.   For a fuller account of this entertaining episode see Professor
      Kathleen Jones, *Mental Health and Social Policy*, 1845–1959
      (London, 1960). She confuses Dr Forbes Winslow, however, with
      his more famous father, the witness at M'Naghten's trial and
      founder of the *Journal of Psychological Medicine*, who had died a
      few years before the Weldon case. The confusion is pardonable,
      because the son not only bore the same names but also pontificated
      on the insanity of murders–as an invited or uninvited expert–
      quite as much as his father.

15.   52 & 53 Vict. c. 41 s. 12 (consolidated in 53 & 54 Vict. c. 5).

16.   See the Prison Commissioners' Annual Report for 1933, p. 34.

17.   See ss. 25-6 of the Criminal Justice Act, 1948 (11 & 12 Geo. VI.
      c. 58) consolidated in s. 26 of the Magistrates Courts Act, 1952
      (15 & 16 Geo. VI & 1 Eliz. II, c. 55).

18.   Juveniles are often remanded, but hardly ever *to prison*. The per-
      centage of persons who are remanded for psychiatric examination
      before trial and *then acquitted* is so small that it is less misleading
      to define the population as convicted persons. Most non-indictable
      offenders–for example, traffic offenders or revenue offenders are
      most unlikely to be even considered for psychiatric remands; but
      we have *included* assaults, drunkenness, indecent exposure, solicit-
      ing, vagrancy offences and Prevention of Crime Act offences,
      since these are both numerous and not unlikely to lead to a hospital
      order or psychiatric probation order.

19.   It is unwise to take the earliest figure in a series such as this, since
      it tends to be subject to errors due to the inexperience of the
      persons who are required to report and record the figures. We
      therefore chose 1922; 1937 was taken next as one of the last pre-
      war years (psychiatric remands in 1938 totalled almost exactly the
      same); 1951 was taken as a year by which the 1948 Act provisions
      were probably in full working order; 1961 was taken as the first
      full year after the coming into operation of the 1959 Act (and
      also the year of Dr Sparks' sample: see p. 54); 1970 was simply
      the latest year for which we had figures.

20.   No doubt a few were disposed of in some of the other ways listed
      in table 5, on p. 78; but as can be seen there these other possi-
      bilities are numerically insignificant. More important, probably, is
      the unknown number who were simply admitted to mental hospitals
      informally or under Part IV of the 1959 Act after court proceedings
      were over, or who were allowed to undergo out-patient treatment
      without any formal requirement to do so. But these cannot have been
      numerous enough to account for much of the residue of 11,947.

21.   'The decision to remand for mental examination', in (1966) 6,
      British Journal of Criminology, 6 ff.

22.   Sparks did not concern himself with remands on bail, of which
      there were 'few'.

Chapter 4. **The Origins of the 1959 Act**

It is time, however, to return to the criminal courts. The legal procedures with which the first volume was concerned were procedures which, with minor exceptions, raised the issue of the offender's *responsibility*. They compelled the court to decide whether the accused was mentally disordered in a way which abolished or reduced his moral culpability for his acts or omissions. The first slight shift towards a new approach seems to have occurred, very unobtrusively and without any realisation of its eventual consequences, in the last few years of the nineteenth century.

Administrative Pressures

Here again the change was the result not of a new philosophy but of administrative pressures created by the sheer volume of humanity which was being fed into the prisons. It was being fed into them not so much by the Assizes and Quarter Sessions as by the magistrates' courts, which since the procedural reforms of 1848[1] had been dealing with ever-increasing numbers of petty offenders. Some of them were of course merely being committed in custody for trial on indictment; but since the reforms successive Acts had empowered magistrates to deal summarily with more and more indictable–and therefore imprisonable–offences which would previously have had to be tried by jury. Large numbers of offenders were also being fined by summary courts and being imprisoned for non-payment. In all probability the 'turnover' of the prisons was being speeded up. Moreover, by the end of the seventies the central Government had been forced to take over the local gaols (again not motivated by zeal for improvement but as a result of an electoral pledge to relieve local rates). The result was to bring the problems of short-term imprisonment more directly to the attention of the administrators. It was the local prisons which had to receive not only those committed for trial without bail but also those whose sentences were of two years or less.

As we saw in the previous chapter, a sizeable minority of these people were recognisably insane even to the sceptical eye of the prison medical officer of that era. In 1889 the Medical Inspector of Prisons reported that in the previous year 'no less than 93 *sentenced* prisoners were found to be insane on reception, and therefore clearly should not have been sentenced at all'.[2] His conclusion was a legal *non sequitur*, for it was of course only certain forms and degrees of insanity which excused from punishment, but he was speaking as a doctor and not as a lawyer.) The Prison Commissioners made urgent representations to the Home Office.

History is not usually made in Home Office circulars, but the one which Clerks of the Peace received in November, 1889 was an exception. The Home Secretary strongly urged on magistrates

> that it is their duty to obtain, in all doubtful cases, evidence as to the mental condition of prisoners. In cases of serious crime it may be necessary to commit for trial persons supposed to be insane, in order that the question of their sanity may be decided by the verdict of a Jury. But where the offence is less serious, it is almost always open to Justices to dismiss the charge, and to deal with the prisoner as an ordinary lunatic, either handing him over to the care of his friends, or sending him as a pauper lunatic to an asylum.

This was a frank invitation to magistrates to deal with petty but insane offenders by suspending the normal process of the criminal law. The charge was to be dismissed and instead of conviction or committal for trial the offender was to be dealt with in the same way as any ordinary lunatic.

The circular was motivated not by any intention of undermining the traditional processes but simply by expediency. To use these processes to try the sanity of dozens of petty offenders would have made inordinate demands on the time of doctors, the patience of courts and – an increasingly important consideration – the resources of local prisons.

The idea of dealing with a petty offender by dismissing the charge was not as revolutionary as it would have seemed a generation before. The Summary Jurisdiction Act of 1879 had regularised a number of unofficial practices which had been developed by enterprising magistrates, and among these was the device of dismissing trifling charges altogether. (An alternative was simply to bind him over to come up for judgment if required, which would happen only if he offended again: Forbes Winslow recounts in his memoirs[3] how his evidence that a well-to-do shoplifter was mentally disordered persuaded a court to deal with her in this way.) It was this provision which, after it had been extended by cautious stages to trial by higher as well as summary courts, eventually developed into the Probation of Offenders Act of 1907. An important feature of that Act was that for the first time it made it clear that among the considerations which could justify a court in dismissing a charge (or discharging an offender on recognisances) was his 'mental condition'.

Legislation 1913–48

The next step was taken when something resembling the procedure suggested in the Home Office circular was made statutory, in the Mental Deficiency Act of 1913. This piece of legislation was based on the monumental report of Lord Radnor's Royal Commission on the Care and Control of the Feeble-Minded (Cd. 4202) which laboured from 1904 to 1908, and produced eight volumes of evidence, reports and other materials, including an account of their expedition to America. The evidence which they received from all sorts of organisations emphasised the important part which mental defect seemed to play in pauperism, illegitimacy, alcoholism and of course crime: they were told of the difficulties of coping with weak-minded offenders within the prison system. Their main recommendations favoured an improved system of institutions and guardianship which would not only protect the community against the mental defective but also safeguard him against abuse and exploitation. Their definition of 'mental deficiency', with its four sub-divisions, 'idiocy', 'imbecility', 'moral imbecility' and 'feeble-mindedness' was based on the advice which they received from the medical organisations. The significance of 'moral imbecility' will be discussed in the chapter on the concept of psychopathy, and it is unnecessary for our purpose to consider the others in detail.

When the Commission came to consider what the procedure should be for dealing with the mental defective who had been accused of an offence, they had to decide between the traditional and the new. Should he be required (assuming that he was capable of being tried at all) to set up a special defence like that of insanity in order to satisfy a jury that he should not be held responsible? Certainly this was sometimes done when a low-grade defective was accused of murder or some other grave offence. But mental defect seemed to be much more a matter of degree than did other forms of insanity, so that the question 'Was he responsible or not?' would be even harder than usual to answer. The King's Bench judges had made it known that they were unanimously opposed to leaving this question to a jury: it should be considered either by the judge (when determining sentence) or by the Home Secretary (in the exercise of his general power to control and dispose of prisoners).

An alternative was suggested by the Inebriates Act of 1898. The era of cheap spirits was also an era of widespread alcoholism, to counter which a system of inebriates' reformatories had been established. If a person was convicted on indictment of an offence punishable with imprisonment or penal servitude, and he admitted to being (or was found by the jury to be) an habitual drunkard, the court could order his detention in an inebriates' reformatory. This procedure, though it had the defect of involving the jury in diagnostic questions, had the merit of separating the question 'Did he do it?' from the question 'Is he an habitual drunkard?' This separation was inevitable where inebriates were concerned, since mere drunkenness was not an acceptable defence in English law. It suggested to the Radnor Commission however that there was a precedent of sorts for separating the issue of guilt from the question of what should be done with an offender whose mental condition was abnormal.

But perhaps the Commission should follow the Home Office's lead, and recommend that higher as well as lower courts should deal with defectives by dismissing the charge and allowing them to be dealt with as lunatics? Since the term 'lunatic' was regarded as including fairly severe degrees of deficiency, many defectives had recently been dealt with in this way. Moreover, the Probation of Offenders Act had just made it plain that both higher and lower courts were entitled to take the offender's 'mental condition' into account when considering whether to dismiss the charge or bind him over.

The recommendations which emerged from all these considerations were magnificently eclectic: in effect the Commission proposed that

1. the issue of guilt should be separated from the question of the alleged

defect, the relative irresponsibility of the offender, and his appropriate treatment. But an exception must be made if his defence was insanity (or if he was dealt with under the Inebriates Act!);

2. summary courts should remand an alleged defective to an institution (or similar place), or adjourn the case, and if subsequent medical evidence justified them in doing so should then adjourn the case *sine die* and order his reception into an institution;

3. as an alternative, a summary court should be able to convict him and then bind him over or allow him to be dealt with by a reception order; and higher courts should be allowed, *mutatis mutandis*, to act likewise;

4. but if a higher court thought the offender sufficiently responsible to merit a custodial sentence, it should be able to impose a sentence of a determinate length, which would be followed by a reception order.

The last of these recommendations resembled the 'double-track' system adopted in 1908 to deal with habitual offenders, which allowed higher courts to sentence them to a fixed term of imprisonment as a punishment for their latest offence, to be followed by a semi-determinate period of preventive detention for the protection of society.

This curious amalgam of civil powers, inebriates' legislation, the 1889 circular and the traditional defence of insanity was never seriously considered. The Government foresaw a major Parliamentary clash between the supporters of reform and reorganisation and those who saw in the report an attempt to segregate and incarcerate large numbers of men and women in the name of eugenics. As session followed session without a sign of a Government Bill, private members tried to force the Home Secretary's hand with Bills of their own, and eventually succeeded. In the spring of 1912 the introduction of a backbenchers' Bill–the Mental Defect Bill–which claimed to be in accordance with the Royal Commission's report was followed almost immediately by the appearance of the Government's Mental Deficiency Bill. Both Bills differed in important ways from the report. For example, their definitions of mental defect were far wider. In addition to idiots, imbeciles, feeble-minded persons and moral imbeciles (see page 211) whom the Commission had meant to include, the Home Secretary's Bill included 'persons who through mental infirmity arising from age or the decay of their faculties are incapable of managing themselves or their affairs'; and the backbenchers' Bill included not only the mentally infirm but also any person 'of unsound mind', who 'by reason of disorder of mind requires care and control and is incapable of managing himself or his affairs'.

Nor did either Bill follow the Commission's recommendations so far as the criminal courts were concerned. In the event, however, the Commons proceeded only with the Government's Bill, and that was so mutilated in Standing Committee by Josiah Wedgwood and other backbench defenders of liberty that it had to be withdrawn, and replaced by a much revised Bill, which reached the statute-book in 1913. Its criminal procedure was a good deal simpler than the Commission's, and was not amended–except in one minor way–during its passage through Parliament:

1. A court which convicted a defective of an imprisonable offence, or found a defective child liable to be sent to an industrial school, could

either postpone sentence and direct that the procedure for civil committal be instituted, or in lieu of sentence commit him to an institution or guardianship just as a civil judicial authority could have done; but a summary court could do so without proceeding to a conviction;

2. the court could either act on evidence given during the trial or other proceedings, or call for further medical or other evidence;

3. pending the actual order of committal it could order him to be kept in an institution for defectives or in a 'place of safety', which could mean a workhouse, police station, institution or place of detention,[4] or any hospital surgery or other suitable place whose occupier was willing to receive him temporarily.

The criminal courts' use of the Act can be studied in table 4. As with all such legislation one should probably not pay much attention to the statistics for the first year of its operation, in which courts and their medical witnesses are feeling their way, while the police whose task it is to keep a statistical record of their decisions may be uncertain as to the exact nature of the decision. For example, in 1914 only a minority of orders made by summary courts were recorded as made without convicting the offender, a picture which is completely reversed in the following and subsequent years.[5] It must be remembered, too, that the first four years of the new regime coincided with the 1914–18 war. It is noticeable that the figures increase sharply in 1919. Summary courts, which handle a much greater volume of prosecutions than higher courts, are of course responsible for the great majority of orders; it also seems, however, that the use of them increased more in summary than in higher courts; at least part of the explanation must be that the volume of indictable offences prosecuted increased somewhat more sharply in the summary courts during this period.

Another point of interest is that the redefinition of 'mental deficiency' in the Act of 1927 (which has been referred to in chapter 2) cannot be said to have led to any definite increase in the number of orders made by criminal courts. The 1913 Act had adopted the Radnor Commission's definition of mental deficiency, which excluded not only 'unsoundness of mind' and senile disorders but also any defect of intelligence which had not been present 'from an early age', with the result that on a strict interpretation the effects of brain damage occurring in adolescence–for example as a result of the encephalitis lethargica epidemics of the twenties which were mentioned in chapter 2–was not mental deficiency. Some doctors stretched the law, but many would not; and the Mental Deficiency Act of 1927 widened the definition by including disorders which had been present before the age of 18.[6] Nevertheless, whatever the effect may have been on other admissions, it does not seem to have affected criminal courts.

More serious, perhaps, was the way in which the Radnor Commission and the 1913 Act drew a definite demarcation line between mental defect and insanity, which had until then been frequently interpreted as including the more severe forms of feeble-mindedness. However beneficial this may have been from the diagnostic or administrative point of view, one result was that the new procedure was not applicable to mentally ill offenders. It is therefore remarkable that for a quarter of a century no move was made to extend the criminal procedures of the 1913 Act to the mentally ill offender. The reason may have been misapprehension about the extent to which the special verdicts met this need: as we shall see, this misapprehension did exist in the Home Office. However that may be, it was not until 1938 and the abortive Criminal Justice Bill that an attempt was made to fill the gap. The Bill contained a clause enabling summary courts which were trying someone for an imprisonable offence to deal with him exactly as the Justices of the Peace could deal with a pauper lunatic under Section 16 of the Lunacy Act of 1890: by a 'reception order' committing him to a mental hospital. The court had to be satisfied on the certificates of at least two duly qualified medical practitioners that the offender was of unsound mind; and it had to be satisfied that 'the offence has been committed'–a very slipshod piece of draftsmanship. The Bill was prevented by the war from reaching the statute-book, but when it was resurrected and passed in 1948 it contained a similar clause. (It was noticeable that two improvements had been made in the drafting. Instead of merely being satisfied that 'the offence had been committed' the court had to be satisfied that the accused himself 'did the act or made the omission charged'. More important, the court had now to be satisfied not only that the accused had done the act, and that he was of unsound mind, but also that he was 'a proper person to be detained': presumably this was intended to discourage magistrates from using this power where they could have adopted a less drastic measure such as a discharge on the understanding that the accused would be cared for by relatives.)

It is by no means certain that the legislators appreciated exactly what they were doing. In the memorandum that prefaced the 1938 Bill it was made plain that this clause was intended to give courts of summary jurisdiction the power to deal with persons of unsound mind in the way in which both higher or lower courts could deal with mental defectives. The implication was that higher courts already had this power, and in the Committee stage of the 1948 Bill the Attorney-General (Sir Hartley Shawcross) explained

> The purpose of this clause is to give the summary courts the powers which quarter sessions and assizes now have of sending such a person, who appears to be of unsound mind at the time when he is brought before them, to a mental institution, and so avoiding the necessity of dealing with him as a criminal at all.[7]

Unless he had failed to distinguish mental deficiency from insanity, he must have had in mind persons who were found to be insane on arraignment, and dealt with under the Act of 1800. If so, there were important differences between the two procedures. Firstly, under the Act of 1800 the court did not have to be satisfied that the accused did the act (indeed, he could be tried on the same charge if he later recovered his sanity). Secondly, the effect of a finding of 'insane on arraignment' was detention during His Majesty's Pleasure; so that the offender could not be released at the discretion of the hospital, as could someone dealt with under the 1913 or 1948 procedures. On the whole the Attorney-General (who had made a bad start to his speech by attributing the M'Naghten Rules to Lord Macnaughton) was oversimplifying his case.

In the event, the wrangle over attempts to introduce the abolition of the death penalty into the Bill distracted Parliament's attention from all but a few of the innovations which the Bill actually contained, and this clause passed unaltered into law. It was later reproduced without amendment in the Magistrates Courts' Act, 1952 (a consolidating measure) and consequently deleted from the Criminal Justice Act.

Although statistics of reception orders did not begin to be published until 1953, it seems possible that cases of a kind which had previously been dealt with under the 1913 Act were by then being made the subject of the new kind of order. It is difficult to explain otherwise the decline in orders made by summary courts which began about 1950, and continued until the slow upward trend was resumed in the late fifties. However that may be, reception orders were never used as frequently as 1913 Act orders, although the gap was smaller where women were concerned.

Probation and Psychiatric Treatment

The 1948 Act also ratified another development of considerable importance: the use of probation as a means of ensuring psychiatric treatment. As we have seen, the Probation of Offenders Act of 1907 had expressly mentioned the offender's mental condition as a possible reason for putting him on probation. This enabled a court to refrain from punishing a mentally disordered offender even if he had not used his disorder as a defence: and it must again be remembered that he could not do so in a summary trial. It did not, of course, ensure that he received treatment for his disorder. Out-patient clinics for such treatment did not yet exist, and the only real possibility was his committal to an asylum or an institution for defectives under civil procedure. It was not until after the First World War, in the late nineteen-twenties, that clinics began to be opened. The earliest of these were for children, and were inspired by examples abroad, such as Adler's clinics in Vienna and the Judge Baker Clinic in Boston. Among them was the East London child guidance clinic established by Dr Emmanuel Miller in 1927. Miller and his work were well known to one of the leading stipendiary magistrates, Clarke-Hall of Old Street Court, on whose bench Miller used often to sit by invitation, especially when young offenders were being dealt with. One result of this association was that in 1927 Clarke-Hall began the practice of putting the occasional child on probation on the understanding that he would attend Miller's clinic.

By the beginning of the nineteen-thirties there were also one or two psychotherapeutic clinics for adults, of which the best known was at the West End Hospital for Nervous Diseases, later known as the Portman Clinic.[8] Moreover, the Mental Treatment Act of 1930 had made it possible for mentally ill people to become voluntary in-patients of approved hospitals. One or two magistrates, following Clarke-Hall's example, were using probation orders as a means of arranging out-patient or in-patient psychotherapy for adult offenders: Claud Mullins was one of them, and describes some examples in his book *Crime and Psychology*.[9] This was an era of great optimism about the efficacy of psychoanalysis and other forms of psychotherapy, not merely as specifics for the neuroses but also as remedies for a wide variety of behaviour disorders, including some forms of anti-social conduct. The Dove-Wilson Committee of 1931–2, although officially concerned with persistent offenders, devoted some of their report to a general discussion of the scope for the psychological treatment of law-breakers. Their optimism was of the cautious kind, but they thought that 'a certain number of offenders might derive benefit by attending for treatment whilst on probation', and they were anxious to see an adequate service of clinics for adults and children established throughout the country.

The Home Office, however, had doubts about the propriety of using probation to compel an offender to undergo psychiatric treatment; in a circular issued in 1934 it pointed out that this would be inconsistent with the principle of the Mental Treatment Act of 1930, which made the treatment of uncertified patients voluntary.[10] Nevertheless the expedient was too popular to be discouraged in this way, and in 1938 a clause to regularise it was included in the Criminal Justice Bill which eventually became law in 1948.

Section 4 of the Act defined the limitations under which a court could include in a probation order a requirement that the probationer should submit to treatment 'with a view to the improvement of his mental condition'. In effect, the limitations were that

1. evidence must be given by a 'duly qualified medical practitioner appearing to the court to be experienced in the diagnosis of mental disorders'. Note that only one such witness was stipulated, in contrast to the two witnesses required for a reception order;
2. the evidence must be to the effect that the mental condition, while it 'required and was susceptible to treatment' was not such as to justify certification under the Lunacy or Mental Deficiency Acts; in other words, the provision was meant for mild disorders;
3. the court must be satisfied that arrangements had been or could be made for the treatment–in other words, that some doctor, clinic or hospital was willing to accept the probationer as a patient;
4. the treatment must be carried out 'by or under the direction of' a duly qualified medical practitioner. This was clearly drafted so as to allow a lay analyst or psychotherapist–of which there were several practising in London clinics and hospitals–to carry out the actual treatment provided that a medically qualified doctor would be answerable;
5. as in the case of an ordinary probation order, the probationer must consent to treatment, and in this case he (or his parent or guardian if he were a juvenile) must also consent to the submission of a report on his mental condition. But his consent would not oblige him to agree to any surgical, electrical or other treatment, if a court thought his refusal to do so was reasonable, in 'all the circumstances';
6. the probation order was to specify the period for which the probationer was required to submit to treatment, and could not specify a period longer than a year. Treatment which lasted longer would thereafter cease to be a requirement of the probation order.

F

TABLE 3. Psychiatric probation orders (made under s.4 of the Criminal Justice Act, 1948)

	Assizes & Quarter Sessions[a]				Magistrates' Courts[a]				Juvenile Courts[a]				Total			
	Residential		Non-residential		Residential		Non-residential		Residential		Non-residential		Residential		Non-residential	
	M	F	M	F	M	F	M	F	M	F	M	F	M	F	M	F
1950	11	10	9	1	235	58	322	61	14	2	98	12	260	70	429	74
1951	71	14	54	3	236	71	300	48	11	1	92	16	318	86	446	67
1952	72	13	48	1	204	70	271	56	28	2	76	5	304	85	395	62
1953	55	15	34	5	234	80	274	52	20	5	95	13	309	100	405	70
1954	56	12	57	3	253	86	250	45	15	2	104	11	324	100	411	59
1955	73	12	64	1	258	87	261	54	26	2	101	11	357	101	426	66
1956	93	11	71	2	280	67	258	57	21	1	96	7	394	79	425	66
1957	110	16	81	4	262	66	265	51	28	–	109	12	400	82	455	67
1958	94	9	66	2	257	67	238	49	21	1	103	2	372	77	407	53
1959	103	9	64	4	308	87	263	43	35	3	100	19	446	99	427	66
1960	131	23	53	7	324	71	263	53	30	2	81	10	485	96	397	70
1961	84	12	57	3	242	54	269	45	31	2	80	10	357	68	406	58
1962	99	18	49	7	258	82	242	82	36	3	110	15	393	103	401	104
1963	79	10	73	7	313	66	306	87	39	3	111	10	431	79	490	104
1964	91	21	70	13	334	72	312	91	42	8	124	12	467	101	506	116
1965	116	18	89	6	332	76	354	93	38	4	90	11	486	98	533	110
1966	96	15	78	16	340	82	383	104	33	6	170	25	469	103	631	145
1967	135	24	80	9	443	93	446	126	45	3	131	16	623	120	657	151
1968	140	30	90	19	411	96	479	118	40	5	121	17	591	131	690	154
1969	153	26	102	18	320	66	521	104	34	2	137	20	507	94	760	142
1970	184	22	113	30	256	63	525	111	26	6	112	13	466	91	750	154

Source: Unpublished tables supplied by the Home Office Probation and After Care Divisions.

[a] A negligible number of juveniles (i.e. persons under 17) are included in the columns for Assizes and Quarter Sessions. In the case of lower courts it has been assumed that such persons were dealt with by juvenile courts, although there must have been a few exceptions.

Since probation orders could not be used for offences carrying fixed penalties, murder and the other crimes punishable with death were outside the scope of this provision, as they were outside the scope of reception orders. But unlike reception orders probation orders could be used to deal with offences which were not punishable with imprisonment, such as simple drunkenness. It thus became possible to induce offenders who could not be 'certified' to undergo what was virtually compulsory treatment. Strictly speaking, the offender's status was that of a voluntary patient, whether he was an in-patient or an out-patient; but since he would be guilty of a breach of the order if he broke off treatment, and since the consequence of such a breach was likely to be imprisonment (or its juvenile equivalent) he was subject to a sanction of sorts.

The extent to which this section was used, and the types of offence and offender to which it was applied, were the subject of the research described in Max Grünhut's last book, *Probation and Mental Treatment*, which must have been one of the first full-scale works of criminology to examine in detail the consequences of legislation designed to deal with mentally abnormal offenders.[11] Since this chapter is historical, it is sufficient for the moment to glance at the trends in courts' use of psychiatric probation orders, which are displayed in table 3 and figure 2.

As these show, orders involving both in-patient and out-patient treatment have been made in considerable numbers. Out-patient orders have always been somewhat commoner, especially for juvenile offenders; but higher courts are an exception, and make markedly more in-patient orders. In-patient orders increased, with fluctuations, during the nineteen-fifties; in the sixties they fell at first—no doubt because of the attractions of the new hospital order—but quickly began to rise again. In contrast, out-patient orders remained at much the same level throughout the fifties, but since 1962 have risen steadily and sharply. The rise in both during the sixties has been sharper than the increase in convictions for indictable offences.

Post-war Ideas

The psychiatric probation order, however, was not suitable—nor had it ever been intended—for the offender whose mental condition fell short of 'certifiability' but who needed special treatment under some sort of compulsory detention. This was recognised in Whitehall, and in 1949 the Home Secretary's Advisory Council on the Treatment of Offenders—under the chairmanship of Mr Justice Birkett—was asked to recommend a solution. They were told that the idea of an 'East-Hubert institution' (see p. 43) had been officially accepted; and they envisaged very much the same sort of establishment,[12] but with an important legal difference. It should be possible for a sentenced prisoner or Borstal trainee to be transferred to it for treatment (and back again), but it should also be possible for higher courts[13] to send an offender direct to it under a new form of sentence. The maximum period for his detention there would be set by the court, which would not, however, be allowed to exceed the maximum term of imprisonment fixed by law for his offence,[14] and it must not be 'unreasonable having regard to the nature of the offence and the history of the offender': in any case he could be released at any time by the

Home Secretary or Prison Commissioners. Before making an order of this kind the court would be obliged to hear independent medical evidence, any medical evidence offered by the defence, and a report from the Prison Commissioners on the offender's suitability for this sort of treatment—a provision copied from the Borstal system.

The Advisory Council's report, which was submitted to the Home Secretary in 1950, received no publicity. It was not at that time the practice to publish their reports officially, although in this case the *Lancet* were given permission to do so in full.[15] No public explanation has ever been given of the reason why the new type of sentence did not find favour. Perhaps it was decided to wait and see how the East-Hubert institution worked in practice, with inmates selected from sentenced prisoners, before allowing courts to take a hand in the selection. Probably not even the Prison Department realised quite how long it was to be before the institution actually came into being (see p. 44); and by the time it did the Advisory Council's idea had been overtaken by the Percy Commission and the Mental Health Act, although to do the Council justice it could be argued that the result did not quite meet the need on which they had put their finger.

The Act of 1959

Both Lord Percy's Royal Commission[16] and the 1959 Act were of course concerned with much wider problems than that of the disordered offender, and especially the tangled state of the law of certification. The development of this part of the law has been ably chronicled by Professor Kathleen Jones,[17] and all that is necessary here is to outline the most important features of the new and simplified system which the Commission designed and the Act created.

Judicial orders were no longer to be required for the compulsory admission of patients. Instead, the essential safeguards against unjustifiably prolonged detention were provided by a regional system of Mental Health Review Tribunals. The old distinction between mental hospitals and hospitals for the physically ill, which had restricted certified patients to the former, was abolished.

The Act also replaced the legal concepts of 'lunacy', 'unsoundness of mind', 'idiocy', 'imbecility', 'moral imbecility', 'feeble-mindedness' and 'mental defect' with a more modern set of categories and definitions. The generic term for all the conditions which could qualify for treatment under the Act was to be 'mental disorder'. This was to be subdivided into five statutory forms, three of which were defined and two deliberately left undefined. The defined forms were

severe subnormality, roughly corresponding to 'idiocy' and 'imbecility', and defined as 'a state of arrested or incomplete development of mind which includes subnormality of intelligence and is of such a nature or degree that the patient is incapable of living an independent life or of guarding himself against serious exploitation, or will be so incapable when of an age to do so';

subnormality, roughly corresponding to 'feeble-mindedness', and defined as 'a state of arrested or incomplete development of mind (not amounting to severe subnormality) which includes subnormality of

intelligence and is of a nature or degree which requires or is susceptible to medical treatment or other special care or training of the patient';
psychopathic disorder, roughly corresponding to 'moral imbecility', and defined as 'a persistent disorder or disability of mind (whether or not including subnormality or intelligence) which results in abnormally aggressive or seriously irresponsible conduct on the part of the patient, and requires or is susceptible to medical treatment': a definition which is discussed in chapters 9 and 10;

The forms of disorder which were left undefined were
mental illness, which included the conditions that in the past would have been categorised as 'lunacy' or 'unsoundness of mind', but could also include less marked conditions, such as severe anxiety states or phobias: and
any other disorder or disability of mind–that is, disorders or disabilities which were not mental illnesses or forms of subnormality, or psychopathic disorder. An example given by the Minister of Health during the Committee stage of the Bill was the after-effects of a head injury.

Finally, the section (s. 4) containing these definitions made it clear that there was no implication that a person could be dealt with as suffering from mental disorder 'by reason only of promiscuity or other immoral conduct'. 'Promiscuity' clearly referred to sexual conduct, but the meaning of 'other immoral conduct' has not so far been the subject of any pronouncement, judicial or ministerial.

The references to subnormality of intelligence in these definitions were important. Under the earlier legislation some psychiatrists had taken the view that a person whose intelligence was average, or at least within what was called 'the normal range'–that is, represented by an intelligence quotient somewhere between 75 and 125–could be a mental defective because in spite of his level of intelligence he was incompetent at the ordinary business of living. This had been especially frequent, of course, in the case of so-called 'moral imbecility', which had been diagnosed in patients whose intelligence was well above the average. The new Act made it clear that low intelligence was an essential feature of subnormality, but not of psychopathic disorder, although it was not incompatible with the latter.

One of the main reasons for this elaborate subdivision of 'mental disorder' was that, as we shall see in the next chapter, the Act made several important distinctions between them for the purpose of compulsory admission to hospital or guardianship. Altogether, it provided seven ways in which a person could be compulsorily admitted:

1. *Removal to a 'place of safety'* by a police officer (s. 136). This is discussed more fully in Appendix A. A 'place of safety' can be–and usually is–a mental hospital. The patient cannot be detained for more than 72 hours under this power (although he can be under those to be described below). This is the only procedure which can take place without the intervention of a medical practitioner. Any form of mental disorder is a sufficient ground.

2. *Admission on a warrant* by a Justice of the Peace who has been told by

a mental welfare officer that there is reason to suppose that a mentally disordered person is living alone and unable to care for himself, or is being ill-treated or neglected or kept without proper control somewhere in the justice's jurisdiction (s. 135). Any form of disorder suffices. The warrant can be executed only by a constable accompanied by a mental welfare officer and a medical practitioner. The patient cannot be detained for more than 72 hours under this power, but can be kept longer under the powers to be described below. The most frequent use of the power is to break into a place in which some elderly person, often with delusions of persecution by neighbours, has barricaded himself.

3. *Emergency admissions* on the application of any relative or mental welfare officer (s. 29), supported by a recommendation of one doctor who believes that the patient is suffering from a mental disorder which warrants detention in hospital for observation, and that this is justified in the interests of the patient's health or safety or for the protection of others. The patient cannot be detained for more than 72 hours under this power, but can be kept longer under the powers described below.

4. *Admission for observation* on the application of the nearest relative or mental welfare officer (s. 25). This differs from an emergency admission (see 3 above) only in that the recommendations of two doctors are required, and that the patient may as a result be detained for not more than 28 days, although he can be detained longer by involving the power described below.

In the case of all these sorts of admission all that is needed by way of diagnosis is a belief that the patient is suffering from a 'mental disorder'. It is only for the remaining types of admission that it is necessary to be more specific.

5. *Admission for treatment* on the application of the nearest relative or mental welfare officer (s. 26), supported by the recommendations of two medical practitioners, on the grounds that the patient is suffering from a mental illness, subnormality, severe subnormality or psychopathic disorder, of a nature or degree which warrants his detention in hospital for treatment, and that this is justified in the interests of his health or safety or for the protection of others. Not only must the diagnosis at least specify the sub-division of mental disorder; it must be one of the four sub-divisions named in section 4, and cannot be 'any other disorder or disability of mind'. Moreover, if the patient is aged 21 or older only 'mental illness' or severe 'subnormality' are sufficient diagnostic grounds: 'psychopathic disorder' or 'subnormality' are sufficient only in the case of younger patients, for reasons which will be discussed later.

The patient can be detained for not more than a year, although authority for his detention can then be renewed for a further year, and thereafter for two years at a time. He has the right of recourse to a Mental Health Review Tribunal if he feels his compulsory detention unnecessary.

6. *Admission or transfer from a prison or other custodial institution* (ss. 72,

73). This provision and its history has already been described in chapter 2, and need not be summarised here.

7. *Admission on a hospital order by a criminal court* (ss. 60, 61[18]). This too requires recommendations by two medical practitioners, who must believe that the offender's mental disorder is of a nature or degree which warrants detention in a hospital for treatment. They are not required, however, to say whether this would be justified in the interests of his health or safety, or for the protection of others. Any of the four specified sub-divisions of mental disorder may be a sufficient ground, and there is no limit to the age at which subnormality or psychopathic disorder may be a ground.

The court must have convicted the offender of an offence for which it could at its discretion have sentenced him to prison (or could have but for his youth). In certain circumstances, however, which will be discussed in the next chapter, it need not convict him, but must merely be satisfied that he did what he is charged with; and in the case of a child or young person it can make a similar order after finding that he is in need of care or protection.[18]

The effect of the order is almost identical with that of a compulsory admission for treatment, with minor differences which will be considered in the next chapter. All that need be mentioned here is that a higher court which does not consider it safe to allow the responsible medical officer alone to decide upon a patient's discharge, transfer or leave may add a 'restriction order' (under s. 65) which in effect means that the Home Office's agreement to any of these steps is required; and this order may either specify the time after which it expires or be for an unspecified period.

It is the last of these procedures for admission with which we are chiefly concerned. So far as prosecuted offenders were concerned, the Commission's hands had been slightly tied by their terms of reference, which expressly excluded 'Broadmoor patients'. This unobtrusive phrase prevented them from taking into their consideration the insanity defence, the procedure for dealing with persons who were unfit to plead, or that for transferring prisoners to mental hospitals. Part of the reason for this deliberate restriction was the current controversy over the death penalty. The report of that other Royal Commission, the Gowers Commission, had been published only the year before the Percy Commission began its work, and had dealt thoroughly with the problems raised by the insanity defence, unfitness to plead, and the reprieve of disordered murderers.[19] If the Percy Commission had tried to say anything more on these topics they would have endangered whatever recommendations they had to make on the trial of other—and numerically more important—sorts of disordered offender, by linking them to the raging controversy over the death penalty. The Commission themselves must have appreciated this, for although persons who benefited from the new defence of diminished responsibility were not outside their terms of reference they forbore to make any comment on their disposal.

Consequently the section dealing with hospital and guardianship orders expressly excluded offences for which the sentence was fixed by law, which for practical purposes meant murder. Even the subsequent suspension of the death penalty for murder did not bring murderers within the ambit of the section, for the law continued to fix the sentence, which was now life imprisonment. Nor did the Act deal with other persons who were found unfit to plead, or who successfully offered the insanity defence, although a few years later the Criminal Procedure (Insanity) Act, 1964 in effect provided a mandatory hospital order coupled with a restriction order for such cases.

At the other end of the scale the section excluded the petty sort of offence that could not be punished with imprisonment. In doing so it followed the lead of the 1913 Act. Its justification was no doubt that it seemed unfair that an offence which could not be the occasion for depriving a mentally normal person of his liberty should make this possible in the case of a disordered person. If so, as we shall argue in the next chapter, the reasoning was superficial, for the aim of compelling the disordered person to enter hospital or guardianship was not to impose a retributive penalty for what he has done but to safeguard him or the community against what he might do. Indeed, the new procedures made it possible to detain in hospital disordered people who had not even been accused of any offence, or indeed appeared before any court. The Percy Commission had therefore intended the hospital order procedure to apply to any offence, whether 'imprisonable' or not,[20] and had pointed out that the offender had plenty of safeguards, in the shape of appellate courts and Mental Health Review Tribunals, against oppressive detention. But the legislators refused to accept this logical conclusion.

Finally the Act preserved yet another important principle of the legislation of 1913. Although the court had considerable freedom of choice, it had to *make* a choice. It must decide either in favour of psychiatric disposal or in favour of penal disposal. No compromise was provided. In this respect both Acts followed the traditional pattern, in which the accused is either to be subject to ordinary punishment or to be dealt with as insane. Perhaps the most interesting aspect of this principle is that both Acts were preceded by Royal Commissions who did not think quite so conservatively. The Radnor Commission, as we have seen, actually proposed a 'double-track' system of imprisonment followed by detention in mental deficiency institutions for offenders whose disorders did not seem to excuse them from all responsibility. The double-track system was of course open to serious humanitarian objections, whether it was applied to recidivists or defectives. But while the Percy Commission did not revive that idea, it did not see the alternatives of penal and psychiatric measures as mutually exclusive.

'The findings of a court . . . would result in appropriate action being taken by the health authorities to provide the required treatment or care. In those circumstances the court could discharge the offender, but that should not necessarily follow. The court should use its normal powers of disposing of cases, having regard to the particular circumstances and the special medical or social care that the offender is to receive. We see no objection to a combination of penal and medical measures in these cases, e.g., by imposing a fine even when the patient

is to receive hospital treatment or training or community care. . . .'
(para. 521).

This did not find favour with the legislators, however, and the Bill expressly declared (s. 60(6)) that a court which dealt with an offender by means of a hospital or guardianship order must not also subject him to a custodial sentence, or put him on probation or fine him. It added, however, that the court could make 'any other order' which it had power to make. Thus it could order the offender to compensate his victim, or could use its powers of confiscation (for example, of firearms) or of disqualification from driving. This suggests that the Home Office's reasons for rejecting the Percy Commission's recommendation were not doctrinaire but practical. As we have seen, mentally disordered prisoners are a nuisance in prison: and to fine a man who is being prevented from earning by being sent to hospital may well impose undue hardship on him—or his family—if indeed there is any prospect of his paying the fine. (By the same token, however, a compensation order might well have been ruled out as well.) It is less easy to argue that probation is impractical or pointless in such cases, since probation orders can be coupled with in-patient or out-patient psychiatric treatment, and are said to be a useful way of providing after-care when the treatment ceases. No doubt in these optimistic days it was expected that mental hospitals would develop their own after-care services more quickly than they have done.

As for psychiatric probation orders, the Commission had expressly forborne to make any recommendations on the subject, on the grounds that Grünhut's investigation of them was in progress and its results should be awaited. The results were not available when the Act was drafted, and it therefore made no real attempt to fit psychiatric probation orders into a consolidated and consistent scheme, although it did include an amendment which made it plain that they were to be used for mental disorders which were not such as to warrant a hospital order.

The Act came into operation on 1 November 1960, and its sharp effect can be seen in table 4. In 1959, the last year of the old procedures, a total of 512 offenders had been compulsorily committed to hospitals: in 1961, the first complete year of the new regime, this number was doubled. In higher courts, which had hitherto been able to commit only under the 1913 Act and not under the 1948 Act (if we ignore the occasional special verdict), the effect was even more marked, and more than three times as many were committed.

Nevertheless, even when powers in the new Act appeared to correspond fairly closely to those in the 1913 Act, it was apparent that they were being more widely used. If the 1961 figures for hospital[21] orders which involved 'subnormal', 'severely subnormal' and 'psychopathic' offenders are compared with the total of orders made under the 1913 Act in 1959, it is clear that here too there has been a sharp increase: from 344 to 521. One possible explanation is that psychiatrists found the definitions of 'subnormality' and 'psychopathic disorder' much easier to satisfy than the definitions of 'feeble-mindedness' and 'moral defect'; and certainly this was intended where psychopathy was concerned. Part of the explanation, however, was probably quite simple: the stimulating effect of what was

TABLE 4. The criminal courts' use of the 1913, 1948 and 1959 Acts
(for notes see p. 75)

Year	Orders under Mental Deficiency Act, 1913		Reception orders by Magistrates' Courts under Criminal Justice Act, 1948[a]	Orders of all types
	by Assizes and Quarter Sessions	by Magistrates' Courts		
1914	3	27 (8)[b]		30
1915	3	91 (83)		94
1916	7	76 (69)		83
1917	1	78 (67)		79
1918	9	88 (70)		97
1919	12	121 (99)		133
1920	26	157(132)		183
1921	27	139(116)		166
1922	19	207(172)		226
1923	21	205(171)		226
1924	31	228(206)	Not applicable	259
1925	26	240(220)		266
1926	18	286(251)		304
1927	23	213(194)		236
1928	32	278(251)		310
1929	39	255(231)		294
1930	29	254(227)		283
1931	34	244(214)		275
1932	26	247(215)		273
1933	18	252(218)		270
1934	34	269(247)		303
1935	38	279(268)		317
1936	24	301(284)		325
1937	32	294(255)		326
1938	46	286(245)		332

1939–45: No figures were published for the war years.

Year	M	F	M	F	M	F	M	F
1946	No		187	41				
1947	figures		251(201)	62(51)	Not		Not	
1948	published		263(201)	47(33)	ascertainable		ascertainable	
1949	65	3	268(183)	47(37)	from		from	
1950	48	3	250	53	published		published	
1951	78	7	206	32	figures		figures	
1952	72	4	216	51				
1953	73	5	191	40	42	17	306	62
1954	55	3	183	53	86	25	324	81
1955	73	3	193	40	85	29	351	72
1956	54	3	190	38	113	35	357	71
1957	68	7	205	30	93	34	366	71
1958	86	3	225	37	109	36	420	76
1959	71	2	230	41	132	36	433	79
1960	116	7	261	68	102	31	479	106

Table 4—*contd.*

Hospital or guardianship orders[c] under Mental Health Act 1959

Year	by Assizes and Quarter Sessions		by Magistrates' Courts after conviction		without conviction		Totals	
	M	F	M	F	M	F	M	F
1961	298	30	510	117	81	23	889	170
1962	275	33	625	143	40	15	940	191
1963	254	35	727	171	47	13	1028	219
1964	304	24	829	142	70	9	1203	175
1965	316	43	765	113	72	8	1153	164
1966	322	35	873	119	77	12	1272	166
1967	372	39	803	120	88	14	1263	173
1968	409	41	760	125	61	11	1227	176
1969	379	52	800	119	73	7	1252	178
1970	417	37	733	107	66	10	1216	154

Source: The Criminal Statistics, England and Wales

[a] And later under the Magistrates' Courts Act, 1952.

[b] Figures in brackets represent orders made without conviction, which are included in the unbracketed totals.

[c] Excluding orders made under s. 61, relating to children in need of care, protection or control, and also a few orders made by appellate courts. The figures shown are taken from what are now tables I(a) and II(a) of the Criminal Statistics, and not from what is now table XV, which is compiled on a different basis.

presented as a 'new deal' for hospital psychiatry in general and for forensic psychiatry in particular.

Indeed, it seems likely that a substantial minority of the hospital orders made in the first year or two of the new Act were being used for cases which would formerly have been dealt with by psychiatric probation orders. Figure 2 shows that in 1961 there was a drop in in-patient but not in out-patient psychiatric probation orders for males, which is what we should expect if hospital orders were being used instead.

The general trend in hospital orders has been slowly but fairly steadily upward, at least until 1969. A closer look, however, reveals that this is really true only so far as concerns males. Orders dealing with women and girls rose for a couple of years but then fell, and since then have hardly risen above their 1961 level. The abnormally high number of women's hospital and guardianship orders for 1963 coincided with a temporary fall in the number of in-patient psychiatric probation orders for women (see table 3). The explanation seems to be that most hospital and guardianship orders affecting women originate in Holloway Prison, which is the remand prison for women tried in the south-east part of England; and a change of medical officers at this time led to a more conservative policy in regard to recommendations for hospital orders.

FIGURE 2. Trends from 1950 to 1970

These graphs are based on the last four columns of table 3 (p. 66) and the last two
columns of table 4 (pp. 74-5); but the crude figures are here shown as percentages
of the figure for 1961, the first year of operation of the 1959 act. The trend in persons
found guilty of indictable offences is shown as a rough indication of persons 'at risk'.

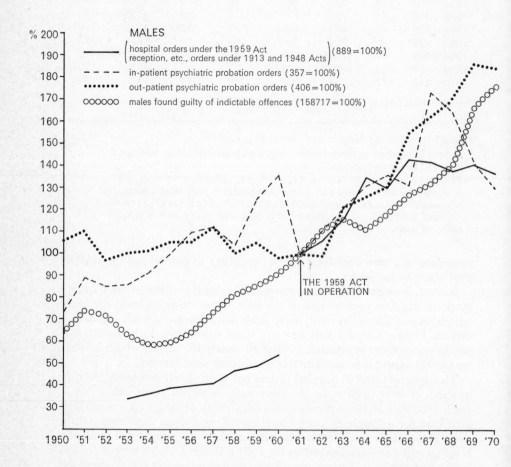

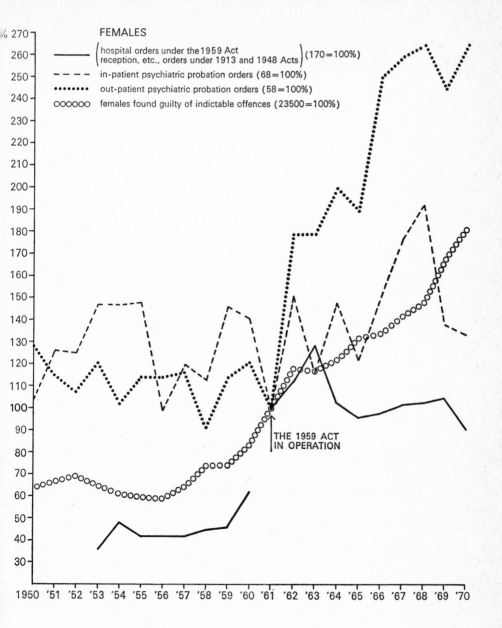

TABLE 5. Official methods of disposing of disordered offenders

	1961	1962	1961 *and* 1962	
Transferred from prison to hospital before trial or sentence	17	5	22	0·5%
Probation with requirement of treatment				
as out-patient	374	380	754	17·8%
as in-patient	392	456	848	20·0%
Made subject to *Guardianship* order	16	14	30	0·7%
Made subject to *Hospital* order				
without a conviction	97	52	149	3·5%
after conviction, but without restriction order	731	892	1623	38·4%
after conviction, and with restriction	150	136	286	6·7%
Found *insane on arraignment*	48	36	84	2·0%
Found *guilty but insane*	10	9	19	0·4%
Found of *diminished responsibility*	36	34	70[a]	1·7%
Found guilty of *infanticide*	13	17	30[b]	0·7%
Transferred from prison to hospital during sentence	182	140	322	7·6%
	2066	2171	4237[c]	100%

Sources: The Criminal Statistics, England and Wales, and unpublished probation statistics supplied by the Home Office.

[a] Since 3 of these were put on probation, probably with a requirement of psychiatric treatment, while 36 were dealt with otherwise than by ordinary sentences, in most cases probably by hospital orders, a substantial number must unavoidably be counted twice in this table.

[b] Since 22 of these were put on probation, probably with a requirement of psychiatric treatment, and 6 were dealt with otherwise than by ordinary sentences, in most cases probably by hospital orders, a substantial number must unavoidably be counted twice in this table.

[c] Since a small number of disordered offenders were almost certainly dealt with more than once during the period, the totals slightly exaggerate the number of *persons* involved.

These two utilitarian procedures–the hospital order and the special probation order–now account between them for the overwhelming majority of cases in which the courts officially recognise that an offender is mentally disordered. The numerical insignificance of the traditional procedures which involve consideration of the accused's mental state by the jury before conviction can be appreciated after a glance at table 5, which covers the years 1961 and 1962, the first two complete calendar years during which the Mental Health Act was in operation. It excludes offenders under 17 because mentally disordered juveniles are much less likely to be dealt with in one of these formal ways. It includes all the procedures whose origins have been traced in previous chapters of this volume or in volume 1, with the inevitable exception of the use of the prerogative of mercy.

Offenders who were found to be insane on arraignment, guilty but insane, of diminished responsibility or guilty of infanticide account in all for slightly less than 5 per cent of the total. Probation orders account for 38 per cent and hospital orders for 49 per cent. The remaining 8 per cent were transferred to mental hospitals before trial or (in most cases) after sentence, at the instance of prison medical officers.

We shall be looking more closely at some of these and other provisions of the Act in later chapters, and particularly those concerned with the courts, with discharge from hospital and with psychopaths. Meanwhile, let us consider what might be called the common philosophy which is shared by all the pieces of legislation which have been chronicled in this chapter. The traditional approach of the law to the problem of the disordered offender was to ask a jury the question 'Could he help what he is charged with?' Instead, the Acts of 1913, 1948 and 1959 asked 'What is the most expedient (or 'suitable') way of dealing with him–psychiatrically or penally?', and they put this question not to the jury but to the sentencer. They did not debar the defence or the prosecution from raising the issue of fitness for trial or the issue of insanity, at least in higher courts; and of course if either of these issues is successfully raised it leaves the sentencer no alternative to committing the accused to hospital. But since the question of expediency is linked not to the offender's state of mind at the time of his act, nor to his fitness for trial, the failure of defence (or prosecution) to raise either of these issues, or to raise them successfully, has no implications for the decision whether to make a hospital order, a guardianship order or a psychiatric probation order.

The new form of question was of course utilitarian. It ignored the extent of the offender's culpability, and invited the court to consider what was 'expedient' or 'suitable', presumably with the future in mind. It is true that, as we have just seen, it did not prohibit the raising of issues which, if successfully raised, prevent the court from treating the offender as culpable; and that, as we shall see in the next chapter, some courts have regarded the degree of his culpability as relevant to the choice between penal and psychiatric disposal. Equally, however, it did not oblige anyone to raise such issues; and indeed–murder apart–it made it unnecessary to do so, since any court could now choose a psychiatric form of disposal without the need for a special verdict. It is also true that it did not bind the court to accept recommendations from psychiatrists, however unanimous, in favour of psychiatric disposal, so that a defending counsel who wanted to make absolutely sure of this would still be justified in considering whether to seek a special verdict; but in practice this seldom seems to happen. It would not be an over-simplification to say that the new approach was one of conciliatory utilitarianism.

It is worth noting, however, that while Bentham would have regarded the Acts of 1913, 1948 and 1959 as steps in the right direction, they were the result not of doctrinaire reforms but of concessions to expediency. The concessions were made by Commissions, civil servants and legislators who were not merely under pressure from the mounting numbers of disordered persons in prisons and in courtrooms, but were also increasingly aware of the restrictiveness with which the traditional tests of the law were operating. Whether the utilitarianism of the legislation would have been more effective if it had been the result of an aggressive campaign rather than a bloodless rear-guard action is an interesting question, on which the following chapters may throw some light.

Notes

1. An Act to facilitate the Performance of the Duties of Justices of the Peace out of Sessions (11 & 12 Vict. c. 43).
2. Medical Inspector's Report for 1889–90, in the annual Report of the Prison Commissioners and Directors of Convict Prisons.
3. L. Forbes Winslow, *Recollections of Forty Years* (London, 1910).
4. The reference was to 'places of detention' provided by police under the Children Act, 1908–the forerunner of 'remand homes'.
5. The making of orders without conviction is discussed in the next chapter.
6. See chapter 9 (p. 211) for a fuller account of the reasons for this amendment.
7. Hansard, Commons Standing Committee A, 12 Feb. 48, col. 1039.
8. E. Glover, *The Roots of Crime* (London, 1960).
9. C. Mullins, *Crime and Psychology* (London, 1943).
10. The Home Office's point of view was supported–perhaps not surprisingly–by a Departmental Committee under the chairmanship of one of their Under-Secretaries: the *Harris Committee on the Social Services in Courts of Summary Jurisdiction* (Cmd. 5122, HMSO, 1936), p. 69.
11. See also Mrs M. Woodside's more recent description of the use of psychiatric probation orders in Edinburgh, in (1971) 118, *British Journal of Psychiatry*, 561 ff. The Scottish statute is very similar to the English so far as this measure is concerned.
12. And accepted that it should be provided by the Home Office or Prison Commissioners.
13. Although summary courts would be allowed to commit offenders to Quarter Sessions with a view to such a sentence.
14. And it was not to be used for non-imprisonable cases.
15. Report to the Home Secretary by the Advisory Council on the Treatment of Offenders (no other title) in (1950), 1, *Lancet*, 1123 ff, with leader on p. 1120.
16. The Royal Commission on the Law relating to Mental Illness and Mental Deficiency 1954–7 (Cmnd. 169, HMSO, 1957).
17. In *Mental Health and Social Policy* (London, 1960).
18. Section 61, dealing with 'care or protection' cases, has now been replaced by section 1(1) and (5) of the Children and Young Persons Act, 1969; but the effect is much the same.
19. See volume 1, chapters 6, 9, 13, 14.
20. See paras. 523 ff.

21. A negligible number of guardianship orders are included in the figures, but do not affect the argument.

Chapter 5. The Act in the Courts

This chapter is concerned with the way in which the criminal courts have interpreted the functions entrusted to them by Part v of the Act, and in particular by the cardinal section 60, which confers the power to make a hospital or guardianship order.

The Medical Evidence. To understand the role of the court under this section it is necessary to compare it fairly closely with the corresponding section (s. 26) that deals with compulsory detention for treatment without trial.[1]

Both sections stipulate that two medical practitioners must be of the opinion that the prospective patient is suffering from mental illness, psychopathic disorder, subnormality or severe subnormality. In both cases the practitioners may have described him as suffering from more than one of these sub-divisions, so long as they agree upon at least one (s. 26(4) and s. 60(5)): and in the case of a hospital order the judge, recorder or magistrate must also be satisfied 'on the evidence' of the practitioners that he is suffering from at least one of these sub-divisions.

Mental Disorder. It is worth noting here that the Act seems to envisage, or at least entertain the possibility of, forms of mental disorder which could not be made the basis of compulsory admission for treatment, whether direct or via the courts. For section 4 sub-divides mental disorders into six main categories: the four already listed plus 'any other disorder or disability of mind'. Thus a condition which was not regarded by psychiatrists as subnormality (severe or non-severe) or psychopathic disorder or mental illness, but was regarded as a 'mental disorder' or 'mental disability' could be the justification for an informal admission to a mental hospital, or even a compulsory admission for a short period of *observation* (s. 25) or compulsory removal to a *place of safety* (s. 136) but could not be the basis for a hospital or guardianship order or for compulsory admission for *treatment*.

That this was intentional was confirmed by the Minister of Health–Mr Walker-Smith–during the Committee stage of the Bill.[2] When Dr Johnson moved to delete the words 'and any other disorder or disability of mind' the Minister explained that there were disorders and disabilities which required care but would not be 'appropriate' for compulsory treatment, and he instanced the effects of head injuries or encephalitis, or 'mental enfeeblement as the result of mental illness'. His argument and examples were not as well chosen as they might have been. For if the aim was to exclude from *compulsory* admission types of case which are thought not to need it, this is supposed to be achieved by the conditions governing compulsory admission, as we shall shortly see. Moreover, to be convincing his examples ought to have been conditions which *in no circumstances* could be regarded as mental illnesses, psychopathic disorders or degrees of subnormality. Yet it is by no means unheard of for the effects of head injuries or encephalitis to be classified by psychiatrists as mental illnesses or forms of subnormality; indeed there were three such cases in our own sample. However that may be, Dr Johnson withdrew his amendment.

In deciding whether a person is mentally subnormal, severely subnormal or psychopathic, doctors are to some extent governed by the definitions in Section 4 of the Act. They cannot very well, for example, label a man as subnormal if tests show his intelligence to be above average. Nor can they label a woman 'psychopathic' (or indeed as suffering from any mental disorder) simply because she sleeps with too many men in too quick succession for the doctors' liking; for the section contains an express warning that it does not imply that someone can be dealt with under the Act as suffering from mental disorder by reason only of 'promiscuity or other immoral conduct'. Nevertheless, there is scope for a wide range of opinion amongst psychiatrists as to what is or is not subsumable under the different subdivisions of disorder. In chapter 10, which we have devoted to the concept of psychopathy, we shall see some of the effects of this. And when we turn to the subdivisions called 'mental illness' and 'other disorder or disability of mind' we find that they are left deliberately undefined. Fortunately, since the residual category of 'other disorders or disabilities' cannot be made the basis of compulsory detention—with the minor exception already mentioned—this absence of definition is less important in that case than where 'mental illness' is concerned. Even so the extent to which the Act relies on the medical profession to apply an unwritten but consistent and reasonable criterion of mental illness is remarkable. For there is no doubt that there are types of behaviour which some psychiatrists would call 'mental illness' while others would not. The commonest examples—all of which are associated with law-breaking—are homosexuality, alcoholism and drug abuse.

Consider homosexuality first. Whether or not it manifests itself in overt sexual behaviour, it is a condition which is discussed in almost every modern psychiatric text-book, and which prompts innumerable men (and smaller numbers of women) to seek psychiatric help. At the same time, psychiatrists and their text-books are increasingly careful to avoid the automatic application of the term 'mental illness' to such people, while emphasising that *some* of them may also exhibit symptoms of what are universally accepted as mental illnesses—acute anxiety, thought disorder, and so on. Many psychiatrists—especially in Britain—would prefer to call homosexuality a 'deviation' or 'abnormality' rather than an 'illness' or 'disorder' or 'disability'. Nevertheless, in certain individuals—and especially, as we shall see in the following chapter, males of low intelligence—the condition is associated with behaviour which is so strongly disapproved that it is prohibited by the criminal law; and when, as often, it takes the form of sexual approaches to boys it tends to be treated seriously by sentencers.

The hospital section of our dossier – which can be studied in Appendix D – asked for a 'clinical description of the disorder' which distinguished the 'predominant' disorder from 'any associated mental disorder (including personality disorders)'. We found three cases in which 'homosexuality' or 'sexual deviation' was given as the predominant disorder. In one of these cases the offender-patient had been classified as suffering from subnormality and psychopathic disorder, so that it could not be regarded as an example of the use of 'homosexuality' *per se* as a justification for a hospital order. The same could perhaps be said of the second case in which the man's offences consisted of larcenies, but the clinical description said 'sexual deviation: homosexual trends creating some secondary anxiety. On former admission there was a distinct schizoid episode, possibly precipitated by amphetamine-like drugs.' Only in the remaining case could it be argued that 'homosexuality' was being used as a more or less uncomplicated diagnosis. The man's criminal record consisted entirely of a series of indecent assaults on young males. The statutory classification given to the court had been 'psychopathic disorder', and the clinical description simply repeated this phrase under 'associated mental disorder', giving 'homosexuality' as the predominant disorder. Thus it seems that there may occasionally be cases in which a person's homosexual behaviour is used as the main, or even sole, ground for a psychiatric diagnosis, in the sense that but for that behaviour he would not have been labelled as disordered. No doubt this is more likely to happen in the case of paederasty than other forms of homosexuality.

As for the abuse of alcohol and other drugs, psychiatric text-books recognise and give definite labels to mental states which are the result of chronic abuse of drugs, such as *delirium tremens*, Korsakov's syndrome, or amphetamine psychosis. At the other extreme, however, the effects of a single overdose of gin or barbiturate are not regarded as mental illnesses. The doubtful territory lies in between, at the point where a person's use of drugs seems to be sufficiently frequent and heavy to be detrimental to his pocket, his work, his family's well-being or his social relations, without affecting his cognition, memory, reasoning, motor control or general health to any substantial extent. In this area some text-books distinguish psychological dependence from physiological dependence, in which withdrawal of the drug leads not merely to unhappiness, anxiety, or tension but to unpleasant physical symptoms.

From the pragmatic point of view there is no doubt that psychiatrists attempt to cure people of dependence on alcohol and other drugs, often using techniques, such as psychotherapy, which have been evolved in treating disorders which are universally accepted as mental illnesses. It has nevertheless been firmly stated in an otherwise excellent article that 'Drug addiction does not appear to come within the definition of "mental disorder" in Section 4 of the Mental Health Act 1959 and accordingly a hospital order cannot be made . . .'[3] Since some types of mental disorder are deliberately left undefined by that section, this statement cannot be founded on what is said there, and could be substantiated only by some sort of poll of psychiatric usage.

The Ministry of Health's statistics (1969, table 18) show that several thousand men and women are admitted each year to mental hospitals with a diagnosis of 'alcoholism' and 'other addictions'. Four out of five are admitted informally, but substantial numbers are admitted compulsorily. Most of these compulsory admissions are in 'emergency' (s. 29) or 'for observation' (s. 25); but some are 'for treatment' (s. 26) and a few are under hospital orders made by criminal courts. It is true that in these cases 'alcoholism' or 'drug addiction' may have been associated with depression, anxiety, schizophrenia or of course 'personality disorder'. But our own correspondence with psychiatrists of our acquaintance suggests that this is by no means always so.[4] Moreover our own dossiers contained seven cases in which either alcoholism or drug addiction was given as the *predominant* disorder. Of the four alcoholics one was also suffering from brain damage, one was described as a schizoid psychopath, one was a psychopathic personality and one (a woman) as an unstable personality. (There were five other cases in which alcoholism–or some equivalent– was given as a disorder associated with some other predominant disorder.) Of the three drug addicts, one was described as an inadequate psychopath, one as a case of personality disorder, and one had no associated disorder at all (his statutory classification in court had been mental illness). Rather surprisingly there was only one case in which drug addiction was given as an *associated* disorder.

To sum up, it seems clear that while some psychiatrists in the middle of the nineteen-sixties were prepared to regard homosexuality, alcoholism or drug addiction as the main diagnostic justification for a hospital order, most–if not all–of them felt happier if they could throw into the scales some other clinical label, of which 'psychopathic disorder' was the popular choice, partly no doubt because of the lack of specificity which we shall discuss in a later chapter, but partly also because it was recognised as a statutory classification.

'Warranting' Detention. Next, the practitioners must be of opinion–and if a court is involved it too must be satisfied–that the disorder is 'of a nature or degree which warrants the detention of the patient in a hospital for medical treatment.[5] Exactly what are the natures or degrees which 'warrant' this are nowhere specified. Section 26, which deals with detention without trial, goes on to add that the practitioners must also be of opinion, and must give reasons for the opinion, that the detention is 'necessary in the interests of the patient's health or safety or for the protection of other persons'.[6] This, however, is plainly an independent stipulation, and not an explanation of the phrase 'nature or degree'. To 'warrant' detention must therefore mean 'to be one of the conditions needed to justify it, but not the only condition'. It is open to the Minister of Health to make regulations prescribing particulars of the grounds for thinking that this condition is fulfilled which must be stated by the practitioners; but his regulations[7] merely ask for a 'clinical description of the patient's mental condition'.

Exactly what then does the word 'warrant' mean? In the original Bill the phrase used was 'renders him suitable to be detained'; but this was criticised in Committee, partly on the grounds that it referred to the patient as if he were an inanimate object, partly because it did not say what it seemed to mean, which—it was suggested—was really 'makes it *essential* for him to be detained'.[8] The Minister of Health pointed out that the grounds for considering detention essential were defined in the other part of the clause (which said that detention must be necessary in the interests of the patient's health or safety or for the protection of others); but he promised to reconsider the wording, and the result was the word 'warrants'. Clearly, then, 'warrants' means something less than 'makes essential'.

On the other hand it means something more than merely 'requiring and being susceptible to' the treatment which goes with detention. For Section 4 of the Criminal Justice Act, 1948, which deals with psychiatric probation orders, was amended by the Act of 1959 to make it clear that they were intended for 'mental conditions' which were 'such as require and may be susceptible to treatment but . . . not such as to warrant detention in pursuance of a hospital[9] order . . .'

The exact meaning of 'warrants detention' has not yet been discussed in any reported case which we have been able to find, and we can only make the tentative suggestion that if it has an exact meaning it must be something like 'will not receive the treatment which it requires without detention'.

The Most Suitable Method. So far there seems to be no difference between the stipulations for compulsory admission with and without the intervention of a criminal court. But now we come to a difference. So far as hospital orders are concerned the medical practitioners do not have to be of the opinion that detention for treatment is necessary in the interests of the patient's health or safety or for the protection of others; nor is the court required to satisfy itself on this score from any other evidence. Instead of what can be called the 'health, safety and protection' condition, the court is required merely to be of the opinion that a hospital order is 'the most suitable method of disposing of the case'.

It is true that in coming to this opinion it must have 'regard to all the circumstances including the nature of the offence and the character and antecedents of the offender, and to the other available methods of dealing with him'. But it is not told expressly what its aims and principles should be in deciding between the 'available methods'.

The Protection of the Public. In particular, the court is not told that 'protection', whether of the offender or of others, is a consideration which points towards hospital, although in the case of compulsory admissions without trial this is an express justification. Indeed, in several cases courts have decided that the protection of others was a consideration which pointed towards prison rather than hospital.

One of these was the case of Morris, a depressed and chronically anxious old man who had put to death his seriously ill wife in what was apparently a 'mercy killing'. At his trial he successfully pleaded diminished responsibility. The Crown tried to call rebutting evidence that he was in fact 'M'Naghten-mad', and though the judge, Mr Justice Jones, refused to allow them to raise the insanity issue[10] he allowed evidence to be heard that Morris' disorder was more serious than the defence's medical witnesses had indicated. Moreover, after conviction, he refused to make a hospital order, seemingly because he did not regard the hospital which had indicated its willingness to receive Morris as a sufficiently secure place for him; and he sentenced him to life imprisonment, although he pointed out that the Home Secretary had powers to send Morris, as a prisoner, 'to the right place', by which he no doubt meant Broadmoor. (It is perhaps of interest that Morris was *not* transferred from prison to hospital by the Home Secretary, but died not long after in prison. It is very unlikely that he could or would have wanted to kill anyone but his wife, and it seems probable that the judge confused severity of disorder with dangerousness to others.) His reasoning was upheld by the Court of Criminal Appeal, although the latter indicated that its decision might have been different if the judge had been told that there was a vacancy for Morris in one of the special hospitals.[11]

A few months later, in Higginbotham's case,[12] the Court of Criminal Appeal seemed to imply that the court has a duty to make rather more enquiries than Mr Justice Jones had done. Higginbotham was a man with a long history of offences connected with motor-cars (including thefts of them) who had during a previous sentence of preventive detention been found sufficiently disordered and dangerous to be transferred from prison to Broadmoor. After his eventual release he incurred two further sentences of imprisonment, but in December 1960 he was among the first offenders to be dealt with by a hospital order with a restriction order, and was committed to Park Prewett, an ordinary hospital. Six months later, while out of the hospital for the day (it is not clear whether with or without leave) he took someone's car was chased by the police and wrecked the car by colliding with a bus. He was sentenced to eight years' preventive detention. Upholding this, the Court of Criminal Appeal said

It may be useful if we say that it is unsafe for courts to assume that the making of a hospital order coupled with a restrictive [*sic* reported] order under section 65 is sufficient by itself to ensure that the convicted person . . . will be kept in safe custody. As far as we can see, the only way in which that result can be achieved is for the court to ascertain first before making the order which mental hospital can receive the man, and further, to find out whether or not the mental hospital is one in which facilities exist for keeping patients in safe custody so that they will not have the opportunity to walk out and commit crime. There are such institutions and if it be discovered *that there is no vacancy in any institution in which the convicted person can be kept in safe custody* one must point out that the powers of the court to make a hospital order are permissive, not mandatory, and if the court thinks it necessary for the protection of the public that the accused man should be incarcerated then the court should use its ordinary penal jurisdiction in order that if the prisoner needs medical treatment, arrangements may be made by the Prison Commissioners . . . for such treatment to be given in a place where he can be kept in safe custody and the kind of thing that happened in this case avoided (our italics).

The implication seems to be that if there is evidence in favour of a hospital order but the court is not satisfied with the degree of security in the hospital which has offered a vacancy it should not simply opt for imprisonment but should first make enquiries about vacancies in more secure hospitals.

In Gunnell's case [13] however, the Court of Appeal went even further, and said in effect that even a secure hospital was sometimes not secure enough. Gunnell, a psychopath with a criminal record who had more than twenty times escaped from ordinary mental hospitals, and who had been in Rampton (without escaping) was discharged from that hospital in 1959.[14] In 1966 he was convicted of a series of rapes, and sentenced to life imprisonment, in spite of evidence in favour of a hospital order returning him to Rampton. Upholding the sentence, the Court of Appeal said

> True, Rampton is said to be a secure hospital, but it does not mean that he would not get away from there. More important, it is to be observed that this dangerous psychopath has already been released on licence from Rampton. Bearing the interests of the public in mind, this court thinks it far safer that he should be kept in prison for as long as is necessary rather than that he should be left to be dealt with as a hospital might deal with him, on a doctor and patient relationship under which it might be considered safe for him to be free, whereas from the public angle he remains a menace.

This amounts almost to a declaration that courts should protect the public not merely against defective security arrangements but also against the mistaken decisions of 'responsible medical officers'—and presumably of Home Secretaries as well, since the court could have made a restriction order.

The court may reach the same decision by different reasoning, as is illustrated by the remarks of the sentencing judge (which were upheld by the appellate court) in R. v. Harvey and Ryan.[15] Rosemary Harvey was a prostitute who had killed one of her colleagues in order to get possession of the latter's child. She was agreed by three medical witnesses to be psychopathic and dangerous, and Broadmoor were willing to take her under a hospital order. Since her crime had been reduced to manslaughter by reason of diminished responsibility, the judge had a choice of sentence, and said:

> It is tempting to do that [sc. make a hospital order] but I don't think it is right. The hospital authorities may very easily take the view that while she is a very evil, bad and dangerous person, they cannot continue to regard her as a person who is mentally sick and they may also take the view that they cannot do anything further to cure her. The pressure to deal with people who are more helpful and less evil might lead them to wish to discharge her, and she probably has some legal rights for consideration for discharge when it is supposed, without any guarantee, that she may be cured. . . .

He went on to impose a life sentence because this would not prevent her from being transferred to a mental hospital (under section 72) but would allow her to be transferred back to prison if the situation which he foresaw were to arise. We shall return to this argument later (on p. 98).

In Greenberg's case, on the other hand, the appellate court seems to have regarded a hospital order (coupled with a restriction order without time-limit) as preferable to a long *determinate* prison sentence, at least from the point of view of public safety. The appellant had been convicted of buggery and indecently assaulting boys. He was a schizophrenic, but at the trial the requisite evidence for a hospital order was lacking, and he was sentenced to imprisonment for thirteen years.[16] On appeal the requisite evidence was called, and the court substituted the hospital and restriction orders, apparently reasoning that Greenberg would be a menace if released uncured.[17]

Restriction Orders. It is impossible however to do justice to the Court of Appeal's policy as regards the protection of the public from disordered offenders without considering their views on the making of what are called 'restriction orders'.

The effect of a restriction order has recently been summed up by them, in the practice note in Gardiner's case[18] as follows:

If . . . a restriction order is made

 (i) there is authority to detain the patient for at any rate the duration of that order, though the Secretary of State may terminate it at any time if satisfied that it is no longer required for the protection of the public;

 (ii) the patient can only be discharged with the consent of the Secretary of State or by the Secretary of State himself;

(iii) the Secretary of State himself has power in discharging the patient himself to make the discharge conditional, in which case the patient remains liable to recall during the period up to the expiration of the restriction order. This power is particularly useful as a means of keeping a discharged patient under the supervision of a probation officer or mental welfare officer for a longer period than would be possible if there were no restriction order;

(iv) a patient who is absent without leave may be taken into custody again at any time.[19]

Only a higher court may make a restriction order, although a magistrates' court may in a case in which the necessary conditions for making a hospital order are fulfilled, commit the offender in custody (or in hospital) to Quarter Sessions with a view to the making of a hospital order with a restriction. Even then, Quarter Sessions are not obliged to make a hospital order, let alone a restriction order. In the years 1964–8, out of 204 offenders committed to them with a view to a restriction order, only three-quarters were eventually dealt with thus: most of the remainder were made the subject of ordinary hospital orders, but 2 per cent were imprisoned, and 2 per cent fined, put on probation or simply discharged.

For the question whether a restriction order is necessary is left very much to the discretion of the judge or recorder. The section itself merely requires that the court, 'having regard to the nature of the offence, the antecedents[20] of the offender and the risk[21] of his committing further offences if set at large', should come to the conclusion that it is necessary 'for the protection of the public' to make such an order. As regards the medical evidence the requirements are the same as for a hospital order, the only extra stipulation being that at least one of the medical practitioners who give evidence must have done so orally. (Note, however, that the medical practitioner who gives oral evidence is not *required* to be the one who has satisfied the local health authority that he has special experience in the diagnosis or treatment of mental disorders.)

The main features of these provisions follow the recommendations of the Percy Commission (pp. 122, 172 ff.), who had been told by the Association of Chief Police Officers about cases in which patients who had committed sexual or violent crimes had been discharged prematurely and committed similar crimes again. In essence, therefore, the restriction order was designed to protect the public against the over-optimism or irresponsibility of psychiatrists, by requiring the psychiatrist who thought that an offender-patient should be discharged to persuade the Home Office that this could safely be done.

It is worth noting that the need for any such provision was questioned in Parliament during the Bill's passage, and by the knowledgeable and experienced Mr Kenneth Robinson. He argued, not without some force, that the offender should either be entrusted completely to the hospital service, or, if this could not be safely done, receive his psychiatric treatment in prison. He quoted in his support the British Medical Association, the Association of Psychiatric Social Workers, the National Association for Mental Health and the National Association of Mental Welfare Officers. He added that the Percy Commission had intended this provision only for psychopathic patients, whom they had envisaged as going to State institutions: an interpretation which their report will hardly bear (see especially para. 520).

The Minister of Health's Parliamentary Secretary–Mr David Renton– had the delicate task of rebutting these arguments without openly casting doubt on the good judgment of some members of the medical profession. He wisely chose as his main argument the advantages of a power which would make it possible to ensure after-care for the discharged patient; but added that there were certain patients, who, though dangerous enough to call for Home Office control over their discharge, were not of a kind which could be properly treated in prison.

This was not a complete answer to Mr Robinson, who could have replied that if there were dangerous offenders who could not be treated in prison the Special Hospitals were the place for them: and that, if so, there was no need to hamper ordinary mental hospitals with restriction orders. Nowadays, a decade later, it is even more questionable whether the combination of a restriction order with committal to an ordinary hospital is a successful expedient. As can be seen from Higginbotham's case–and several others in our sample (described on pp. 197-8)–a restriction order does not guarantee secure custody, for it does not oblige an ordinary hospital to impose any physical restraint on the offender-patient. This was not understood by some judges and recorders, at least in the first few years, with the result that they were encouraged to trust ordinary hospitals with dangerous offenders whom they would otherwise have insisted on sending to a Special Hospital or prison.

Another feature of restriction orders whose value is questionable (although it was not in fact questioned in Parliament) is the power of the court to specify a time-limit. This seems to be based on the assumption that there will be cases in which it is at first inadvisable to leave the responsibility for discharge wholly in the hands of the hospital, but will later become safe to do so. It is not easy to imagine what sort of cases these could be. For the section makes it clear that in deciding whether to make a restriction order the court is to 'have regard to the nature of the offence, the antecedents of the offender and the risk of his committing further offences if set at large'. The nature of the offence cannot change with time, nor can the antecedents of the offender. The risk of his committing further offences may well decrease; but how is the court to predict the date by which this decrease will have so altered the situation that the decision can safely be left to the responsible medical officer? It is possible to conceive of a case in which some definite changes in circumstances is foreseeable—such as the emigration of a paranoid offender's fancied enemy. The Court of Appeal has suggested—in Gardiner's case (loc. cit.)—that the *only* type of case in which a time-limit may be justifiable is 'where the doctors are able to assert confidently that recovery will take place within a fixed period'; but situations in which a responsible psychiatrist is confident both that the offender will recover by a certain date and that his offence was so closely connected with his disorder that recovery will guarantee no repetition of it must be rare indeed.

(It must be noted, by the way, that in the past at least the Court of Criminal Appeal itself had been known to make use of restriction orders with time-limits. One such case—in our sample—was that of a man who had been convicted at Quarter Sessions of attempted housebreaking and larceny on separate occasions, and received two concurrent sentences of twelve months' imprisonment. He appealed against these sentences, and the Court of Criminal Appeal substituted a hospital order with a restriction order of three years' duration. Since he had been diagnosed as subnormal and mildly psychopathic, this could not have been a case in which 'the doctors are able to assert confidently that recovery will take place within a fixed period'.)

In any case, a restriction order without a time-limit does not exclude the possibility of discharge at any time, and while three-quarters of our restriction order cases were still in hospital two years after the making of the order (see pp. 172-3) there were cases in which the offender-patient was discharged very early indeed. Perhaps the most striking example was a Welshman in his fifties, who had formed an association with a woman in his village; when she told him that she wanted to end it because she had met someone else he tried to suffocate her with a pillow. He was diagnosed as suffering from reactive depression, 'mixed type', and after medication and 'superficial psychotherapy' was discharged with Home Office consent eight months later. Although he had telephoned his former mistress while in hospital he eventually accepted that their relationship was at an end, and by the end of our follow-up had remained steadily at work, with no recorded reconviction.

It was understandable—if not excusable—that even the experienced lawyers who made the restriction orders should sometimes have reasoned as if by setting a time-limit they were in effect sentencing the offender-patient to detention for a fixed period. One such order, for example, was for a nine-month period, another for six months, and one for three months. The three-month order was imposed on a mother who had murdered her mongol child while in a post-puerperal schizophrenic state. The charge of murder had been reduced to infanticide by the Director of Public Prosecutions. The six-month order was applied to a psycho-pathic man in his twenties with a record of fourteen sexual offences against under-age girls. In hospital he was very soon given 'complete freedom of movement', and allowed out to work. Nine months after the making of the order he was discharged, and shortly afterwards convicted again, although not of a sexual offence. The nine-month order was imposed on a man who had committed a breaking and entering offence in concert with another man (who received an ordinary prison sentence, not of nine months).

As table 6 shows, the use of fixed periods was at first popular. In the first year of the Act's operation 44 per cent of restriction orders were of this kind. Its popularity quickly declined, however, until just before Gardiner's case it was only 20 per cent. In Gardiner's case the Lord Chief Justice said that 'since in most cases, the prognosis cannot be certain the safer course is to make *any* restriction order unlimited in point of time' (our italics). He added, however, that there might be exceptions (of the kind which we have just discussed); and the result has been that orders with fixed periods have not yet fallen into complete disuse, but still account for about one restriction order in ten. Even if one believes in the sort of exception which the practice note described it is hardly credible that so many cases belong to that category.

We also found several cases in which the offender seemed so obviously dangerous that it was difficult to see why the court had not thought a restriction order necessary. Later in this chapter we shall see that the use of the magistrates' power to make a hospital order without convicting may prevent the adding of a restriction order. There were other cases, however, in which the magistrates convicted an offender and then made a hospital order themselves although committal to Quarter Sessions with a view to a restriction order might have been wiser. One such case was that of a twenty-nine-year-old colliery worker, a paranoid schizophrenic, who had some sort of grudge against a neighbouring family. He paid them several visits to threaten violence, and on one of these was found by the police to have concealed a pair of scissors in the leg of his sock. For this he received fourteen days' imprisonment. On the day of his release he began to make a wire garotte, saying that he was going to use it on the family in question. Later in the day he went round to their house, and after a struggle with the head of the household grabbed a knife from the table and threatened to kill husband, wife and children. He had a long history of convictions, most of which were petty, but some of which emphasised his tendency to violence (for example, 'firing a gun on the highway'). We surmised that if this last incident had actually culminated in bloodletting he would probably have been committed to a higher court for trial or sentence, and would probably have been put under a restriction order.

Another such case was that of a woman in her forties, who had immi-grated with her husband from eastern Europe not long after the last war.

Her husband had left her, their children had been taken into care, and she herself was living on National Assistance. For some years she had been complaining to the police that she was being spied upon by Russians, and she had spent two short periods in local mental hospitals. Shortly after being discharged from one of these, she rushed out of her house with an iron bar in her hand and attacked a neighbour, who was passing the house with a baby in her arms. In spite of the fact that one of the psychiatrists' reports gave a clear warning of the likelihood of further violence to her neighbours, possibly in a more severe form, the magistrates' court made her the subject of an ordinary hospital order. A few months later she was allowed to go home again. Nine months after that she picked up a fellow-countryman in a public house, took him home and there killed him with an axe.

Even higher courts, however, may sometimes unaccountably refrain from making a restriction order. One such case was that of a fifty-year-old man who had made a serious attack on his wife. He had no previous convictions and–apart from some out-patient treatment for hypochondriac anxiety in the early nineteen-fifties–no history of serious mental illness. A month or two before the incident he had received an anonymous letter telling him that his wife was having an affair with a man at her place of work. Although she denied this, he was not convinced, and became depressed, moody and menacing. His wife later told the police that only by persuasive talking had she managed to stave off violence during this period. A few weeks after receiving the letter he tried to cut her throat, and succeeded in wounding her badly. The diagnosis was 'depressive state', with 'psychopathic personality'. The assize judge made an ordinary hospital order committing him to a local hospital without restrictions. The responsible medical officer, however, very sensibly put him in a maximum security ward, and refused to relax his precautions until the divorce proceedings which his wife instituted were complete. He was still inside and under maximum security precautions at the end of a year. It is possible, although we do not know, that the sentencer in this or other such cases was handicapped by the absence of both the medical witnesses, of whom at least one must give *oral* evidence before a restriction order can be made. In theory, of course, the offender can be remanded again so that a medical witness can attend, but this may present difficulties, especially in the case of an itinerant judge of assize.

In contrast, a case in which it was difficult to see the need for a restriction order was that of a seventeen-year-old subnormal, whose offences involved nothing worse than homosexual acts with consenting adults– usually for money–and one or two very petty thefts. He was described by the medical witnesses as suffering from both subnormality and psychopathic disorder, and it may have been this–or his homosexual activities– which prompted an assize judge to add a two-year restriction to the hospital order. Another case in which it was not easy to see the need for a restriction order was that of a nineteen-year-old subnormal who had been found guilty of sexual intercourse with a subnormal girl, not much below the age of consent. His only other recorded offence was one of wilful damage, committed while he was *on bail*. It may have been this which prompted Quarter Sessions to impose a restriction order. However that may be, they were evidently half-hearted about it, for they limited it to a period of a year. Since this was the period for which an ordinary hospital order would have remained in force without renewal, the only logical justification for this step would have been that they wanted the Home Secretary to bear the grave responsibility of any decision to discharge him within the year. (In the event, the Home Office did consent to his discharge after eleven months, and he settled down to work with a building firm, incurring no further convictions during our two year follow-up.)

The Practice Note in Gardiner's Case. We must now point out, however, that the offenders in our sample were dealt with before Gardiner's case. The details of the case itself are of little interest: it was clear that the Court of Appeal merely used it as the opportunity to issue a 'practice note' on the use of restriction orders, since they emphasised the number of cases which had convinced them that 'some courts do not fully appreciate the advisability in some cases of making a restriction order'. The practice note went on to give a very clear statement of the effect of an ordinary hospital order and of a restriction order. It continued

. . . a restriction order enables the Secretary of State to exercise the function . . . of a central authority which pays special regard to the protection of the public in controlling the discharge of dangerous patients. Apart from a restriction order it is inevitable that the hospital's first concern is the welfare of the patient and this does result in some cases in a patient who is subject to a hospital order alone securing his discharge earlier than he would do if he were also subject to a restriction order. The Secretary of State might well feel that although the patient was apparently no longer in need of medical treatment a further period in hospital under observation was advisable or was required to guard against the possibility of relapse leading to further crime.

This of course is not meant to suggest that restriction orders should be made in every case but it is very advisable that they should be made in all cases where it is thought that the protection of the public is required. Thus in, for example, the case of crimes of violence, and of the more serious sexual offences, particularly if the prisoner has a record of such offences, or if there is a history of mental disorder involving violent behaviour, it is suggested that there must be compelling reasons to explain why a restriction order should not be made. Nevertheless experience has shown that there are an alarming number of cases in which in such circumstances no restriction order has been made. As an example, a woman with a history of mental disorder attacked a neighbour with an iron bar and was made the subject of a hospital order alone. Four months later she obtained her discharge and within less than a year she killed a man with an axe, was found unfit to plead and removed to Broadmoor. . . .

There have also been cases in which a court has decided that the prisoner must be detained under conditions of special security in one of the special hospitals and yet no restriction order has been made. In the

result he may well be able to secure his discharge on application to a
Mental Health Tribunal on the ground that he is not at the time
suffering from mental disorder, even though relapses may be expected.
The effects of this note, which was issued early in 1967, can be seen in
table 6. The percentage of hospital orders which were coupled with
restriction orders, having averaged just over 13 per cent in the first six
years, rose sharply to 19 per cent in 1967, and has averaged over 18 per
cent in 1967–9. Secondly, as column G shows, a substantial part–but by
no means the whole–of the increase was due to the way in which magistrates' courts seem to have been stimulated to commit more cases to
Quarter Sessions with a view to a restriction order.

In contrast, committals to Special Hospitals without a restriction order,
though strongly condemned in the practice note, were only slightly reduced after its publication. What was the reason for the existence and
persistence of this small minority of cases? One conceivable explanation
was that these orders were made by summary courts, which have no
power to make restriction orders, but are on occasion presented with an
offender whose offence can be tried summarily and who has been offered
a vacancy in Broadmoor, Rampton or Moss Side. Rather than commit
him to Quarter Sessions with a view to a restriction order, which would
delay his arrival in hospital, they may prefer simply to make a hospital
order. This could not be the sole explanation, however, for about two in
every five such orders were made by *higher* courts.

Our own sample contained 30 such orders, 13 made by higher courts,
and we examined them to see what the explanation might be in each case.
In some cases the offence was relatively trivial, and the obvious question
was 'Why a Special Hospital?'. In four of these cases the answer was
clearly that the offender had already been in one of the Special Hospitals,
and was being returned there because that was where he was known: an
example was an ex-Broadmoor patient whose offence was being 'drunk
and disorderly', although he was also very violent towards the constables
who arrested him. In ten other cases the offender was a known absconder
from ordinary hospitals, or had made himself objectionable to those
hospitals by violent or suicidal behaviour. In four more cases the offender
had a long criminal record, but of relatively trivial offences, so that the
courts may have felt that the security of a Special Hospital was necessary
but that the date of release could safely be left to the responsible medical
officer. In contrast were the cases in which it was easy to see why a Special
Hospital had been preferred, but difficult to see why a restriction order
had not been made. In six of these cases the current offence or the man's
record or both were so serious that we could only suppose that the court
thought that the security of a Special Hospital was sufficient safeguard,
and overlooked the point made in the subsequent practice note. In five
other cases the offender's youth may have been a consideration, although
again an illogical one. Finally in one case the offender was said to have
been 'unfit to plead', which probably indicated that he was sent to
hospital without conviction (see the later section of this chapter on summary courts).

We were struck, too, by the fact that in all but one of our cases the

TABLE 6. The use of restriction orders[a]

Year	Total number of hospital orders	Total number of restriction orders	Col. B as % of col. A	% of B with time-limit	% of B involving Special Hospitals	% of B made as a result of committal from lower court	Offenders committed to higher court with a view to a restriction order[b]	Restriction orders made as a result of committals shown in col. G	Committals to Special Hospitals without restriction orders	Col. I as % of col. A
	A	B	C	D	E	F	G	H	I	J
	N	N	%	%	%	%	N	N	N	%
1961	1059	154	14·6	44·2	33·1	18·2	22	c	20	1·8
1962	1131	138	12·2	39·1	50·0	15·9	13	c	25	2·1
1963	1247	159	12·8	40·3	47·2	13·8	7	c	33	2·6
1964	1378	185	13·4	21·6	47·6	10·3	21	13	31	2·3
1965	1317	196	14·9	17·8	42·4	11·2	22	14	45	3·5
1966	1438	180	12·5	20·0	54·4	11·7	28	21	41	2·8
1967[d]	1436	271	18·9	11·0	47·6	20·7	65	49	32	2·2
1968	1403	255	18·1	10·2	53·3	24·3	74	57	38	2·7
1969	1430	256	17·9	7·1	50·1	23·5	47	33	38	2·8

[a] Source: The Criminal Statistics for England and Wales. Numbers of committals to Special Hospitals without restriction orders were supplied by the Department of Health and Social Security.

[b] Source: The Assizes and Quarter Sessions tables of the Criminal Statistics for England and Wales.

[c] The tables for these years do not give the information.

[d] The practice direction in Gardiner's case was issued early in 1967.

diagnosis included subnormality or psychopathic disorder (under one or other of its synonyms: see chapter 10). This contrasted strongly with the diagnoses of our restriction order cases, only 55 per cent of which were of this kind. Although the odds against this being due to sampling error were very small indeed (less than 1 in 1,000) we were glad to find it confirmed by another observation. This was that over a longer period (1961–6) nearly three-quarters (73 per cent) of Special Hospital admissions under hospital orders without restriction went to Rampton and Moss Side (which specialise in dangerous subnormal or psychopathic patients); whereas only 42 per cent of *all* offender-patients admitted by the Special Hospitals from criminal courts went to Rampton or Moss Side. The probable explanation is that a higher percentage of Broadmoor cases are seen in prison by one of the hospital's own consultants, who can thus draw the attention of those concerned to the desirability of a restriction order.

Is it possible, then, to sum up the views of the Court of Appeal on the protection of the public against the mentally disordered offender, as they are reflected in the practice note and the Court's *dicta* in the cases of Morris, Higginbotham, Gunnell, Greenberg and Harvey and Ryan? It does not seem too fanciful to suggest that it seems to have in mind a rank order of security on the following lines:

1. a sentence of life imprisonment (the cases of Gunnell and Harvey and Ryan: and see also R. v. Hodgson [1968] Crim. L.R. 46);
2. committal to one of the Special Hospitals, which should always be coupled with a restriction order (Morris' case, and the practice note);
3. a determinate prison sentence (Higginbotham's case);
4. committal to an ordinary hospital with a restriction order, which, the practice note implies, provides more protection than
5. committal to an ordinary hospital without a restriction order.

Finally, the court thinks that, with rare exceptions, a restriction order should be without a time-limit.

If this is not too crude a summary, it is worth considering for a moment whether it will stand up to a critical scrutiny. In the first place, is a life sentence really a better protection than committal to a Special Hospital? Only on two assumptions: that the lifer will be allocated to a maximum security prison, and that the question of his release will be considered with more care than if he had gone to one of the Special Hospitals. How safe are these assumptions? It is true that men such as Straffen, whose case was described in volume 1 (p. 116), are kept in maximum security wings: but this is by administrative decision, and the court cannot ensure this. As for release, this is a matter for the Home Office whether the offender is a lifer or a Special Hospital patient, unless the court has ignored the Court of Appeal's advice, and sent him to a Special Hospital without a restriction order.

As for the courts' argument (for instance in R. v. Harvey and Ryan) that a life sentence is preferable to a hospital order because the latter allows the patient to claim a right to discharge if 'cured', it is strange that even the appellate court should fail to draw the important distinction between ordinary hospital orders and those to which the court has attached a restriction order. This probably explains the trial judge's reference,

H

vague as it was, to Rosemary Harvey's right to discharge in the event of 'cure'; for as we shall see in chapter 7 (p. 168) she could then more or less demand that a Mental Health Tribunal order her to be discharged, *but only if no restriction order had been made.* Had one been made, a Tribunal could at most have recommended her discharge to the Home Secretary. The latter would not have been obliged to accept this advice, and could have refused to authorise her discharge. The Home Office does not regard itself as bound in law to agree to the discharge of such a patient simply because he or she is regarded as 'cured', but has regard to the risk of further harm by the patient.

The judge's argument would have been sounder, however, if he had not tried to give it a legal flavour. For it did draw attention to an administrative defect of the system. It is a fact that some offender-patients for whom no mental hospital can do more than provide a more tolerant form of security than a prison have to continue to occupy valuable beds because they are regarded[22] as too dangerous to discharge and yet cannot legally be transferred to any other kind of establishment. It is arguable, of course, that what is needed is simply extension of the Special Hospitals to cater for patients who cannot be given anything more than understanding care and supervision. Yet it is also arguable that many long-term prisoners would benefit from exactly the same sort of regime, and that such establishments should therefore be part of the prison system rather than the Special Hospital system. The moral argument—that someone whose law-breaking is to some extent attributable to mental disorder *deserves* to be in hospital rather than prison—has force only so long as hospital is preferable to prison. If, as is likely, there are offenders of this sort who would prefer Grendon to one of the Special Hospitals, a logical moralist would give them the choice.

Secondly, it is open to doubt, as we have seen, whether there is much point in a restriction order which gives an ordinary hospital complete discretion in the degree of security to which the patient is subject. As our cases illustrate, some responsible medical officers apply the strictest security of which their hospitals are capable, even in cases where the court has omitted to make a restriction order; but they are not obliged to do so when a restriction order *has* been made, and in some cases they do not do so. Where security is concerned, a restriction order acts as a warning, but is not an injunction. It is arguable that there is a type of case in which the offender is not an immediate danger, and will become one only if discharged and allowed to drift back into his former situation; an example is the man who becomes violent only after prolonged drinking bouts, and who is unlikely to harm anyone, even on day parole, so long as he is a 'dried-out' patient. For such cases a restriction order at least ensures some degree of after-care, which *may* be all that is required. But it goes further than that. Its basic inconsistency, in its present form, is that it assumes that the responsible medical officer cannot be trusted to decide when to discharge the offender in question, but *can* be trusted to decide the degree of security required while he is a patient. It would be more logical if restriction orders gave the Home Office a say in the latter as well as the former.

Thirdly, we have cast doubt on the need for a form of restriction order which sets its own time-limit. Even if there are cases in which it can confidently be predicted that the offender will cease to be a danger within a definite period–and this too is questionable–they must be rare. Since a time-limit neither safeguards the offender against longer detention, nor guarantees to the public that he will not be released earlier, it is difficult to argue that anything would be lost if even these exceptional cases were subject to an indeterminate restriction. The fixed period could well be abolished, and is now sufficiently unfashionable to make it unlikely that it would be mourned.

Other Considerations. Let us turn, however, to cases in which the protection of the public either *can* be secured by a hospital order, or is not a consideration at all (as when the offender's offences are not dangerous to others). How is the court supposed to reason in these cases?

Perhaps it is fair to assume that in straightforward circumstances the courts reason as Mr Justice Marshall did in the case of Mrs Russell, a woman of 41 who had tried to gas herself and all her children. The youngest child did in fact die, but her defence of diminished responsibility was successful, evidence being given that she was suffering from schizophrenia with depressive features. The judge merely said that he had come to the conclusion that 'the public interest would best be served by her being cured', and he made a hospital order committing her to an ordinary hospital.[23]

Indeed, writing in 1965 a leading authority on sentencing, Mr Thomas, summed up his impressions thus:

A survey of decisions of the Court [of Criminal Appeal] since the passing of the Mental Health Act, 1959, suggests that the powers given by the Act are being used whenever possible. The Court is quite prepared to abandon concepts of retribution and deterrence when dealing with a mentally disturbed offender who has committed even a serious crime of violence which would in the normal way attract a deterrent sentence, and sentences of imprisonment are used only where a hospital order or probation order with a condition for treatment are unsuitable. . . .[24]

The picture painted here is one of quite consistent utilitarianism. But how realistic is it? There have been cases–one or two are mentioned by Mr Thomas himself–in which the Court of Criminal Appeal clearly implied that the utilitarian approach was subject to the overriding demands of retributivism: in other words, that the public interest was the proper consideration only if there were no need for 'punishment'. The first plain statement to this effect was an *obiter dictum* of the Court of Criminal Appeal in Morris' case, already mentioned:

. . . the basic principle must be that where punishment as such is not intended, and where the sole object of the sentence is that a man should receive mental treatment and be at large as soon as he can safely be discharged, a proper exercise of the discretion demands that steps should be taken to exercise the powers under Section 60. . . Of course there may be cases where, although there is a substantial impairment of responsibility, the prisoner is shown on the particular facts of the case nevertheless to have some responsibility for the act he has done, *for which he must be punished* [our italics] and in such a case, although ... this was not such a case, it would be proper to give imprisonment, allowing the Secretary of State to exercise his powers under Section 72 in order that any necessary mental treatment should be given. . . .

It is a nice illustration of the close connection in the judicial mind between the retributive and the denunciatory aims of sentencing. There may be cases, Lord Chief Justice Parker was saying, in which the responsibility of the accused was not sufficiently diminished to excuse him from retributive punishment, in which case the court 'must' (not 'may') sentence him to imprisonment, even in the knowledge that he *may* in the event be transferred from prison to hospital, perhaps the very hospital to which it could have committed him by means of a hospital order. The main point of this extract, however, is that it makes clear the view of the Court of Appeal that the need for retributive punishment overrides the utilitarian case for committal to hospital, at least as far as the sentencer is concerned.[25]

(It must be noted that even retributive reasoning of this sort can lead to the opposite decision. In 1967 a Mr Rafi was convicted of stealing rare books worth £17,000, and sentenced to nine months' imprisonment. The Court of Appeal, however, were satisfied that his mental condition was such that treatment, not punishment, was the proper course, and substituted a hospital order.[26])

Nevertheless, the Court of Criminal Appeal have also taken a view which is not easily reconcilable with their *obiter dictum* in Morris' case, namely that a hospital order can properly be made even if there is no connection between the disorder and the offence. The case in which they did so was one of those very rare ones in which an appellant who *had* been dealt with by hospital order wished to be sentenced in the ordinary way instead. Hatt, a mortuary attendant who like Higginbotham was addicted to car-stealing and dangerous driving, was also one of those eccentric people who repeatedly seek admission to hospitals in order to undergo unnecessary operations, and indeed one operation which had been performed on him—whether necessarily or not is unclear—was a leucotomy. On the occasion leading to his appeal he had been made subject to both a hospital order and a restriction order without a time-limit. Fearing perhaps that this would result in longer detention than any prison sentence which he might otherwise have received, he sought leave to appeal, on the ground that there was no connection between his disorder and his offence, and that in the absence of such a connection a hospital order should not be made. Refusing leave to appeal, Mr Justice Streatfeild pointed out that the section did not require such a connection.[27]

Certainly it does not. But if the *obiter dictum* in Morris' case is followed, the absence of any connection would strengthen rather than remove the court's obligation to punish the offender. For if a man can have a mental disorder which is so closely connected with his act as to diminish his responsibility for it, and yet still be held responsible enough to oblige the court to punish him, then a man whose disorder is unconnected with his offence must *a fortiori* call for punishment.

It could be argued that Mr Justice Streatfeild's reasoning in Hatt's case was not irreconcilable with that of the Court of Appeal, if what the former had in mind was an offence so trivial that it did not demand punishment. It is probably significant that the cases in which the Court of Appeal have reasoned retributively have been ones in which the offence was a very grave one, such as homicide or rape, and sometimes also cases in which a defence of diminished responsibility has understandably focused the court's attention on the culpability of the accused. But Mr Justice Streatfeild does not seem to have argued in this fashion. He had been the chairman of the important Departmental Committee on the Business of the Criminal Courts (1961, Cmnd. 1289) which had emphasised the non-retributive aspects of sentencing; and it is likely that he was interpreting the section in the purely utilitarian sense which had been in the minds of the Percy Commission and the Parliamentary draftsmen.

The trouble is that the section as drafted neither expressly permits nor expressly forbids courts to think in terms of retribution and responsibility. It is true that, by requiring medical evidence about the mental condition of the accused at the time of disposal but not at the time of the offence, it seems to imply that a man who had been sane at the time of his act could nevertheless be considered suitable for a hospital order by the court. But it is arguable that, by enjoining the court to have regard to all the circumstances, including 'the nature of the offence', it readmits by the back door, as it were, the offender's mental condition at the time of the offence; and that 'suitable' could mean, among many other things, 'retributively right'. Courts are in the habit of weighing an offender's culpability not only in the course of his trial but also when they sentence him; and if it was intended that they should not do so when the requisite evidence in favour of a hospital or guardianship order had been given, this should have been expressly stated. To do so would not have been to compel the courts to follow the medical recommendations, for they could still have been permitted to take into account the prospects of successful treatment and any need to protect the public.

'*Occasionalism*'. On the whole, however, Mr Thomas was probably right if he meant that in the ordinary case in which a hospital order is proposed courts tend to reason in a utilitarian way. If so, legislation on the disposal of disordered offenders seems to have reached a very interesting stage. This can be defined briefly by saying that in their case the offence itself seems to be in process of relegation from the position of *justification* for the measures applied to the position of a mere *occasion* for them.

The concept of 'occasion' needs little explanation. At one extreme, a trivial offence may draw the attention of an agency to a situation which seems to call for official efforts to remedy it. Thus, to take an imaginary example, a boy who is detected in riding a bicycle without lights at 2 a.m. may be found by the police to have a grossly abnormal home, and the incident may eventually lead to supervision and even removal from home under the statutes which give local authorities power to take children into their care. This may happen in cases in which nobody would question the need to care for the child, although at the same time nobody would argue that the incident itself offered any justification for more than the mildest of penalties. At the other extreme, an incident of serious violence may not only be the occasion for arrest and trial but also be offered by the court as justification for an extremely long sentence.

It is of course only on retributive reasoning that the offence by itself can ever be the whole of the justification for the court's measure. If the court is thinking in purely utilitarian terms it must in addition have reasons for fearing that the offender may do further serious harm before it can feel justified in imposing a long custodial sentence. It is true that in some cases the court argues from the nature of the offences which have been proved that the risk of further offences is substantial enough to be a justification. An example is a case in which a man has attempted but failed to murder an avowed enemy of his. Such cases are rare, however, and there is an increasing tendency for courts to feel the need for additional information. Usually the offence is only part of the justification. But it is an important part.

One of the differences between the courts' approaches to the sentencing of presumptively normal adult offenders and their approach to the disposal of the immature is that in the case of the latter they seem willing to entertain the proposition that the offence itself may be no part, or at most a negligible part, of the justification[28] for the measure which is applied, whereas in the case of normal adults they seem unwilling to concede this. This unwillingness–if anyone doubts it–can be demonstrated by pointing to the very restricted way in which courts use precautionary sentences of a length greater than that which they regard as 'justified' by the offence itself.

From this point of view the offences of the mentally disordered seem to fall into an intermediate position, but to be moving towards the position of offences committed by children. The importance of this will become clear when we see–in chapter 22–how long a period of detention in hospital can result from a fairly trivial offence. It is true that the 1959 Act is still to some extent based on the concept of the offence as justification; for it limits hospital orders–and even guardianship orders–to offences for which the statute allows imprisonment. In practice, this can be–and often is–circumvented: if an offender who is likely to be found guilty of a non-imprisonable offence seems in obvious need of compulsory admission, this can be arranged under Section 25 of the Act, either after the charge has been dealt with or after it has been dropped. Another expedient is the use of the psychiatric probation order, which can be employed to arrange in-patient as well as out-patient treatment, and which, because it was developed out of a non-custodial measure, is not limited to imprisonable offences. It is a less satisfactory expedient, partly because it cannot be used without the offender's consent, partly because his status in hospital is that of a voluntary patient, who can be prevented from leaving[29] only by the speedy use of one of the compulsory sections of the Act (a very rare step in such cases), and partly because–if the wording of the statute is honoured–it should not be used for conditions which warrant hospital orders.[30]

For the present, however, we are concerned with theory rather than the awkward realities of practice. Can the limitation of Section 60 to imprisonable offences be justified by utilitarian reasoning? To argue, for example, that this in effect limits protection by hospitalisation to offences against which Parliament permits protection by imprisonment is too far-fetched. Not only is it impossible to argue that the short prison sentences which are the maxima for many offences function as any sort of protection; it is also impossible to argue that a guardianship order is more than a nominal form of protection.

In contrast, the Act implies—and the Court of Criminal Appeal has confirmed—that there need be no connection between offence and mental disorder to justify a hospital order. The corollary of this is that the order may be justified solely by having regard to the offender's mental condition, together with any information which the court may have about his 'character and antecedents'.

Further, while courts also seem to be saying—when they take into account culpability or the need to protect others—that the offence itself can be a justification for *refusing* to make a hospital order, it seems to be implied at the same time that if neither the offender's culpability nor his dangerousness is a bar to a hospital order then other considerations extraneous to the offence can, as it were, take over. All this comes very close to saying that so far as ordinary sentences are concerned the offence is still an important element of the justification, but that so far as psychiatric measures are concerned it is little more than occasion.

One obvious implication of a consistent 'occasionalism'—if we may mis-apply a philosopher's word—would be that hospital orders (and *a fortiori* guardianship orders) should not be limited to offences which are punishable with imprisonment. For this limitation can be justified only by arguing that it is unjust to confine a man in a hospital as a result of an offence for which he could not have been deprived of his liberty had he been sane. Only a retributivist can use this argument; a utilitarian cannot. Even a retributivist must have difficulty in defending a system which allows some non-offenders to be confined compulsorily in mental hospitals at the discretion of psychiatrists, but forbids criminal courts even on the recommendation of psychiatrists to deal similarly with a group of offenders. Nor could any lawyer—retributive or not—be happy about a system which in such cases forbids a court to entertain a recommendation from two psychiatrists which the psychiatrists themselves can put into effect (under Part IV of the Act) as soon as the offender walks out of the court.

Another way in which the Act stops short of complete occasionalism can be seen in the case of restriction orders. A court which is deciding whether to make one must have regard to the nature of the offence. Presumably this means—although it has not yet been confirmed by the Court of Appeal—that the current offence must itself be of a kind against which the public needs to be protected in this way. Yet there are cases in which, though the current offence is not seriously harmful, investigation by the police or by a psychiatrist shows that the offender is dangerous. We have already told the story of the immigrant woman who was discharged within a few months in spite of a psychiatrist's warning that she was likely to repeat her violence in a more severe form. Another case was that of a young man with a compulsive tendency to steal cars, which led—

TABLE 7. Hospital and guardianship orders in summary courts[a] (based on table 4)

Year	Summary courts' orders as % of orders in all courts[a] %	Orders made without conviction, as % of all summary courts' orders %
1961	69·0	14·2
1962	72·8	6·7
1963	76·8	6·3
1964	76·2	7·5
1965	72·8	8·4
1966	75·3	8·2
1967	71·4	9·9
1968	68·1	7·5
1969	69·9	8·1
1970	66·8	8·3

[a] Excluding small numbers of orders made by juvenile courts under s. 61 of the Act, relating to children in need of care, protection or control, and also a few orders made by appellate courts.

via borstal and prison–to a hospital order. His record also included, however, two assaults (and indecency with a ten-year-old-girl) and his tendency to violence was confirmed when after his early discharge from hospital he was convicted of assault with intent to rob, and sentenced to four years' imprisonment. In the next chapter too we shall be pointing out that although indecent exposure by itself is not regarded as very harmful some of our exhibitionists had previously been convicted of more serious forms of sexual molestation. It is difficult to see why courts should not be enabled to make restriction orders in such cases.

Summary Courts

Virtually all the reported cases have occurred in higher courts, and it is therefore the reasoning of recorders, judges and the Court of Appeal with which we have so far been concerned. A glance at table 7 reminds us however that the majority of hospital and guardianship orders are made by summary courts.[31] Even in the first year of the Act's operation magistrates made about two orders for every one made by higher courts, and in later years the proportion has often been higher still.

This being so, it is remarkable how few points of difficulty have been reported from summary courts, even in the journals which concern themselves with summary proceedings. We could not be sure to what extent we should attribute this to the fact that–with rare exceptions such as Hatt–offenders have little incentive to appeal against hospital orders (especially the experienced offender-patient who knows how easy it is to get out of a mental hospital), and to what extent it reflects the lower frequency of legal representation in summary courts.

Orders Without Conviction. Nevertheless, summary courts have one power which is not in the hands of higher courts[32]: to make a hospital or guardianship order on being merely satisfied that the accused did what he is charged with, and without proceeding to convict him. This power can be traced back to the Home Office Circular of 1889 (see p. 59) which encouraged magistrates to use their civil powers of committal to lunatic asylums in petty cases, and dismiss the charge. The 1913 Act preserved this procedure by allowing summary (but not higher) courts a choice between convicting and not convicting the accused before arranging for him to go to an institution for mental defectives. The 'reception orders' by which summary (but not higher) courts could commit persons of unsound mind to mental hospitals did not require the court to convict—merely to be 'satisfied' that the accused did what he was charged with (indeed, it is by no means certain that they could properly be used after a conviction). The 1959 Act allowed summary courts a choice between convicting and merely being satisfied that the accused did what he was charged with, but limited the choice to cases in which the accused was mentally ill (as reception orders had been limited) or *severely* subnormal (although the 1913 procedure had made it possible to deal in this way with the 'feeble-minded', who corresponded to what could now be called the 'subnormal').

The reason for the preservation of this power was never officially explained. It may be that, as Sir Hartley Shawcross implied in the 1948 debate (see p. 63), summary courts seemed to need a power which was a rough equivalent to higher courts' powers to find offenders who had been found unfit to plead or guilty but insane. If so, this was rough equivalence indeed, as has been pointed out. This explanation, however, would be consistent with the exclusion of mere subnormality and psychopathic disorder from the sub-section, since these are disorders which are hardly ever regarded as rendering a person unfit to plead or wholly excusing him from responsibility for his act; and as we shall see the power is sometimes used as a substitute for such a verdict.

At some point after the 1939–45 war there seems to have been a change of practice. The great majority of orders by summary courts under the Mental Deficiency Acts—about four in every five—had until then been made without conviction, according to the Criminal Statistics. Unfortunately, this publication ceased in 1949 to distinguish between orders made with and those made without a conviction, and we have no estimate of their proportions for the nineteen-fifties. Under the 1959 Act, as table 7 shows, the proportions have been very different: apart from the first year of the Act's operation, less than one in ten hospital or guardianship orders made by magistrates have been of this kind, and the average percentage over the whole period has been roughly 8 per cent. It is not easy to explain this marked change: the introduction of reception orders cannot do so, for they too were made without conviction. The most likely explanation is the way in which the 1959 Act limited orders without conviction to cases of severe subnormality and mental illness, thus excluding the numerous high-grade defectives and moral defectives who would have been eligible under the old legislation. Even this seems hardly enough, however, to account for a drop from about 80 to less than 10 per cent.

Our own sample contained 52 such cases, which seemed to fall into four groups. First, there were at least four cases in which the magistrates seem to have acted improperly in making the hospital order without convicting, since the accused was not described as suffering from mental illness or severe subnormality. An example was a subnormal and psycho-pathic man in his forties who committed a minor indecency with a ten-year-old boy on a river-bank. It would have been quite proper to make the order in his case after convicting him; but he seems to have been dealt with under s. 60(2). Another was a seventeen-year-old boy of 'borderline intelligence', whose own father accused him of stealing £9 from his jacket. The boy–who had £8 which he could not account for–later rang up the police himself to confess. No doubt the circumstances moved the magis-trate to refrain from convicting him; but in fact they had no power to make the order without doing so. Such cases may well have been a legacy from the days when the 1913 Act allowed moral imbeciles and feeble-minded persons to be disposed of without conviction.

The largest group, however, which accounted for fully two-thirds of our cases, had no feature in common except the triviality of the act which had led to the order, and we could only conclude that this was what had led the magistrates to make it without convicting, although we could easily have pointed to acts of similar triviality of which they had convicted the accused before making a hospital order. Examples were minor assaults on police who stopped the accused (probably because he was behaving oddly); a schizophrenic who broke a café window in some quarrel with the owner; a middle-aged paranoid man who revenged himself on a pub-keeper after a quarrel by bombarding the premises with bottles labelled 'with the compliments of R. F. Jones'. Sometimes there were other cir-cumstances which no doubt moved the magistrates: old age (in the case of an eighty-year-old woman charged with 'wandering abroad'), a long history of hospital treatment (in many cases), voluntary confession (in the case described above of the boy who stole from his father).

'Triviality', however, cannot be the explanation in cases such as the following, in which a depressed old man, also described as suffering from senile dementia, suddenly hit his wife from behind with an axe. When he saw her bleeding he exclaimed 'Oh, your poor head. What have I done? Come and get help.' They walked out of the house together and got assistance. The account of the incident suggests strongly that the man hardly knew the nature and quality of his act, and this may well have been a case in which the magistrates thought that his mental state should excuse him from the stigma of conviction.

There were other examples of what might have ended as homicide. A severely subnormal man, who had twice been convicted of sexual offences against children, was certified as a defective in prison and transferred to an institution. Eventually he was discharged, and had been living for about five years with his parents. One day he approached a ten-year-old girl on some derelict land. Forcing her into a depression in the ground he sat on her feet and made her undress. When she was completely un-dressed he forced her back with a stick across her throat, making various threats. He told her that if he didn't choke her 'the boss would cut his face with a knife'. The girl seems to have had the presence of mind to ask to see his 'boss', and he allowed her to dress and go away with him. It can only have been the severity of his mental subnormality which moved the magistrates to make a hospital order without convicting him; and we thought it likely that had he appeared before some other court he might well have been committed to a higher court with a view to a restriction order.

More interesting still were the cases in which the magistrates had clearly decided not to convict because they felt that they could not communicate sufficiently with the offender to try him. In three or four of these cases the police report in our dossier actually said that the accused had been found unfit to plead. It is quite possible that in those cases the magistrates actually heard medical evidence on the subject of fitness to plead, for this is not unheard of.[33] In two other cases the accused was 'mute' or 'stuporose', and in another he was so obviously incapable of understanding the proceedings that the nonplussed magistrates remanded him on bail for nine days. Their object was probably to enable the police to consider whether to drop the charges (which arose out of the unauthorised use of a milk float); but on consulting the Director of Public Prosecutions the police were advised not to withdraw them, in order that the case could be dealt with under the 1959 Act.

From the purist's point of view it could be argued that to use section 60(2) in this way is rather too rough justice, and an example of occasionalism at its worst. If the magistrates felt it so impossible to communicate with the accused, how could they feel justified in finding that it was he who did the act charged? Might he not, if he had been less disordered, have put forward an acceptable defence? Might he not yet be fit to do so at a later date? And does not a hospital order, whether with or without conviction, prevent him from being properly tried on a later occasion? It is true that under section 70(1) he can appeal against the order even if it was made without conviction; but a right of appeal is no substitute for a postponement of trial. Nor can it be argued that the act which the accused is 'found' to have committed is bound to be so trivial that he cannot suffer from the stigma. One of the persons who was 'found unfit to plead' in this way was a thirty-year-old man who was stopped in the street by the Metropolitan police in the small hours. When they began to question him he punched them, biting one policeman's finger. At the police station he was searched and found to have a packet containing cannabis. The diagnosis was 'affective psychosis', but he had no record of previous mental disorder, and no record of convictions. Henceforward, however, his record will show that he assaulted the police and was in possession of cannabis.

It is easy to develop an argument on these lines; but it is not so easy to suggest what else the court should have done. It is true that since he was in custody awaiting trial he could have been transferred to hospital untried (under s. 73); and perhaps the court should have remanded him with a view to this. If it wished, however, to ensure that he went at once to hospital its only course was to make a hospital order, and it could do so only under section 60, which makes no provision for persons who cannot be properly tried. Nevertheless, these five cases lend some point to the suggestion in volume I (p. 239) that magistrates' courts should be given the power to deal with such persons without trial and without committal to a higher court.[34]

Pleas of Guilty. Akin to the problem posed by unfitness to plead is the danger of a plea of guilty by a disordered offender who is really innocent. As we saw from Mary Davis' case (volume 1, p. 65) this is a danger which has long been recognised by people with experience of the strange mental processes of some offenders. Although we did not, unfortunately, include in our dossiers any question about the plea offered by the accused, we did come across such cases. One, which reached the Court of Appeal's Criminal Division in 1968,[35] was that of Forbes, a thirty-three-year-old man of low intelligence who had been in various institutions for mental defectives since the age of nine. He also had a criminal record, and on this occasion had pleaded guilty at Inner London Sessions to burglary, larceny and similar offences, asking for no less than 142 other offences to be taken into consideration. He was sentenced to concurrent terms of three years' imprisonment. He later managed, with the help of the police, to establish that he could not possibly have committed at least one of the offences to which he had pleaded guilty and 88 of those which he had asked to have taken into consideration[36]; and he explained that he had admitted all these offences in order to show that he was capable of committing so many crimes that he could not be a mental defective. As a result he was set free by the Court of Appeal (Criminal Division) after serving about half his sentence. Our own sample, too, included a twenty-five-year-old man with a long history of petty offences, short prison sentences and mental hospital admissions, who while in hospital confessed to a murder: the Birmingham police proved that his confession was untrue.

Remand. Finally, we were interested to know where the offender had spent the period between detection and the making of the order—whether he had done so in custody, in hospital or at liberty. This period might be several months, or—in a few cases—as short as one week. Our dossiers had not been designed in sufficient detail to enable us to account for the whole of the period with complete certainty; but it was possible to form some fairly clear impressions. Seventy-nine per cent of our offender-patients had spent most or all of the time in a prison or—in the case of some young adults—a remand centre. Five per cent had been in hospital, on bail, with the exception of five cases who had been committed to hospital (under section 68) while awaiting a possible restriction order by Quarter Sessions. Four per cent had been on bail and living at home: most of these were subnormal. In another 6 per cent of cases we could not tell where the period of bail had been spent. The remainder were for the most part cases in which there appeared to have been no remand, usually because they were juveniles who had been brought to court on a summons complete with the necessary medical evidence.

It is obviously desirable that an offender who is eventually to be committed to a hospital should be admitted to one at the earliest possible stage in the process which leads to trial and sentence. The Act, however, provides for this in only two ways. As we have seen in chapter 2, an offender who is mentally ill or severely subnormal can be transferred from prison to hospital before trial or sentence; but this requires special justification, and is relatively infrequent. Secondly, if a magistrates' court commits an offender to Quarter Sessions with a view to a restriction order, it can also commit him to hospital for the interim. Otherwise, however, its only way of arranging that he goes to hospital is to grant bail on this condition: and this, as we have seen, is how all but a few of those who spend the interim period in hospital were sent there.

In contrast, the Scottish Act permits a court to commit to hospital a person charged with any offence who appears to be mentally disordered, whether he is simply being remanded or committed for trial (section 54 of the Mental Health (Scotland) Act, 1960). It is not easy to see why an English magistrates' court should not have the same power (subject, as in Scotland, to the readiness of a hospital to receive the offender and to safeguards). For the makeshift of bail gives the hospital no power to prevent the offender from leaving: to do so it would have to resort to compulsion under section 25 or 26. One or two cases in our sample illustrated this.

For example, a council house tenant, who had recently spent several short periods in the local mental hospital, quarrelled with two of his lodgers and fired a shotgun at them as they ran out of the house. He went straight to the police station to say he was sorry for the brawl (but denied the shooting). His odd behaviour caused the police to arrange for an emergency admission to the local hospital. There he was made the subject of a compulsory admission for one month's observation, after which he became an 'informal' patient, but almost immediately left hospital. A month later he was re-arrested, but released on bail on condition that he stayed at the hospital until the committal proceedings. A fortnight later, however, he again left the hospital and went home, where he took an overdose of sleeping tablets. After treatment for the overdose it was understandably decided to keep him in custody until he appeared in court. He eventually pleaded guilty to actual bodily harm and other offences, and was sent under a hospital order with a twelve-month restriction order to the same local hospital.

Altogether, there were no less than ten cases in our sample in which offenders who were later made the subject of restriction orders were on bail between their appearance at magistrates' courts and the making of the orders. In one such case an eighteen-year-old subnormal youth who had been on bail at home for four months after a couple of housebreakings was made the subject of a four-year restriction order by Quarter Sessions. (It must be granted that although he had a record of several petty thefts and housebreakings he did not seem a likely candidate for a restriction order, nor had the magistrates committed him to Quarter Sessions with a view to one.) In another case a man in his thirties, who had tried to set fire to the house where he lived with his father and brother, seems to have been left at home for a week before being admitted to hospital for observation, as a result of which he was committed to the same hospital under a three-year restriction order. A third offender-patient, who had been remanded on bail and spent the period in hospital, was eventually admitted to Broadmoor under an unlimited restriction order. A fourth man, who had been charged with several acts of buggery and indecency with boys over seven months, and had been committed to prison, was let out on bail so that his defence could arrange a medical examination. He was diagnosed as schizophrenic, and made the subject of an unlimited restriction order, from which he had not been discharged by the end of our follow-up. It must be admitted however that in none of these cases does anyone seem to have suffered any harm from the bailed offender.

Since this chapter has drawn attention to several imperfections – or what seem to be imperfections – in the drafting of the Act, it is only fair to conclude by pointing out that nevertheless ten years of operating the Act do not seem to have produced any difficulties serious enough to make amendments to it imperative. (The minor amendments which are consequential to other legislation, such as the Criminal Procedure (Insanity) Act, 1964, are not really exceptions.) Yet perhaps this is not so surprising after all. We have shown in the historical chapter that the Act was a less revolutionary innovation than is sometimes supposed. Moreover, it was based on the report of a very thorough Royal Commission, and its draftsmen had behind them the combined experience of the Home Office, the Ministry of Health and the Board of Control. Nevertheless it is worth noting that legislation concerned with mental disorder seems to be revised at much greater intervals than legislation concerned with criminal law and sentencing. Part of the explanation must be that it is more flexible, and leaves psychiatrists and mental welfare officers more freedom to adapt their decisions to changing circumstances than does penal legislation. Certainly, as we have seen, the sections of the Act concerned with the criminal courts allow plenty of scope for differing philosophies amongst both sentencers and psychiatrists: and where the sections creak, expedients have been devised to lubricate the joints.[37]

Notes

1. For the moment, guardianship orders are ignored.
2. See the proceedings in Standing Committee E, for 12 February 1959, cols. 65-6.
3. By D.A. Thomas, commenting on R. v. Molyneaux [1968] Crim. L.R. 229.
4. And see a psychiatrist's letter in the *Daily Telegraph* of 2 January 1971.
5. 'Medical treatment' includes nursing, and also includes care and training under medical supervision: see the definitions in s. 147.
6. It would not, apparently, be enough that the patient is likely, if at large, to maltreat animals.
7. The Mental Health (Hospital and Guardianship) Regulations, 1960 (S.I. 1960 no. 1241).
8. Standing Committee E, col. 218.
9. Note that section 4 does not appear to exclude conditions which warrant a guardianship order.
10. This was in 1961, before the Criminal Procedure (Insanity) Act, 1964 made it clear that this was permissible: see volume I, p. 152 ff.
11. R. v. Morris (1961) 45 Cr. App. R. 185 ff.

12. R. v. Higginbotham (1961) 45 Cr. App. R. 379.

13. R. v. Gunnell (1966) 50 Cr. App. R. 242.

14. In fairness to Rampton it should be pointed out that the previous
     offences in his record had been neither sexual nor violent. More-
     over, Rampton's escape-rate in recent years has been very low, if
     not quite as low as Broadmoor's: see p. 14.

15. [1971] Crim. L.R. 664: the quotation, however, is from the
     transcript.

16.   It must be remarked that at that time the Court of Criminal
     Appeal had the power (which they later lost) to substitute life
     imprisonment for a determinate sentence, and it is perhaps odd
     that they did not do so.

17. But this is reported only briefly in [1964] Crim. L.R. 236.

18. In the practice note in Gardiner's case [1967] Crim. L.R. 231.

19. Whereas without a restriction order the power to retake him would
     expire after a certain period: see s. 40.

20. Note that whereas in considering whether to make a hospital order
     the court must have regard to both the *character* and antecedents
     of the offender, here it is only his antecedents which seem to be
     regarded as relevant. It is not easy to see a reason for the difference.

21. At this point the corresponding Scottish provision adds the words
     'as a result of his mental disorder': see s. 60(1) of the Mental
     Health (Scotland) Act, 1960. These words were inserted in order
     to allay the fear of Scottish psychiatrists that restriction orders
     would be made in too many cases in which the persistence of law-
     breaking was really not attributable to mental disorder.

22. It is of course arguable that some of them could be conditionally
     discharged, say to specialised hostels, without as much risk as is
     assumed. But that is a side-issue: the main point is that so long as
     it is assumed, rightly or wrongly, that they are too dangerous to
     discharge the system can be criticised for failing to make sensible
     provision for them.

23. R. v. Russell (1963) 3 All E.R. 603: [1964] Crim L.R. 138.

24. D. A. Thomas, 'Sentencing the Mentally Disturbed Offender' in
     [1965] Crim. L.R. 685 ff.

25. There have been later cases in which the principle has been
     reaffirmed; e.g. Gunnell, loc. cit. (n. 13).

26. R. v. Rafi [1967] Crim. L.R. 715, and *The Times*, 27 September.

27. R. v. Hatt [1962] Crim. L.R. 647.

28. This point of view has indeed been ratified recently by section 1
     of the Children and Young Persons Act of 1969, which—so far at
     least as children between 10 and 14 are concerned—was intended
     to relegate the offence to the status of occasion, and insists that
     the court's order must be justified on the grounds that 'he is in
     need of care or control which he is unlikely to receive unless the
     court makes an order . . .'.

29. The fact that by leaving hospital he has breached a requirement

of his probation order seems to be almost completely inoperative as a sanction.

30. Although it can apparently be used for conditions which warrant a guardianship order.

31. In our sample, 6 per cent were made by juvenile courts, 69 per cent by adults' summary courts, 13 per cent by Quarter Sessions and nearly 12 per cent by Assizes. One was made by the Court of Criminal Appeal.

32. Except in the very special circumstances described on p. 29.

33. See the anonymous case reported in [1961] CXXV, *Justice of the Peace*, 759.

34. It is worth a passing mention that we found three cases in our sample in which the offender had previously been found unfit to plead by a higher court–in one case to a charge of murder–but had subsequently been convicted of offences by other courts, usually summary courts. In all three cases the finding of unfitness to plead had occurred in the early nineteen-fifties, before the marked decrease in such findings which was probably attributable to the introduction of the phenothiazine drugs (see volume 1, pp. 238-9); and all three offenders suffered from disorders which are responsive to these drugs. In other words, they were probably offenders who could nowadays be rendered fit for trial.

35. R. v. Forbes (1968) 52 Cr. App. R. 585

36. Since the 88 offences which had been erroneously taken into consideration had actually been committed, though not by him, he could hardly have known of them if the police had not brought them to his attention.

37. As this book was going through the press, however, the Home Secretary (Mr Maudling) announced the setting up of a committee 'to examine to what extent, and on what criteria, the law should recognise mental disorder or abnormality as a factor affecting the liability to trial or conviction of a person accused of a criminal offence, and his subsequent disposal'. The committee would also, he said, be asked 'to consider whether changes are desirable in the powers, procedure and facilities for enabling appropriate treatment–including treatment in the community and supervision after discharge–to be given to such offenders'. (Commons Hansard for 29th June, 1972, col. 1684). The Chairman of the committee was to be Lord Butler, a former Home Secretary. The occasion of this announcement was a Parliamentary statement about the release from Broadmoor of Graham Young, who had been sent there under a 15-year restriction order for administering poison to members of his family and a schoolfellow. He had been conditionally released nine years later, and had then poisoned several of his work-mates, two fatally. It is clear, however, from the wide scope of the committee's terms of reference, as well as the speed with which the announcement was made, that it had been planned before the re-arrest of Young.

Chapter 6. **The Offender-Patients**

This chapter and the next two will be concerned with the offenders who are made the subject of hospital orders, and whom we shall for the sake of simplicity call 'offender-patients'. Most of what we have to say about them will be based on our survey of hospital orders made in the twelve-month period from April 1963 to March 1964.

It is important to emphasise what the Oxford survey (as we shall call it for brevity's sake) was not intended to do. It was not a study of decision-making by the courts, of the kind carried out by Dr Sparks (see pp. 54-5). Nor was it a study of psychiatric practice, either in the field of diagnosis or in the field of treatment. A sample confined to offender-patients, and moreover offender-patients who were the subject of only one of the main procedures for disposing of disordered offenders, would be far from suitable for this purpose. It is true that when in a later chapter we come to the subject of psychopathy, a diagnosis which is closely linked with anti-social behaviour, we have felt justified in making some observations on this particular psychiatric label; but only because it seems to us that our sample happens to provide relevant information.

The fact is that the subject of our survey was not what might be called 'the natural history' of either offender-patients or psychiatrists, but the operation of a system, in this case the hospital order system. We were not trying to answer the question 'What sorts of offence are associated with serious mental disorder?' (although our data can probably give a better answer to this than has hitherto been given) so much as the question 'What combinations of disorders and behaviour tend to lead to a hospital order, and what sorts of people therefore tend to reach mental hospitals by this avenue?' Again, we were not trying to describe in detail what psychiatrists and other hospital staff do to these patients, or its effect on their symptoms, but what their careers seem to be like in the year or two immediately following a hospital order. We believe, of course, that an operational study of this kind will have interest and value not only for sentencers and other agents of law enforcement but also for psychiatrists, psychiatric social workers and other hospital staff. But we must emphasise its limitations.

In order to answer these operational questions we decided to collect a sample consisting of all the hospital and guardianship orders made in twelve months. Ideally we should have liked the twelve months to coincide with a calendar year, but our arrangements were not complete by January

I

1963 and rather than wait until January 1964 we chose the twelve months beginning with April 1963.

There is always a risk in a study of this kind that the period chosen will turn out to be atypical. On the whole, however, we were fortunate. By April 1963 the new procedure had been in operation for nearly two and a half years, and police, sentencers and psychiatrists were reasonably familiar with it. On the other hand, experience had not yet dictated any changes of policy, nor—with one exception—did any occur during the period chosen.

The exception was the use of hospital orders to deal with women. As we have seen (table 4) the number of such orders had been increasing steadily since the Act came into operation, but fell sharply—by about 22 per cent—in 1964, and by the end of 1969 had not regained the level of 1963. There was no corresponding fall in hospital orders involving men. Since between a third and a half of all hospital orders involving women originated in Holloway (the large women's prison in London) during the sixties, it is probably significant that the fall coincided with a change of senior medical officer at that prison, and that it was largely—though not wholly—compensated by an increase in psychiatric probation orders involving women, and especially orders requiring in-patient treatment. At all events, it is clear that our sample may not be quite as representative of the sixties where women are concerned as where men are concerned.

With the help of the Home Office and our psychiatric advisers we worked out the following procedure for collecting the information about our sample:

a. every time a hospital order was made the local police force would complete the first part of a special yellow dossier which we had designed, and which will be found in Appendix D;

b. this would be sent to the Home Office's Statistical Division, where the police sent most of their statistical returns. This had several advantages: the Division were anxious to learn more about the new procedure for statistical purposes, and they were already experienced in checking such documents for minor errors;

c. the Division would then send the dossier to the receiving hospital, where the second part would be completed before it was returned to the Home Office. The Ethical Committee of the British Medical Association, to whom the project was explained, agreed that there was no objection to the disclosure of clinical information for this purpose;

d. the Home Office would then send the dossiers to the Penal Research Unit at Oxford, where they would be kept under lock and key, and where the information in them would be transferred to cards for eventual consumption by the Atlas Computer at Harwell.

The follow-up is described in chapter 8 and Appendix C.

We did not of course manage to collect 100 per cent of our intended sample. In all, 1,332 hospitals or guardianship orders were made during the chosen period. Despite all our efforts, however, only 1,200 dossiers, representing 90 per cent of 1,332, eventually reached us in a usable condition. In 16 of these cases the hospital, in spite of the Ethical Committee's agreement, had refused to give information about the patient. In 14 more cases the order dealt with a patient who was already in our sample, but who had left hospital and again become involved with the criminal law. Nine were guardianship orders, a type of case which is so infrequent that we shall ignore it throughout these chapters. One offender-patient died before the order could take effect. This left us with usable information on 942 males and 218 females.

This result is by no means unsatisfactory, and a great deal of the credit for it must go to the police forces which took so much trouble to answer all the questions in their part of the dossiers, to the hospital staffs who completed their part, and to the Statistical Division of the Home Office which so carefully checked each dossier for discrepancies. We were particularly impressed with the meticulousness of the police information. In many cases this must have given the hospitals facts about the patient which would not otherwise have been known to them: a point to which we shall return later.

We should also like to record our gratitude to the two psychiatrists who acted as our advisers. One was Dr P. G. McGrath, Physician Superintendent of Broadmoor Special Hospital; the other was Dr I. Skottowe, at that time Consultant at the Warneford Hospital, Oxford. Without their help we should have made many more mistakes than we did.

The cost of the whole operation was met by a grant from the Home Office. We received more than financial assistance, however, from that Department. Not only did its Statistical Division play an important part in the collection of dossiers (and the tracing of missing cases), but we received a great deal of invaluable information and advice from the Criminal Divisions, as well as other branches of the Department.

In reporting and discussing the results of a survey such as this, it is impossible to be exhaustive: one can only be more or less selective. Even so, there is always a tendency to compile a Homeric catalogue of ships, in which a few points of interest are lost in a recital of facts. We have tried to marshal our ships into a relatively small convoy of tables, and to put into our text, with a minimum of figures, only those observations and reflections which seem to us worth singling out for the reader. A summary will be found at the end of this chapter. If the result appears imprecise or over-compressed, we can only plead that there are worse defects, one of which is total recall and another is unreadability.

Histories and Background

Before discussing our offender-patients' current offences and diagnoses, let us look at their histories, so far as these could be gleaned from official records of conviction or admission to mental hospitals, or from the information which police forces and hospitals were able to insert in our dossiers.

For the most part these histories were a depressing series of convictions, short custodial sentences and admissions to hospital, the last of these usually beginning somewhat later in life than the criminal records. Only a small minority (11 per cent of the men and 22 per cent of the women) had no recorded convictions or hospital admissions: and as we shall see

TABLE 8. Previous penal and psychiatric histories

	Males %	Females %
A. No previous convictions or hospital admissions	10·7 ⎫	21·7 ⎫
Previous convictions but no hospital admissions	23·7 ⎪	14·3 ⎪
Previous hospital admissions but no convictions	16·0 ⎬ p < 0·001 ⎨	27·6 ⎪
Both previous convictions and previous hospital admissions	49·6 ⎭	36·4 ⎭
Totals	100·0 (= 908[a])	100·0 (= 203[a])

B. Prior hospital admissions			C. Previous convictions		
	Males %	Females %		Males %	Females %
0	34·3	36·0	0	25·7 ⎫	45·9 ⎫
1	26·3	22·2	1	14·5 ⎪	11·9 ⎪
2	15·5	13·8	2	11·4 ⎪	18·3 ⎪
3	8·3	11·3	3	11·6 ⎪	8·2 ⎪
4	4·5	3·4	4	8·9 ⎬ p < 0·001 ⎨	2·8 ⎪
5	3·0	5·4	5	5·8 ⎪	3·7 ⎪
6	2·3	3·4	6	3·3 ⎪	0·9 ⎪
7	1·9	1·5	7	3·2 ⎪	2·3 ⎪
8+	3·9	3·0	8+	15·6 ⎭	6·0 ⎭
Totals	100·0 (= 908[a])	100·0 (= 203[a])	Totals	100·0 (= 942)	100·0 (= 218)

[a] Excluding 34 males and 15 females whose dossiers were incomplete.

even these figures were artificially inflated. As for the remainder, it was noticeable that men were more likely to have previous convictions without hospital admissions than *vice versa*; but that for women the opposite was true. The same—though to a differing extent—is probably true of the male and female population in general.

Small as it is, the minority with completely clean penal and psychiatric records is exaggerated by the table. If we had been able to trace all previous hospital admissions and all previous convictions, its real size would undoubtedly have turned out to be smaller still. For we had to rely partly on the information supplied by local police, but chiefly on the receiving hospital, to tell us of any previous psychiatric treatment received by the offender-patient. If this had taken place in the same hospital, it would in all probability be remembered and reported to us. But if it had occurred elsewhere, the hospital which completed our dossier would be likely to learn of it only from the offender-patient or his relatives. The Ministry's Mental Health Enquiry index of mental hospital patients is not allowed to be used to help psychiatrists to trace previous hospital admissions of their patients, and although as research workers we were subsequently allowed to use it to trace the re-admissions of our offender-patients, it was in any case too recent a creation to record the earliest admissions of most of our sample. Consequently a mobile offender-patient without traceable relatives who wished to conceal the fact that he had previously been a mental hospital patient would have had a good chance of doing so. On the other hand, when the hospital's part of our dossier did indicate that he had previously been in another hospital, we were often able, by writing to that hospital, to find out that it had records of even earlier stays in other hospitals, and so on. Even so, table 8 B must somewhat underestimate the numbers of offender-patients with multiple previous admissions, and especially those in the higher part of the range.

Similarly, but for slightly different reasons, the most precise thing that could be said about our sample's penal histories was that *at least* 71 per cent had been previously convicted, although that percentage is impressive enough. Quite apart from the fact that even mentally disordered offenders sometimes commit offences which are never traced to them,[1] our information about those which had been traced to our sample could not be quite complete. The police forces which gave us this information relied–as they do when preparing 'antecedents reports' for courts–chiefly on their own records and the national Criminal Records Office. The latter, however, does not in most cases receive reports of cautions, convictions for non-indictable offences[2] or findings of guilt in the case of juveniles outside the Metropolitan area. Consequently, a mobile offender might have a history of convictions, cautions and juvenile court appearances which is not fully recorded in any single filing system.

Nevertheless, many police forces take a great deal of trouble to build up as complete a record as possible by addressing enquiries to forces in areas where the offender is known to have lived, and later (on pp. 137-9) an example will be given of the result of this thoroughness in the case of an itinerant schizophrenic. Some police forces even included previous cautions and acquittals in the information supplied to us.

In the case of immigrants (whom we shall discuss later) a clean record must sometimes have been extremely misleading. The police records sometimes supplied us with information about previous convictions in Eire, but in the case of other countries–at least so far as our dossiers were concerned–this would have involved an excessive amount of correspondence. In one case, however, a very thorough police force was able to tell us that a Goanese man who had been sending libellous letters was a paranoid schizophrenic who had tried to assassinate Radakrishnan in Nairobi. (The magistrates committed him without conviction to a local mental hospital.)

Change of Name. The tracing of previous convictions and hospital admissions was made no easier by the considerable number of offender-patients who used different names. Although we had expected this, and had asked for 'aliases' in the police section of our dossiers, we were surprised to find that no less than 25 per cent of our women and 20 per cent of our men were known to have used different names and no doubt there were more cases unknown to the police. In the case of women–who are expected to change their name when they marry, and often do so when co-habiting with a man–there may well have been this rational explanation in many cases; but the high percentage for males cannot be explained away on these lines. Some of them might, of course, have been rational devices adopted by petty criminals to hamper the efforts of the police to

link them with previous offences; but it is likely that most of them were
the product of delusions or persecution or of confused identity. When—
for reasons that will be explained later—we matched 62 male psychopaths,
one to one, with 62 schizophrenic males and 62 subnormal males of
equal ages, we found that of the psychopaths and subnormals, who might
be expected to behave more like rational criminals than the schizophrenics,
only 3 per cent and 6 per cent respectively were known to have aliases,
compared with fully 19 per cent of the schizophrenics: strong evidence
that the 'aliases' were associated with the nature of the disorder.

Even so, the psychiatric and criminal careers of our offender-patients
were impressive. Table 8B, which gives the numbers of previous admissions
to mental hospitals, shows the 'revolving door' hard at work. Practically
one in every four of our offender-patients had been in mental hospitals
not once or twice before, but three or more times: and about 4 per cent
had eight *or more* previous stays in their dossiers. Male and female
distributions were very similar.

Using tables specially supplied by the Ministry of Health, we compared our percentages of 'non-first admissions' (to use the Ministry's
term) with non-first compulsory admissions under the non-criminal
sections of the Act (ss. 25, 26, 29, 135[3]) during 1964, the nearest year to
that of our sample for which they could provide such figures. Unfortunately, whereas our figures represented *persons*, the Ministry's represented
admissions, and therefore counted a person more than once if he or she
was admitted more than once during the year. The effect of this from our
point of view was to inflate artificially the Ministry's percentages of non-
first admissions. Consequently, nothing could be inferred from the somewhat higher percentages of non-first admissions among the Ministry's
subnormals. On the other hand, we were on firm ground when we
observed that only 55 per cent of the Ministry's non-subnormal male
admissions were non-first admissions, compared with our 72 per cent;
for if the Ministry's percentage could have been deflated to correspond
exactly with ours the difference would have been greater still.[4] The same
was true of the non-subnormal female admissions, for which the percentages were very much the same as those of the males.

'*The First-timer.*' Finally, the minority with no previous records of
conviction or hospital treatment—what we nicknamed the 'first-timers'—
seemed to merit a closer look. When we examined their dossiers the result
was interesting. Some of them showed that the offender-patient was a
recent immigrant, so that his or her clear record meant little. Others,
though without recorded convictions or hospital admissions, had in fact
been in trouble with the police but had been fortunate enough to be let
off without prosecution; or had been under psychiatric treatment either
by general practitioners or by out-patient clinics. Some of the subnormals
had been in E.S.N. schools, residential or non-residential. When all these
were eliminated, male first-timers had fallen to 4·5 per cent of the total,
women to 12·8 per cent: but the difference was still significant (p < 0·001).
Moreover, some of these were only juveniles, so that it was hardly surprising that this should have been their first contact with law enforcement
and psychiatry.

What really interested us was the very small group of *adult* first-timers: 36 men and 21 women. Some–especially amongst the women–were well on in years. One was a woman of 80, arrested for vagrancy and found to be in a confused and paranoid state. Another woman was 73 years of age, who had committed a theft and some damage while in the early stages of senile dementia. Although the numbers were too small for significance, male first-timers tended more often to be in their thirties or late twenties, mostly schizophrenics but with a few depressives and even some subnormals. Indeed, a remarkable feature of our adult first-timers of both sexes was the number of subnormals amongst them: no less than 12 out of 58. Some of these were *severely* subnormal individuals who had apparently managed to attract no attention from health services or police until middle age or even later. One farm-labourer of very low intelligence had worked in an extremely rustic area until the age of 55 before repeated acts of unlawful sexual intercourse with a young girl got him into trouble at last. A pair of vagrant women who were taken into custody for 'sleeping rough' turned out to be a subnormal woman of 63 and her twenty-year-old daughter, also subnormal. We shall be dealing in more detail with the subnormals later, and one or two of the non-subnormal first-timers will be mentioned in other contexts.

Age. We shall return to our offender-patients' psychiatric histories when we come to their diagnoses, and their criminal careers will be discussed in more detail in the next section. Meanwhile, since age is a variable that is important when considering the vicissitudes of almost any sample, we must look at tables 9 and 10 (which are fully explained in the Notes on p. 122). An obvious question was 'Did the age-distributions of the Oxford sample differ from those of ordinary offenders, or from those of non-offenders admitted compulsorily to mental hospitals, and if so how?' We have therefore set out, side by side with our own figures, age-distributions for indictable offenders and for admissions to ordinary mental hospitals for the nearest possible years to those of our sample (the comparability of these groups is discussed in the Notes on the tables).

Juveniles. The most striking difference is between the very small percentages of juveniles (i.e., persons under the age of 17) in the Oxford sample and the very large percentage (21 per cent) amongst ordinary indictable offenders. Part of the reason is that, as we shall see in the section dealing with the diagnoses, so many of our sample were suffering from schizophrenia or depression; for these are disorders which seldom manifest themselves–at least in a clinical degree–until adulthood. Yet even subnormality, which is nearly always diagnosable from an early age, seems unlikely to lead to a hospital order in the juvenile courts. Most of the subnormals in the 15-19 age-group were past their 17th birthday. To a lesser extent the same was true of psychopaths. We shall discuss in the diagnostic section the factors which protect juveniles from hospital orders.

Since juveniles seem to be largely exempted, as it were, from Part v of the Act, whether by the nature of mental illnesses or by the system for dealing with troublesome adolescents, it seemed both legitimate and worth while to see whether the age-distributions of indictable offenders would not resemble ours more closely if those below the age of 15 were

TABLE 9. Age-distributions of Oxford sample and other selected groups shown as cumulative percentages (see note 1, p. 122)

MALES	10-	15-	20-	25-	30-	35-	40-	45-	50-	55-	60-	65 +	N = 100%	Significance of differences
Found guilty of indictable offences in 1963	20·8	47·3	64·2	75·3		88·3		95·5		98·8		100·0	181,640	p < 0·001
All in Oxford sample	0·6	14·2	33·3	46·0		71·6		88·5		95·6		100·0	942	
Schizophrenia — all in 1964	0·4	11·4	26·8	55·8			77·4		88·5		95·0	100·0	4,837	NS but p < 0·05 if females are included
First admissions in Oxford sample	—	8·4	21·7	56·7			86·8		92·8		98·8	100·0	83	
Schizophrenia — all in 1964	0·01	4·2	15·4	45·7			76·8		91·2		97·6	100·0	11,419	p < 0·01
Non-first admissions in Oxford sample	0·3	2·7	8·9	42·1			77·5		94·8		99·0	100·0	302	
Subnormality — all in 1964	25·1	60·1	70·8	81·0			89·5		96·6		99·4	100·0	1,595	p < 0·001
First admissions in Oxford sample	2·1	45·4	80·4	90·9			96·5		98·6		100·0	100·0	143	p < 0·005
Part IV in 1964	11·3	64·5	74·2	90·3			96·8		100·0		100·0	100·0	62	
Subnormality — all in 1964	18·8	41·4	56·2	74·3			86·3		94·0		98·8	100·0	2,591	p < 0·001
Non-first admissions in Oxford sample	0·5	12·2	44·7	71·3			90·4		98·4		98·8	100·0	188	p < 0·001
Part IV in 1964	0·9	33·7	59·8	80·4			91·6		99·1		100·0	100·0	107	
Personality disorder — all in 1964	7·3	29·5	48·5	72·5			87·8		95·5		98·7	100·0	2,170	NS
In Oxford sample	2·1	39·5	56·2	81·1			93·7		95·8		95·8	100·0	48	
Personality disorder — all in 1964	1·5	12·0	29·0	57·3			81·9		93·6		98·9	100·0	2,266	NS
Non-first admissions in Oxford sample	—	12·7	36·6	66·1			81·6		98·5		98·5	100·0	71	
Depressive — all in 1964	0·1	5·9	8·8	22·6			42·8		63·5		85·1	100·0	9,391	NS but p < 0·05 if females are included
First admissions in Oxford sample	—	—	13·6	31·8			63·6		81·9		90·9	100·0	22	
Depressive — all in 1964	0·07	1·1	4·2	14·7			34·9		57·1		82·7	100·0	9,966	NS but p < 0·05 if females are included
Non-first admissions in Oxford sample	—	—	8·9	24·5			49·0		64·6		80·0	100·0	45	

(Age-groups)

TABLE 10. Age-distributions of Oxford sample and other selected groups shown as cumulative percentages (see note 1, p. 122)

FEMALES	10-	15-	20-	25-	30-	35-	40-	45-	50-	55-	60-	65+	N = 100%	Significance of differences
Found guilty of indictable offences in 1963	15·1	34·2	45·7	54·8	70·0		84·4	84·4		94·5		100·0	27,468	
All in Oxford sample	—	18·3	37·6	48·6	65·1		84·4			92·7		100·0	218	p < 0·001
Schizophrenia First admissions — all in 1964	0·6	7·5	16·7		35·2	57·3			73·6		85·8	100·0	5,772	
Schizophrenia First admissions — in Oxford sample	—	5·6	22·2		38·9	50·0			77·8		94·4	100·0	18	NS
Schizophrenia Non-first admissions — all in 1964	0·1	3·0	9·8		31·9	61·2			81·7		93·5	100·0	13,175	
Schizophrenia Non-first admissions — in Oxford sample	—	3·2	9·5		19·1	60·3			81·0		93·7	100·0	63	NS
Subnormality First admissions — all in 1964	19·1	50·9	60·2	71·8		83·2			93·0		98·5	100·0	1,366	
Subnormality First admissions — in Oxford sample	—	63·5	90·3	95·1		95·1			100·0		—	100·0	41	p < 0·001
Subnormality First admissions — Part IV in 1964	1·6	57·5	67·3	77·1		83·7			93·5		98·4	100·0	61	p < 0·01
Subnormality Non-first admissions — all in 1964	11·5	30·4	44·6	65·1		81·4			93·2		98·2	100·0	2,167	
Subnormality Non-first admissions — in Oxford sample	—	15·2	52·2	89·2		93·5			97·8		100·0	100·0	46	p < 0·001
Subnormality Non-first admissions — Part IV in 1964	—	29·6	51·5	78·1		91·4			97·7		100·0	100·0	128	p < 0·05
Personality disorder First admissions — all in 1964	8·2	37·2	54·9	74·9		86·2			92·5		96·1	100·0	1,284	
Personality disorder First admissions — in Oxford sample	—	—	—	—		—			—		—	—	—	not applicable
Personality disorder Non-first admissions — all in 1964	1·9	18·7	37·4	64·8		84·7			93·8		97·8	100·0	1,826	
Personality disorder Non-first admissions — in Oxford sample	—	5·9	35·2	70·5		88·2			88·2		100·0	100·0	17	NS
Depressive First admissions — all in 1964	0·1	3·0	8·5	23·7		42·8			63·2		82·9	100·0	16,996	
Depressive First admissions — in Oxford sample	—	—	—	28·6		71·4			100·0		—	100·0	7	NS
Depressive Non-first admissions — all in 1964	0·03	1·0	3·7	14·3		32·4			55·3		79·4	100·0	22,116	
Depressive Non-first admissions — in Oxford sample	—	—	16·7	33·4		50·0			66·7		83·3	100·0	12	NS

ignored. Even when this was done, however, most diagnostic groups were still markedly older than ordinary indictable offenders. Only one group, composed of male subnormals and psychopaths, resembled them at all:

Age-group	Male indictable offenders, 1963 % (cum.)		Oxford sample of male subnormals and psychopaths % (cum.)
15–	33·4		24·9
20–	54·7		55·5
25–	68·7		69·9
30–	85·1	p < 0·001	85·4
40–	94·2		94·2
50–	98·3		98·7
60 +	100·0		100·0
	N = 143,907		N = 445

Notes to tables 9 and 10 on pp. 120-1

1. Distributions are shown as cumulative percentages for two reasons. First, comparisons are easier if one can see at a glance what percentage of a given group was *under* a certain age. Second, the Home Office's age-groupings differ from the Ministry's where persons aged 25 or older are concerned, and the use of cumulative percentages simplifies the presentation of our distributions side by side with the Home Office's and the Ministry's.

2. The groups selected for comparison were:
   (*a*) all offenders convicted of indictable offences during 1963, the nearest year to that of our sample (which was April 1963 to March 1964). The source was Appendix III of the Criminal Statistics, England and Wales. Since about 30 per cent of our sample were non-indictable offenders, we would have liked to include a corresponding percentage of non-indictable offenders in this comparison group; but the Home Office could not provide age-distributions for non-indictable offenders.
   (*b*) patients admitted in 1964 (the nearest calendar year to ours for which the Ministry could provide figures) to mental hospitals run by Regional Hospital Boards. They do not therefore include admissions to Special Hospitals or Teaching Hospitals. They include not only informal admissions but also compulsory admissions, whether through the criminal courts or not: but these are small in number when compared with informal admissions.

3. Where a comparison is appropriate the probability of its being due to chance has been calculated and shown as 'p' in the final column.

4. First admissions are tabulated separately because they are represented in different proportions in different diagnostic groups, and are obviously likely to be associated with a lower age than other admissions.

5. Because the same individual may be convicted or admitted to hospital (as the case may be) more than once in the same year in the Home Office's figures for indictable offenders and the Registrar-General's figures for admissions *other than first admissions*, these figures are not strictly comparable with ours, in which no individual is counted more than once even if more than once dealt with by hospital order in the same year. But this difference cannot affect the comparability of first admissions, and probably does not seriously affect the comparability of non-first admissions.

Even so, although practically the same percentages of both groups were under 25, most of our under twenty-fives were in their early twenties, whereas most of the ordinary indictable males were in their late teens.[5]

If on the other hand we compared our subnormals[6] with admissions to mental hospitals in 1964, the latter too tended to be younger. For subnormals we were able to obtain from the Ministry the age-distributions of compulsory admissions under non-criminal procedures (i.e., Part IV of the Act); but these proved even younger.

So far as non-subnormal patients were concerned, the Ministry could provide age-distributions for diagnostic groups which corresponded to our main ones, but could not at the same time sub-divide them into compulsory and non-compulsory admissions; so that we had to be content to compare our offender-patients with admissions of all kinds, whether formal or compulsory. Because of the relatively small numbers involved when diagnostic groups and first and non-first admissions are distinguished, most of the differences in age-distribution did not reach even the 0·05 level of significance unless males and females were combined. With this reservation, the result of the comparison can be summed up thus:

1. Our schizophrenic first admissions were rather older than schizophrenic first admissions in general, with a peak in the thirties; the same was true to a more marked extent of non-first admissions.
2. Our depressives, whether first or non-first admissions, were somewhat younger than depressive admissions in general, but largely because the latter included very substantial numbers of elderly admissions, after the age of 65. Even so, 15 per cent of our depressives were over 65.
3. Unlike our subnormal admissions, our psychopathic admissions did not differ significantly from such admissions in general (but we shall be discussing them in more detail in chapter 10).

Work. Not unexpectedly, the work records of our men were for the most part intermittent and unstable. No less than 70 per cent were unemployed at the time of their current offence. Even when the jobs they had previously had were examined, the overwhelming majority had held them for less than a year: more than half had held eight or more jobs for less than that time. The impression given by the women was of somewhat greater stability, but where women are concerned employment records are more difficult to interpret.

Occupations were for the most part unskilled or semi-skilled, and fully two-thirds of the men had no training for any sort of employment. About 4 per cent were said to have had full-time technical or professional training, but by the time of the hospital order not all of them were making use of this training. There was a noticeable tendency for the stated occupation to be of a kind which is associated with intermittent and independent work: 'scrap-metal merchant', 'self-employed salesman of minor articles', 'self-employed tar-macadam worker' are examples. Other descriptions may well have included an element of fantasy or wishful thinking, as seemed probable in the case of the 'free-lance navigator of yachts'.

Marital Status. The percentages of our sample who had either never married or had been divorced or separated were strikingly high:

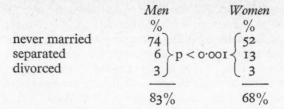

	Men %		Women %
never married	74		52
separated	6	p < 0·001	13
divorced	3		3
	83%		68%

Women were more likely to have been married than men, a tendency which could not be ascribed to age-differences, for they were slightly younger. This difference was apparent in every diagnostic group, but was especially marked amongst the depressives and manic-depressives: in spite of the relatively middle-aged composition of this group, a third of the men had never married, compared with only one of the 19 women. Even when compared with highly recidivist samples of male prisoners our men were remarkably ineligible for, or allergic to, marriage.[7]

Residence. Tables 11 and 12 show where the offender-patients were said by their hospitals to have been living at the time of their offence. Most frequently they were in the parental home, with lodgings or 'no fixed abode' second equal. The subnormals and psychopaths, being young on the whole, were the most likely to be still living with father or mother, although this was more marked in the case of men than of women, who were more likely than men to be living with a spouse or cohabiting. Adult male first-timers were also particularly likely to be living with parents, who may well have sheltered them from trouble: but the same did not seem to be true of adult *female* first-timers. Not surprisingly, the percentages with 'no fixed abode' were especially high in the case of schizophrenics, and highest of all for the female non-paranoid schizophrenics. Among the male schizophrenics it was at first sight interesting to note that those with a paranoid diagnosis were more likely to be living with a spouse or cohabiting, until one realised that this situation is of course associated with paranoid jealousy, and consequently with criminal violence. Finally, a small but substantial minority of both men and women were already in institutions–usually mental hospitals–when they committed their offences.

Criminal Behaviour

It is time to examine our sample's penal careers, together with their 'current offences'–that is, the behaviour which led to their hospital orders. When we turn to previous convictions, the male and female patterns, which were so similar in the case of hospital admissions, differ markedly, as can be seen from table 8 (A) and (C). At least three-quarters of our males had records, compared with a little more than half of our females; and at least 22 per cent of our males had been convicted on six *or more* separate occasions, compared with 9 per cent of our females. Depressing as these percentages are, they compared well with the 1963 intake of sentenced prisoners, in which only 12 per cent of the men and 30 per cent of the women were said to have clean records, while no less than 48 per cent of the men and 33 per cent of the women had been convicted on six or more separate occasions.

TABLE 11. Residence at time of arrest

MALES	Schizophrenia	Paranoid schizophrenia	Subnormal	Depressive	Personality disorder	Other	Total
Living with parents	21·8	24·4	57·7	12·0	36·2	37·9	36·5
Living with brother or sister	2·4	4·5	4·5	6·0	1·7	2·7	3·5
Living with spouse	3·0	15·5	2·1	26·8	10·9	18·9	7·2
Living with children	0·3	—	—	—	0·8	—	0·2
Living with paramour	0·7	1·1	—	1·5	1·7	—	0·6
Living with someone else	2·4	4·5	2·1	7·5	0·8	2·7	2·6
Living in lodgings	22·8	22·2	12·1	17·8	14·3	10·8	17·1
Living in an institution	6·7	4·5	6·7	3·0	10·9	5·4	6·7
Living elsewhere	11·7	12·2	4·2	14·9	6·7	8·1	8·6
No fixed abode	28·2	11·1	10·6	10·5	16·0	13·5	17·0
N = 100% =	298	90	331	67	119	37	942

TABLE 12. Residence at time of arrest

FEMALES	Schizophrenia	Paranoid schizophrenia	Subnormal	Depressive	Personality disorder	Other	Total
Living with parents	14·0	9·7	42·3	10·5	29·4	7·1	24·8
Living with brother or sister	8·0	3·2	2·4	5·3	—	—	3·6
Living with spouse	16·0	9·7	5·9	36·8	17·6	14·3	12·9
Living with children	—	3·2	—	—	—	—	0·5
Living with paramour	4·0	6·4	5·9	5·3	11·8	14·3	6·9
Living with someone else	—	3·2	4·7	10·5	—	7·1	4·1
Living in lodgings	12·0	29·0	10·6	10·5	23·5	21·5	15·2
Living in an institution	4·0	3·2	4·7	—	5·9	21·5	5·0
Living elsewhere	6·0	16·2	8·2	15·8	—	7·1	8·7
No fixed abode	36·0	16·2	15·3	5·3	11·8	7·1	18·3
N = 100% =	50	31	85	19	17	14	218

The sample's current offences (and diagnoses) are set out in tables 13 and 14. The grouping of them into a manageable number of categories was not an easy task. It had to be based on the Home Office offence-classification used by the police. But this involves nearly 200 sub-divisions, and although these are broadly subdivided into motoring offences, other non-indictable offences and six classes of indictable offences, these groupings were often based on legal distinctions—for example between the possible methods of trial—which were not the most relevant when we were trying to present a picture of what it was that our offender-patients had *done*. In the end we had to work out our own broad groupings, which are set out in the table in descending order of frequency. Most are self-explanatory, but one or two call for comment. 'Acquisitive' includes all forms of robbery, theft, fraud and breaking and entering for gain. 'Sexual' includes not only serious offences such as rape but also trivial ones such as indecent exposure: on the other hand those involving the death of or a violent attack on the victim are both included under 'personal violence'. This last heading excludes *minor* assaults on the police, which, together with obstructing or refusing to obey the police are shown under 'assaulting police'. This does not mean that we take assaults on police less seriously (those that caused real harm are included under personal violence): the reason was simply that—whether the offender is mentally disordered or not—an assault on a police officer is often the result of the officer's initiative rather than a spontaneous action by the offender. A constable who sees a man behaving in a suspicious or bizarre way will accost him, and the result may be to provoke the man to what is classified as an assault on a police officer, especially if the officer asks the man to accompany him to a police station. Sometimes these assaults are serious affairs, with real injury to the police although often they are more technical than injurious—a raised fist, a brandished stone or an attempt to jostle the policeman aside. The Home Office classification groups these trivial brushes with the police separately, and we think that by excluding them from 'violence' we have presented a more accurate picture. Similarly, we have distinguished 'Arson' from other methods of 'Damage to Property', in this case to see whether its alleged association with subnormality was confirmed (it was).

Tables 13 and 14 differ from all other tables in one respect: we have deliberately included in them not only a few cases whose dossiers were too late for inclusion in most of our tables, but also persons who were committed to mental hospitals after being found unfit to plead or 'guilty but insane'. We did so because otherwise these tables could have been criticised as under-emphasising the extent to which mentally disordered offenders are responsible for the types of crime which cause great concern, and especially personal violence and sexual molestation; and certainly unfitness to plead and verdicts of insanity tend to be associated with charges of serious violence, sexual assault or arson.

In discussing the nature of the current offences it is again necessary to be selective in order not to be tedious. We shall concentrate on four groups: dishonest acquisition, personal violence, sexual offences and damage to property. The first of these must be mentioned, if briefly, because it is by far the most numerous group: the next two partly because they too were comparatively numerous. For if this had been a sample of ordinary indictable and non-indictable offenders who were convicted in 1963, rather less than 3 per cent of their offences should have consisted of personal violence, and less than 2 per cent should have been sexual. Damage to property also seemed to be over-represented, especially amongst our women's offences, and will be briefly mentioned in that connection.

Acquisitive Offences. As can be seen at a glance from the tables, the

TABLE 13. Male offender-patients' current offences and diagnoses[a]

Type of offence	Diagnoses								Percentages	
	Schizophrenia		Subnormality		Personality disorders	Affective disorders	Other	Total	Males	(Females)
	non-paranoid	paranoid	non-severe	severe						
Acquisitive	116	21	141	32	57	24	14	405	41·6	(42·0)
Sexual	29	7	72	20	15	7	5	155	15·9	(4·4)
Personal violence	46	30	11	3	24	21	7	142	14·6	(15·9)
Damage to property	26	10	5	1	5	7	—	54	5·6	(8·0)
Frequenting with criminal intent	27	4	—	1	—	1	2	35	3·6	(—)
Arson	7	3	14	2	6	—	2	34	3·5	(3·1)
Assaulting police	13	7	1	—	3	3	2	29	3·0	(1·3)
Vagrancy	15	2	1	1	2	—	1	22	2·3	(9·3)
Taking and driving motor vehicles	5	1	8	1	1	2	—	18	1·9	(0·9)
Drunkenness	5	—	—	—	2	1	2	10	1·0	(2·7)
Others	23	9	10	4	5	5	3	59	6·1	(8·4)
No offence[b]	5	—	2	—	1	1	—	9	0·9	(4·0)
Total	317	94	265	65	121	72	38	972	p < 0·001 (11 d.f.)	
Percentages Males	32·5	9·7	27·3	6·7	12·5	7·4	3·9 ⎫	100·0		
(Females)	(23·5)	(14·2)	(33·6)	(4·4)	(7·5)	(10·2)	(6·6) ⎬ p < 0·005 (6 d.f.)	(100·0)		

[a] This table also includes those found 'guilty but insane' or unfit for trial (see p. 126) but excludes guardianship orders.
[b] i.e., juveniles in need of 'care, protection or control' (see s. 61 of the Act) or probationers breaching their orders.

TABLE 14. Female offender-patients' current offences and diagnoses[a]

	Diagnoses								
	Schizophrenia		Subnormality		Personality disorders	Affective disorders	Other	Total	Percentage
Type of offence	non-paranoid	paranoid	non-severe	severe					
Acquisitive	20	11	36	5	10	5	8	95	42·0
Sexual	2	—	6	1	—	1	—	10	4·4
Personal violence	9	7	4	—	3	10	3	36	15·9
Damage to property	3	8	5	—	—	1	1	18	8·0
Frequenting with criminal intent	—	—	—	—	—	—	—	—	—
Arson	3	—	2	1	—	1	—	7	3·1
Assaulting police	2	—	1	—	—	—	—	3	1·3
Vagrancy	10	4	4	—	1	1	1	21	9·3
Taking and driving motor vehicles	—	1	1	—	—	—	—	2	0·9
Drunkenness	—	—	2	—	1	2	1	6	2·7
Others	4	1	8	2	2	2	—	19	8·4
No offence[b]	—	—	7	1	—	—	1	9	4·0
Total	53	32	76	10	17	23	15	226	
Percentage	23·5	14·2	33·6	4·4	7·5	10·2	6·6		100·0

[a] This table also includes those found 'guilty but insane' or unfit for trial (see p. 126) but excludes guardianship orders.
[b] i.e., juveniles in need of 'care, protection or control' (see s. 61 of the Act) or probationers breaching their orders.

current offence was acquisitive in a very large percentage of cases: no other type of offence came anywhere near it. It is this sort of criminal act (together with 'vagrancy' offences such as begging or sleeping in un-authorised places) which poses a real problem for lawyers who are un-happy about excusing such offenders from punishment without some test of their responsibility for their acts. In the case of, say, a violent or sexual offence it is usually possible to connect the act plausibly with the mental disorder, and to infer in effect that the offender would not have done what he did had he not been schizophrenic or subnormal or depressed, as the case may be. This is often much less plausible with offences of dishonesty, especially if they are well-planned or involve a considerable amount of money or valuable property. One offender-patient, a schizo-phrenic woman, took part in a housebreaking which relieved her uncle of £2,700. In our society a desire for money cannot be regarded as abnormal, although one's method of trying to acquire it may indicate extreme stupidity or lack of conscience. Indeed, it is a complete disinterest in worldly goods which is the mark of the eccentric nowadays.

It is true that we did encounter one or two cases in which the acquisitive motivation was obviously abnormal. An example was a thirty-nine-year-old nurse, suffering from depression and 'personality disorder', who during years of shoplifting had filled a large room with an extraordinary miscellany of stolen goods. Another was a subnormal man who had been convicted of a considerable number of book-thefts: his room was found to contain about 350 volumes, stolen at different times. More often, however, the acquisitive offences were petty affairs, committed without planning or skill, for food, small sums of money or minor saleable articles. Each of these could be ascribed to a motive which we regard as normal: hunger, desire for money, need for sleep and shelter. In these cases it is hardly possible to say with confidence that the offender would not have done it if he had not been disordered, for they are indistinguishable from the acts of a large number of ordinary, if incompetent, people. What *can* often be argued is that the disorder, by rendering him unemployable and unwelcome to friends, relatives or others who might have assisted him, had reduced him to straits in which stealing, begging, or sleeping rough seems the easiest—perhaps the only—solution. In this sense the behaviour of many of our petty thieves and vagrants may well have been indirectly attributable to their disorders, although not in a way which the law recognises as an excuse. An example was a homeless twenty-five-year-old woman, an ex-patient of several mental hospitals, who was checked twice on a January night by a constable. On the second occasion she was found huddled in a doorway, wearing a coat which she had not had earlier, and which she admitted stealing from a nearby shop window. How else could a homeless vagrant get a coat to warm her in the small hours of the morning?

Sexual Offences. Even sexual offences can in some cases be regarded as an understandable attempt to satisfy more or less normal impulses on the part of people whose mental, physical or social handicaps make it difficult or impossible for them to do so legally, although in other cases the need itself takes an abnormal form, such as sadism or paederasty.

The sexual offences with which our offender-patients had been charged

K

ranged from rape and attempted rape to minor indecencies (such as rub-
bing oneself against women in a market place) and included indecent
exposure. It is always difficult to be sure from the legal category of a
sexual offence how serious it was in terms of physical or psychological
harm. 'Indecent assault' in particular seems to be interpreted by courts–
and therefore by police–so as to cover a wide range, from forcible acts
of great indecency committed against struggling victims to indecent exposure accompanied by an invitation to intercourse and a movement
towards the victim.[8] In one of our cases, for example, a depressed rather
dull man of 23 placed his hand on the leg of a twelve-year-old girl who
was sitting beside him on the bus, and was charged with indecent assault
(the magistrates made him the subject of a hospital order without convicting him). In some cases the offender has merely invited a child to partici-
pate in an indecency–for example to touch what is usually described as
'his person'–and the illogicality of calling this an assault led to the
creation of a new offence, 'indecency with a child', in 1960. Even if–as
happened in at least one of our cases–the child refuses the invitation and
is not subjected to any physical pressure the offender can still be charged
with inciting him or her to commit an act of indecency. Indeed, children
have been known to invite the indecency, although this probably happens
rather less often than paederasts themselves allege. It was therefore necessary to examine the police reports in order to gain some impression of the
seriousness of the incident, and often it was still not possible to tell how
much lasting harm had been suffered by the victim.[9] For example, a
severely subnormal man of 22 entered a house to which he was delivering
oil while the parents were out and sat down on the sofa beside two girls,
one aged 8, the other 5. After some preliminaries, he tickled the younger
girl's pudenda, and went away. A week later, he again entered the house
in spite of resistance by the girls, and tried to jam the door shut behind
him. While he was talking to them their mother returned and forced the
door open. He admitted his offence to the police and was found to have
committed previous 'indecent assaults' on two boys and a 'female'. With
some hesitation we classified this as 'unlikely to have affected the victims
seriously', although we do not question the wisdom of committing him
to a mental hospital (he had previously been cautioned, conditionally discharged and put on probation!) An example of a case which was classed
as 'trivial' was that of a subnormal man in his thirties who had been paying boys for mutual masturbation. When they increased their charges he
found himself in debt, and went to the police for advice.

At the other extreme were cases in which the sexual offence was accompanied by homicidal violence. One of these involved a twenty-three-
year-old man with a long record of petty acquisitive offences, going back
to the age of nine. He took an eight-year-old girl into a field and attempted
to have intercourse with her, ejaculating over her clothes; then strangled
her. He was found guilty of manslaughter by reason of diminished responsibility, and sent to Rampton under an indeterminate restriction order. At
the time of the crime he was already under suspicion of a similar homicide,
committed in exactly the same spot a year before. Police enquiries also
revealed that he had several times 'indecently assaulted' his niece, and

that 'the family generally are regarded as mentally retarded'. He was diagnosed as a case of 'personality disorder'.

Our tentative classification of the harmfulness of the sexual offences by males was as follows:

A. Involving death or serious bodily harm   7 cases
B. Involving some violence to the person   7 cases
C. Likely to have shocked the victim, and in some cases
   involving threats of violence   27 cases
D. Unlikely to have affected the 'victim' seriously   69 cases
E. Trivial incidents   17 cases
F. Indecent exposure   34 cases
                                                            ———
                                                            161 [a]

[a] These include a few offences which are classed as 'personal violence' in table 13, but were sexually motivated.

Subnormal males were decidedly over-represented among the sexual offenders. Only a third of our sample were labelled subnormal, but they accounted for 59 per cent of the sexual offences: and the severely subnormal were even more over-represented than the moderately subnormal. All other diagnostic groups were under-represented, although the 12 per cent with 'personality disorders' accounted for nearly that percentage (10 per cent) of sexual offences.

In the majority of cases the victims[9] of the offences were children. Even if we leave aside the 34 cases in which the current offence was merely indecent exposure, 94 (74 per cent) of the remaining 127 involved at least one boy or girl under the age of 14; and in another 9 (7 per cent) the boy or girl was under 16.

Sexual Recidivism. Leaving aside the very small number of female sexual offenders for the moment, to what extent were the males sexual recidivists, in the sense that they had committed sexual offences in the past? In view of the large numbers of sexual offences which are said never to be reported to the police, and the considerable percentage of the reported offences which the police do not succeed in tracing to the offender, any estimate based on the official records of our sample can be regarded only as a minimum figure. We found that 81 (52 per cent) of our 155 male sexual offenders had previously been convicted of sexual offences, while another 6 per cent had been charged with more than one such offence at trial, or had had others taken into account, or were known[10] by the police to have committed other sexual offences. Even when we excluded those whose current offence was indecent exposure—a notoriously repetitive type of behaviour—we were still left with a group of which half had previous convictions for sexual offences.[11]

Indecent Exposure. One in five of our sexual offenders' convictions were for that fairly harmless offence, indecent exposure (sometimes called 'exhibitionism'). There is a popular belief, for which psychiatrists must take some responsibility, that exhibitionists do not commit more serious sexual offences. We have not found any real support for this in the major studies

of sexual offenders. The Cambridge survey found that half its exhibitionists had previously been convicted of indecent assaults, the victims in
most cases being usually young girls.[12] In the U.S.A., Gebhard *et al.*
could only say, at best, that 'some two thirds' of the previous sexual
offences of exhibitionists were for the same type of offence.[13] Of our 34
exhibitionists, nearly half (16) had earlier been convicted of other types
of sexual offences, usually indecent assault on females (intermingled in
most cases with non-sexual offences). Moreover, amongst the men whose
current sexual offences were of other types were another 10 men who in
the past had been convicted of indecent exposure. In one such case a
thirty-eight-year-old man with a conviction for indecent exposure when
he was in his twenties (and a history of petty thefts interspersed with
admissions to mental hospitals) had twice enticed children – of both sexes
– into his car, driven them to a wood and asked them to take part in some
sort of sexual activity; when they refused he attacked them, stabbing one
of the children in the stomach. Clearly, at least where mental disorder is
involved, the notion that exhibitionists never do any harm is a myth.[14]

There were several cases in which we could not help feeling that the
offender should have been identified as dangerous earlier in his penal
career and dealt with accordingly. An example was that of a twenty-year-
old psychopath, who had at 16 been fined £5 by a juvenile court for
indecently assaulting a boy of 9, at 17 put on probation for indecently
assaulting a girl of 11, and at 19 had received two consecutive six-month
prison sentences for indecently assaulting two girls of 10 and 12, with
three similar offences taken into consideration! All these ineffectual sentences were imposed by magistrates' courts. On the latest occasion he had
pulled a girl of 7 into his car with his hand over her mouth, driven her to
a lonely road, dragged her into some bushes and tried to rape her. The
police report described him as neurotic, lacking in confidence and apt to
get quickly depressed when things go wrong. It said that he 'had always
pleaded that he required medical treatment'. One medical witness had
been unable to find evidence of any mental disorder, but the trial judge
ordered a further examination with the result that he was diagnosed as a
psychopath and committed to Broadmoor under an indeterminate restriction order.

Personal Violence. Third in frequency – but practically 'second equal' so
far as our men were concerned – was personal violence. As has been indicated already, this category has been pruned of acquisitive violence (i.e.,
robbery), and of minor assaults on police. Even if these had been included,
however, personal violence would still have fallen far behind acquisitive
offences. On the other hand, if we compare our men with those received
into prisons or Borstals under sentence in 1963, of whom about 8 per
cent had been imprisoned for violence, current offences of violence are
significantly ($p < 0.001$) more frequent in our sample, if not markedly
so.[15]

As can be seen, violence was not common among the current offences
of our subnormals, and still less common amongst the severely subnormal.
There was, however, one example of serious violence by a severely handicapped man in his twenties, who suffered from cerebral palsy and slight

hydrocephalus. He was looked after by his mother, and was said to have no aggressive tendencies; nor was there any record of earlier offences. While attending the local training centre, however, he wandered into a storeroom, picked up an axe and went out into the road, where he struck a three-year-old child with it. He was then allowed to remain at liberty until his trial and committed to a rural hospital without a restriction order, and later discharged by a Mental Health Review Tribunal (see p. 169). Violence was a little more frequent among the non-paranoid schizophrenics (14 per cent) and the cases of personality disorder (20 per cent). The groups which had high percentages, however, were the paranoid schizophrenics (31 per cent) and the depressives (29 per cent).

Unlike the violent offences of mentally normal males, which tend to have a peak around the age of 20, the probability of violence among our sample seemed to reach its height in later life, as table 15 shows. To what

TABLE 15. Age-distribution of violence by men in Oxford sample

Age-group	Cases involving violence as percentage of N in age-group %	N in age-group
under 17	3·7	27
17-	10·5	143
21-	9·0	144
25-	9·2	119
30-	16·5	127
35-	18·3	115
40-	15·6	109
45-	8·0	50
50-	16·0	50
55-	11·7	17
60-	11·7	17
65 and over	16·7	24
		942

extent were our violent men 'chronically' violent? It is fashionable to be sceptical about the concept of the violence-prone individual,[16] and to emphasise both the extent to which the previous recorded offences (if any) of men convicted of violence consist of non-violent offences, and also the extent to which the records of men convicted of non-violent offences are interspersed with occasional violence. Indeed, there is evidence that with each successive conviction for a non-violent offence there is a slight increase in the small probability that the offender will later be convicted of violence; and in this sense some violence seems to be, as it were, an occupational risk of a career of petty crime.[17] Even in our somewhat abnormal sample quite a sprinkling of violent offences could be observed in the records which preceded a non-violent offence, while a violent offence, if it was not the first recorded offence, was often preceded by non-violent offences.

It was important, too, to remember that our histories of earlier convictions, supplied by local police forces, would not necessarily record every incident of violence in the offender's career. The police, as we have said, made use of both their local records and of the central Criminal Record Office; but common assaults are not usually reported to the latter. Consequently, if an offender had moved from one area to another, the police who dealt with his latest offence might not learn of earlier convictions for minor violence. Secondly, by no means all violence results in prosecution, even when the offender is known to the victim. This is especially true of violence between members of the same household. Sometimes police enquiries uncovered an unrecorded history of violence, as in the case of a seventeen-year-old schizophrenic patient who absconded from a mental hospital and stabbed the male nurse who traced him to the nearby town. His criminal record was clean, but even before his first admission to hospital there had been more than one violent incident between him and members of his family. One man, whose current offence was a trivial acquisitive one and whose record was innocent of violence, was under suspicion of more than one murder, of which he was later found guilty.

Even so, there could be no denying the evidence of a moderate degree of 'specialisation' so far as personal violence is concerned. Table 16 shows,

TABLE 16. Previous recorded convictions for violence

Current offence	Number of men with				Total	Probability of 1+ previous recorded violent offence
	0	1 or more	2 or more	3 or more		
Homicide and attempts	22	6	3	1	28	0·21
Assaults	69	24	9	6	93	0·26
Assaults on police	20	8	6	2	28	0·29
Robbery	9	3	1	0	12	0·25
Drunkenness	7	4	2	2	11	0·36
Unlawful intercourse	6	3	1	1	9	0·33
Shoplifting	22	3	2	2	25	0·12
Other larceny	175	22	7	4	197	0·11
Damage	48	7	6	3	55	0·13
Burglary	116	16	8	6	132	0·12
Heterosexual	61	9	2	1	70	0·13
Homosexual	38	5	4	1	43	0·12
Frequenting	30	4	1	1	34	0·12
Arson	29	4	1	1	33	0·12
Indecent exposure	30	3	1	0	33	0·09
Fraud	29	2	0	0	31	0·06
Begging	19	2	2	1	21	0·10
Taking and driving	16	2	0	0	18	0·11
Cruelty to child	2	0	0	0	2	0·00

for different types of current offence, the probability that a male offender-patient had at least one previous recorded conviction for personal violence. It can be seen that there is a sharp division between a group of six offence-types (shown as the first six in the table) for which this probability was at least 21 per cent, and the remainder, for which it did not exceed 13 per cent. With one exception, all the offence-types carrying high probabilities are of a kind which it is plausible to associate with violence, the exception being unlawful intercourse. Conversely, the low probability group did not include any offence-type which one would expect to be associated with personal violence, with the possible exception of cruelty to children, of which however there were only two instances.

Victims of Violence. In the great majority of cases the victim of the violence was someone closely associated with the offender-patient: a wife, husband, paramour, parent, child or lodger. Women were especially likely to kill or injure their children, often as a preliminary to an attempt on their own life. In other cases it was someone who came upon the offender while he was trespassing, or a policeman who stopped and questioned him because of his odd behaviour. In the case of men—but never of women—it was sometimes the manager or barman of a public-house who refused to give him more drink, a bus-conductor who tried to stop him from smoking, or a labour-exchange clerk who in some way annoyed him. Occasionally it was a fellow-patient who had in some way irritated him, or a hospital nurse who was trying to control him, although there must be many minor incidents of this kind which hospitals do not report. In one case a motorist who gave a lift to a man in his thirties was later struck in the face by him for taking the wrong route (the hitch-hiker was found to be a psychopath with no less than 28 previous convictions, the last four for assault). Such cases apart, however, attacks 'out of the blue' on complete strangers, without any previous contact, accounted for about 1 in 7 of our cases of violence by males, but only 2 out of our 36 female cases.

These attacks on strangers usually took place in the street, although in one case a paranoid schizophrenic attacked a man in front of him in a Post Office queue, and in another an Irishwoman attending Mass in a London church asked another woman to change her seat, and stabbed her when she refused. In the more typical cases, however, the victim would be passing the offender in the street, who would strike him with his fist, using no weapon, and without pressing the attack home. Even so, it would often be found that there had been some sort of communication between the two, however fleeting. For example, a woman in our sample, who suffered from deluded jealousy of her husband's relations with other women, was standing with him at a bus-stop. A strange woman came up and asked him the time of the next bus, whereupon our offender-patient attacked her. In the great majority of cases these attacks on strangers were committed by paranoid schizophrenics, although the nature of their persecutory delusions was not always explained as clearly as it was in this case.

McClintock has drawn attention to the substantial amount of violence which centres on public-houses and cafés; and in this respect many of the men in our sample seemed to behave like their more normal contemporaries. One forty-year-old epileptic was in frequent trouble as a result of drink. Of his 22 convictions, 9 were for being 'drunk and disorderly', 7 were for assaulting the police, one was for refusing to leave a pub, and the one which led to his hospital order was an assault on a pub-manager who refused to serve him at closing time. At least 10 per cent of the current offences of violence in our sample were connected with drinking, and most of these took place in or just outside public-houses. None of these were assaults on police, but several were assaults on staff who refused to serve the offending man a drink.

Preventable Violence. In one or two cases the offender's behaviour had given warnings which, if they had been taken more seriously, might have led to action which would have averted serious violence. One such case was that of a man in his early thirties who shot his brother in the face with a shotgun. He was a paranoid schizophrenic who had first come to police attention through using a false name when enrolling as a voter. A year before the shooting he had attacked the same brother, though only with his fists. Even before that his GP had been told by his family that he had an obsession about the police, talked about doing someone in, and kept an axe under his bed, together with many other details which would suggest paranoid delusions even to a layman. Arrangements had apparently been made for him to see a psychiatrist, but he had failed to keep the appointment.

Another preventable act of violence—this time fatal—was committed by a severely subnormal woman of 33. She and her husband—also of low intelligence—had been convicted two years before of assaulting and ill-treating their three-year-old boy, on information laid by the NSPCC. Both were imprisoned for three months, and it was probably at this time that their six children were taken into care by the local authority. By the time of the homicide, however, she was again trying to look after them, and had given birth to a seventh baby. One morning when bathing him she lost her temper with him, banged his head on the floor and drowned him in the bath-water. When her husband came home they took the baby to the infirmary saying that he had been accidentally drowned, but investigation revealed skull fractures and the story came out. When one reflects not only on the homicide but on the sort of upbringing which her six other children must have been undergoing, it is difficult to see why they were allowed to return to her.

Some of our offenders had clearly been known as violent outside their families if not to the police. One of these, a man in his twenties, lived with his elderly mother, and when his paranoid schizophrenia developed lived on her savings and gave up work. He was obsessed with the idea of developing his physique and winning prizes for it: as the police report said, 'he became a health and strength addict . . . and his mental condition seems to have deteriorated since then'. When his mother complained about his refusal to work he reacted violently; and was so well known as a violent and quarrelsome man that he was banned by several of the local pubs. Eventually he struck a pub-keeper who refused to serve him, was charged with occasioning actual bodily harm, and became the subject of a hospital order.

Arson and other Damage to Property. Arson and other damage to property deserve a brief mention. The association between arson and subnormality has been well known for many years, and was observable in our sample: nearly half of the offences of arson had been committed by the third of our men and women who were subnormal. For most of the acts of incendiarism the motive was not plain; but in some cases it was clearly aimed at specific people. For example, a sixteen-year-old schizophrenic girl who had just been told by her mother to keep her clothes tidy attacked her mother and sister, then ran upstairs and set fire to her bedroom. Some of these cases of arson had been prosecuted as mere malicious damage, presumably in order that they should be dealt with by a magistrates' court.

In contrast, damage to property which does not involve incendiarism seemed to be more characteristic of schizophrenics than of subnormals, for the 42 per cent of our men and women who were schizophrenic had been responsible for 65 per cent of the malicious damage. Indeed, the 10 per cent who were *paranoid* schizophrenics had been responsible for 25 per cent of the damage. It is worth noting that this same diagnostic group was also over-represented so far as personal violence was concerned.

Predominant Offence. In discussing the previous offences, however, of our violent, sexual and destructive offenders it must be made clear that in the vast majority of cases their previous records were not of these kinds. What might be called petty dishonesty and social untidiness—that is, 'vagrancy offences'—were predominant. With the exception of the dangerous types of offender which have been mentioned, the general picture is one of nuisance rather than real harm. Although three-quarters of our men had previous convictions, less than a third had been sentenced to a prison, Borstal or other penal institution.

Even so, some of the penal histories were of impressive length and variety. An example—admittedly one of the most spectacular—is the penal career of a schizophrenic Scottish vagrant, who was only 39 by the time he entered our sample. One of the remarkable features of his dossier—which is summarised below—is the fact that it contains no record of psychiatric treatment, although there is an unexplained period of about two years (around 1950) during which no convictions were recorded, and which he *may* have spent in a mental hospital. If so, it is even more deplorable that he should have continued for another ten years to be dealt with by nothing more than a series of conditional discharges and short terms of imprisonment. Nor can this be wholly excused by pointing out that the Mental Health Act was not in operation during most of his career, for even after it was he incurred two conditional discharges and five prison sentences.

Recorded offences of a 39-year-old male schizophrenic vagrant

Date	Nature of conviction	Disposal
1945		
March	Convicted at age 20 in his home town Sheriff Court of 6 house-breakings	Sentence deferred 3 months, then admonished
September	At home town police court, of theft	Fined £4 or 30 days'
November	At home town Sheriff Court, of 3 postal thefts	Fined £5 or 30 days' on each count
1946		
May	At home town Sheriff Court, of 3 thefts	30 days' imprisonment

Recorded offences af a 39-year-old male schizophrenic vagrant—contd.

Date	Nature of conviction	Disposal
1946		
July	At home town Sheriff Court, of housebreaking	30 days' imprisonment
November	At a northern English magistrates' court A, of stealing a coat from a house	4 days' imprisonment
November	At home town Sheriff Court, of theft and housebreaking	4 months' imprisonment
1947		
May	At home town Sheriff Court, of 2 thefts	6 months' imprisonment
September	At magistrates' court B, of stealing food from an hotel	Bound over for 2 years, in sum of £5
November	At magistrates' court C, of stealing cheese and syrup from a house	2 and 3 months' imprisonment concurrent
1949		
May	At a Scottish police court D, of breach of the peace	Fined £1, imprisoned for default
May	At English magistrates' court E, of being drunk and disorderly	Fined £5, imprisoned 6 months later
July	At magistrates' court F, of stealing a wallet from a jacket	2 months' imprisonment
1950	No recorded convictions: an unexplained gap of two years	
1951		
August	At magistrates' court G, of begging	1 month's imprisonment
1952		
November	At magistrates' court H, of begging	Conditional discharge
December	At magistrates' court I, of begging	1 month's imprisonment
1953		
March	At London magistrates' court J, of stealing a pint of milk	14 days' imprisonment
April	At a south coast magistrates' court K, of begging and indecent exposure	1 and 2 months' imprisonment, concurrent
November	At a northern Assizes, of buggery	3 years' imprisonment
1954 } **1955** }	In prison: released November, 1955	
1955		
December	At a magistrates' court L, of 'sleeping out'	Conditional discharge
1956		
January	At magistrates' court M, of loitering with intent near cars	3 months' imprisonment

Date	Nature of conviction	Disposal
1956		
April	At magistrates' court N, of begging	1 month's imprisonment
July	At magistrates' court O, of stealing a towel	1 month's imprisonment
1957		
April	At a London Sessions, of loitering with intent	9 months' imprisonment
November	At a provincial Quarter Sessions, of indecent assaults on boys of 12 and 13	9 and 9 months' imprisonment
1958		
June	At a London Sessions, of indecent exposure	12 months' imprisonment
1959		
April	At a northern Quarter Sessions, of indecent exposure	12 months' imprisonment
1960		
January	At a south coast magistrates' court, of begging	1 month's imprisonment
February	At the same court, of begging	3 months' imprisonment
May	At another south coast magistrates' court, of begging	1 month's imprisonment
July	At a western magistrates' court, of begging	2 months' imprisonment
September	At a Midland magistrates' court, of indecent assault on a 16-year-old boy	6 months' imprisonment
1961		
February	At a Midland magistrates' court, of begging	Conditional discharge
April	At a south-eastern magistrates' court, of indecent exposure	12 months' imprisonment
December	At a home county magistrates' court, of begging	14 days' imprisonment
1962		
January	At a Midland magistrates' court, of begging	Conditional discharge
February	At a western magistrates' court, of begging	1 month's imprisonment
May	At a northern magistrates' court, of begging (door to door) and false pretences (with a 'deaf and dumb' placard)	1 and 2 months' imprisonment, consecutive
September	At a Midland Quarter Session, of indecent assault on a 15-year-old boy	12 months' imprisonment
1963		
1 July	At a Midland magistrates' court, of indecency with boys aged 14	Hospital order (bringing him into Oxford sample)
7 July	While a patient, committed an indecent assault on a boy just outside the hospital	
22 July	Absconded from hospital, retaken a week later	

Diagnostic Groups

It is now time to turn to the diagnoses. These must of course be distinguished from the statutory sub-divisions into which medical witnesses are compelled to sort offender-patients when recommending hospital or guardianship orders. Our dossiers showed both statutory sub-divisions and the diagnoses of the responsible medical officers in the receiving hospitals, some but not all of whom had been medical witnesses at the court appearance. There was of course a close correspondence between the statutory sub-divisions of 'subnormality', 'severe subnormality' and 'psychopathic disorder' on the one hand, and diagnoses of 'subnormality' (with or without more specific labels) or 'personality disorder' on the other. Most other diagnoses appeared in court as 'mental illness'. Our tables, however, are based on the diagnoses of the responsible medical officers. Our dossiers had asked the hospitals not only for the 'predominant disorder' but also for 'any associated mental disorder', as well as 'associated physical disorders' and 'contributory environmental factors'. The hospitals seemed to have no difficulty, however, in giving the predominant disorders, most of which fell clearly into one of four familiar diagnostic groups—the schizophrenias (with paranoid schizophrenia a common sub-division), the various forms of subnormality, 'severe' or 'non-severe', affective disorders (depressive or manic-depressive states) and personality disorders, often called psychopathic disorders. These are the groups which we have distinguished in our tables. The remainder, which include epilepsy, disorders peculiar to old age, brain damage, and syphilitic infection of the central nervous system, were too insignificant in number to list separately, and are grouped under 'Other'. The groups are ranged from left to right in descending order of frequency.

The Schizophrenics. From the point of view of anti-social behaviour, by far the most important of the main diagnostic groups is the schizophrenias. So far as ordinary hospital admissions are concerned they are outnumbered only by depressive disorders of one kind or another. But schizophrenics have the lowest percentage of voluntary admissions—lower even than alcoholic psychoses—and if we consider only admissions which take place under some sort of compulsion, the schizophrenics soar to the top of the list. Moreover, although in total numbers of voluntary and compulsory admissions they are outnumbered by depressives, they seem to yield larger numbers of long-stay patients, and larger numbers of re-admissions. Our sample confirmed and indeed accentuated this picture. Schizophrenics accounted for no less than 42 per cent of our males, while only 7·4 per cent were diagnosed as depressive. A comparison with the Ministry of Health's statistics for admissions to ordinary mental hospitals in 1964[18] showed that our schizophrenics included a rather low percentage of 'first admissions' (22 per cent compared with 30 per cent, irrespective of sex).

On the other hand, the age-distribution of our schizophrenics, which can be seen in table 9, was not startlingly different from that of the general run of schizophrenic admissions, especially when the under-representation of first admissions was taken into account. There was the usual peak around the age of thirty, with very few in their teens, but a long tail extending into old age. Indeed, the oldest offender in our sample was a chronic paranoid schizophrenic who had been born in the year of the Criminal Lunatics Act, 1884. *Half a century ago* he had been tried and found unfit to plead after an insane attempt to shoot a man. After fourteen years in Broadmoor he had been transferred to a local mental hospital, probably as a prelude to his release, which took place in 1935. For nearly two decades more he seems to have managed to avoid any trouble–at least so far as police records were concerned–but in 1963, soon after his 79th birthday, his persecutory delusions caused him to strike someone with a rubber cosh and try to stab him with a kitchen knife. He was committed to a local hospital, where he was giving no trouble two years later, and where he would probably remain for the rest of his life.

It was noticeable that the older the schizophrenic the more likely was the disorder to take paranoid form. This being so, it might have been expected that paranoid schizophrenics, being older than the others, would have a higher percentage of histories of previous admissions but in fact the opposite was the case.[19] Taken together, these observations support the widely-held view that the paranoid form of schizophrenia tends to have a later onset than other forms, or more precisely that the age at which it leads to the first hospital admission is later.

The Subnormals. Next to the schizophrenics, the largest diagnostic group consisted of the subnormals, who presented a very different picture. To see this picture clearly it is necessary to look first at the pattern of subnormal admissions in general. Half of all first admissions take place before the age of 15, and three-quarters before the age of 20: the percentages and admission-rates for the sexes are not very different. The early first admissions tend to be cases of severe subnormality, the later ones being increasingly the result of failure on the part of moderately handicapped boys and girls to adapt to the behavioural standards of their families or schools. Many of these cases attend special schools or training centres, while living at home, until the age of 16 (the minimum leaving age for such establishments), after which it is a question of survival in an increasingly complex world of adults. Those who cannot support themselves and are not supported and sheltered by their families gravitate into mental subnormality hospitals.

The vast majority of admissions of subnormals are 'informal', even when the patient is an adult. In 1964 only 169 men and 189 women were received into mental subnormality hospitals for compulsory observation or treatment under Part IV of the 1959 Act–fewer even than the subnormals who were made the subject of hospital orders; and no doubt some of these Part IV admissions were 'psychopaths' rather than ordinary subnormals. This is a striking contrast to the pattern of admissions to hospitals for mental illness, where only about 2 per cent of compulsory admissions are the result of orders by the courts. No doubt part of the explanation is that non-severe subnormality and psychopathic disorder cannot be made the basis of a Part IV compulsory admission after the 21st birthday; but when we see how many of our hospital order cases were in their late teens it seems surprising that there are not more Part IV admissions at this age.

For no less than 28 per cent of our subnormals were between their 15th and 20th birthdays. The concentration was particularly striking in the case of females, of whom 38 per cent were in this age group. Nevertheless, what is surprising is not so much this concentration–which is simply the result of emerging from the shelter and control of the family and the school–as the fact that so few are committed by compulsory procedures which do *not* involve the courts. The explanation may be that their behaviour, unlike that of schizophrenic or depressive patients, is seldom such that it is seen by doctors as endangering the 'health or safety' of themselves or others. Certainly we have seen that subnormals do not often commit serious personal violence, although we have also seen that they are responsible for more than their share of arson and sexual offences, both of which can do considerable harm.

For most of these subnormals in their late teens the hospital order which brought them into our sample was apparently their first introduction to a mental hospital: three-quarters of the males and four-fifths of the females had no previous institutional histories apart from special schools–and some of them had not even been in special schools. Indeed, out of all our subnormals, 93 had been educated at secondary modern schools or the equivalent, and of these 14 were described as severely subnormal! One man and one woman were said to have attended technical colleges.

Although we have emphasised the youth of our subnormals, it must also be pointed out that among the men at least there were rather more in their twenties and thirties than would have been predicted from a study of the age-distribution of admissions in general. Again we considered whether this was attributable to the provisions of the 1959 Act (s. 44), which forbid the detention of a subnormal patient against his will after his 25th birthday without a special report to the effect that he is dangerous to himself or others. Our age-distribution, however, showed no sign of a sudden spate of subnormals in their late twenties with previous admissions: all that could be observed was a rather slower decline in the number of admissions than might have been predicted from the general age-distribution. We have already (on p. 119) mentioned the phenomenon of the subnormal first-timer who is getting on in years.

The pattern is reasonably consistent with the hypothesis that for the most part our subnormals are near the ill-defined borderline that separates the incompetents who are cared for in subnormality hospitals from those who have to fend for themselves in the community. In these cases it is only when there is trouble with the law, and the problem of disposal arises, that admission to hospital appears as a solution.

One difficulty in comparing the careers of different diagnostic groups such as schizophrenia and subnormality arises from differences in their age-distribution. If we are looking for attributes such as 'having been found guilty at some time in the past' or 'being married', the older a man or woman is the more time he or she has had to acquire such attributes; so that a group containing a higher percentage of younger people might give an illusory impression of greater law-abidingness or celibacy, as the case might be. The simplest way to meet this difficulty, if one has enough individuals in one's samples, is to take sub-samples in which the individuals are matched for age. In the course of our study of our psychopathic males (see chapter 10), we were able to match each of 62 'pure' psychopaths (see p. 226 and pp. 228-9) with a 'pure' schizophrenic and 'pure' subnormal of approximately the same age (other diagnoses were not numerous enough to be included); and the resulting comparison is sufficiently relevant and interesting to be shown here (table 17), although we shall leave the discussion of psychopaths until later.

It must be remembered, of course, that the sub-samples of schizophrenic and subnormal males on which table 17 is based were selected not randomly but so as to match our pure psychopaths in age. The table does seem, however, to confirm that subnormal males tend to have their first encounters with the criminal law earlier than schizophrenics, though not as early as psychopaths, but that their offences seem less likely to be taken seriously by the courts. Their probability of being in employment at the time of their offence was much the same as the schizophrenics', but they were even less likely to be married than the schizophrenics.

Affective Disorders. The 'affective disorders' consisted partly of 'the English disease' – that is, depressive states – or manic-depressive conditions. As table 13 has already demonstrated, they were strikingly associated with current offences of violence. This was the only diagnostic group in which such offences outnumbered acquisitive offences (if men and women are counted together). It is true that petty thefts, often from shops, were still common amongst their offences, and British psychiatrists[20] have drawn attention to the association between depression and shoplifting. Nevertheless, the chief risk of depression – next to solitary suicide attempts – is that the sufferer, in despair for the future of his family, will try to kill one or all of them, usually as a preliminary to ending his own life. This is especially true of mothers with young children, although occasionally a grown child will attack his or her parents. One example of this less common situation also illustrates the way in which a depressive state can lead to violence 'out of the blue' by a person with no previous history of violence or psychiatric treatment. This was the case of the 'very reserved' thirty-year-old typist who lived with her mother. She had few friends, and had been depressed since her father's death a few years before. She came home from the office early one day saying that she did not feel well; and in the evening, when her mother was looking for a needle she had dropped she hit her over the head with a flat-iron, and tried to strangle her with electric flex. Her mother feigned unconsciousness, and was dragged into the kitchen, where her daughter put her head into the gas-oven and turned on the tap. After a struggle the daughter collapsed, and her mother was able to get help.

In men, the affective disorder seemed more likely to take the manic-depressive form, which accounted for 63 per cent of the males' affective disorders, as compared with only 37 per cent of the females'. The peak age for affective admissions in general seems to occur in the late fifties; but for ours it was earlier – around the age of 40, although there was another concentration of men in the over-60 age-group. The first of these peaks seemed to be wholly attributable to manic-depressives, the great majority with histories of previous admissions. There were so few women

TABLE 17. Sixty-two age-matched[a] trios of male psychopaths, schizophrenics and subnormals

Notes: see p. 145

	Psycho-paths	Schizo-phrenics	Sub-normals	Significance of differences[c]		
Mean no. of court appearances	6·79	3·68	4·18	Ps *v* Sc	z = 3·61	p < 0·001
				Ps *v* Sb	z = 3·17	p < 0·01
				Sc *v* Sb	z = 2·11	p < 0·05
Mean age at first conviction	17·2	23·0	18·8	Ps *v* Sc	z = 4·02	p < 0·001
				Ps *v* Sb	z = 0·35	NS
				Sc *v* Sb	z = 3·16	p < 0·01
Predominant type of offence[b]						
Acquisitive	58·1%	61·3%	64·5%	Ps *v* Sc	Y = 0·25	NS
				Ps *v* Sb	Y = 0·48	NS
				Sc *v* Sb	Y = 0·21	NS
Sexual	14·5%	8·1%	24·2%	Ps *v* Sc	Y = 0·94	NS
				Ps *v* Sb	Y = 1·23	NS
				Sc *v* Sb	Y = 2·24	p < 0·05
Against public order	9·7%	14·5%	11·3%	Ps *v* Sc	Y = 0·69	NS
				Ps *v* Sb	Y = 0·15	NS
				Sc *v* Sb	Y = 0·43	NS
Personal violence	17·7%	16·1%	–	Ps *v* Sc	Y = 0·11	NS
				Ps *v* Sb	Y = 3·17	p < 0·01
				Sc *v* Sb	Y = 3·00	p < 0·01
With any recorded personal violence	56·4%	38·7%	22·5%	Ps *v* Sc	Y = 1·95	p < 0·06
				Ps *v* Sb	Y = 3·37	p < 0·001
				Sc *v* Sb	Y = 1·80	p < 0·10
Mean no. of previous hospital admissions	1·55	0·87	1·03	Ps *v* Sc	z = 3·19	p < 0·01
				Ps *v* Sb	z = 1·66	p < 0·10
				Sc *v* Sb	z = 1·57	NS
With three or more previous hospital admissions	16·1%	16·1%	20·9%	Ps *v* Sc	Y = 0·10	NS
				Ps *v* Sb	Y = 0·69	NS
				Sc *v* Sb	Y = 0·55	NS
Sent to Special hospital	33·9%	11·3%	4·8%	Ps *v* Sc	Y = 2·76	p < 0·01
				Ps *v* Sb	Y = 3·57	p < 0·001
				Sc *v* Sb	Y = 1·11	NS
Put under restriction order	37·0%	17·7%	12·9%	Ps *v* Sc	Y = 2·55	p < 0·01
				Ps *v* Sb	Y = 2·69	p < 0·01
				Sc *v* Sb	Y = 0·60	NS
Using aliases	3·2%	19·3%	6·4%	Ps *v* Sc	Y = 2·27	p < 0·05
				Ps *v* Sb	Y = 0·61	NS
				Sc *v* Sb	Y = 1·87	p < 0·10
Ever married	17·7%	12·9%	8·1%	Ps *v* Sc	Y = 0·69	NS
				Ps *v* Sb	Y = 1·38	NS
				Sc *v* Sb	Y = 0·69	NS
Unemployed at time of offence	54·9%	69·3%	61·3%	Ps *v* Sc	Y = 2·18	p < 0·05
				Ps *v* Sb	Y = 1·07	NS
				Sc *v* Sb	Y = 0·56	NS
Manually employed	40·3%	22·6%	38·7%	Ps *v* Sc	Y = 2·02	p < 0·05
				Ps *v* Sb	Y = 0·08	NS
				Sc *v* Sb	Y = 1·97	p < 0·05

that nothing definite can be said about their age-distribution. Irrespective of sex, only about a third were 'first admissions'.

Other Diagnoses. 'Other diagnoses' were very miscellaneous, including such disorders as 'puerperal psychosis', 'senile dementia' and in one case 'general paralysis of the insane'. There were a handful of cases in which the responsible medical officer was frankly doubtful about the presence of any genuine disorder. One such was that of a man in his thirties, who had quarrelled with his father, went to the latter's place of work and struck him. His father obtained a summons for common assault, with the result that the son appeared before the magistrates. He had been in a local mental hospital a couple of years before for hypochondriac complaints, but had been discharged as free from mental illness, although he was described by a psychiatrist as a 'dull, backward, idle, scrounging, malingering, inadequate psychopath', with a 'great dislike for work'. On this occasion he seems to have decided to feign madness, and by conduct such as publicly masturbating he managed to be remanded in custody for a medical report, in which the prison medical officer said that he was schizophrenic. The magistrates committed him to the same local hospital, where the responsible medical officer, to whom he was well known, soon got him to boast of having outwitted the prison medical officer. Since his offence would probably have earned him only a fine or a short period of imprisonment, if not probation, it is doubtful whether he gained much, although he may have regarded a stay in hospital at public expense as preferable to life outside.

Another offender-patient suspected of malingering was a thirty-two-year-old Scot with a long record of theft, fraud, receiving and travelling on trains without paying the fare. On this occasion he was convicted of several frauds, one of which involved persuading his employer into advancing him £140 from his future wages in order to settle the estate of his mother (whose death he had announced in a telegram which he had addressed to himself). He had at different times been a patient in four mental hospitals, at least one of which had diagnosed him as psychopathic. Having arrived at his current hospital, however, under a hospital order which classified him as mentally ill, he maintained to the responsible medical officer that he was not and never had been mentally ill, but had simply been able to pick up enough knowledge to deceive psychiatrists into thinking that he was. The medical officer could neither find any objective evidence of mental illness nor get him to admit to any symptoms of it. His subsequent career, however, suggested that this man was more disordered than he himself would admit (see pp. 197-8).

Notes to Table 17

[a] By finding a schizophrenic and a subnormal whose age did not differ by more than one year from that of each psychopath, or three years in middle-aged cases.

[b] I.e., the type of offence which appeared in the offender-patient's record more often than any other.

[c] z is calculated by Wilcoxon's signed-rank test: Y by Stuart's modification of the χ^2 test for matched pairs, using Yates' correction. See A. Stuart, 'The Comparison of Frequencies in Matched Samples', (1957), X, 1, *British Journal of Statistical Psychology, 29.*

Epileptics. One small group worth mentioning is the epileptics. The association between epilepsy and crime—especially violent crime—in which the nineteenth-century psychiatrists such as Lombroso and Maudsley firmly believed, has since been discredited but more recently rehabilitated. Scandinavian surveys[21] found that epileptics were no more likely to have convictions than any other members of the population, and were unlikely to have committed serious violence: but unfortunately these turned out to be surveys of hospital and clinic patients, which excluded prisoners. In contrast, a survey of the English prison and Borstal population in 1966 by Dr J. C. Gunn found significantly more epileptics, especially in the 25-44 age-group, than figures from general practices would lead one to expect, with a tendency to over-representation amongst violent offenders which might have proved significant had the sample been larger.[22]

Our sample contained only 4 men and 1 woman whose predominant disorder was described as epilepsy, but 2 other men were described as having epileptic personalities, and in the case of 24 other men and 6 other women epilepsy was mentioned as an associated physical or (less often) mental disorder: a total of 37. In most cases there was no obvious connection between the offence and the epilepsy. Like other disorders which handicap a person's work and social life it may simply reduce the sufferer to a condition in which he is driven to commit an offence to satisfy his needs. One case was said to be an example, however, of the classic—if rare—phenomenon of 'post-ictal automatism'. A twenty-nine-year-old man, who had received a severe head injury some twelve years before and suffered from fits, was known as a violent and domineering individual, with convictions for attempted robbery as well as shop-breaking and brothel-keeping. On three occasions he had made murderous and quite inexplicable attacks on virtual strangers without warning, immediately after a fit.[23]

Female Offender-Patients

Table 14 is the female counterpart of table 13. Before it is examined, a word or two must be said about the sex-ratio. Our males outnumbered our females by slightly more than 4:1. In the following year, however, there was a fall in the number of female hospital order cases, and the sex-ratio in the second half of the sixties was more like 7:1. A ratio of this order is close to the ratio for indictable offenders in general[24] for this period. The important fact about the sex-ratio for hospital orders, however, is that it is quite different from the sex-ratio for other compulsory admissions to mental hospitals, in which women slightly outnumber men. So far as the distribution of the sexes is concerned, offender-patients resemble offenders much more than patients.

Given this marked disproportion in numbers, one might have expected to find differences in the distributions of the current offence-types and diagnoses. In fact tables 13 and 14 are more striking for their similarity than for their differences. For easier comparison the percentages for women have been inserted in brackets beside those for men, and are remarkably similar.

Female Diagnoses. For example, the women's diagnoses were very similar in distribution to the men's. There was the same over-representation of schizophrenics and under-representation of depressives in comparison with other compulsory admissions. Amongst the schizophrenics, however, it was noticeable that women were somewhat more likely to be diagnosed as paranoid: and that the paranoid women were a much older group than their male counterparts. Again, relatively fewer women were diagnosed as cases of personality disorder. Neither of these differences will surprise psychiatrists: Lombroso himself observed that 'moral insanity' (see p. 209) was less frequent amongst women.

So far as offence-types are concerned there are two differences which are highly significant ($p < 0.001$). Female offender-patients were more often charged with a vagrancy offence, and less often with a sexual one. The female vagrants had in almost all cases been found 'sleeping rough', and in most cases refusing to go to a place of shelter when directed by the police; but one had been found begging. The great majority were in their forties or older: one first-timer was 80 years of age, a confused paranoid woman with hypertension whose history could not be obtained from her. Most of them were schizophrenic, but a small group of four were subnormal. Of the ten sexual offences committed by the women, seven consisted of soliciting by women with records of similar behaviour in the past. Three of them were the subnormal daughters of one Irish tinker, who were said by the police to have solicited in a trio in cafés. The remaining three sexual offenders were more unusual. One was a manic-depressive woman of about 70 years of age who seems to have seduced three boys of about 14. The second was a severely subnormal girl of 20 who scandalised the passengers on a London bus by lifting her clothes, making obscene gestures and shouting indecencies. The third was a young subnormal woman who had been in a training school till she was twenty. She then married a youth of 17 and had a child. Her offences were indecent assaults on several young boys and on a young girl.

The numbers of sexual offences would have been larger if we had included the 'care or protection' cases, most of which involved sexual misconduct by subnormal girls of 15 or 16 years of age. In some cases they could have been charged with soliciting or incest; but it is exceptional for the police to bring charges of soliciting or other types of sexual offence against girls under the age of 17.

Female Violence. Interestingly, offences of violence were no less common amongst the women,[25] accounting for 16 per cent of their current convictions. Of this 16 per cent (7) had killed or tried to kill their own children, usually but not always intending to take their own lives as well. In most other cases the victim was also a member of the woman's immediate family circle: her husband, brother, mother or grandmother. In one case the victim was a woman who had married the offender-patient's former boy-friend, and the motive was presumably jealousy. In two other cases, the victim was a neighbour.

Women were slightly more often convicted of drunkenness ($p = 0.025$). What was noticeable, however, was that whereas a substantial minority of the violent men had been drinking, there was no mention of alcohol in the police reports of women's violence. Another feature of women's violence was that it was more often homicidal in intention, although unfortunately the figures were too small for significance.

Most but not all of the female thieves had committed nothing worse than one or two shopliftings or other minor larcenies – usually of money, clothes, watches, rings or cosmetics. There were exceptions, however, including the forty-four-year-old Irishwoman who met a young housewife at a chapel, and as a result of a hard-luck story was taken to her home for the night. The housewife found a revolver in her guest's room, but was told reassuringly that everyone carried one in Eire. Next day the guest had disappeared, taking £18 from her benefactor's desk; and when she was arrested some months later in Northern Ireland she still had the revolver with her. She turned out to be a schizophrenic with a long record of larceny and housebreaking.

Immigrants

Increasing interest has been taken by British criminologists in the relationship between immigration and crime. Reviewing the rather sparse and patchy results of empirical studies published by 1967, A.E. Bottoms summed them up as follows:

> Crime among Irish immigrants appears to be relatively high in
> most offence groups even after allowance has been made for age.
> Qualifications need to be made however in respect of many social
> factors.
> Crime among Commonwealth immigrants tends to be generally low,
> except in crimes of violence, where, however, domestic disputes play
> an important part. . . . Similar qualifications of the data need to be
> made as in the case of the Irish. . . .[26]

A few studies have also been published on the relationship between immigration and mental disorder, with results which we shall mention in due course. We ourselves had asked hospitals for the offender-patients' places of birth and upbringing, nationality and colour: and table 18 shows the birth-places of foreign-born members of our sample, distinguished by diagnostic groups.

Several facts emerge. First, no less than 14 per cent of our men and 10 per cent of our women came from countries outside the United Kingdom: percentages considerably higher than those of foreign-born people in the general population. The biggest single source of this country's immigrants – at least in the early sixties – was the Irish Republic. Even so, that country was more strongly represented in our sample than would have been expected. It was possible to calculate, from the age-specific tables for immigrants in the 1961 Census Reports, that our sample might be expected to contain 18 men and 4 women from Eire: but the numbers were in fact 46 and 13 respectively. Jamaica, too, contributed nearly thrice the expected number of men but decidedly fewer than the expected number of women. India and Pakistan contributed no women at all, and slightly fewer than the expected number of 6·5 men. (It was not possible to make similar comparisons for other countries, either because the expected numbers were so small or because the Census classifications did not correspond with ours. Nevertheless, the numbers of men (22) from eastern Europe seemed remarkably high, even when one recalls the Polish Army and the Ukrainian and Hungarian refugees.)

Secondly, by far the commonest diagnosis amongst the immigrants was schizophrenia, which accounted for no less than 75 per cent of the males (compared with 42 per cent of all our males). Particularly striking was the over-representation of the paranoid form (20 per cent compared with 10 per cent for the whole sample). In contrast only about 5 per cent of the male immigrants were subnormal, compared with 34 per cent of our whole male sample. The women immigrants, on the other hand, showed percentages of schizophrenia and subnormality which corresponded almost exactly to those of the whole sample, and although schizophrenia among immigrant women seemed more likely to take a paranoid form, the numbers were too small for significance. (Other diagnoses were too small in numbers to make comparisons reliable.) Since schizophrenia, especially in the paranoid form, is associated, as we have seen, with offences of violence, it was not surprising to find that a very high percentage (26 per cent) of the immigrants' current offences took this form, although the percentage was even higher than was to be expected from the diagnoses alone (had they *all* been male schizophrenics one would have predicted only 20 per cent).

The extent and seriousness of the violence, however, must not be exaggerated. Only ten coloured immigrants had become offender-patients as a result of violence. In three cases the victim[9] was a policeman, and in a fourth he was a carpenter who found the offender trespassing and asked him to leave, thus provoking the attack. In no other case was the victim a stranger. More or less the same could be said of the little group of seven violent Irishmen, four of whom had become violent only when accosted by police or taken into custody. (One of the other Irishmen struck a stranger, a woman who, he said, had been staring at him; one struck a man with whom he had been arguing; and one–a heavy drinker–attacked his mistress and her mother.) The only striking crime of violence by an immigrant was that of the paranoid woman, described in chapter 5 (p. 93), who attacked a neighbour, was admitted to hospital, discharged, and then killed a man.

Since the male immigrants included so few subnormals it was not surprising to find that only a handful of their current offences were sexual. Only four of these offences involved anything more than indecent exposure: two of them were committed by European immigrants, and two by coloured men.

It is tempting to dismiss the excess of schizophrenics among our male immigrants as simply due to the under-representation of subnormals, whose handicap might be expected to hinder them from emigrating to this country, at least as adults. But this can be refuted simply by removing the subnormals from both the immigrant and the home-grown males, and comparing the percentages of schizophrenics amongst the remainder: the immigrants are still well ahead with 79 per cent as compared with 51 per cent ($p < 0.001$). Even within the limits of our sample there seems to be an association between being an immigrant and being diagnosed as schizophrenic.

TABLE 18. Diagnoses and country of origin

	Diagnoses							
	Schizophrenia				Subnormality			
Country of origin	non-paranoid		paranoid		non-severe		severe	
	M	F	M	F	M	F	M	F
Eire	28	1	5	1	4	7	1	1
North America	1	—	—	—	—	—	—	—
Australia & N.Z.	1	—	—	—	—	—	—	—
Jamaica	18	—	7	—	1	1	—	—
India & Pakistan	5	—	—	—	—	—	—	—
China & Japan (& other Asian countries)	1	—	—	—	—	—	1	—
Africa	8	—	3	—	—	—	—	—
Western Europe	1	2	4	—	—	—	—	—
Eastern Europe	10	1	8	3	—	—	—	—
Middle East	—	—	—	1	—	—	—	—
United Kingdom	223	46	63	25	256	69	66	9
Not known	2	—	—	1	2	—	—	—
Total	298	50	90	31	263	77	68	10

Reported research into the psychiatric morbidity of immigrants into Britain has been concentrated almost entirely on West Indians[27] and tends to be based on samples which seem likely to exaggerate the difference between the immigrants and the native-born population. Thus Hemsi's comparison of mental hospital admissions of West Indians and native English in Lambeth and Camberwell was unfortunately restricted to *first* admissions, so that newcomers were more likely to be included than inhabitants of long standing, who were more likely to have had their first admission before the year of the sample. Nevertheless, all the literature on immigrants, whether in Britain or in other countries, does suggest the hypothesis that in comparison with indigenous populations they are more likely to be diagnosed as mentally ill, usually with disorders of a schizophrenic or psychoneurotic type. At least one study,[28] which compared Norwegian immigrants to Minnesota with Norwegians who remained in Norway, suggested that the type of man who is likely to become schizophrenic is somewhat more likely than others to emigrate: a finding which would explain why female immigrants (who tend to accompany male emigrants rather than emigrate of their own accord) should show a lower prevalence of mental illness. Certainly our sample, with its heavy over-representation of male (but not female) schizophrenics, was consistent with the Norwegian study.

Summary

So far as age was concerned, our offender-patients were not simply a random sample of either offenders or patients. They were markedly older on the whole than the typical thief, robber, or man of violence. On the other hand, our schizophrenics—and especially those with previous

| Diagnoses | | | | | | | |
| Affective disorders | | Personality disorders | | Others | | Total | |
M	F	M	F	M	F	M	F
3	1	3	1	2	1	46	13
1	—	—	—	—	—	2	—
—	—	1	—	—	—	2	—
5	—	2	—	1	—	34	1
—	—	—	—	—	—	5	—
1	—	—	—	—	—	3	—
1	—	1	—	—	1	13	1
—	—	1	—	1	1	7	3
1	—	1	—	2	—	22	4
—	—	—	—	—	—	—	1
5	18	109	16	31	11	803	194
—	—	1	—	—	—	5	1
7	19	119	17	37	14	942	218

admissions—were somewhat younger than other compulsory and informal admissions in this diagnostic category. In contrast, our subnormals were older than those admitted in other ways. The explanation seemed to be that there was a substantial group of our subnormals who were in their late teens, having got into trouble with the law soon after emerging from the shelter of homes and schools. Nevertheless, some of our sample were surprisingly aged and active.

Yet although adult—at least in the chronological sense—most of our offender-patients were either unmarried or had broken marriages, and were living with their parents or in lodgings or institutions or had 'no fixed abode'. Work records—at least amongst the men—were very poor.

Their previous histories of admissions, convictions and trouble with police and hospitals were discouraging. At least 8 in every 9 had previously been either in hospital or in criminal courts, and half had records of both. A substantial minority of 16 per cent had records of 8 or more previous convictions, and there were striking instances of long series of (mostly trivial) convictions without any recorded psychiatric treatment. Fourteen of our sample had even incurred a hospital order twice in a twelve-month. In short, what we were sampling was largely a 'stage-army' which could appear from the direction of the hospital or the prison.

Of those with apparently 'clean' hospital and criminal records, some were juveniles, some immigrants whose records in their country of origin could not be ascertained. The percentage of genuine first-timers was very low, though higher among women than among men. There were considerably more men from Eire and Jamaica in our sample than would have been predicted from the 1961 Census, and eastern Europe was also well represented, though whether over-represented was impossible to say. Very few of our male immigrants were diagnosed as subnormal, but a remarkable number as schizophrenic.

As for the rest of our sample, three-quarters were either schizophrenic or subnormal, the former including a strong minority with a paranoid diagnosis, the latter a substantial number of severely subnormal men. In comparison with non-criminal admissions depressives were distinctly under-represented. Epilepsy was seldom diagnosed as the predominant disorder, but more often as an additional complication.

Whatever the diagnosis, by far the most common current–and previous –offence consisted of acquisitive dishonesty: theft, burglary, breaking and entering or robbery. Most were trivial, a few quite lucrative. Some were clearly irrational and attributable to a compulsion, but more often they seemed to be perfectly understandable attempts to meet the need for food, clothing, shelter or money on the part of someone whose disadvantages made it very difficult for him to meet the need legitimately.

Second equal, but far behind, came sexual offences–most of them by subnormal men–and violence, chiefly on the part of schizophrenics and depressives; and these two types of offence were much commoner than in an ordinary sample of offenders. Many of the sexual offences were trivial, involving little physical or psychological harm so far as one could tell from the police description; but some were homicidal and others must have done serious harm. About one in five of our sexual offenders had been previously convicted–some several times–of sexual offences, usually against children (who were most commonly the victims of the current offence too). So far as our sample at least was concerned, the belief that indecent exposers never or hardly ever do anything worse is a myth.

Violence, too, ranged from the homicidal to the trivial. It was seldom directed at complete strangers, although sometimes the victim was a policeman or citizen who had alarmed or provoked the offender by asking him to explain his behaviour or entering into some kind of argument with him. At least 10 per cent of our violent men had been drinking, usually in public-houses. Current violence, robbery or drunkenness were at least twice as likely to be associated with previous violence as other current offences. There were several cases in which it seemed that homicidal or serious violence could have been foreseen and prevented either by compulsory admission to hospital or by prolonging the detention of a patient already in hospital.

True to the literature, incendiarism was associated with subnormality; but other kinds of damage to property seemed more characteristic of schizophrenia, especially in its paranoid form. In this and other ways there seemed to be a tendency–though not very marked–for damage and personal violence to be associated.

Women. The similarities and differences between the two sexes are worth summarising. Although there were fewer women in our sample than there would have been had it been a sample of informal or compulsory non-criminal admissions, there were roughly as many as one would expect in a sample of ordinary indictable offenders; and while violence was over-represented amongst the men's current offences it was similarly over-represented amongst the women's. Again, though women are very rarely convicted of sexual offences–apart from soliciting–one or two of our women were; and one should not overlook the handful of 'care, protection or control' cases which involved juvenile promiscuity. On the whole, apart from a greater tendency to be convicted of vagrancy, the women's offences resembled the men's; but their violence was more often domestic–and fatal–and less often (in fact hardly ever) associated with drinking. Like ordinary women offenders, they had far fewer previous convictions, and more of them had completely 'clean' records so far as both convictions and admissions were concerned.

Excluding those with neither previous convictions nor previous hospital stays and those with both, men were more likely to have previous convictions than previous admissions, women the reverse: an observation which suggests that the female members of the stage-army make somewhat different entrances.

On the other hand, their distributions of previous hospital admissions and current diagnoses were very similar, with a minor tendency for more women schizophrenics to be diagnosed as paranoid. Their overall age-distribution was not very different, although their subnormals tended to be younger and their depressives older than their male counterparts. Proportionately more of the women had married, and fewer were living with parents, brothers or sisters. Where immigrants were concerned, Irish-women–like Irishmen–seemed over-represented, but not women from Jamaica, India or Pakistan; and the over-representation of schizophrenics among the male immigrants was absent where the women immigrants were concerned.

What final comment can be made about our cohort? To call it a 'stage army' is to some extent justified by the frequent entrances which most of its members had made, either by way of the prison gates or through the revolving doors of the mental hospitals. A stage-army, however, is a harmless group, and not all of our sample could be dismissed so lightly. Indeed, in the course of our follow-up–described in chapter 8–it seemed to us that in several cases the receiving hospitals cannot have appreciated the dangerousness of the offender-patient; and we learned with some surprise that in the ordinary course of events hospitals would not receive from the police (or the court) the details of the current offence, let alone the offender-patient's criminal record. An exception must be made in the case of those under restriction orders, police reports on whom are sent by the Home Office to the receiving hospitals. If it could be assumed that every offender-patient who had ever inflicted serious harm on someone would be subject to a restriction order this practice would be fairly reassuring; but as we have seen this is far from being the case.

A striking example of this occurred while this book was being written. A schizophrenic man in his thirties, called Michael Johnson, was admitted to a West Country hospital under a hospital order in March 1969. He had gone with a carving knife to the home of his wife, who had left him because of his violent and callous behaviour. When his wife let him in he put an arm round her neck, and with the knife in his hand pulled her towards him, saying 'I've got to do it'. A scream from one of their children caused him to release her, and the police were summoned. After a considerable struggle he was overpowered, and taken into custody. He was charged merely with 'having with him in a public place a knife', and all that the Clerk to the Justices told the prison governor about the nature of the offence was that 'the defendant took a knife to frighten his wife'. He was dealt with by means of a hospital order without restrictions on discharge, kept only for a month, and then allowed to become an out-patient. While he was an out-patient letters expressing concern were received by the hospital from his wife and from her doctor. In November he failed to keep an appointment at the hospital, and was 'discharged' (i.e., taken off the list of out-patients) in spite of the fact that his charge nurse in hospital had placed on record that Johnson would fail to take his Stelazine when not forced to. A week after his 'discharge' he stabbed his wife and himself to death. The responsible medical officer at the hospital later told a public enquiry[29] that if he had known the real circumstances he might not have admitted him (i.e., presumably might have insisted on a more secure hospital being approached).

We must not, however, over-emphasise either the dangerousness of hospital order cases or the carelessness of ordinary hospitals. As we shall see in chapter 8 (pp. 193 ff.) very few of our cohort committed really serious offences within the period of our follow-up, and of those that did even fewer were predictably dangerous. The great majority seemed to be a social nuisance rather than a menace, requiring care and management rather than strict security. The Attorney-General who introduced the Insane Offenders Bill in 1800, after Hadfield's trial, referred to *his* stage-army in his peroration:

> When we consider the circumstances of these unhappy persons, that generally they are of low habits and connexions, and seldom have any friends to take care of them, it will appear to be humane to give the executive government some discretion to dispose of them.

His language was not quite that of modern sociology or psychiatry, but otherwise it is not a bad description of *our* stage-army.

Notes

1. For that reason it is more precise to talk of 'penal careers' than of 'criminal careers'.
2. A few exceptions, such as indecent exposure, are on the Standard List of centrally recorded offences.
3. The number admitted under this section was negligible.
4. It was significant at the 0·001 level as it was.
5. Nor would the correspondence have been closer if our age-groupings had excluded members of our sample under the age of 17; in fact, the age-grouping shown seems to achieve about the closest correspondence possible.
6. Our psychopaths were not numerous enough to make the differences in distribution significant.
7. See for example, the review in W. H. Hammond and E. Chayen, *Persistent Criminals* (HMSO, 1963), 149.

8. See for instance R. v. Rolfe (1952) 36 Cr. App. R. 4.

9. The term 'victim' is used here simply to mean the other person involved, without implications as to the harm done or the initial responsibility for the act.

10. To say 'known' when the person was not tried is sometimes justifiable, for the police may have convincing evidence which cannot be used in court: for instance if parents do not wish children to give evidence.

11. The Cambridge survey of sexual offenders convicted in 1947 (see n. 12 *infra*) reported much lower percentages for a sample in which mentally disordered men were not distinguished from others. But many of their so-called 'first offenders' must have committed sexual offences which were not traced to them, as the Cambridge investigators themselves appreciated.

12. Cambridge Department of Criminal Science, *Sexual Offences* (London, 1957), 161.

13. P. H. Gebhard, J. H. Gagnon, W. B. Pomeroy, C. V. Christenson, *Sex Offenders: an analysis of types* (London, 1965), 393.

14. It is possible that some of the incidents which led to a conviction for 'indecent exposure' were in fact abortive sexual assaults, and that a conviction for indecent exposure was simply the most that the police could manage on the evidence; but we doubt whether all our examples could be explained away by this means. In any case, our point is that a record of 'indecent exposure' is not a guarantee of harmlessness.

15. We have no means of comparing our sample in this respect with compulsory admissions to hospitals without prosecution.

16. See, for example R. A. Carr-Hill, 'Victims of our Typologies' in *The Violent Offender – Reality or Illusion*? (Oxford, 1970).

17. See N. D. Walker, W. Hammond and D. J. Steer, 'Repeated violence' in [1967] Crim. L.R. 465.

18. The first year covered by the 'Ministry's Statistical Report Series no. 4' (HMSO, 1969). We were unable to obtain from the Ministry corresponding figures for compulsory admissions.

19. 71 per cent of paranoid schizophrenics had had previous admissions compared with 81 per cent of other schizophrenics: $p < 0.01$, using a one-tailed test.

20. See G. Woddis, 'Depression and Crime', in (1957) 8, *British Journal of Delinquency*, 81 ff.

21. See P. Juul-Jensen's monograph in (1964) 40, *Acta Neurologica Scandinavica* suppl. no. 5; but also the article by Gudmundsson in (1966) 43, ibid., suppl. 25, which showed that in Iceland epileptics *were* over-represented in police records.

22. See J. C. Gunn and G. Fenton, 'Epilepsy in Prisons: A Diagnostic Survey', in (1969) 4, *British Medical Journal*, 326 ff. and J. C. Gunn 'The Prevalence of Epilepsy among Prisoners', in (1969) 62, *Proceedings of the Royal Society of Medicine*, 60 ff.

23. Dr J. C. Gunn, however, has suggested that even some of the infrequent cases of post-ictal violence are the result not of automatism but of the confused and alarmed state of mind which may follow a fit. See his article 'Epilepsy, Automatism and Crime' in (1971) 1, *Lancet*, 1173 ff.

24. It is true that a substantial minority (varying from 25 to 30 per cent) of offences which lead to hospital orders are non-indictable, and that the sex-ratio for non-indictable non-motoring offences is much higher (19:1 in 1963, increasing to 30:1).

25. If men with current sexual offences are excluded from the comparison (since women are rarely accused of imprisonable sexual offences), 17 per cent of the men's current offences consisted of personal violence against persons other than police: so $p > 0.1$.

26. See A. E. Bottoms, 'Delinquency amongst Immigrants' in (1967) VIII, 4, *Race*, 357 ff.

27. See L. K. Hemsi, 'Psychiatry Morbidity of West Indian Immigrants' in (1967) 2, *Social Psychiatry*, 95. Other inconclusive studies are those of A. Kiev, 'Psychiatric Morbidity in West Indian Immigrants in Urban Group Practice' in (1965) 3, *British Journal of Psychiatry*, 51 and R. J. F. H. Pinsent, 'Morbidity in an Immigrant Population' in (1963) 1, *Lancet*, 437, whose data came from general practice and thus excluded persons whose conditions had led to hospitalisation.

28. See Ø. Ødegaard in (1932) *Acta Psychiatrica et Neurologica*, Suppl. 4. An obvious query is whether hospitalisation was not a more likely consequence of mental disorder in Minnesota than in Norway. But if so one would expect (*a*) that rates for *other* mental disorders would be higher in the Minnesota immigrants than amongst stay-at-home Norwegians; (*b*) that the reported duration of the schizophrenic disorder before hospitalisation would tend to be shorter in Minnesota than in Norway; and neither of these expectations was confirmed. As for the possibility that it was the stress of coping with a new environment and unsympathetic native population that increased the schizophrenia rate, 9 per cent of the schizophrenic Norwegian immigrants were reported to have been disordered before arrival, while 70 per cent were reported to have shown no symptoms until at least 5 years after arrival; in other words only 21 per cent appear to have developed the disorder in their first five years in Minnesota. Moreover, the age-distribution of onset did not differ significantly from that of stay-at-home Norwegian schizophrenics.

29. The report of which was made available to the Press—and to us—by the South Western Regional Hospital Board. Consequently, we felt free to use the patient's name.

Chapter 7. In and Out of Hospital

When tracing the careers of our offender-patients after their entry into hospital[1] we had perforce to be content with a 'paper follow-up', based on information supplied either by the hospitals themselves in answers to questionnaires or else by the Criminal Records Office, the Mental Health Enquiry Statistics Office or the records office of the then Ministry of Social Security. We should have liked to organise a more personal follow-up of offender-patients who left hospital, but were dissuaded by one of our psychiatric advisers, who felt very strongly that this would be regarded by many psychiatrists and ex-patients as an improper intrusion. The procedures which we used instead are described in Appendix C.

We also wrote to all the 229 hospitals which had not received any of our cases, asking the reason. Most of them replied helpfully and informatively. In one or two cases the fact that the hospitals in question–which included one or two very large ones–received no hospital order cases in the year of our sample seemed due to pure chance. Some of the small hospitals turned out to be little more than convalescent homes or hostels, receiving only specially selected patients from other hospitals who needed minimal care. Others said simply that they had not been asked to receive any, although they tended to add that there would be difficulties about secure detention. In some cases Regional Boards or Management Committees had decided that patients requiring compulsory detention, and especially those from the criminal courts, should be received only by selected hospitals, so as to allow the remainder to operate with the minimum of restraint on patients' movements. One or two hospitals accepted offender-patients but preferred them to be under psychiatric probation orders, either because of the after-care which the probation officer provided or because they believed that offenders responded better if they were 'informal' patients. (Strictly speaking, this reasoning was illegitimate, since the 1948 Act expressly limits psychiatric probation orders to mental conditions which are not such as to 'warrant' detention under a hospital order; but as we saw in chapter 5 the meaning of 'warrant' is so unclear that any psychiatrist could be forgiven for overlooking this.)

It was also plain, not only from our sample but also from published statistics for the years 1964–6[2] that teaching hospitals accepted only a handful of cases from the criminal courts each year. The reason may be partly that offender-patients tend to be clinically uninteresting; we saw in the previous chapter how few of ours received any of the rarer psychiatric labels. No doubt, however, the troublesome behaviour of many offender-patients in hospital is another disincentive. Ironically, now that Bethlem is a teaching hospital it seldom receives an offender-patient.

The Special Hospitals. Psychopaths apart, only 6 per cent of our men went to Special Hospitals. (The percentage for women was suspect, for the reason given in the footnote to table 21.) Not surprisingly, however, the percentage for psychopaths was much higher: 34 per cent. If psychopathic males were excluded, the other main diagnostic groups were represented in the Special Hospitals to a strikingly proportionate extent:

	Ordinary hospitals %	*Special hospitals* %
Schizophrenia	47·3	44·9
Subnormality	40·2	40·8
Affective disorder	8·0	10·2
Other disorder	4·5	4·1

Broadmoor, Rampton and Moss Side are under considerable pressure to accept prospective hospital order cases which are believed to be dangerous or even merely troublesome, partly because ordinary hospitals fight shy of such patients, partly because courts have more confidence—and rightly, as we shall see—in the security of the Special Hospitals. Requests from prison medical officers for beds in one of these hospitals are channelled through the Department of Health and Social Security as the authority responsible for them. In deciding, however, whether to accept a patient that Department have regard not merely to the wishes of the medical witnesses and the vacancies in the appropriate Special Hospital, but also to the opinion of the latter's senior staff as to whether the proposed patient really could not reasonably be sent to an ordinary mental hospital. Broadmoor, in particular, being under the greatest pressure of all, is frequently asked by the Department of Health and Social Security to send one of its consultants to examine the offender and discuss his case with the medical witnesses before advising his acceptance or rejection.

The Unplaced Patient. Occasionally it seems to happen that an offender who is recognised by psychiatrists and the court to be in need of a hospital order cannot be made the subject of one because the court has not been told that a hospital has made arrangements to admit him. The reason is usually that the local hospitals have refused to admit him. In one such case an offender was sentenced early in 1961 to five years' imprisonment. When questions were asked about him in Parliament the Minister of Health (Mr Enoch Powell) replied that he had 'every reason to believe that suitable hospital accommodation was available if the doctor responsible had made due inquiry'.[3] Nevertheless our survey showed that three years later it was still possible for a hospital order to be frustrated in much the same way. A man in his twenties was made the subject of a hospital order by a magistrates' court, apparently in the expectation of a vacancy at a local hospital. For some reason this did not materialise, nor would any hospital in the region accept him. The Act lays down that the offender must be admitted to the hospital named in the order within 28 days of the date of the order, although if within that period some special circumstances or emergency (such as, presumably, a fire at the hospital) makes this impracticable the Minister of Health can substitute another hospital. If neither of these things is done within the 28 days, the order lapses. Consequently, our prospective offender-patient had to be set free.

Regional Differences. Leaving aside the Special Hospitals, which are the direct responsibility of the Department of Health and Social Security, the 151 receiving hospitals were under the general management of the 15 Regional Hospital Boards. Table 19 therefore subdivides our offender-patients according to region, omitting those who went to Special Hospitals. It can be seen at a glance that two-fifths of them went to hospitals in one of the four Metropolitan regions, and indeed that 18 per cent of them went to one region, the South West Metropolitan.

How disproportionate were the different regions' shares of our cohort? A rough answer can be got by showing them as rates per 100,000 population of each region, as has been done in columns C and D. But this would fail to take account of two factors. In the first place, some hospitals in some regions accept patients from neighbouring regions: in 1963 – and for some years afterwards – subnormality hospitals in the Manchester region admitted cases from the Liverpool region. This factor is of particular importance where the South West Metropolitan Region is concerned; for in the mid-sixties four of its large hospitals – Cane Hill, Horton, Long Grove and Springfield – admitted substantial numbers of patients from the other three Metropolitan Regions. Consequently, to relate admissions to regional population in these cases would be misleading. Secondly, psychiatric morbidity varies in prevalence from one area to another. For both reasons it is better to relate the regional distribution of our cohort to the numbers of admissions of all kinds to mental illness and mental subnormality hospitals in each region: and this has been done in columns E and F. It can be seen that there is still a striking variation in the percentages of admissions which are arranged by the criminal courts.

Here again, of course, administrative factors are at work. At least part of the reason why the South West Metropolitan Region still tops the league is the fact that its catchment area embraces busy criminal courts such as Bow Street and Marlborough Street. It also includes Brixton Prison, through which a very large percentage of the whole country's hospital order cases pass. It is true that not all hospital order cases from these courts or this prison go to local hospitals; for hospitals will often refuse to admit people who live outside their catchment areas. A high percentage, however, of cases passing through Brixton are 'homeless' – that is, are living in lodgings, or institutions, or are of 'no fixed abode' (the last being so common that it is abbreviated to 'N.F.A.'). It is difficult for hospitals to apply the catchment area principle to such cases, and this no doubt largely explains why the South West Metropolitan Region's cases contain such a high percentage of homeless cases (see column K).

It seems likely that at least some of the variations in subnormality rates (shown in column J) are also due to an administrative factor: the distribution of large mental subnormality hospitals. As we have seen, the

TABLE 19. Hospital orders and Hospital Board Regions. Notes: see p. 161

Region		Hospital order cases in the Oxford Survey cohort[a]						Discharges by operation of law per 100 hospital orders[d]	Abscondings per 100 hospital orders[d]	Schizophrenia rate[e,d]	Subnormality rate per 100 hospital orders[f,d]	Homelessness rate per 100 hospital orders[g,d]
		Numbers		As rate per 100,000 of population[b]		As rate per 100 hospital admissions[c]						
		A	B	C	D	E %	F %	G	H	I	J	K
		Men	Women	Men	Women	Men	Women	Men only %	Men only %	Men only %	Men only %	Men only %
Newcastle		22	1	1·45	0·65	0·47	0·16	9·1	22·7	69·2	40·9	45·5
Leeds		47	12	3·05	0·74	0·91	0·16	12·8	25·5	83·9	34·0	44·7
Sheffield		40	10	1·71	0·44	0·73	0·14	10·0	15·0	64·0	37·5	37·5
East Anglia		17	2	2·14	0·25	0·81	0·06	5·9	5·9	44·4	47·1	52·9
Oxford		11	3	1·26	0·34	0·53	0·10	—	18·2	50·0	27·3	18·2
South Western		67	9	4·61	0·59	1·50	0·12	7·5	23·9	43·3	55·2	41·8
Welsh		42	10	3·19	0·74	0·95	0·19	2·4	16·7	39·5	9·5	38·1
Birmingham		97	19	3·98	0·76	1·33	0·20	5·2	24·7	51·4	25·8	44·3
Manchester		87	30	4·02	1·29	1·65	0·39	10·3	23·0	45·6	34·5	37·9
Liverpool		23	5	2·28	0·43	0·54	0·09	4·4	26·1	52·6	17·4	56·5
Wessex		32	6	3·47	0·65	1·03	0·12	—	18·8	66·7	15·6	34·4
North West ⎱ Metro-		48	23	2·40	1·03	0·98	0·35	6·3	25·0	45·2	35·4	52·1
North East ⎰ politan		30	8	1·94	0·46	0·84	0·14	—	20·0	68·0	16·7	36·7
South East ⎱		78	24	4·80	1·33	1·59	0·33	5·1	20·5	51·3	50·0	51·9
South West ⎰		182	46	11·87	2·70	2·16	0·39	18·1	20·9	78·8	14·3	73·1
Combined Metropolitan		338	101	5·65	1·36	1·56	0·32	11·8	21·3	69·3	25·7	61·9
All regions		823	208	3·57	0·86	1·17	0·28	9·0	21·3	60·7	29·5	49·9
				p < 0·001	p < 0·001	p < 0·001	p < 0·001	p < 0·001	NS	p < 0·001	p < 0·001	p < 0·001

Manchester Region took some of the Liverpool Region's subnormal patients. This cannot, however, explain the variations in the schizophrenia rate, since we have deliberately excluded subnormality cases when calculating this, in order to ensure that any variations were not merely the complement of variations in subnormality rates. Since mental illness hospitals admit a mixture of diagnostic categories, variations in the schizophrenia-rate cannot be explained administratively. Nor can it be explained as a reflection of different diagnostic ideologies: this is plausible where different countries are concerned, but not where the problem is regional variation. There are even marked differences between the London Regions. It is difficult to escape the conclusion that this particular regional variation –if no other–does reflect differences in the types of disordered offender with which different courts are being presented. The drift of schizophrenics to the Metropolis is a well-known phenomenon, and the areas to which they tend to drift were in most cases those from which the South West Metropolitan Region admitted patients at this time: Paddington, Notting Hill Gate, Southwark, Camberwell, Lambeth, Bethnal Green, Poplar and Stepney. Quite apart from the drift, however, these were areas with high prevalences of social pathology, including in many cases high schizophrenia rates.[4]

These points may also help to explain other regional anomalies, although we have neither the time nor the knowledge to discuss them all, and will confine ourselves to a few points. Wales, nearly all of whose rates are low, has exceptionally small percentages for both schizophrenia and subnormality; the reason may be the over-representation of psychopaths, due to the attractions of Dr Craft's unit for them in North Wales. Manchester's high rate for women's hospital orders probably results from the presence of a remand prison for women, just as Holloway must contribute to the high rate in the North East Metropolitan Region (but note that the South West Metropolitan Region, with no women's prison, still tops the league: a clear indication of social pathology in the population). Other aspects of our regional comparison will be discussed later in this chapter as they become relevant.

In Hospital. Although we were concerned with the operational aspects of hospital orders rather than psychiatric practice, our six- and twelve-

---

Notes to Table 19

[a] Excluding cases received into Special Hospitals, which are not the responsibility of Regional Hospital Boards. (Teaching hospitals did not receive any of our offender-patients.)

[b] As estimated for 1964. *Source:* Ministry of Health Statistical Report Series No. 4

[c] *Source:* Ministry of Health Statistical Report Series No. 4.

[d] The numbers of women involved were too small for significant comparisons.

[e] Calculated on the basis of hospital orders minus diagnoses of subnormality, for reasons given in the text above. In view of Oxford's small numbers, it was combined with the South West when 'p' was calculated.

[f] Calculated on the basis of all hospital orders, including those with a diagnosis of subnormality.

[g] Defined as 'not living at the time of the current offence with parents, spouse, relatives, cohabitee or friend'.

M

month questionnaires asked, 'What forms of treatment has he received?' Drugs apart, the commonest reply was 'occupational therapy', which was mentioned in 45 per cent of cases. Next most frequent were 'habit training' and 'supervision' (35 per cent): the former, of course, was particularly common where subnormal patients were concerned. Psychotherapy was mentioned in 20 per cent of questionnaires, and group therapy in 5 per cent. Only one of our cohort underwent leucotomy—which had gone out of fashion by the early sixties in most hospitals—although one of our offender-patients had undergone it about a year before the incident which brought him into our sample: in neither case were the results impressive.

Although we did not regard the replies to this question as a very reliable indication of what was actually being done to the offender-patient, we were struck by the fact that where information about treatment *was* given the three most frequently mentioned forms (apart from drugs) were non-medical; that is, of kinds which are usually left to occupational therapists and nursing staff. It is true that psychotherapy, too, is sometimes given by non-medical staff; but if anything this reinforces our observation. Indeed, it would be possible to go further, and point out that the activity which must take up most patient-hours in any type of mental hospital (apart from sleep) is occupational therapy, and that very much the same could be said of prisons, although the term used in their case is 'work'. Invidious though this comparison sounds, it is not intended as a criticism of occupational therapy. What is interesting to the detached observer is the intense criticism to which prison work is subjected, and the comparative rarity of any critical examination of the nature of occupational therapy.[5]

Security. Since security is a consideration which is very much in the minds of sentencers who are considering the making of a hospital order, we asked (both in the dossier and in the six- and twelve-month questionnaires) about the restrictions on the offender-patient's freedom which were thought necessary at the moment. Since few of the follow-up questionnaires indicated much change in the original restrictions, the latter are summarised here, Special Hospital patients being excluded:

	Men	Women
	%	%
Under no restrictions	10	12
Allowed parole in grounds	35	35
Under observation by nurses	18	23
In locked wards	35	28
Under maximum security	2	–

It can be seen that so far as the ordinary hospital is concerned, only 37 per cent of our men and 28 per cent of our women were in locked wards. Nor is even a locked ward a precaution of high security. Dr Rollin, writing of Horton Hospital, says that it offers 'no more than token security'.[6] Dr Antebi, writing of All Saints Hospital, Birmingham, is even more concrete: 'the absconder is as likely to escape from a locked ward as from an open one', although he admits that escapes from locked wards occurred during 'periods of freedom . . . granted . . . in an attempt at rehabilitation'.[7]

In her survey of subnormality hospitals in 1965,[8] Mrs Morris found that nearly a third of her sample of subnormal patients compulsorily detained in ordinary hospitals were allowed to wander freely in the grounds, while another third were allowed out of the ward alone or with other patients, only a third being confined to the wards. Although we could not categorise our replies in precisely the same way, our percentage of subnormal offender-patients who were in locked wards or under maximum security precautions was also about one third, while the percentage allowed 'ground parole' or greater freedom was considerably higher than in her sample. In other words the statistics strongly suggested that as a whole our sample of subnormals were not subjected to more restrictions than they would have been had they been admitted as compulsory patients without having been convicted of an offence. No doubt there were cases in which restrictions were imposed because of the offender-patient's breach of the law; all we can say is that so far as ordinary subnormality hospitals were concerned these cannot have been numerous.

Leaving Hospital. Perhaps the most important aspect of any system for dealing with mentally disordered offenders is the procedures by which they can obtain their legal freedom. From this point of view English mental hospital patients fall into three main categories, which are set out schematically overleaf.

An informal patient may walk out of the hospital whenever he pleases. In theory the medical staff can prevent this by arranging quickly for his compulsory 'admission'.[9] In practice, however, this seems to be a rarely used expedient, probably because its use would discourage people from entering voluntarily. Consequently even a probationer whose probation order includes a requirement that he shall be an in-patient at a named mental hospital is free to leave at any time. Grünhut, studying a sample from the mid-nineteen-fifties, found that as many as one in four probationer-patients did so.[10] It is true that the defecting probationer-patient risks being brought back to court, where he may well receive an ordinary custodial sentence, but this seldom happens.[11]

Quite a few compulsory patients are reclassified as informal within a few months of admission, so that they can leave whenever they wish, although most of them probably abide by their psychiatrist's advice. The need for compulsory detention must in any case be reviewed by the responsible medical officer in the tenth or eleventh month of their stay, and if he reports to the managers that it should continue the authority for detention is automatically renewed for a year (or two years if it has been renewed before). Another possibility for some patients is that their nearest relative will exercise his or her power to demand their discharge; but this demand can be vetoed by the responsible medical officer if he considers that the patient would be dangerous to himself or others.

The intention of the Act was that the offender-patient should be so far as possible in the same position as other compulsory patients, unless a higher court had placed the patient in a special category by adding a restriction order (which will be discussed in the next chapter). Consequently, nearly all the escape-routes which we have mentioned are open to them. Understandably, on the whole, an offender-patient's nearest rela-

Category	Mode of discharge
'Informal' (i.e. voluntary)	by 'discharging oneself'[a] on medical advice[a] on arrest by the police[a]
Compulsory (including hospital order cases not under a restriction on discharge)	with permission from the responsible medical officer[b] (s. 47)
	at the request of one's nearest relative (except in hospital order cases) but subject to medical veto (s. 47)
	'by operation of the law' (i.e., by absconding for the necessary period) (s. 40)
	as a result of a court decision (e.g., on appeal against a hospital order) (ss. 69, 70)
	by direction of a Mental Health Review Tribunal (ss. 122-4)
	by the expiry of a time-limit (e.g., the first twelve months) without renewal of the authority (s. 43)
	on being reclassified as informal and discharging oneself (s. 38)
	on spending more than six months under a custodial sentence (s. 46)
Under restriction (including persons found not guilty by reason of insanity, or unfit to plead, and transferred prisoners whose date for release is not past)	at the instance of the responsible medical officer,[b] but with the Home Secretary's consent (s. 66)
	as a result of the expiry of a time-limit on the restriction, in one of the ways open to compulsory patients (see above) (ss. 63, 65)
	by direction of the Home Secretary (s. 66)

[a] Since an informal patient is under no legal restraint, these are not strictly speaking ways of obtaining one's legal freedom from compulsory detention.
[b] Or the hospital managers, who very occasionally overrule the responsible medical officer.

tive is not allowed to demand his release if he has been committed by a criminal court, just as a prisoner's freedom cannot be demanded by his nearest relative. But with this exception the offender-patient has the same rights as the man or woman in the next bed who has been admitted compulsorily without prosecution.

Absconding. A simpler and more popular road to freedom is absconding. As we have seen above, Special Hospitals apart, the open door policy means that only a minority of compulsory patients are in locked wards.[12] Others are restrained from leaving by being deprived of day clothes, or by a system of passes at the hospital gates; but in most cases the restraint is psychological. Some compulsory patients are allowed to leave the hospital grounds on 'day parole', on week-end visits to their families, or on longer absences with permission. 'Absconding' therefore includes everything from breaking out of a locked ward to a mere failure to return from leave. There is no automatic hue and cry when a compulsory patient absconds. On the contrary the Ministry of Health's memorandum of advice[13] says that 'calls on the police for this purpose should be kept to a minimum', although it makes it clear that the police should at once be informed of the absence without leave of a 'dangerous' patient.

Indeed, although absconders have received little attention in what has been written about the Act,[14] the medical profession has coined its own euphemisms for this unofficial type of exit. The patient who leaves without his doctor's approval is said to 'discharge himself',[15] and if he remains at large for the necessary period is said to have been 'discharged by operation of the law' (or 'd.o.l.'). Historically, this means of securing one's freedom was instituted–in the Lunacy Act of 1890–as a safeguard for the patient against unjustified or unnecessarily prolonged detention. It was based on the rough-and-ready assumption that if he could not only escape but also contrive to evade recapture for a substantial period he could not be so incompetent after all. The situation has now changed. The locked gates and high walls of the Victorian asylum have been replaced by 'the open door'. Moreover, as we have pointed out, there is no automatic hue and cry after the great majority of absconders; indeed, they are often regarded as nuisances whom the hospital is only too glad to be able to 'take off its books' after the statutory period has elapsed. Consequently, remaining at large for this period is no longer the test of ingenuity which it was–or was assumed to be–in Victorian times.

One of the minor curiosities of the 1959 Act is the way in which this provision was applied to hospital order cases in the same way as to other compulsory admissions. The Percy Commission simply recommended the extension of the period[16] to 28 days (but 6 months in the case of psychopaths over the age of 21 because 'it might take more than 28 days to find such a patient'!). Since they were at pains to place hospital order cases on all fours with other compulsory patients so far as possible, the only exceptions which they recommended were restriction order cases.

It has been argued by Dr P. Grahame Woolf,[17] on the basis of his experience with subnormal patients at Darenth Park, that 28 days is too short a period for hospital order patients, who are attracted by what they–often rightly–regard as a very easy way out of hospital. He suggests that the period should be six months for all hospital patients, and not merely (as at present) psychopaths and subnormals who are over the age of 21. Indeed, one might go further, and argue that the justification for extending this protection against unnecessary detention to hospital order cases re-quires consideration. *Pace* the Percy Commission, such cases cannot be regarded as completely on all fours with other compulsory patients, as has been acknowledged by their exclusion from the provision which allows their nearest relative to demand their release. Discharge by operation of the law makes sense of a sort when the choice is between compulsory hospitalisation and freedom. But in the case of hospital order patients the choice is between compulsory hospitalisation and some other measure open to the courts; and in practice the alternative which is in the mind of most sentencers in such cases is prison or Borstal. A prisoner or Borstal inmate cannot obtain his legal freedom by absconding, and a probationer who tries to terminate his supervision in this way can be brought back to court to be dealt with for his original offence. If, of course, one could argue that hospital order patients are assumed to have so little responsibility for their offences that they should be excused punishment, one might then be able to argue that they should enjoy whatever protection other compulsory patients have; but as we have seen in chapter 5 this is not the assumption upon which Section 60 is based. The court's reason for deciding that a hospital order is 'the most suitable method of disposing of the case' *may* be based on the view that the offender's culpability is diminished by his disorder; but it may equally well be based on the assumption that in-patient treatment is most likely to reform him, however culpable he may be. If so, should he be allowed to terminate treatment when he, rather than his responsible medical officer, thinks fit? It cannot be argued in the case of offender-patients that the ability to remain at large for the necessary period is good evidence that they need no further treatment, for—as we shall see—being d.o.l. is significantly associated with a probability of further reconviction.

The truth is that discharge by operation of the law is a very crude and questionable safeguard even where other compulsory patients are concerned. It dates from a time when the only other safeguard against the unscrupulous relative and the complaisant doctor was the Justice of the Peace. Now that the patient—including the hospital order patient—can have recourse to a Mental Health Review Tribunal (see p. 167), is there a need for it? So far as hospital orders are concerned the issue is by no means academic. No less than 78 of our men and 26 of our women gained their legal freedom in this way within twelve months of being committed to hospital. Indeed, one man had to be excluded altogether from our sample because he succeeded in absconding while being escorted from prison to hospital, and remained at large long enough to gain his legal freedom, so that his dossier was never completed.

On the other hand, there is at least one practical argument in favour of the provision. Without it, the ex-patient remains a perpetual fugitive, at risk of being retaken at any time. This may drive him into a more unnatural way of life, such as vagrancy. A time-limit allows him to 'come out into the open', and does not prevent his being rehospitalised if his later behaviour appears to justify this. It is an argument which must carry some weight, and for this reason we content ourselves with presenting the two points of view.

None of our cohort succeeded in absconding for long from a Special Hospital. In contrast, absconding was common amongst unrestricted offender-patients in ordinary hospitals, and especially amongst schizophrenics and psychopaths, of whom one in every seven absconded during his or her first year. There were even five restricted offender-patients who managed to abscond in their first year, a fact which emphasises that a restriction order is no guarantee of secure custody: we shall return to this subject later.

There was considerable variation between regions in the percentage of our offender-patients[18] who managed to gain their legal freedom in this way (see table 19). This was in contrast to the rate of ordinary absconding, which did not vary greatly. Only one region, East Anglia, had a markedly abnormal absconding rate (in this case well below the national average) and it had too few of our offender-patients for any calculation of significance. The d.o.l. rate, however, varied from nil (in Oxford, Wessex and the North East Metropolitan Regions) to 18 per cent in the South West Metropolitan Region. A nil rate must be at least partly a matter of luck; but the same cannot be said of a rate of nearly one in every five. It was the South West Metropolitan Region, it will be recalled, which topped the league for admissions per head of population and hospital orders per head admitted. Its d.o.l. rate was twice the national average, whereas the other metropolitan regions' rates were below it. No other region came anywhere near it: Leeds was a poor second with 140 per cent of the average.

Mental Health Review Tribunals. Next, there is the possibility of discharge by the direction of one of the Mental Health Review Tribunals. These were created by the 1959 Act,[19] on the recommendation of the Percy Commission,[20] as a new kind of safeguard against the unnecessary use of compulsory powers of detention. Instead of requiring that the power of compulsory detention should be exercised by Justices of the Peace or other judicial authority,[21] the Act simply allows the patient to apply to the tribunal for his Hospital Board Region[22] for a direction that he be discharged.

If he is to exercise this right he must do so within six months of his admission[23] (or his sixteenth birthday, whichever is the later). Offenders subject to hospital or guardianship orders and sentenced prisoners transferred to mental hospitals[24] have the same right, unless the offender is subject to a restriction which gives the Home Secretary control over his discharge. Since the compulsory detention of these offenders has been initiated by a judicial body—in this case a criminal court—the case for providing them with the same substitute for judicial protection is not so obvious. The Percy Commission did not explain it, but seem simply to have assumed that in this respect, as in almost all others, the offender-patient should be on all fours with the non-criminal patient who has been compulsorily admitted for treatment. Perhaps the soundest argument is that since the authority for detention conferred by a hospital order can be renewed without reference to the court (see p. 164), quite a trivial imprisonable offence can result in detention for several years (see p. 177), so that some sort of safeguard is required. If so, however, it would be more logical to confine it to cases in which the authority for detention *has* been renewed.

The powers and duties of the tribunals, too, are not altogether self-explanatory where offender-patients are concerned. First, a tribunal *may* direct discharge *in any case* which is the subject of an application to them; and while they are obliged by rules[25] to record their reasons for doing so there seems to be no statutory limitation on the grounds on which they may come to such a decision. On the other hand, they are *obliged* to direct discharge in certain situations. If they are satisfied that the patient is not *at the time of application* suffering from mental illness, psychopathic disorder, subnormality or severe subnormality, they must order him to be discharged. It is true that the same section (s. 123) also obliges them to direct discharge if satisfied that his continued detention is 'not necessary in the interests of the patient's health or safety, or for the protection of other persons'. But this is an *alternative* and not an *additional* necessary condition. In other words, a patient (or his legal representative) could argue that while he had been sufficiently depressed at the time of admission to make an attempt to kill himself and his family, he had now made a good recovery, and was no longer mentally ill. If it were objected that his past history demonstrated a tendency to relapse after discharge, making him a danger to himself and his family, he could safely admit this. For he would be able to insist that if satisfied that he was at the moment no longer mentally ill the tribunal *must* direct his discharge.[26] It could not properly ask whether the other necessary condition was fulfilled; for, as has been pointed out, this is not an additional but an alternative consideration.[27] So far as offender-patients are concerned the law is thus curiously reminiscent of the eighteenth century, when offenders who had successfully pleaded insanity were held to be entitled to release from custody if they recovered their sanity, sometimes with dire results.[28]

This being so, it is fortunate that an attempt by Mr Kenneth Robinson during the passage of the Bill[29] to extend this provision to restriction orders was unsuccessful. The Parliamentary Secretary (Mr David Renton) pointed out that the Bill gave the Home Secretary the right to refer such cases to a tribunal for advice (which would not, of course, be binding). As a concession, however, he initiated a Government amendment which gave the patient the right to insist on having his case referred to a tribunal for advice (see s. 66(6) and (7)).

The operation of these tribunals has been described by Professor Greenland,[30] who was able to attend personally a considerable number of hearings in the first half of the year 1967. All that we need therefore do is examine the twelve cases from our cohort in which offender-patients were discharged by direction of a tribunal. With the help of the Ministry and the consent of the chairmen of the tribunals concerned we were able to ascertain the officially recorded reason for the tribunal's decisions. In nearly all the cases this was simply that in the tribunal's view it was not 'necessary in the interests of the patient's health or safety or for the protection of other persons that he should continue to be liable to be detained'. In one case the tribunal had added that it was satisfied that the patient was not suffering from mental illness: he was a man with no criminal or psychiatric record who had sent a threatening letter to a person whom he suspected of having him dismissed from his job, and had been diagnosed as being a 'paranoid personality' in a 'paranoid state'. In one remarkable case a man who had originally been classified as 'severely 'subnormal' (with hydrocephalus) was described by the tribunal as of 'average intelligence'.[31]

Five out of twelve offender-patients whom the tribunals discharged were reconvicted during our two year follow-up, some of them several times, and one of them within nine days of discharge. In most cases the offences involved only petty dishonesty or disorderly conduct, which did not cast doubt on the wisdom of the tribunal's view that continued detention was not needed for the protection of others. One was a case of the kind deprecated in the Lord Chief Justice's practice direction in Gardiner's case (see pp. 94-5): an offender-patient who had been considered dangerous enough to be sent to a Special Hospital, but who had not been made the subject of a restriction order. The tribunal were thus able to direct his discharge, on the grounds that while he was still suffering from subnormality his continued detention was not necessary in the interests of his own health or safety or for the protection of others. (He was subsequently reconvicted, first for stealing and later for possessing an offensive weapon.) Another subnormal, young and obstreperous, was later convicted of 'wounding with intent'. And there was one case in which the tribunal's reasoning was questionable, both *prima facie* and in the light of the consequences. This involved a psychopathic paedophile in his thirties, with a long record of indecent assaults on boys. The responsible medical officer's prognosis, which we quote with his leave, was 'pretty hopeless: custody for the rest of his life if it were left to me'. The tribunal, however,

> were of the opinion that, although it might be desirable for the protection of other persons that the applicant should be liable to be detained in some institution, the applicant is not able to benefit from medical treatment and that accordingly it would not be proper that he should be liable to be detained in a mental hospital.

This reasoning seems open to two criticisms. In the first place, it rests on the assumption that detention in a mental hospital is justifiable only if the patient is able to benefit from 'medical treatment': an assumption based on a very questionable interpretation of Section 4 of the Act which we discuss on pp. 223 ff. Secondly, even if we overlook the first criticism, the decision argues as if the Tribunal felt that it would be improper to detain the patient further; that is, *as if they had no choice* but to order his discharge. We have seen that in certain situations tribunals *are* obliged to do this; but the situation which they describe here is not one of these. The tribunal therefore had discretion whether to direct that this offender-patient should be discharged. This being so, it is legitimate to question the wisdom of directing the discharge of a person from whom, on the tribunal's own admission, other persons needed protection. The tribunal might argue that this case points to a defect in the statutory system, which does not allow such an offender-patient to be transferred to prison, or even brought back to court with a view to a prison sentence for the protection of the public. Arguable as this is, it does not absolve them from the duty of operating the system as it happens to be; and to order a dangerous patient to be set free because he cannot be transferred to prison is an odd way of doing so. It is worth recording that within a few months of discharge this particular offender-patient had been reconvicted of three more indecent assaults, with a fourth 'taken into consideration', and had been made the subject of another hospital order.

Further Prosecution. Whatever a patient's status–informal, compulsory or under hospital order–it does not *in law* protect him against arrest or prosecution. It is true that police are reluctant to prosecute inmates of psychiatric hospitals. In the small survey of unprosecuted offenders which we describe in Appendix A there was a case in which the police said that it was 'impossible' to prosecute because the person involved was a compulsory patient, meaning no doubt that it was morally rather than legally out of the question. Indeed, in the majority of cases in that survey the decision not to prosecute was attributable to the knowledge that the suspect was an in-patient, out-patient, ex-patient or absconder from a mental hospital. Some offenders are aware of this policy and enter hospital in an attempt, which sometimes succeeds, to avoid criminal proceedings.

Nevertheless, a small percentage of our first-year leavers departed under arrest. All were in ordinary hospitals. We expected to find that they had committed crimes so grave that the police must have felt they could not have been left unprosecuted. In fact most of their offences seemed trivial. One depressive inadequate youth was arrested in a town near his hospital for being drunk and disorderly and sentenced to two months' imprisonment. Another subnormal young man absconded and after several larcenies was sent to Borstal. More dangerous was the twenty-eight-year-old schizophrenic, who had been committed to an ordinary hospital after his 'voices' had made him attack an eight-year-old girl (in a non-sexual way). He believed that 'all children are monsters', and nine months later, apparently while under 'nursing observation', stole a child and its pram from a shopping centre. He was found by the police on a cliff top, from which he said he was going to throw the pram and its contents. Convicted of child stealing, he was committed to Broadmoor by Quarter Sessions, with an indeterminate restriction order.

It should be noted, by the way, that neither arrest nor prosecution terminates the hospital's authority to detain the patient. Indeed, the authority remains in force even if he is convicted and sentenced, unless the sentence is a custodial one for a period of more than six months (see s. 46) or unless he is made subject to a new hospital or guardianship order (see s. 63(5)). Moreover, if he is subject to a restriction order, not even a custodial sentence of any length, or a new hospital or guardianship order, supersedes it (Third Schedule and s. 65(4)). Our impression is, however, that in practice hospitals very seldom reassert their right to detain the offender-patient after he has been dealt with again by a court, unless he is subject to a restriction order.

Discharge on Medical Advice. The great majority who left hospital, however, did so with the approval of the responsible medical officer. Depressive patients, for whom electro-convulsion therapy and chemotherapy offer real hope of lasting improvement, were especially likely to leave early, and about one in four did so within the first three months. The length of time spent in hospital by offender-patients in our cohort who, within the first two years, were discharged from ordinary hospitals by their responsible medical officers was interesting:

	Males	*Females*
	%	%
Under 1 month	3·7	8·0
1-3 months	16·8	14·1
3-6 months	20·7	18·6
6-9 months	12·2	15·9
9-12 months	15·3	15·0
over 12 months	31·3	28·4

There was no difference worth consideration between the distributions of men and women. Two-fifths of those discharged within two years were out within six months, and almost 70 per cent within a year. Moreover, when we looked more closely at those who were discharged in their second year, we found that in the majority of cases this had happened within a month or two of the end of their first year. Our impression is that when the time comes at which the responsible medical officer must decide whether to go through the procedure for extending the statutory twelve-month period of compulsory detention his solution is often to allow the patient's status to become 'informal' by simple lapse of time, but to persuade him or her to stay in hospital a little longer. Another type of situation is that in which the patient is on trial leave when the first year comes to an end, and after a few weeks his name is simply removed from the books.

The follow-up of what we shall call our 'first-year leavers' and our restriction order cases will be described in the next chapter. In the remainder of the current chapter we shall be concerned with the lengths of time which the members of our cohort spent in ordinary hospitals. The results of our 1971 review are displayed in tables 20 and 21, which show what percentages–subdivided by type of hospital, type of order and diagnostic group–left hospital within one, two, etc., years of committal, or were still in hospital in the spring of 1971 *as a result of the order*. What it does not include are the offender-patients who left hospital but were later readmitted, whether voluntarily, compulsorily or as a result of a further court appearance; so that it should not be used to estimate, for example, what percentage of any cohort is likely to be in hospital after a given period. Nor can it be assumed that all those who were still in hospital in March 1971 are still there today. Within these limitations, however, the table gives a rough indication of the length of stays in hospital to which hospital orders lead.

From this point of view the most interesting section of the table is that which shows offender-patients who were sent to ordinary hospitals without a restriction order. Almost half (48·7 per cent) of these left–whether with or without the agreement of their responsible medical officer–within a year of admission; another 22 per cent in their second year; and so on until by the end of the sixth year only 10 per cent remained. By means of our questionnaires to hospitals we were able to ascertain the manner

TABLE 20. Leaving-years of Oxford cohort

MALES

Type of hospital	Type of order	Diagnostic group	1st year %	2nd year %	Leaving hospital in 3rd year %	4th year %	5th year %	6th or 7th year %	Still in hospital on 31 March 1971 %	Total (=100%)
Ordinary mental illness or mental subnormality hospitals	Hospital order without restriction	Schizophrenic	63·0	17·3	3·6	3·6	2·1	2·1	8·3[a]	336
		Affective	78·0	4·0	10·0	—	2·0	2·0	4·0[a]	50
		Psychopathic	44·7	29·9	3·0	4·5	—	10·4	7·5[a]	67
		Subnormal	20·5	32·6	13·2	6·6	4·0	9·2	13·9[a]	273
		Other	67·8	3·2	3·2	9·7	—	3·2	12·9[a]	31
		Total	47·2	22·5	7·4	4·8	2·5	5·4	10·2	757
	With restriction	Total[b]	17·1	18·3	14·6	6·1	8·5	15·9	19·5	82[d]
Special Hospitals	Without restriction	Total[b]	12·5	12·5	—	—	16·7	25·0	33·3	24
	With restriction	Total[b]	3·1	6·2	1·5	6·2	4·6	18·4	60·0	65[c]

[a] χ^2 for 2 d.f. = 7·91 (p < 0·025).

[b] the numbers involved were so small that sub-division into diagnostic groups would be misleading.

[c] χ^2 (3 d.f.) for the distributions of restriction order cases in ordinary and Special Hospitals = 33·5 (p < 0·001).

TABLE 21. Leaving-years of Oxford cohort

FEMALES

| Type of hospital | Type of order | Diagnostic group | 1st year % | 2nd year % | Leaving hospital in | | | | Still in hospital on 31 March 1971 % | Total (=100%) |
					3rd year %	4th year %	5th year %	6th or 7th year %		
Ordinary mental illness or mental subnormality hospitals	Hospital order without restriction	Schizophrenic	63·1	14·4	5·3	—	—	4·0	13·2	76
		Affective	64·6	5·9	5·9	5·9	—	—	17·7	17
		Psychopathic	71·5	21·4	—	—	—	—	7·1	14
		Subnormal	38·7	31·2	7·5	6·3	1·3	7·5	7·5	80
		Other	66·7	8·3	8·3	—	16·7	—	—	12
		Total	54·3	20·6	6·0	3·0	1·5	4·5	10·1	199
	With restriction	Total^a	11·1	44·5	11·1	—	11·1	11·1	11·1	9
Special Hospitals	Without restriction	Total^a	16·7	16·7	16·7	16·7	—	16·7	16·7	6
	With restriction	Total^a	b	b	b	b	b	b	b	b

a The numbers involved were so small that sub-division into diagnostic groups would be misleading.
b Information about women offenders sent to Special Hospitals was not received in time to be included in the computerised data. There are therefore no women shown as being received under restriction orders in Special Hospitals.

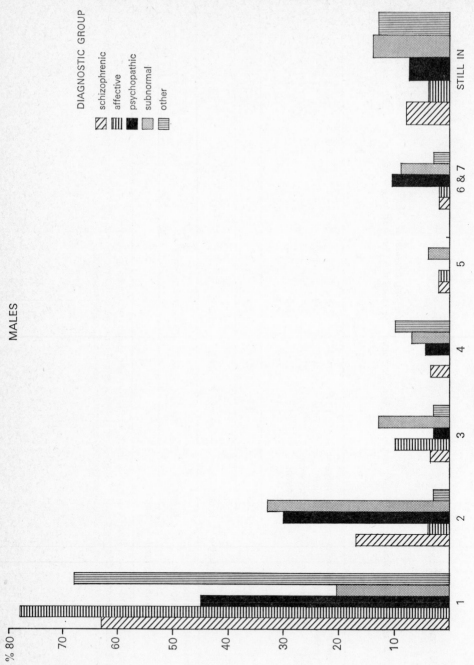

FIGURE 3. Leaving-years of unrestricted offender-patients

FEMALES

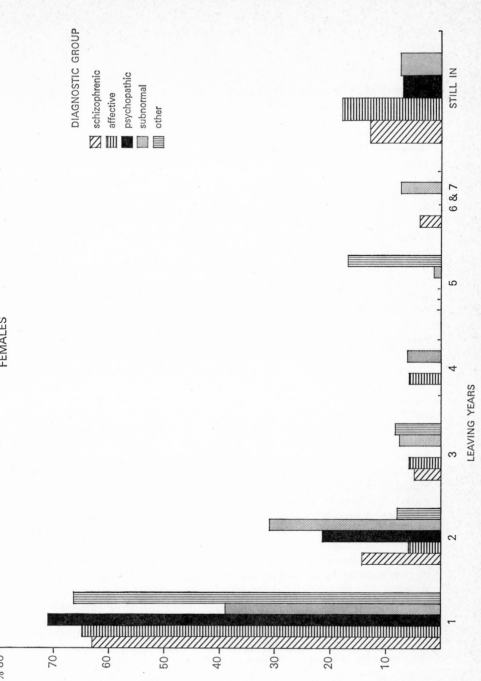

in which those who left during their first[32] year had done so. For ordinary hospitals the percentages (including restriction order cases) were

	Men %	Women %
Discharged by responsible medical officer	70	71
Discharged with Home Secretary's consent (s. 65)	2	1
Absconded and not returned to same hospital	21	23
Discharged by Mental Health Review Tribunal	2	3
Removed by police	3	1
Died	2	2

The percentages are very similar for men and women, and contrary to our expectation women were quite as likely as men to leave by absconding. In contrast, so few of our Special Hospital patients left in their first year –only five all told–that they are not worth tabulating. None of them left by absconding.

From another point of view it is those who remained in hospital for longer periods who are interesting. The moralist, for example, who is worried by what we have called 'occasionalism' (see p. 101) is bound to ask how justifiable was the detention of a substantial minority of our cohort for more than seven years. In the case of the Special Hospital patients, of course, the fact that over half were still inside in 1971 requires little explaining or excusing: these were after all the most dangerous members of our cohort. To a lesser extent the same might be said of the restriction order cases who remained for several years in ordinary hospitals, although these were proportionately fewer. It is the unrestricted offender-patients in ordinary hospitals who seem to call for a closer look. Ten per cent of them were still inside in 1971. The percentages did not differ between the sexes, but varied significantly ($p < 0.025$) with diagnostic group. The psychopaths, rather surprisingly, were under-represented, having for the most part left in their first two years, in some cases by absconding, but in others with the permission of their hospitals–who must often have been relieved to get rid of them. It was the subnormals who were over-represented amongst those still inside. It would be wrong, however, to assume that they were all detained against their will. Many subnormals settle down fairly contentedly in hospital, and the absconding-rate of the male subnormals in our cohort was low in comparison with that of psychopaths or schizophrenics although it was higher amongst our women.

Nevertheless, some people would question whether all contented sub-normal residents in institutions should be allowed to remain there, and might argue that they were contented merely as a result of 'institutionalisa-tion', which can be regarded merely as a more subtle form of injustice than forcible detention. Without swallowing this argument whole, we examined the dossiers of the subnormals who were still inside ordinary mental hospitals in 1971 to see how serious their misbehaviour had been. Leaving aside the nine who had been subjected to a restriction order–and who must therefore have been regarded as dangerous by a court at least–

there were 38 men and 6 women. Rather more than a third of the men had been convicted of sexual offences, whether on the occasion of their hospital order or previously. A few had been beyond the control of their parents, although it is impossible to say whether this meant that they were still unsuitable for life outside an institution. Some had already spent many years in institutions before the hospital order. Several, however, were just petty thieves or vagrants. One man and one woman, who had reached their late twenties without any convictions, had been committed to hospital as a result of a theft and a vagrancy offence respectively. One can only hope that their prolonged stays in hospital were necessary and voluntary.

Notes

1. We did not trouble with the guardianship order cases, which were too few to be treated as a representative sample.

2. The Ministry of Health's Statistical Report Series no. 4 (HMSO, 1969).

3. See Hansard (Commons) for 13, 20 and 27 February 1961. One of the authors also happened to be in an Assize Court by chance when the judge, who had twice remanded a subnormal young arsonist so that another effort could be made to find him a hospital vacancy, at last sentenced him to borstal training. It seems to be especially difficult to find places in subnormality hospitals in the London area: see the complaints from prison medical officers in the annual Report of the Prison Department for 1970, para. 158 (HMSO).

4. See for instance the findings of the Psychiatric Rehabilitation Association's Research Unit, in *The Mental Health of East London* (London, 1966; cyclostyled 1968).

5. One of the authors was present when a party from the staff of a large mental hospital visited Grendon Psychiatric Prison. Some of the party were critical of the monotony of the work offered in the prison to intelligent inmates. When asked by the author what sort of work they gave to intelligent patients in their hospital one of them replied, after some thought, 'putting mottoes in Christmas crackers'. In fairness, we do not know whether this really did represent occupational therapy at that hospital; but it did illustrate a failure to apply the same standard of criticism to both types of institution, perhaps because of the magic of the term 'occupational therapy'.

6. H.R.Rollin, *The Mentally Abnormal Offender and the Law* (Oxford, 1969), 103-4. His whole chapter on security is well worth reading.

7. 'Some Characteristics of Mental Hospital Absconders', in (1967) 113, *British Journal of Psychiatry*, 1087 ff. Dr Antebi does not give figures to support his comparative estimate.

8. P.Morris, *Put Away: A Sociological Study of Institutions for the Mentally Retarded* (London, 1969), 75.

9. Section 30 of the Act specifically permits this, but only for a 72-hour period, so that the need for longer compulsory detention can be properly considered.

10. See M. Grünhut, *Probation and Mental Treatment* (London, 1963), 29.

11. Often because the probation officer is not told what has happened. When he is, the probationer may be untraceable; or the probation officer may not consider it worth the trouble to bring him back before the court.

12. See s. 40 of the Act.

13. Memorandum on Parts I, IV-VI and IX of the Mental Health Act (HMSO, 1960).

14. See Rollin and Antebi loc. cit. *supra* (notes 6 and 7) and P.G. Woolf, 'The Back Door: Discharge by Operation of the Law after 28 Days' Absence', in (1966) 6, *British Journal of Criminology*, 59 ff.

15. Informal patients are said to leave 'a.m.a.', i.e., against medical advice.

16. The original period (specified in section 85 of the Lunacy Act, 1890, 53 & 54 Vict. c.5) was 14 days. As under the 1959 Act, he could be re-admitted compulsorily even if the period had expired, but only after the whole procedure had been gone through again.

17. P.G.Woolf, loc. cit. *supra* (note 14).

18. In this paragraph, as in table 19, there is no reference to d.o.l. or absconding rates for women, in view of their small numbers.

19. The composition and work of the Tribunals is governed by ss. 3, 122-4 and the First Schedule of the Act, together with the Mental Health Review Tribunal Rules, 1960 (S.I. 1960 no. 1139).

20. Paras. 438-54.

21. With exceptions described by the Percy Commission in paras 120-5.

22. Each consists of a panel of legally qualified chairmen, doctors (who are usually qualified psychiatrists) and laymen with 'experience in administration', 'knowledge of social services' or 'such other qualifications or experience as the Lord Chancellor considers suitable'. At least one member of each of these groups must be present at any sitting of the Tribunal.

23. He may also apply after any decision to extend the period of his compulsory detention. But note that patients merely detained for observation, or under emergency powers, cannot apply to a Tribunal, presumably because their period of detention is short.

24. 'Nearest relatives' also have the right to apply in certain circumstances, but apparently seldom do. Professor Greenland (loc. cit. *infra*, note 30) found only four examples of this in 180 applications.

25. The Mental Health Review Tribunal Rules, 1960 (S.I. 1960 no. 1139).

26. This interpretation has been confirmed by the Lord Chief Justice in R. v. Gardiner (see pp. 94-5).

27. A third alternative consideration, concerning only Part IV admissions, is also set out in s. 123, but is not relevant here.

28. The only important difference is that whereas the eighteenth-century offender-patient had at least been officially declared guiltless, his modern counterpart has usually not.

29. During the Commons' Committee stage: see the Proceedings of Standing Committee E for 19 March 1959, cols. 566 ff.

30. C. Greenland, *Mental Illness and Civil Liberty: a study of Mental Health Review Tribunals in England and Wales*, Occasional Papers in Social Administration no. 38 (London, 1970).

31. This was the twenty-four-year-old man who wandered out of a training centre with an axe and hit a child with it: see p. 133.

32. See Appendix D. We did not feel that we could reasonably continue to send questionnaires to hospitals after the end of the first year.

Chapter 8. The Hospital-Leavers

Although we had to confine ourselves to a 'paper' follow-up (for the reasons explained on p. 157) we nevertheless managed to improve on the usual form of penological follow-up, which relies solely on information about subsequent reconvictions, obtained from the Criminal Records Office. In the first place, since hospital admissions were obviously another form of 'relapse' to which our cohort was prone, we were allowed to obtain information from the Mental Health Enquiry Index about re-admissions to mental hospitals, although for reasons of confidentiality we were told no more than the date (and not, for example, whether the readmission was informal or compulsory).

It is true that even centrally recorded convictions and admissions to hospital are to some extent incomplete information. As was mentioned in chapter 6, not all convictions are reported by local police to the Criminal Records Office, so that some of our ex-offender-patients may have been convicted of minor offences, such as begging or 'wandering abroad' without our being informed of this. Even if an offence is centrally recorded, it may or may not be one which is usually regarded as serious. Fifty (11 per cent) of our ex-offender-patients who left within their first year were centrally recorded only as a result of convictions which did not lead to imprisonment or a further hospital order, and were therefore in all probability trivial.

Moreover, both reconvictions and readmissions to hospital are negative information, in the sense that they record only failure of one sort or another. Admittedly until quite recently some penologists have simply subtracted persons known to have been reconvicted from the total, converted the remainder into a percentage, and called this 'the success-rate'.[1] Indeed, even those penologists who were sophisticated enough to talk instead of the 'known reconviction-rate' did not hesitate to use it as an index of the failure of a penal measure. By supplementing this with re-admissions we did in fact show that whereas 40 per cent of our hospital order cases who left hospital in their first twelve months were reconvicted of centrally recorded offences in the next two years, 46 per cent were known to have been readmitted to mental hospitals, whether direct or via criminal courts; and only 39 per cent had avoided both reconviction and rehospitalisation.

Yet whether the cohort to be followed up consists of ex-patients, ex-prisoners, ex-probationers or any other category of sentenced offender, one ought always to wonder how 'successful' this residue of unrecorded cases really is. And even for a paper follow-up something more than mere speculation is possible. With the co-operation of the Ministry of National Insurance we were able to get information about the periods for which our ex-patients had been in contributory employment. Here again, confidentiality debarred us from getting as much information as we should have liked, but what we did get was valuable. It is true that payment of insurance contributions is a better index of success in the case of men than in the case of women; but three-quarters of our ex-patients were men. It must also be admitted that some of our ex-patients probably obtained casual employment without paying contributions; so that to this extent our information from the Ministry may slightly have underestimated the extent of their subsequent employment. Strictly speaking, therefore, our frequent references to 'employment' throughout the rest of this chapter ought to be to 'reported contributory employment during the follow-up period'; but that would be tedious.

The Follow-up of First-Year Leavers

Table 22 is a rather depressing combination of these three types of follow-up information. Distinguishing men from women, it shows that only a little over a third of the former, and rather less than half of the latter, succeeded in keeping out of the criminal courts and the mental hospitals; and had the follow-up been a longer one the percentages would doubtless have been more discouraging still. In terms of employment the results are also disappointing. Although none of these ex-patients was so old as to be unemployable on grounds of age (all our first-year leavers were under 65) less than two-thirds of the men and less than a third of the women were in contributory employment for any of the time, let alone for most of it. It is arguable, of course, that when one recalls the poor penal, psychiatric and occupational records of most of our cohort the fact that as many as a quarter managed not only to keep out of courts and hospitals but also to keep jobs for at least some of their first two years at large is not so discouraging as it appears at first sight.

It was obviously necessary to carry out a more thorough analysis of our 'outcomes' (as we shall for the sake of brevity call the results of this particular follow-up). For example, table 22 suggests that even this unusual sample of ours exhibits the usual marked difference which is to be found between men and women so far as concerns the likelihood of reconviction–or at least reconviction of offences serious enough to lead to another hospital order or a prison sentence. But this might be the case merely because our women were so selected by the system as to be less likely 'recidivists' than our men. For instance, as we saw in chapter 6 relatively fewer of them had previous convictions; and this is a variable which is associated with subsequent reconviction in any normal penal sample. It was necessary to analyse the relationship between our 'outcomes' and variables which seemed likely to be associated with them in such a way as to allow for possibly spurious associations of this kind. The method by which this was done is described in Appendix B, so that in this chapter the results can be discussed with the minimum of technicalities.

TABLE 22. Results of two-year follow-up of first-year leavers

A.	Males %	Females %
Reconvicted, and committed to hospital or penal custody as a result	30·8	21·9
Reconvicted, but not committed to hospital or penal custody as a result	11·6	8·6
Re-admitted to hospital, but not reconvicted	21·1	21·0
Neither reconvicted nor re-admitted to hospital, but not in contributory employment	9·7	30·4
Neither reconvicted nor re-admitted to hospital, and in contributory employment, however short	26·8	18·1
	100·0 (= 351[a])	100·0 (= 105[a])

(Males, middle four categories: $p < 0.001$ (4 d.f.). Males last two categories bracketed = 36·5; Females last two categories bracketed = 48·5)

B.

In contributory employment, irrespective of reconviction or re-admission to hospital

	Males	Females
for no period	39·0	69·5
for 1 month or less	2·9	2·9
for more than 1 month	58·1	27·6
	100·0 (= 351[a])	100·0 (= 105[a])

$p < 0.001$ (2 d.f.)

[a] These totals exclude persons under 17, for whom the criterion of employment was likely to be inappropriate; and there were no first-year leavers over the age of 65.

To conclude the discussion of sex-differences, however, we established by this method that in our sample of offender-patients the apparently strong association between being male and being reconvicted was reduced to an insignificant level (p being rather over 0·1) when our other variables were allowed for. On the other hand, when it was a matter of contributory employment during the follow-up period, the sex-difference was still highly significant (p < 0·001).

This should remind us, however, that so far as women are concerned subsequent employment is not a very satisfactory criterion of 'success'. A female ex-patient (or ex-prisoner, for that matter) often goes back to housekeeping for her family, a parent or a relative; and to classify her as 'unsuccessful' simply because she is not recorded as having any contributory employment would be quite wrong-headed. It must also be remembered that it is easier for a woman than for a man to obtain a paid non-contributory job, for example as a 'daily help'.

We wanted, however, to analyse the results of the follow-up in rather more detail, in order to see what sort of person is likely to be a 'success' or 'failure' in terms of these criteria. We had recorded data about a considerable assortment of variables. On the one hand, we had information about the offender-patients' previous histories, age, nationality and so forth: information which, in theory at least, was available when he or she was disposed of by the court: these can be referred to as 'pre-order variables'. To what extent could these be used to predict success or failure? On the other hand, we had information which, by its very nature, could become available only after the offender-patient had entered hospital: the current diagnosis (which would not necessarily be the same as previous diagnoses), how long he or she was kept in hospital, whether he or she absconded (and if so whether this was the method of discharge) and whether any after-care was planned. These can be referred to as 'post-order variables'.

The Variables. The choice and definition of our outcomes are discussed in Appendix B; but before proceeding further a few general remarks about our variables are needed. Since we had to depend on hundreds of different individuals for the information in our dossiers, the information which we asked for had to consist of more or less 'hard' data,[2] although 'hardness' is a matter of degree, and such information as 'predominant disorder' is not as hard as 'date of birth' (especially when 'psychopathic disorder' is concerned, as we shall see in chapter 10). Again our information had been asked for, or recorded by us, in quantifiable form wherever this seemed reasonable. Instead of asking whether the offender-patient had a large family we had asked for the number of his children; and his employment record—so far as this could be got—was reduced to variables such as 'previous jobs held for less than one year' and 'employed at time of offence'. This process of selection and quantification, though obviously necessary in a survey of this kind, has its disadvantages. As one of us has already pointed out, the easier a variable is to measure, the less likely it is to be what one really wants to measure.[3]

Perhaps the best example of this dilemma is the concept of 'institutionalisation', a state of mind which is believed to result from prolonged or repeated stays in more or less 'total' institutions such as prisons and mental hospitals, and which is said to reduce the inmate's capacity for independent living, or even to leave him with a preference for institutional life which may prompt him to seek readmission when faced with the difficulties of outside life. How reliably can institutionalisation be assessed? Research workers are studying this problem; but until they produce some kind of test for the purpose the best one can do is to record how much time the ex-inmate has spent in custodial institutions, how long he has been at large since his last stay, and so on. This is obviously a very indirect method, which assumes that institutionalisation increases with each period 'inside' and is not entirely cured by intervals of freedom, and that every inmate is subject to it, if in varying degrees. But it is not completely unsatisfactory, for—as we shall see—the total time spent in penal custody was a useful predictor of future reconviction even in our rather abnormal cohort.

Pre-order Information. The results can be briefly stated. (Readers who want more precision can turn to table 29 in Appendix B). The rather surprising weakness of the sex-difference in reconvictions has already been mentioned. Another surprise for penologists will be the absence of any significant association between age and any of the outcomes, with the not very surprising exception of women's employment (the older the woman the less likely she was to be employed after discharge). Being foreign by birth did not seem to matter. Offenders who had been living at home when they offended were slightly less likely than others to be reconvicted, presumably because most of them went back to a sheltered and supportive home of some sort on discharge. In spite of what has been said about women's occupations on p. 182, women who had been employed at the time of their offences were less likely than others to be rehospitalised, more likely to be employed after discharge, and if employed to remain employed. So far as men were concerned, however, this variable was not significantly associated with any outcome except remaining in employment if they entered it.

The number of previous hospital admissions was associated with re-admission after discharge, and so far as women were concerned the longer the interval between the previous and the current hospital stay, the less likely the patient was to be readmitted, although the latter association was not strong, and did not reach a significant level in men. Similarly, the number of previous convictions was associated with the likelihood of reconviction, whether serious enough to lead to further custody or not: a relationship which is encountered in almost every kind of penal sample. In other words, the rough rule that if you want to know what *will* happen to someone it is a good idea to ask what *has* happened to him holds good for the sort of social casualties with which we are concerned.

Similarly, time spent in previous penal custody (which, as we have explained, was intended as an indirect measure of institutionalisation[4]) was associated with the likelihood of reconviction, whether or not this led to reimprisonment or rehospitalisation. This too has been observed in penal samples.

Post-order Information. The post-order data which we selected for study consisted of abscondings, time spent in hospital, after-care and of course diagnosis.[5]

We distinguished absconding which led to 'discharge by operation of the law' ('d.o.l.'—see p. 165) from what might be called 'temporary absconding', which was somewhat less frequent. So far as men were concerned, being d.o.l. was associated with reconviction (whether leading to further custody or not), with failure to enter contributory employment and with shorter periods in such employment; but in the case of women these associations were negligible.

Temporary absconding was another matter. If the whole sample of 942 men and 218 women is considered, 19 per cent of the men and 15 per cent of the women were reported to have absconded at least once in the course of their first year, and 3 per cent of the men and 2 per cent of the women absconded on eight or more occasions. In most cases their absences lasted only a few days, although as we have seen substantial numbers succeeded in remaining at large long enough to gain their legal freedom. So far as our follow-up was concerned, temporary absconding was not associated with reconviction or readmission to hospital, and only in the case of women was it significantly associated with failure to take up contributory employment.

Our interpretation of these observations is that being d.o.l. is an indication that the offender-patient is sufficiently sophisticated to realise that he can obtain his legal freedom in this way, and sufficiently competent– in a short-term sense at least–to subsist for the necessary period without running into trouble: in short, that he is criminally experienced. The temporary absconder, on the other hand, is more likely to have behaved in a confused or impulsive way.

Duration of Stay. The shorter the time before the offender-patient's departure the more likely he or she was to be reconvicted and recommitted to custody, whether in prison or hospital, and the less likely a man was to obtain contributory employment for more than a negligible period. This cannot be dismissed as due to the d.o.l. cases. It is true that d.o.l. cases were–not surprisingly–over-represented among the early leavers; but the method of analysis allowed for this and still showed a significant ($p < 0.01$) negative association between time in hospital and serious reconviction for both sexes combined.

There were at least two plausible interpretations of this:

(a) that offender-patients whose conduct would have been improved by by a longer stay were being allowed to leave earlier than–on this criterion at least–they should have been;

(b) that those whose chances of reconviction were unlikely to be improved by further detention were simply being recognised by the hospitals and allowed to leave.

In an attempt to see which was the more likely hypothesis we made use of our second-year leavers, whom we had followed up for one year after their departures. There seemed to be enough schizophrenics and psychopaths amongst them to enable us to match substantial numbers with first-year leavers, using sex, age, diagnosis, previous convictions and previous hospital stays as criteria; and we did in fact manage to find 42 matched pairs of schizophrenics and 22 matched pairs of psychopaths. We reasoned that on hypothesis (a) we should expect more first-year leavers than second-year leavers to be reconvicted, whereas on hypothesis (b) the reconviction-rates should be roughly equal. The latter turned out to be the case:

	Reconvictions (within 12 months) of	
	1st-year leavers	*2nd-year leavers*
Schizophrenics (42 pairs)	15	12
Psychopaths (22 pairs)	10	8

There was a slight excess of reconvictions amongst the first-year leavers, but it was far too small for significance.[6] On the other hand, it was noticeable that more second-year leavers–whether schizophrenic or psychopathic–had been *rehospitalised* within twelve months of leaving ($p < 0.025$ for schizophrenics and psychopaths combined). The explanation may be that offender-patients who have remained in hospital after the end of their first year are more likely to have done so voluntarily, and are thus more likely to seek or at least accept readmission if they get into difficulties. On the whole, therefore, our data seemed more consistent with the hypothesis that hospitals were simply recognising that some offender-patients were unlikely to be improved by a longer stay, and allowing them to leave without fuss.

After-care. Our six-month and twelve-month questionnaire about each patient (see Appendixes C and D) asked:

> If he has ceased to be a patient, has the hospital had any subsequent contact with or information about him? If so, what?

The answers were very varied. In many cases they amounted to 'no contact'; in others it was clear that the hospital had taken considerable trouble to ensure not only contact but some degree of supervision. The two most common forms of contact were attendance at the hospital's out-patient clinic ('he is attending the hospital's out-patient department regularly') and reports from the Mental Welfare Officer of the local authority ('. . . returned to former lodgings . . . where contact is being maintained on friendly basis by Mental Welfare Officer'). Sometimes the ex-patient was 'seen by probation officer'.

When trying to assess the efficacy of what can roughly be called 'after-care' in preventing relapse or helping the ex-patient to hold down a job it was necessary to draw a line somewhere. We classified the ex-patient as having received after-care only if the hospital's answer indicated something more than casual, unplanned contacts, or single visits to out-patient departments. Trial leave was treated as after-care, although in a strict sense it preceded 'discharge'. Even so, we felt that we were stretching the term 'after-care' to its reasonable limit; and were therefore glad that our restriction order cases gave us an opportunity of measuring the effectiveness of after-care of a somewhat more rigorous standard.

We shall deal with them later, however. For the moment we are concerned with the relationship between after-care of however low a standard and the outcomes. It was interesting to find that in the case of women the association with any of our outcomes was negligible; but that in the case of our men there were slight but significant associations with favourable outcomes (keeping out of court, substantial employment and employment without relapse). On the other hand, even amongst the men the association between after-care and *keeping out of hospital* was negligible; but the explanation may well be that good after-care entails timely readmission in some cases.

Diagnosis. We were also interested in the extent to which the psychiatrists' diagnoses were related to outcome. The function of psychiatric diagnoses will be discussed in chapter 10, when we come to consider the utility of the label 'psychopathic disorder'. At this point it is sufficient to point out that a psychiatrist's diagnosis is not normally expected to imply an automatic prognosis, good or bad. Still less is it expected to tell us whether the patient will need to be rehospitalised or brought before a criminal court again.

It is therefore no criticism of the diagnoses of our sample – though it is rather surprising – that none of the main diagnostic groupings (paranoid schizophrenia, other schizophrenia, subnormality, affective disorder or psychopathy) was significantly associated with rehospitalisation. Had the rehospitalisation rate for our first-year leavers been low this absence of association could perhaps have been explained away on the hypothesis that only the good risks were being allowed to leave in their first year: but since no less than 42 per cent of our men and 31 per cent of our women were rehospitalised, with or without prosecution, this will not wash.

Paradoxically, the diagnostic group was a better predictor of reconviction than of rehospitalisation. Indeed, the negative association between schizophrenia (especially in its paranoid form) and reconviction was the strongest coefficient that emerged from our whole analysis.[7] It is not easy to interpret this with confidence. Is the explanation simply that schizophrenics are more easily recognisable as such when they come to the notice of the police, and are thus more likely to be dealt with in ways that do not involve prosecution? Or that treatment – which in their case usually means psychotropic drugs – has more effect on them than on the other diagnostic groups? On the latter hypothesis one would expect schizophrenics to be significantly less likely to be rehospitalised than the other diagnostic groups: but this was not borne out. On the whole it seems slightly more likely that some process of discrimination is at work.

Weakness of Associations. Having reached this point, however, we must now emphasise how weak were all the associations which we have mentioned. Although we mentioned only those which were strong enough to make it unlikely that they were the effect of mere chance, they were far from being impressive. Moreover, when we studied the fraction of the total variance in each outcome criterion that was accounted for by all the variables we had tabulated,[8] this too was remarkably low in most cases. The point may be clearer if made the other way round, and more concretely. An outcome such as rehospitalisation can be called 'unexplained' *so far as our variables are concerned* to the extent that, in combination, they fall short of accounting for 100 per cent of its variance. In the case of men, rehospitalisation was 87 per cent 'unexplained', reconviction ('serious' or non-serious) was 74 per cent 'unexplained' and the favourable outcomes were roughly speaking 80 per cent 'unexplained'. (The degree of 'inexplicability' was less in the case of women, apparently because this cohort contained a small group of women with long histories of imprisonment and hospital stays, who were extremely likely to reappear in court and be readmitted to hospital.)

What is the reason for this 'inexplicability'? There are several possibilities. Beginning with the least likely, they are:

(*a*) that it is wholly or substantially the result of a high degree of *inaccuracy in our information* about either the outcomes or the variables or both. For example, we pointed out in chapter 6 that we could not be sure of having ascertained every previous conviction or hospital admission. On the other hand, these were among the variables that were associated with *re*-conviction and *re*-admission in a plausible, if weak way, so that the worst that can be suggested is that the associations would have been stronger if our information had been more complete. On the whole, inaccuracy does not seem a sufficient explanation. For instance, it is most unlikely that the surprising absence of any significant relationship between age and outcome so far as men were concerned is due to incorrect information about their ages, for these were usually confirmed by police from criminal records, and ages confirmed in the same way have been found by penologists to be strongly related to reconviction.

(b) that a follow-up period of two years is simply too short to distinguish between 'successes' and 'failures'. It has been suggested, for example, by the Carr-Hills[9] that if one is trying to distinguish between men who are going to be reconvicted and men who are not one must allow for a very large element of chance in the timing of their relapses (especially since some relapses may go undetected); and that consequently even follow-ups of two or three years may not be long enough. We were able, however, to submit our data about the timing of our cohort's reconvictions and rehospitalisations to Mr R. A. Carr-Hill, who confirmed that their distribution over time did not appear to be consistent with a high degree of randomness. In other words, some factor or factors which we had not succeeded in measuring were at work.

(c) that we were measuring, or trying to measure, the wrong variables. As has been emphasised already, it had been necessary to concentrate on 'hard' data because of the number of different individuals on whom we had to rely for our reported information, and the harder the data the less likely it is to be what one really needs to measure. Here there are two things which must not be confused: the crudity of one's yardstick and the concept which one is using it to measure. A good illustration of the point is 'age'. A penologist who studies its relationship to outcomes such as reconviction is not—unless he is very stupid—testing the hypothesis that mere lapse of time since birth is causally related to a tendency to crime; he must have in mind some concept such as 'maturation', 'learning' or (perhaps) 'burning out'. The interesting thing is that whatever age does measure (and it may be a mixture of changes in the individual and in his situation) it does seem to be related to a declining probability of reconviction in ordinary samples of offenders. So however crude it may be as a measure, it is not a mistaken choice. The fact that in our sample age showed remarkably little association with outcomes such as reconviction does not show that it was a mistaken choice of variable. All that can be said is that so far as *disordered* offenders[10] are concerned our data do not support the notion that 'maturity' (or whatever it is that age is supposed to measure) is predictively useful.

On the other hand, what is possible is that there are variables which we did not attempt to measure, however crudely, but which would have sub-stantially reduced the 'randomness' of the outcomes. An example is what might be called the offender-patient's 'way of life'. Was he, for example, a 'respectable' individual, with a stable family life and job, and non-criminal friends? Or an isolated, rootless vagrant? Or a hard-drinking associate of delinquents? If he had a home, how much 'support' and 'shelter' did it provide? Was he or she antagonistic to authority, or genuinely willing to accept help? 'Soft' as this sort of data may be, it would in theory be possible, with the help of trained interviewers, to categorise it: it is after all no softer than much of the contents of the social enquiry reports which probation officers render to the court. The problem arises from the fact that one could not rely on reports compiled by the local social worker (whether probation officer or psychiatric social worker), since one social worker might describe as 'supportive' a family which another, more perceptive or cynical, would call 'subtly destructive'. It would be necessary to recruit and brief a small army of highly special-ised interviewers.

Moreover, one must not overlook the very real possibility that the sort of variables which would have substantially reduced the 'inexplicability' of the outcomes were not merely difficult to categorise at the time of the offender's court appearance, or even while he was in hospital, but could have been ascertained only after his discharge. A family which is 'sup-portive' before a man is charged with some form of violence, dishonesty or sexual molestation may well be 'unsupportive' when he is returned to it. He may even turn into a man without a home. Consistent with this hypothesis is the negative association between after-care and reconviction amongst our cohort.

Predicting Reconviction

Whatever the reason for the rather low 'explicability' of our outcomes—and it may well have been a mixture of those we have suggested—we were somewhat discouraged about the prospect of extracting a useful prediction formula from our data. The main[11] point of attempting this was that such a formula can be of help to decision-makers. Suppose that one has grounds for thinking that some expedient helps to reduce the frequency of relapse (however defined), but that one's resources will not allow it to be applied to all one's patients. An example might well be after-care, which seems, from our findings, to be associated to some extent with 'success'. If one could separate one's patients into sub-groups with different probabilities of relapse (which in essence is what predictive techniques do) one could select the high-risk sub-groups for intensive efforts to provide after-care.[12]

As has been said, we were not very optimistic about the possibility of constructing a useful prediction formula from our data. Not only was the 'explicability' of our outcomes rather low in most cases (though higher in the case of women): a recent Home Office report[13] had also emphasised that such formulae have so far been found to discriminate efficiently only so far as extreme sub-groups are concerned. They may identify high-risk or low-risk groups, but these tend to be minorities, and the majority are left with rather middling probabilities (such as 45 per cent or 53 per cent) which are of no use in decision-making. Nevertheless it seemed that even if we could do no more than identify high-risk or low-risk minorities this could be of practical use to hospitals—for example, in deciding how much effort to devote to after-care.

If the scoring system was to be used in this way, it would be a mistake to include variables which either could not be known to the hospital decision-makers in time for any proper decision (e.g., whether the offender-patient was d.o.l.) or else was subject to the very sort of decision for which they might want to use the prediction formula (e.g., whether after-care had been planned or not). This left us with not many variables that seemed to be significantly associated with relapse: homelessness, unemployment at the time of the offence, previous convictions (or hospital stays), previous time spent in penal custody, nature of current offence and diagnosis. Even so, it was possible to be selective. One does not greatly increase the discriminatory power of a prediction formula by including all possible variables, because some of them are highly correlated. Scoring systems involving only a few variables have been found almost as powerful as those involving large numbers.

Again, there are several highly sophisticated methods of constructing prediction formulae, most of which result in weighted scoring systems in which different variables are assigned different values (e.g., '12', '17' or '1·2', '1·7'). The same Home Office study, however, also points out that these are only a slight improvement on unweighted scoring systems which simply assign '1' for the presence and '0' for the absence of the relevant variable. We therefore constructed one or two scoring systems of this simple kind.

We concentrated on the outcome of 'reconviction' for two reasons. First, its 'explicability' was higher than that of any other outcomes in our analysis, more variables being associated with it to a significant degree. Second, it seemed to us that the outcome which hospitals would most want to prevent was reconviction. Readmission to hospital is not always a pity: it may be the way in which a more serious incident can be prevented. The prevention of unemployment, too, is an unrealistic aim where many offender-patients are concerned, especially women.

As was to be expected from our data,[14] we had more success with our female than our male first-year leavers. One simply but fairly powerful scoring system was to give the woman one point for:

1. any previous convictions;
2. a history of previous custodial sentences (with an additional point if they had totalled 5 months or more);
3. a diagnosis of subnormality or psychopathic disorder.

The result was the following table:

Total score	Women in sub-group	Number reconvicted as % of sub-group
0	36	5·6
1	31	25·8
2	25	44·0
3	7	71·4
4	6	100·0
Whole sample	105	3·05

A fairly similar scoring system for men discriminated less well. If one point was given for:

1. a history of previous custodial sentences (with an additional point if they had totalled 13 months or more);
2. a diagnosis of subnormality or psychopathic disorder;
3. having been unemployed at the time of the offence which led to the hospital order,

the following table resulted:

Total score	Men in sub-group	Number reconvicted as % of sub-group
0	49	20·4
1	131	32·8
2	95	43·2
3 or 4	76	71·1
Whole sample	351	42·4

As is usual with prediction tables, the majority of the cohort fell into groups with middling frequencies, which are of little use for decision-making purposes. But substantial numbers—accounting for 37 per cent of the cohort—were selected as being either high-risk or low-risk individuals.

How does one judge the success of a prediction formula? It depends on the way in which one means to use it. If it is intended to select bad risks for some special treatment which is likely to be distressing (such as longer detention) then one should look closely at the percentage of the whole sample which would have been treated as a bad risk but which was *not* in fact reconvicted: what can be called 'false positives'. If all the women who scored 4 had been treated as bad risks, there would have been no false positives, since all were in fact reconvicted. But if all who scored 3 or 4 had been treated as bad risks, 2 out of the whole sample of 105 would have been false positives; and if this had been done with the men there would have been 23 false positives—7 per cent of the whole sample of 351.

Conversely, if one were trying to pick good risks for some measure (such as early release) which involved the possibility of a dangerous mistake, one would worry about the percentage of 'false negatives'. If on the other hand the expedient which is to be applied to the selected sub-groups involves no risk of serious harm or distress to anyone—and again after-care seems a good example-the percentage of false positives or negatives hardly matters, and the important question is 'How large a percentage of the whole sample can the formula help us to identify as bad or good risks (depending on which we want)? In this situation a formula which identified 12 per cent of the sample—even with a fair number of false positives—would be of more use than one which identified only 6 per cent however few the false positives. In concrete terms, if one is trying to select high-risk groups for an unobjectionable expedient such as special after-care, it would be rational to take men or women scoring 3 or 4 on the systems outlined above.

We suggest this with three reservations. First, the scoring systems have not been validated; that is, tried out on an entirely new sample.[15] Second, we do not claim to have devised the best possible scoring systems, since these were arrived at by inspection, trial and error. Third, our cohort of women may not have been as representative of female hospital order cases as our male cohort, since as we have seen, 1963 was the year in which an abnormally high number of women was dealt with in this way. On the other hand, the variables in our scoring system are all plausible. If we had found that, say, the number of a patient's children was a powerful predictor of future reconviction the difficulty of explaining this would have made us sceptical. The association, however, between reconviction and previous penal record, or unemployment, is supported by other penological research.

Finally, since our analysis had in fact shown that after-care was associated with a lower probability of reconviction amongst our men, we proceeded to find out whether this was true of both high-risk and low-risk groups. For it was conceivable that the association was confined to one or other; and if, for instance, it had proved to hold only for low-risk groups the case for recommending more intensive efforts to provide it for high-risk groups would have been seriously weakened. In fact, it proved to hold for most risk-groups, as table 23 shows.

TABLE 23. After-care[a] and risk-group

	Score-group[b]	Number in group	After-care[a]	Percentage reconvicted	
Men	0	24	yes	8·3	
		25	no	32·0	
	1	58	yes	34·5	
		73	no	31·5	C.R. = 3·43
	2	37	yes	21·6	p[c] < 0·00034
		58	no	56·9	
	3 & 4	19	yes	47·4	
		57	no	78·9	
Women	0	18	yes	5·6	
		18	no	5·6	
	1	17	yes	17·6	
		14	no	35·7	
	2	8	yes	25·0	C.R. = 1·93
		17	no	52·9	p[c] < 0·027
	3	4	yes	50·0	
		3	no	100·0	
	4	2	yes	100·0	
		4	no	100·0	

[a] As defined on p. 186.

[b] As explained on pp. 191-2.

[c] Using W. G. Cochran's criterion for combining 2×2 contingency tables (see his article in (1954) 10, *Biometrics*, 417 ff.).

The exceptions were rather interesting. In the largest score-group of our men, which accounted for 37 per cent of our first-year leavers, there was no association between after-care and non-reconviction. These were men with a moderately low likelihood of reconviction (33 per cent as the table shows). For this group, perhaps, the difference between reconviction and non-reconviction was very much a matter of chance. Again for women in the extreme score-groups, who were either very good or very bad risks, it did not matter whether they had been the subject of after-care or not. For all other groups, however, the association was strong: so strong that in the case of men the probability of its being due to sampling error was more or less negligible. Moreover, it was noticeable that even amongst the high-risk groups—the psychopaths and subnormals with substantial experience of penal institutions—the percentages for whom the hospitals appeared to have had some hope of providing after-care were considerable. In other words, being in a high-risk group neither rules out after-care nor is an indication that it will be useless.

We must point out, of course, that these tables do not prove conclusively that after-care reduces the reconviction-rates. An alternative interpretation is that offender-patients for whom it is easier to arrange after-care were for other reasons less likely to be reconvicted. They may have been more co-operative, or less likely to drift out of touch than those for whom hospitals, realistically, did not forecast after-care. But if so one would have expected the association to be absent from the high-risk groups. Since after-care is *intended* to reduce the ex-patient's likelihood of relapse, and the results are *consistent with* the hypothesis that it does, our data provide a strong case for experimenting with more intensive efforts to provide after-care, especially for high-risk groups.

Dangerous Offenders

So far we have talked simply of 'reconvictions' without differentiating between the really dangerous and the trivial. Many reconvictions were indeed trivial. Petty thieves committed further petty thefts. Soliciting prostitutes went back to soliciting. Disorderly drunks got drunk and disorderly again. When we sifted the reconvictions for those which involved real harm to people, however, we found rather few.[16] Our first- and second-year[17] discharges, totalling 673, yielded only ten cases in which the ex-patient had been convicted of serious violence, nine in which he had been convicted of a serious sexual offence, and five in which he had been convicted of arson. In one case the ex-patient was convicted of murders committed *before* his admission to hospital (for a fairly trivial offence), and which were no doubt unknown to his psychiatrist. He is excluded from the table below. Two were cases whose discharge at the direction of Mental Health Review Tribunals has already been mentioned. Three of the violent offences, one of the sexual offences and three of the cases of arson involved patients who had been the subject of restriction orders: a category which will be discussed shortly.

What interested us most was the extent to which the harmful behaviour of these 23 ex-patients could be said to have been predictable. Their numbers were too small for a reliable statistical exercise, and in any case

o

the more clearly dangerous the offender the less likely he or she was to have left hospital (although some alarming exceptions are mentioned later in this chapter). We can do no more therefore than enumerate those whose previous careers (including the offence which had brought them into our cohort) exhibited similar behaviour to that which led to their reconvictions.

Subsequently reconvicted of	*Previous convictions of a similar kind*		
	None	*1*	*2 +*
Serious violence	5	2	2
Serious sexual molestation	2	1	6
Arson	2	3	–
	9	6	8

As can be seen, most of the serious violence involved ex-patients with no records of violence. (One, however, had a long record of aggressive behaviour, and one was the paranoid woman immigrant whose murderous attack on a neighbour has been described on p. 93, and who had been rightly labelled as dangerous by a hospital doctor: it will be recalled that she was subject to an ordinary hospital order, was discharged, and then murdered a man whom she picked up in a pub.) In contrast, most of the sexual offences were by men with records of sexual molestation, usually of children. Only five of these sexual offenders were subnormals, the rest being an assortment of schizophrenia, alcoholic dementia and 'psychopathy'. Contrary to expectation, none of the arsonists were diagnosed as subnormal. This under-representation of subnormals amongst the sexual offenders and incendiaries is no doubt attributable to the tendency of subnormality hospitals to keep their inmates for longer than other psychiatric hospitals: see p. 176.

It must be remembered that this table shows only offender-patients in a single year's cohort who were allowed to leave (or succeeded in escaping from) hospitals and within a limited period were detected in and convicted of serious offences. It does not show those who might have been in the same position had they not been prevented from leaving. Nor of course does it show the total number of such ex-patients who are at large in the community. At most, therefore, it indicates what might be called one year's 'vintage' of cases in which the hospital order system failed to protect the public against serious personal harm. Seen in this light, 23 failures out of 1,160 hospital orders–2 per cent–is not a large number. It is true that it could have been lower if a few obviously dangerous individuals had been looked after with more care, and if the courts had been more sensible in their use of restriction orders. One or two members of our cohort who gained their freedom were clearly men of violence; and several of our discharged paedophiles were plainly so compulsive as to be very poor risks. But, those cases apart, so long as hospital order patients[18] are committed to ordinary hospitals, and so long as these operate on the principle of minimum security, there will continue to be a few virtually unpredictable failures which involve serious harm.

Restriction Orders. Nevertheless, these cases should lead us to look with all the more interest at the safeguard which restriction orders are intended to provide. As was explained in chapter 5 (p. 90) their aim is to give the public a higher degree of protection against such offender-patients by ensuring that their discharge is subject to the control of the Home Office. Their effect, in brief, is that the patient cannot be given leave of absence, transferred to another hospital or discharged from hospital without the Home Secretary's consent. The order remains in force even if the offender-patient is subsequently sentenced for another offence. Nor can he have recourse to either of the two main safeguards against unnecessary detention which are available to ordinary patients. Whereas an ordinary patient who has been compulsorily admitted (whether under a hospital order or simply 'for treatment') can regain his right to freedom by absconding and remaining at large for the necessary period (see p. 165), a patient under a restriction order can be retaken however long he remains at large. (The only exception is the case in which the restriction order has expired: another anomaly which would be removed if all restriction orders were for unlimited periods of time: see p. 91.)

Secondly, he does not have the ordinary compulsory patient's right to ask a Mental Health Review Tribunal for a direction that he be discharged. All he can do is request the Home Secretary to refer his case to a tribunal 'for their advice', which is not binding. Indeed, it is quite frequently not accepted. In the first ten years of the Act's operation 2,447 cases were referred to tribunals, who recommended discharge or other changes in the offender-patient's status in 775 (32 per cent) of these cases. This advice, however, was accepted in only three-quarters of these 775 cases. Moreover, when the figures for each year were studied, it was clear that while there had been fairly steady *increases* both in the annual numbers of references and in the percentage of cases in which a relaxation of some sort was recommended by the tribunals, these trends had been accompanied by a *decrease* in the percentage of recommendations which were accepted by the Home Office.[19]

Rejection of a tribunal's advice is almost always based on considerations of public safety, and so far as purely medical questions are concerned (for example, whether the offender-patient is still mentally ill) the Home Office seem to be very mindful of the fact that if the case were a non-restricted one the tribunal would have the final say. Even where the advice is not accepted, the review of the case may stimulate the responsible medical officer to give further thought to it, and the result is sometimes a recommendation from him which leads to some relaxation. Nevertheless, the fairly substantial rejection-rate (which in recent years has been rather over a quarter), calls for some thought. It should be contrasted with the very much smaller percentage of rejected Parole Board recommendations for the release of prisoners. Out of more than 2,000 such recommendations each year only a handful are not accepted. Even if it is argued that it would be fairer to compare restriction order cases with 'lifers' rather than ordinary prisoners, the percentage of rejections for this type of prisoner is only 2·5 per cent. This raises the question whether the tribunals are the best bodies to entrust with the function of advising the Home Office on restriction order cases—a question to which we shall return later in the chapter.

To sum up: the patient who is subject to a restriction order can be detained without any formal renewal until one of the following things happens:

(*a*) the period specified in the restriction order comes to an end: but as we have seen, most restriction orders are for unlimited periods;

(*b*) the Home Secretary, being satisfied that the need to protect the public no longer requires him to be under the restriction, directs that he should become an ordinary hospital order patient, in which case his hospital order is treated as if it had just been made and in due course will need renewal if he has not by then been discharged;

(*c*) the Home Secretary authorises his discharge.

The last of these possibilities is the most usual way of ending a restricted patient's stay.

If our cohort of restriction order cases is representative, at least half such patients regain their liberty within about six years, as table 24 shows.

TABLE 24. Status in mid-1970 of restriction order cases in the Oxford survey

Discharged			
before expiry of order	58 ⎫		
on expiry of order	8 ⎬	85	54·6%
after expiry of order	19 ⎭		
absconded and dealt with afresh by courts		3	1·9%
died		6	3·8%
transferred to Scottish hospitals		2	1·3%
Still compulsorily detained in hospital			
discharged conditionally, but recalled	3 ⎫		
others (including a few retaken	⎬	60	38·4%
absconders),	57 ⎭		
		156	100·0%

This table requires some explanation. Since our main follow-up of patients who left hospital within a year of the making of their hospital orders would have included very few of our restriction order cases (only 16 to be precise), we had to arrange a longer follow-up. Fortunately, the Home Office record the discharges, reconvictions and movements from hospital to hospital of such cases so long as the restriction orders remain in force; and we were thus able to review the position of each of our 156 restriction order cases in the middle of the year 1970.[20] As the table shows, 55 per cent had been deliberately allowed to leave hospital, while 2 per cent had absconded and been dealt with for further offences.[21] Apart from eight who had died or been transferred to Scottish hospitals, the remainder (38 per cent) were still in hospital (although some had achieved short periods of freedom by absconding). Since the main aim of the restriction order is the protection of the public, the most pertinent question that can be asked is 'How many of this cohort committed further serious offences during the follow-up period?' Thirty of them in all had centrally recorded reconvictions.

In all but three cases the further offences had been committed after the offender-patient had been deliberately discharged. The exceptions were absconders. One of these was a schizophrenic immigrant who had taken a knife to a policeman who asked him what he was doing. He escaped twice from a locked ward of an ordinary hospital, and on the second occasion avoided recapture. Ten weeks later the Home Office agreed to the hospital's requests to be allowed to remove his name from their books. A couple of years later he was found by the police in possession of an offensive weapon, with the result that he was recommitted to the same hospital under an ordinary hospital order. The hospital, not realising that his restriction order was still in force, regarded him as an ordinary hospital order patient, and discharged him a month or two later. By the time the Home Office learned what had happened he had been living in the community for over a year without giving any trouble, and it was therefore agreed to terminate his liability to detention under the original order. Another absconder was the psychopathic hitch-hiker who had quarrelled with and struck the motorist who gave him a lift. In spite of his long and violent record he was at first placed in an open ward, and although his abscondings led to his being placed in a 'closed ward' his medical officer admitted that security was 'non-existent'. On the occasion of his last escape eleven months after admission, he robbed and seriously injured a householder. For this he was sentenced to five years' imprisonment. An effort was made to have him transferred to a Special Hospital during his sentence, but this failed on the grounds that he was unlikely to respond to treatment (a view already expressed by the hospital from which he had absconded). For this reason[22] his liability to detention under the restriction order was eventually terminated by the Home Office shortly before his release from prison.

The third absconder was the fraudulent Scot described on p. 145, who had told his responsible medical officer that he could feign mental illness. He had been troublesome and aggressive in the ordinary hospital to which he had been sent, threatening and attacking staff and setting fire to bedding. A transfer to a Special Hospital had just been arranged when he absconded from a locked ward (from which he had been allowed to go out in the company of staff). That same day he knocked at the door of a house, hit with a milk bottle the woman who answered the door, and stabbed her husband when he went after him. This resulted in a seven-year prison sentence, for the doctors who examined him on that occasion took the view that his mental condition did not warrant a hospital order. Later in the same year, however, he was transferred from prison to the Special Hospital which had earlier agreed to receive him. There he told his doctor that he had feigned mental illness to get out of prison (just as he had said when he arrived at the ordinary hospital after the making of his hospital order). Though the doctor doubted this, he did seem to improve, and was returned to prison to finish his sentence (by the end of which his restriction order would in any case have expired). His subsequent career was very similar. First came several frauds and a prison sentence followed by another hospital order. He absconded from hospital and stabbed a stranger in the street, in order, he said, to kill him and so get his case reviewed. The judge who sentenced him to life imprisonment directed that his medical reports should be sent to the Home Secretary so that his transfer to the same Special Hospital could be considered, and he was duly transferred there. His psychotic symptoms then improved–whether as a result of treatment, spontaneous remission or deliberate choice–and he was returned to prison to continue his life sentence.

Of those who had been deliberately discharged, six were cases in which the period of the restriction had been extremely short (twelve months or even less), so that after a few months the responsibility for discharging the offender-patient devolved on the responsible medical officer. One such case was that of a psychopathic sexual offender with a record of repeated indecent assaults on young girls. His restriction order specified a period of only six months. When it expired, he was detained under the powers of the hospital order, but while on leave committed robbery and assault. After serving a prison sentence for this, and another for malicious wounding he was again convicted of indecency with children. Another offender-patient was the subject of a restriction order which expired twelve months later (perhaps because his record included only one act of minor personal violence). He remained for a short time as an informal patient, but was soon reconvicted, this time of arson, and sent to Broadmoor under an indeterminate restriction order. Another was a subnormal who had been convicted of a petty shopbreaking. Although there was nothing in his record to suggest that he was dangerous, he had been made the subject of a nine-month restriction order (we have suggested on pp. 91-2 that the court must have calculated by reference to the prison sentence which it would have regarded as appropriate). He was discharged soon after the order expired, but was reconvicted twice a few months later, again for petty acquisitive offences.

Altogether, however, the six-year follow-up disclosed only 12 out of the 156 restriction order cases in which it was clear from the legal label of the subsequent offence that the offender-patient had behaved dangerously.[23] The reconvictions were not of an alarming kind, involving for the most part thefts, frauds, forgeries, burglaries and damage to property. Our dozen included three men convicted of robbery, but as this can involve anything from actual violence to the mere threat of it we could not tell how much of a danger they represented to life or limb. Three others were found guilty of arson. (One of these was a psychopathic Sunday school teacher who had set fire to his church in a fit of pique. When his restriction order expired a year later he went home and was shortly afterwards moved by some other minor frustration to set his own house alight, but immediately regretted this and raised the alarm.)

One of the less serious cases demonstrated vividly the almost fortuitous ways in which the system rings the changes in its handling of the mildly disordered but apparently incorrigible recidivist. This was a twenty-five-year-old psychopath, who was said by at least one psychiatrist to be able to simulate psychosis. After a career of petty shopbreaking which began before the age of 12, and led him via approved schools to Borstal and several prison sentences, he was eventually made the subject of an ordinary hospital order soon after the coming into operation of the Act. He was soon at liberty, however, and on being tried for yet another burglary was found guilty but insane and sent to an ordinary hospital. From this he seems to have absconded and committed three more burglaries in 1963, for the last of which he was made the subject of the five-year restriction order which brought him within our cohort. While in hospital he absconded repeatedly, committing petty thefts during his absences, and also gave the police a good deal of trouble by confessing untruthfully to a murder. (His treatment was succinctly described by his psychiatrist as 'chlorpromazine and prayer'.) He was discharged with the Home Office's consent in 1966, and made five court appearances, all for burglary, over the next fourteen months, the first within two months of discharge. The sentences alternated between probation and imprisonment!

What was particularly worth noting was the small percentage of the 30 reconvicted restriction order cases who had been conditionally discharged.[24] A conditional discharge, which is possible only if the period of the restriction order has not yet expired, enables the Home Secretary to insist on arrangements being made for the ex-patient's after-care. In 50 out of the 58 cases in which he could have done so he did, and only 5 were reconvicted, none of them for serious offences.

In order to see how good this result is, it should be compared with the reconvictions during the first two years at liberty of our offender-patients who were discharged within a year of their order. To make this comparison as exact as possible we excluded from the 50 conditionally discharged patients 4 who were immediately repatriated, 1 who died, and 19 who were discharged too late for a two-year follow-up. We also excluded one of our conditionally discharged patients who had been reconvicted because this conviction occurred after more than two years at liberty. This left us with four convictions in a two-year follow-up of 25 men; a rate of 16 per cent. The overall reconviction rate for male offender-patients released in their first year was 42 per cent: nearly three times as great; and if we had been able to exclude from them all those who left the country during their first two years at liberty, and all those whose after-care was comparable to that insisted on by the Home Office, it would no doubt have been higher still.

(One obvious possibility, of course, was that the conditionally discharged restriction order cases were being saved from reconviction by being recalled to hospital, either just in time to prevent them from committing offences, or in time to prevent a prosecution. Amongst our 25, however, we could find only one whom the Home Office had recalled. This was a psychopath who had been conditionally discharged from a Special Hospital to live in a hostel under the supervision of a probation officer. He immediately infringed the conditions of his discharge by spending nights away from the hostel and avoiding his probation officer. He eventually disappeared altogether, but was traced to another town, where he had come to the notice of the police by creating a disturbance at the home of the husband of a woman with whom he was now living. He was recalled to the Special Hospital, but eight months later was discharged again as untreatable but unlikely to be violent. This did not prevent him from being recorded as a failure in our follow-up, for he was reconvicted–of shopbreaking and false pretences–within two years of his original discharge. He was committed to an ordinary hospital under a restriction order, absconded, was reconvicted, and when last heard of was in another Special Hospital.)

Special After-care. We have been able to show on p. 192 the rather encouraging association between 'after-care' and favourable outcomes so far as most of our male first-year leavers were concerned. It was so difficult, however, to assess the thoroughness of after-care where ordinary hospital order cases are concerned that we decided to make use of these conditionally discharged restriction order cases as the basis of a better test.

Accordingly we took as *propositi* all our restriction order cases who had been conditionally discharged in time to allow of a two-year follow-up (i.e., before the autumn of 1968), although several had to be discarded for various reasons. These we matched, one-for-one, with 'controls' from amongst those ordinary hospital order cases who had been discharged in time for our two-year follow-up, without any apparent arrangements for after-care. The criteria for matching were sex (all were male), diagnosis and previous criminal record. This gave us 22 matched pairs; and we found that of those who had received official after-care only 4 had been reconvicted during the follow-up period, compared with 13 of those who had received no apparent after-care. Small as the numbers were, this difference was marked enough to be highly significant.[25]

The comparison is open to the criticism that whereas all our controls were first-year leavers our *propositi* had in many cases spent more than a year–indeed in one or two cases over four years–in hospital; and that this might have rendered them in some way less likely to be reconvicted. It is true that our follow-up of first-year leavers did indicate a negative association between time in hospital and serious reconvictions. But in the case of men (and all our matched pairs were male) this association was very weak ($\beta = 0.10$: see Appendix B) and of doubtful significance ($t^2 = 3.18$). When serious and non-serious reconvictions were considered together it practically disappeared. Our comparison of second-year leavers with first-year leavers did not suggest that the former were any less likely to be reconvicted, at least in their first year at large, and it is quite possible that the weak negative association between time in hospital and serious reconvictions applies only to the first twelve months in hospital.[26] On the whole this criticism does not seem a strong one. When it is remembered that our *propositi* had been selected for restriction orders largely because of their persistence in serious crime, their relative freedom from reconviction for at least two years is remarkable. It may, of course, owe something to the selectiveness with which they were allowed to leave hospital; but it is more plausible–and consistent with the results of our main follow-up– to conclude that after-care was an important factor.

It is time, however, to return to the subject of the restriction orders. Since this is one of the most important devices for protecting the public against the dangerous offender-patient, its efficacy needs the closest appraisal. Several important points emerge from what has been said in this chapter and in chapter 4:

(a) On the credit side is the relatively low reconviction-rate of
    restriction order patients whose discharge is conditional; that is,

who are under some sort of supervision with the possibility of recall to hospital. Whether this is attributable to the selectivity with which conditional discharge is granted or to the thorough arrangements for after-care (or more probably to both), it shows that the restriction order system does reduce the frequency of offences by these offender-patients.

(b) This makes it all the more difficult to justify a restriction order with a time-limit. The circumstances in which the Lord Chief Justice's practice direction suggested that it might be justified are unlikely to occur, and difficult to identify with confidence if they ever do occur (see p. 91). Short time-limits can give rise to the premature discharge of dangerous offender-patients, as we have illustrated.

(c) It is questionable whether restriction order cases ought to be sent to ordinary hospitals. They are even less welcome there than ordinary hospital order cases,[27] partly because of anxiety about their behaviour, partly because responsible medical officers dislike the necessity of seeking Home Office agreement when they want to send the patient on leave or discharge him. The ideology of the 'open door' means that few, if any, ordinary hospitals can guarantee to contain a sophisticated absconder.

(d) It is questionable whether Mental Health Review Tribunals are a satisfactory safeguard against unjustifiable detention for this category of offender-patient. The trouble is not so much that in these cases they can only advise, and not decide upon discharge; for as we have seen their decisions can be unwise. (Nobody criticises the Parole Board system on the grounds that it is merely advisory.) Their real defect is that their advice is bound to carry less weight with the Home Office than that of the Parole Board. Their decisions are not subject to scrutiny, by follow-up or otherwise, whereas the Parole Board publishes annual reports, with statistics and justifications of its policy. The Home Office has no say in the choice of their members, as it has in the case of the Parole Board. Those who feel that the offender-patient who is under a restriction order needs a more adequate safeguard might well consider the suggestion that the Parole Board would be preferable. It has more experience of assessing offenders' careers than any Mental Health Tribunal could acquire in a decade of sittings. It includes psychiatrists and criminologists (as well as judges) amongst its members. And it pays close attention to the circumstances in which the offender will be living if he is given his freedom.

Notes

1. For a fuller discussion of reconvictions as a measure of 'success' see N. Walker, *Crimes, Courts and Figures* (London, 1971).

2. In the language of social science, 'hard' means 'unaffected by the judgement of the person recording the data', while 'soft' means the opposite. Thus 'age', 'sex', 'number of previous convictions' and

and 'place of birth' are 'hard data', while 'aggressiveness', 'inadequacy', 'unemployability' are 'soft', since a person who is classified
as 'aggressive' (etc.) by one interviewer may not appear so to
another. 'Hardness' must not of course be confused with 'accuracy':
a person's age may be wrongly recorded as a result either of his
untruthfulness or the interviewer's carelessness.

3. See 'A Century of Causal Theory', in *Frontiers of Criminology*,
    H. J. Klare and D. Haxby (edd.) (Oxford, 1967).

4. We could, perhaps, have added to this 'time previously spent in
    mental hospitals'. But our information about this was much less
    reliable. We felt able to use 'previous hospital admissions' as a
    variable (in spite of the difficulties of ascertaining these, which
    were mentioned in chapter 6, they did prove to correlate with
    readmission) but the length of each stay was often not recorded.

5. We could also have included type of treatment, conduct in hos-
    pital (as reported by staff) and prognosis; but did not consider
    that our information on these points was sufficiently complete or
    'hard'.

6. Nor was it plausible to argue that it would probably have reached
    an acceptable level of significance had the numbers been larger;
    for we were dealing with 62 matched pairs.

7. It was almost as marked for women as for men, but did not reach
    significance level in their case because of their smaller numbers.

8. See table 29 in Appendix B. It must be pointed out that the
    'inexplicability' could almost certainly have been reduced
    somewhat by special methods of analysis: see the discussion in
    Appendix B.

9. R. A. Carr-Hill and G. A. Carr-Hill, 'Reconviction as a Process', in
    (1972) 12, *British Journal of Criminology*, 35.

10. More precisely, those who leave hospital in the first year.

11. Another function of prediction formulae is to provide a method
    of group-matching samples and controls in a study of the effective-
    ness of some 'treatment'. This is how we use our scoring systems
    on p. 192.

12. We realise of course that objections are raised to the use of pre-
    dictive methods. One sort of objector believes that they are inferior
    to non-arithmetical methods of using one's data. The evidence does
    not support this: see the review in Mrs F. H. Simon's *Prediction
    Methods in Criminology*, Home Office Research Unit Report Series
    (HMSO, 1971), 143-4. The other sort of objector is more worried
    about the possibility that a prediction formula may be misused –
    or, more precisely, used for inappropriate decisions. To take an
    example from our own study: it is conceivable that a sentencer
    who was over-impressed with our prediction tables might decide
    not to use hospital orders for our high-risk sub-groups. This
    would be rational only if hospital places were so scarce that he was
    forced to be selective. A third sort of objector is simply repelled by
    the idea of using so impersonal a method – however efficient – in

arriving at decisions affecting human beings: but this is essentially an aesthetic reaction with which one cannot argue.

13. Loc. cit. (n. 12).

14. See the R^2 values in table 29 in Appendix B, which were 0·26 for men and 0·45 for women.

15. We fear that we must leave this to other research workers. They will find, almost certainly, that the percentages in our tables have shrunk towards the mean; but this cannot be prevented when one constructs a formula to fit one sample and tests it on another.

16. We extracted every case in which the legal label of the offence indicated personal violence, arson or a sexual offence; but then excluded indecent exposure, soliciting, assaulting the police (for the reason given on p. 125) threatening behaviour and possessing an offensive weapon. The last of these never involves a firearm, and it is a charge which tends to arise out of an arrest for some other offence, such as shopbreaking or being drunk and disorderly.

17. It must be remembered that we had information about reconvictions for only the first year after discharge for the second-year discharges, as compared with two years for the first-year discharges.

18. We are not implying that predictably harmful patients are confined to hospital order cases. They are also to be found amongst those admitted compulsorily without prosecution or even informally, as Dr Rollin has shown in chapter 5 of *The Mentally Abnormal Offender and the Law* (Oxford, 1969). Indeed some of our own cases had previously been admitted in these ways.

19. The figures were supplied at our request by the Home Office.

20. Since their original orders were spread over a 12-month period, whereas our review was carried out at a single date, their periods 'at risk' are not of uniform length. But since they were of considerable length – being in no case less than 6 years – this matters less than it would have done if the follow-up period had been short.

21. These were not of course the only absconders: merely those whose abscondings had led to their being dealt with afresh by criminal courts.

22. A contributory consideration was that he intended to go on a government training scheme on release.

23. We did not count as dangerous: acquisitive offences not charged as robbery, sexual offences which did not involve assault, offences against public order or decency, or assaults on the police (for the reasons given on p. 125). On the other hand, we included murder, attempted murder, grievous bodily harm, robbery, assault with intent to rob, arson, indecent assaults, indecency with children and an attempted buggery.

24. Not counting one who had been reconvicted of housebreaking while still on the hospital books. He was sentenced to imprisonment, transferred to hospital and a year later repatriated to the West Indies with a conditional discharge.

25. $p = 0 \cdot 01$, approximately, using Stuart's test for matched samples (loc. cit., p. 145 n.).

26. It might, for example, merely reflect willingness to co-operate in treatment.

27. It is even said that some responsible medical officers try to stipulate that if they accept a hospital order case a restriction order should not be made: see for example Commons Hansard for 23 January 1962 (written answers, col. 8).

Chapter 9. **From Moral Insanity to Psychopathy**

Before our review is concluded, there is one diagnostic category which needs a chapter or two of its own because of the peculiar difficulties which it has created for courts, legal draftsmen and philosophers. Psychopathic disorder differs from most, if not all, other psychiatric diagnoses in several ways. With the possible exception of 'maladjustment' no other diagnosis has had such difficulty in establishing its status as a genuine clinical label; and there are signs that both are proving too vague and unsatisfactory for professional use. Other disorders have symptoms which only occasionally bring the sufferer into conflict with the codes of behaviour of his society; but the symptoms of psychopathy almost invariably do so. At the same time they are less specific than the signs of most mental illnesses, and less easily measurable than mental subnormality. For the lawyer it raises in its most acute form the difficulty of distinguishing between those sufferers who should be held responsible for their conduct and those who should not.

The history of 'psychopathy' begins with the formation of a concept in the minds of philosophers and mad-doctors. Thereafter, the concept becomes linked with a succession of ill-defined terms of art, until one of these is seized on by legislators and bundled into the statute-book. The resulting trouble takes half a century to recognise and remedy, and today it remains uncertain whether the remedy is entirely successful.

The Concept

In tracing the history of the concept it is important to distinguish it clearly both from causal theories and from the word 'psychopathy' itself. As we shall see, the former depend largely on the fashionable ideology of the day, while the word itself meant something quite different for much of its history. Essentially, the concept is of a disorder, or group of disorders, which in the first place falls short of more definite forms of mental disorder and secondly is associated with antisocial conduct. The first of these notions–that the gulf between the sane and the mad might be an illusory one, filled with differing degrees of abnormality, is older than is usually supposed, although it was unfashionable amongst the mad-doctors of the so-called Enlightenment. It is at least as old as Burton's *Anatomy of Melancholy* (1621), which is prefaced by a few lines of not very elegant rhyme reminding the reader that between him and the madman there is no difference.[1] It is unlikely that Burton meant this to be taken very seriously; it was an aphorism, intended–like so many sayings of Oxford dons–to produce both shock and humility with a single sentence.

About the same time, however, Hobbes was writing into his *Leviathan* (1651) a passage which the twentieth-century Schneider would have approved:

> . . . to have stronger and more vehement passions for anything, than is ordinarily seen in others, is that which men call Madnesse . . . and if the excesses be Madnesse, there is no doubt but the Passions themselves, when they tend to Evill, are degrees of the same . . .

Even Hobbes' contemporary, Hale, though a judge, was prepared to recognise the existence of 'partial insanity' for practical if not judicial purposes (see volume I, p. 38). By the middle of the eighteenth century the theory that there is no sharp line of distinction between madness and sanity was being put forward as a serious scientific thesis by at least one physician, David Hartley (1705–57):

> Mad Persons differ from others in that they judge wrong of past or future Facts of a common Nature; that their Affections and Actions are violent and different from, or even opposite to, those of others upon the like Occasions, and such as are contrary to their true Happiness; that their Memory is fallacious, and their Discourse incoherent; and that they lose, in great measure, that Consciousness which accompanies our Thoughts and Actions, and by which we connect ourselves with ourselves from time to time. These circumstances are variously combined in the Various kinds and Degrees of Madness; and some of them take place in Persons of sound Minds, in certain Degrees and for certain Spaces of Time; *so that here, as in other Cases, it is impossible to fix precise limits, and to determine where Soundness of Mind ends and Madness begins* . . . (our italics).[2]

Hartley, however, had more influence on poets and philosophers–such as Coleridge–than on his own profession. Doctors were more impressed by his contemporary Battie, and Battie was influenced not by Hobbes' definition of madness, but by Locke's, with the result that in England–as we saw in volume I (p. 71)–a mental state which did not involve hallucinations or delusions was not regarded by most physicians as real madness.

One or two, however, were less rationalistic. Among them was Thomas Arnold, owner of a large private mad-house in Leicester, whose scholarly but eccentric two-volume treatise[3] offered such engaging diagnoses as 'scheming insanity', 'appetitive insanity' and 'nostalgic insanity'.[4] He pointed out that:

> . . . there is indeed some difficulty in determining the boundaries between what may not improperly be called moral and medical insanity. Several of the philosophers considered every foolish or vicious person as insane or morally mad; and only to be distinguished from the actually or medically mad by the degree of disorder . . .

Note the term 'moral insanity', which was to be the subject of so much discussion in the nineteenth century. Arnold writes as if he were coining the phrase, and uses it quite as ambiguously as did his successors. Did it mean 'anti-socially mad'? Probably not at this date. More likely is the possibility that it meant 'affectively (as opposed to "cognitively") mad' or 'functionally (as opposed to "organically") mad'. It is even more probable that it simply meant 'virtually mad', as in the phrase 'a moral certainty'. However, that may be, his treatise was not well received and he was criticised for confusing moral with medical—i.e., real—madness.[5]

In France, however, Pinel found readier acceptance for his notion of 'manie sans délire'. His often-quoted example of this sounds so like an 'aggressive psychopath' that it will bear one more repetition:

> The following relation will place in a conspicuous point of view, the influence of a neglected or ill-directed education, in inducing upon a mind naturally perverse and unruly, the first symptoms of this species of mania. An only son of a weak and indulgent mother, was encouraged in the gratification of every caprice and passion, of which an untutored and violent temper was susceptible. The impetuosity of his disposition increased with his years. The money with which he was lavishly supplied, removed every obstacle to his wild desires. Every instance of opposition or resistance, roused him to acts of fury. He assaulted his adversary with the audacity of a savage; sought to reign by force, and was perpetually embroiled in disputes and quarrels. If a dog, a horse, or any other animal offended him, he instantly put it to death. If ever he went to a fête or any other public meeting, he was sure to excite such tumults and quarrels as terminated in actual pugilistic rencounters, and he generally left the scene with a bloody nose. This wayward youth, however, when unmoved by passions, possessed a perfectly sound judgement. When he came of age, he succeeded to the possession of an extensive domain. He proved himself fully competent to the management of his estate, as well as to the discharge of his relative duties; and he even distinguished himself by acts of beneficence and compassion. Wounds, law-suits and pecuniary compensations, were generally the consequences of his unhappy propensity to quarrel. But an act of notoriety put an end to his career of violence. Enraged at a woman, who had used offensive language to him, he precipitated her into a well. Prosecution was commenced against him, and on the disposition of a great many witnesses, who gave evidence to his furious deportment, he was condemned to perpetual confinement at Bicêtre.[6]

But would Pinel have grouped along with this man the sort of people who are now diagnosed as psychopaths? This is very doubtful. He cites this case, as has been said, to illustrate 'mania without confusion' which, he says 'may be either continued or intermittent. No sensible changes in the function of the understanding, but perversions of the active faculties, marked by an abstract and sanguinary fury with a blind propensity to acts of violence.' The other examples he gives are of sudden, unprovoked outbursts of violence: a cobbler, for example, who could feel the approach of one of his abnormal states, and warn his wife so that she could keep out of harm's way. These do not sound like psychopathy.

The idea that there could be 'madness' without any damage to understanding was a difficult one for British mad-doctors. Yet one of the chief sceptics eventually became a convert, and was largely responsible for securing acceptance for the notion in the English-speaking world. This was James Prichard (1786–1848) who managed to combine the post of Physician at Bristol Infirmary with research into anthropology and Egyptology, and was sufficiently respected as a psychiatrist to be made one of the Commissioners in Lunacy shortly before his death. His *Treatise on Insanity and other Disorders affecting the Mind* published in 1835, conceded that Pinel was right, and that there could be madness without delusion.

Prichard is not infrequently credited with having been the first British psychiatrist to recognise the psychopath. His definition of 'moral insanity' is often quoted:

> . . . madness, consisting in a morbid perversion of the natural
> feelings, affections, inclinations, temper, habits, moral dispositions, and
> natural impulses, without any remarkable [*sc.* observable] disorder
> or defect of the interest or knowing and reasoning faculties, and
> particularly without any insane illusion or hallucinations.[7]

But an examination of the case-histories which he gives as examples of moral insanity (as well as his later definition[8]) makes it very doubtful whether he was describing what a modern English psychiatrist would call a psychopath. One was a gentleman who in adult life developed an obsessional tidiness and feelings of inferiority to his wife; another developed persecutory delusions; another was a manic-depressive country magistrate; another was an alcoholic squire; another was probably a rare case of infantile schizophrenia; and another was a middle-aged gentlewoman who developed a strange restlessness and lack of concentration after 'a severe inflamation in the lungs'. It is noticeable that practically all these case-histories trace the onset of the disorder to a definite point in time, often to a specified illness or event. Nor do the symptoms described include the easily provoked aggressiveness or the irresponsibility, inadequacy or callousness that are offered nowadays as the distinguishing features of one or other type of psychopathy.

The mistaken idea that Prichard was describing a disorder which was necessarily associated with sinful or anti-social conduct arose from his use of the word 'moral'. Although the word was not uncommonly used in its modern sense in his day (and long before that), it could also, as we have seen mean nothing more than 'psychological' or 'emotional'. An example was another psychiatric phrase, 'moral management', which meant simply the control of the insane by non-mechanical, psychological methods. When Bucknill and Tuke, the authors of the standard mid-Victorian textbook of psychiatry, discussed Prichard's notion they used the less ambiguous term 'emotional insanity'.[9] Whatever Prichard's contribution to Egyptology or anthropology, he was not a very original psychiatrist, and was simply importing the view of Pinel and Esquirol that there was a group of disorders which were brought about by psychological as opposed to physical accidents, and which consisted essentially in emotional imbalance. Examples of 'moral' causes were 'disappointment in love', 'political events', 'reverses of fortune', 'excess in study' and 'reading romances'. It was the merit of this classification that it recognised two important possibilities. One was that mental illness was not always characterised by delusion or hallucination; the other that they were not always attributable to physical injury, disease, poisoning, sunstroke or masturbation.[10] There is no doubt, however, that Prichard used his term so as to include, though not exclusively, behaviour which was in the modern sense immoral, and this was what the phrase came to mean to psychiatrists by the last decades of the nineteenth century.

Moral Imbecility.[11] In this sense, however, moral insanity was a disorder which could manifest itself at almost any stage of life. Equally, if not more, important, was the observation that some individuals behaved badly from a very early age. Again, English psychiatrists had apparently to have their attention drawn to this by Continental or American doctors. Benjamin Rush noticed it[12]; and so did Dr Woodward of the State Lunatic Asylum in Massachusetts. But interest in the varieties and causation of mental deficiency was greatest on the Continent. There was an important school of thought in France and Germany which believed in the congenital origin of a wide range of abnormalities, whether of the mind or body. It had many adherents in European psychiatry, and its leading exponent was of course Morel, whose 'Traité des dégénérescences physiques, intel-lectuelles et morales de l'espèce humaine . . .' (1857) attributed not only epilepsy and idiocy but also insanity and criminality to this conveniently vague concept. (It was the combination of Morel and Darwin which gave the Italian alienist, Lombroso, the idea that 'born criminals' were a form of atavism.) It was in Germany however, that mental deficiency was most scientifically studied, and where a certain degree of it was most readily accepted as a legal defence in criminal cases. While Prichard was writing about moral insanity, Heinroth and Griesinger were recording the be-haviour of cretins and other mental defectives. In particular, Griesinger, who had worked in a state asylum for defectives in Württemberg, and whose text-book was translated into French and English in the eighteen-sixties, was drawing attention to:

> An extremely dangerous class . . . those weak-minded children with instinctive (congenital) evil desires to mischief, cruelty, theft, drunkenness, etc., which sometimes nothing can suppress. These individuals, when their intelligence is such as to permit them to remain out of an asylum, afterwards furnish a numerous contingent to our prisons and houses of correction; their state is frequently evidently hereditary and their habits are by no means identical with the evil desires which are developed in children through the example of their seniors.[13]

In England, Charles West, who specialised in and lectured on the diseases of children, observed amongst them a 'mental disorder' (his own very modern term) of the kind normally described as moral insanity. The term for this phenomenon which eventually gained currency in English-speaking countries was 'moral imbecility'. It appears in Prichard, but only as a translation of Heinroth's phrase, 'Blodsinn mit Willenlosigkeit' i.e., feeble-mindedness with lack of self-control. Prichard simply said that moral insanity could sometimes be 'native or congenital'. Nevertheless, the orthodox were sceptical. Bucknill and Tuke poured cold water on the idea:

P

It must of course be admitted that ordinary idiots are idiotic *morally* as
well as intellectually; but we have not yet seen enough evidence to
prove that a condition of moral idiocy exists (loc. cit.).

Had England not lagged behind Germany in the provision of institutions
for the mentally defective they might have had more opportunities of
observing what West and Griesinger were describing. But with the growth
of such institutions the evidence became only too abundant. Henry
Maudsley (1835–1918), who had been much influenced by Morel, was
more receptive. When he published his *Responsibility in Mental Disease*
(1872)–a book so popular that a second edition was needed within the
year–he pointed out that 'many cases of moral insanity will be found to
be connected with more or less congenital moral defect or imbecility'. His
belief in Morel's notion of degeneracy led him to regard insane or epileptic
patients as a major source of moral imbeciles.

The Law

Unfortunately, the alarm over the apparently increasing numbers of
mental defectives in the population led the legislators to take a hand in the
game, with consequences which were doubly misleading. Not only did
they inscribe indelibly into the statute-book the notion that there was a
distinguishable mental condition which was closely associated with anti-
social behaviour; they also linked it–more or less by accident–with low
intelligence. The second of these consequences was eventually remedied,
but not the first.

What happened was this. When the Royal Commission on the Care and
Control of the Feeble-Minded was set up in 1904, the evidence which
they received from the medical profession, and in particular the Royal
College of Physicians, clearly assumed the existence of two sorts of
patient whose main symptoms were their anti-social conduct. On the one
hand there was the morally insane person 'who, after many years of
reputable life, all at once unaccountably exhibits vicious propensities, or
takes to criminal courses' (Royal College of Physicians' evidence). On the
other hand there was the 'moral imbecile', who 'from an early age displays
some mental defect coupled with strong vicious or criminal propensities
on which punishment has little or no deterrent effect'. The former should
be treated as cases of 'unsoundness of mind', the latter as examples of
'mental defect'.

At this point, however, the Commission came to a conclusion which
was to have important consequences. On the one hand, it would not be
'scientifically correct' to make the morally insane a separate subdivision
of 'unsoundness of mind', although they did not say why not. On the
other hand, 'moral imbecility' should be distinguished from other sorts
of mental defect, apparently because the essence of this form of defect
was not an incapacity for looking after one's self but an abnormality of
'will and judgement'.

Since their other three subdivisions[14] of 'mental defect' were 'feeble-
mindedness', 'idiocy' and 'imbecility', it was inevitable that the phrase
'mental defect' should become firmly associated with the notion of low

intelligence, although this was not the Commission's intention, nor, on a strict interpretation, the legal effect of the definition. It is doubtful whether this would greatly have worried the Radnor Commission, who had been assured by the Lord Chancellor's visitor in Lunacy[15] that the vicious or criminal propensities of the moral imbecile were 'generally associated with some slight limitation of intellect'. Nevertheless, as we shall see, it had important practical consequences.

Since one of the Radnor Commission's aims was frankly to segregate mental defectives for eugenic reasons, its report was highly controversial, and (as we saw in chapter 4) the Government hesitated for several years to bring in the necessary legislation. When they were eventually forced to do so by back-bench pressure, their Bill did not deal with 'persons of unsound mind', although the Royal Commission had made proposals for bringing them within its comprehensive scheme of control. The result was that almost by accident the 1913 Act was silent on the subject of moral insanity. As for moral imbeciles, its definition differed only in a few words from that proposed by the Royal College: they were

> persons who from an early age display some permanent mental defect coupled with strong vicious or criminal propensities on which punishment has had little or no effect.[16]

It was some years before the restrictiveness of this definition began to be a subject of complaint, although it might have been earlier if it had not been for the First World War. When complaints began they were directed not at the apparent linking of moral imbecility with intellectual incapacity, but at the insistence that this must have existed 'from an early age'.

It took several epidemics and a Departmental Committee to bring about legislation. The post-war outbreaks of *encephalitis lethargica*–of which the worst occurred in 1924[17]–left in their wake several hundred children with permanent brain damage and anti-social traits which could not be said to have existed from an early age. Independently, in 1925 the Report of the Committee on Sexual Offences against Young Persons[18] drew attention to cases in which men with long records of indecent exposure or worse, who clearly ought to be in some institution, could not be certified because the doctors could trace nobody who would confirm that they had behaved anti-socially in childhood. The Government were prodded into action; but their first Bill, which simply redefined mental defectiveness as a condition which was 'innate or induced after birth by disease, injury or other cause' was wrecked in the name of liberty by the same Colonel Wedgwood who had so successfully delayed the legislation of 1913 (see p. 61); and the second Bill succeeded only because it included the words 'before the age of eighteen'. As for moral imbeciles, the requirement that punishment should have been found to be ineffective was dropped, and they became persons

> ... in whose case there exists mental defectiveness coupled with strongly vicious or criminal propensities and who require care, supervision and control for the protection of others.[19]

Even so, in practice the definition still excluded many men and women whose anti-social behaviour appeared to have psychological origins. Most doctors were unwilling to diagnose a patient as a moral imbecile unless his behaviour was accompanied by some limitation of intelligence.[20] Although strictly speaking neither the 1913 nor the 1927 definitions had said anything about 'intelligence', this interpretation was understandable, not only because of the way in which the definitions were drafted, but also because the scientific measurement of intelligence which had been popularised by educational psychologists had influenced both laymen's notions of mental defect and psychiatrists' diagnoses. The phrase 'mental defectiveness coupled with strongly vicious or criminal propensities' thus came to be understood as meaning that the patient must be stupid as well as wicked. In fact mental defectiveness meant nothing more specific than 'arrested or incomplete development of mind', and a minority of doctors did appreciate that this could mean no more than a failure to develop normal self-control or emotional reactions. But for most the change in the non-legal meaning of 'mental defectiveness' and 'imbecile' had been decisive.

The Word

As so often happens, a new word was needed to clear up the muddle, and the word was 'psychopathic'. To understand how it came to have the necessary meaning we must hark back again to the German psychiatrists of the middle of the nineteenth century. In the writings of the German psychiatrist Ernst von Feuchtersleben in the eighteen-forties 'psychopathy' meant what the etymologist would expect; that is, psychological damage or defect. Von Feuchtersleben referred to 'psychopathies, or diseases of the personality (insanity in the more comprehensive sense) . . .'[21] The word 'psychopathology' continued to mean 'the study of psychopathological defect' long after 'psychopathic' had come to have a more restricted meaning.

The second meaning is traceable to Koch, the German author of *Die Psychopathischen Mindwertigkeiten* (1891).[22] Struck by the ambiguity of 'moral insanity', he preferred the term 'constitutional psychopathic inferiority' to cover a wide range of disorders which did not amount to insanity in the strict sense. It was the more widely-known Kraepelin, however, who popularised this 'residual' meaning, as I shall call it. In his nosology it included neurasthenia, 'compulsive' and 'impulsive' insanity and sexual perversions. (The last of these categories, by the way, had been taken by Krafft-Ebing as the subject for his book *Psychopathia Sexualis* (1886). Its popularity with readers who were unfamiliar with Kraepelin gave the impression that psychopathy was associated with sexual perversion, an impression which has been perpetuated in the USA by what are called 'sexual psychopath laws'). Kraepelin clearly distinguished psychopathic inferiority from moral imbecility, although the eighth edition of his text-book emphasised the anti-social behaviour (such as lying and swindling) which accompanied many psychopathic states. However that may be, the 'residual' meaning rapidly became popular in the USA, where 'psychopathic clinics' were set up and in some cases staffed by 'psychopathic doctors'. In 1902 William James could call Fox the Quaker and John Bunyan 'psychopathic': the former for his eccentricities, the latter for his oversensitive conscience.[23]

Adolf Meyer, who emigrated from Switzerland to the USA and helped to popularise the ideas of Koch and Kraepelin there, is credited with narrowing the residual meaning. Certainly his psychobiological approach made it difficult for him to attribute too many disorders to wholly 'constitutional' factors, so that in his nosology 'constitutional inferiority and abnormal make-up, with or without out-breaks' was relegated to the status of a minor rather than a major waste-basket and was clearly distinguished from neurasthenia, psychasthenia, and hysteria (not to mention epilepsy, idiocy and imbecility).[24] Note, however, that he did not here use the word 'psychopathic', and where he does it seems to have a fairly wide, loose sense.

In England too this residual meaning became popular. Well after the First World War Cyril Burt classed a child as 'psychopathic' only if he 'showed pathological as well as abnormal symptoms – slight delusional tendencies, slight manic-depressive tendencies, or something of the morbid negativism of *dementia praecox*'.[25] Even in the nineteen-fifties a prison medical officer explained that when he talked of 'psychopaths' he was not referring 'to the clinical entity now generally recognised as true psychopathic personality, but using it in the somewhat generic or etymological sense to include imperfectly remitted schizophrenics, chronic and more or less conditioned psychoneurotics, and high-grade feeble-minded people . . .'[26]

The third, 'ethical', usage, in which 'psychopathic' means 'anti-social' (whatever else it denotes), is a development which is very hard to date with confidence, and even harder to trace to its source. It crops up as early as 1885 in a report in the *Pall Mall Gazette* of a murder trial in St Petersburg:

> The evidence all through the trial was dead against Mdlle. Semenova, and it would have fared badly with her but for the declaration of an expert M. Balinsky, a Russian mad-doctor, who, pointing out to the jury the hysterical bearing of the culprit, persuaded them that she was suffering from 'psychopathy', and therefore morally irresponsible. For the benefit of those who are as yet ignorant of the meaning of psychopathy – a term which before long will be naturalised in our courts – we give M. Balinsky's explanation of the new malady. 'The psychopath', he says, 'is a type which has only recently come under the notice of medical science. It is an individual whose every moral faculty appears to be of the normal equilibrium. He thinks logically, he distinguishes good and evil, and he acts according to reason. But of all moral notions he is entirely devoid. . . . Besides his own person and own interests, nothing is sacred to the psychopath, etc., etc.'[27]

It took longer than the Gazette predicted for the term to be 'naturalised in our courts'; but the journal's concluding sentiment is one which a modern judge might have echoed:

> The short and the long of it seems to be that if egotism is fully developed in a human being, he becomes 'morally irresponsible' – a very convenient doctrine, to which, however, mankind will have to

add a corollary that whenever a fully developed psychopath is discovered
he shall be immediately hanged.

It seems quite possible that Balinsky, one of the leading Russian psychiatrists of his day, was in fact using the term in a more or less modern
way. The psychiatric examination of persons accused of serious crime was
a well-established practice in Russia, and while Balinsky did not specialise
in forensic aspects of his subject he frequently appeared in court. His
school of thought seems to have made distinctions between different kinds
of psychopathy, and to have believed in an amoral variety. His successors,
however, notably Gannushkin and Kerbikov, discredited his subdivisions,
and adopted a point of view resembling Kraepelin's original one.[28] It is
true that Kraepelin eventually came to emphasise the anti-social behaviour
of many psychopaths, but it was in the USA that the ethical meaning came
to rival or even supersede the residual sense. This was the result of increasing psychiatric interest in criminals, and especially prison populations.
The classic example is Bernard Glueck's attempt to classify 608 inmates
of Sing Sing Prison, not long after the First World War.[29] Fully 19 per
cent seemed to him to be 'psychopaths with delinquent tendencies'. Clearly
for him 'psychopathic' did not of itself mean 'delinquent'. But by the
middle of the nineteen-thirties the author of a well-known American text-
book of psychiatry said that 'there has at times been a tendency to include
practically all habitual criminals in this group, or even to limit it to the
anti-social'.[30]

It was Sir David Henderson (1884–1965), a Scottish disciple of Adolf
Meyer, who imported the ethical usage into Britain. Although he worked
under Meyer's guidance, and clearly took many of his ideas from him,
he seems to have borrowed this one from other American psychiatrists.
His own contribution to the concept[31] was his threefold subdivision of
psychopaths into

1. *the predominantly aggressive.* This linking of psychopathy with
   aggression can be traced back, via moral insanity, to Pinel's famous
   case-history, and needs little comment. It is worth noticing, however,
   that violence does not figure among the symptoms of Koch's or
   Kraepelin's psychopathic inferiority.

2. *the predominantly inadequate.* It was into this category that Henderson
   put Kraepelin's liars and swindlers, together with compulsive
   wanderers and a wide assortment of hysterical and neurotic
   conditions. It is reminiscent not only of Koch's psychopathic inferiority
   but also of Janet's 'psychasthenia'. Henderson himself realised how
   elastic a waste-basket it was, but does not seem to have been deterred
   by this; and it was adopted not only by the Royal Commission on
   Lunacy and Mental Deficiency, but also, as we shall see, by British
   criminologists.

Henderson added a third category

3. *the predominantly creative.* This was dramatic rather than original.
   Cox,[32] Lombroso, Moebius[33] and Healy[34]—to mention only a few of
   Henderson's predecessors—had drawn attention to the fact that not a
   few people of high ability suffered from behavioural disorders, if not
   occasional insanity. Henderson, however, seems to have believed

that 'genius' was something more than a matter of degree, and that it
was associated with 'mental imbalance' to a more-than-chance extent.
He did not improve his case by his very careless choice of examples,
which consisted of Joan of Arc and Lawrence of Arabia.

The result was that his last category, the only one which was not closely
associated with delinquent behaviour, received little attention, and his
already very simple subdivision was still further simplified, so that it
became virtually a system for classifying delinquents. A good example of
this is Dr West's important and influential book *The Habitual Prisoner*,[35]
which explicitly used Henderson's pre-war dichotomy. West classified no
less than 52 per cent of his hundred recidivists as 'passive-inadequates'
and 36 per cent as 'active-aggressives', leaving a residue of 12 per cent
which he regarded as 'normal'. In other words, either a recidivist fitted
into one of Henderson's main categories, or he was psychologically
normal.

Psychopathy in Court

Moreover, psychopathy was so resounding a term of art that it persuaded
many a psychiatrist of the existence of a specific disorder for which at last
a name had been found. In 1949 Dr Edward Glover referred to 'perfectly
valid scientific discoveries such as the nature of psychopathy', and complained that judges had ridden roughshod over it.[36] Even judges, however, eventually bowed before the word, although it was some time before
their obeisance became a willing one. When 'psychopath' began to be
heard in roughly its modern sense in British criminal courts about the end
of the 1939–45 war, it carried little weight. Even in Scotland, the home
country not only of Henderson and Glover but also of the defence of
diminished responsibility, the term cut no ice with lawyers. When Patrick
Carraher, who had committed two homicides and had a record of attempted suicide, was described as psychopathic by medical witnesses
because of his lack 'of moral sense', the appellate court commented simply
that 'much of the evidence given by the medical witnesses is to my mind
descriptive rather of a typical criminal than of a person of the quality
of one whom the law has hitherto regarded as being possessed of diminished
responsibility'.[37]

In England, where psychopathy, along with several other diagnoses,
was clearly outside the scope of the insanity defence, the Gowers Commission of 1949–53 echoed Lord Normand's sentiments. Not only was
the term employed so loosely as to be a 'psychiatric waste-basket for cases
otherwise difficult to classify'; even when it was more precisely used it was
often applied to character and conduct that seemed typical of the confirmed criminal or simply of a wicked man. Nevertheless, the Commission
was convinced by the medical witnesses who appeared before it–notably
Sir David Henderson–that as a concept it was 'necessary and legitimate'.
They were especially impressed by the results of electro-encephalographic
studies, which showed a high frequency of abnormalities in the brains of
aggressive psychopaths, and especially of 'motiveless' murderers. This led
them to the belief that 'the moral and emotional immaturity . . . of
the psychopath is related to a constitutional immaturity in the development of the brain'. Consequently, though the difference between the

psychopath and normal people was quantitative rather than qualitative, and his legal responsibility could not be regarded as totally abolished, it could in many cases be regarded as diminished.

This conclusion seems to have had more effect in England than in Scotland, where judges remained sceptical. When the Homicide Act, 1957 became law, the first defence of diminished responsibility was based on a diagnosis of psychopathic personality (Shirley Campbell's case: see volume I, p. 152). It succeeded, but several subsequent defences of the same kind did not, and it was not until Matheson's case that the Court of Criminal Appeal gave a decision which by implication confirmed that a diagnosis of psychopathy could in their view sustain a defence of diminished responsibility. Albert Edward Matheson was a fifty-two-year-old casual labourer in Newcastle, who had spent much of his life in penal institutions, and had been a voluntary patient in a mental hospital. He indulged in sodomy and other abnormal practices, and used to push his nails up his urethra. He had a homosexual relationship with a boy of 15, to whom he probably paid money. A day or two after the boy had missed an appointment with him he met him, took him to a boxing hall, and killed him by hitting him on the head with a bottle full of water. After cutting up and disembowelling the body, which he hid in a sump, he left Newcastle for Edinburgh, from where he posted anonymous postcards to the boy's mother, abusing him and saying he was dead; eventually he gave himself up to the Glasgow police.

For the defence, a prison medical officer and two psychiatrists testified that he had a mental age of about ten years, and a psychopathic personality; and that he was shallow, unstable, sexually perverted and lacking in moral responsibility. The prosecution called no evidence to the contrary, but the jury, probably because of the shocking nature of the crime, rejected the plea of diminished responsibility and found him guilty of capital murder. The Court of Criminal Appeal substituted a verdict of manslaughter by reason of diminished responsibility, and a sentence of twenty years' imprisonment,[38] on the grounds that

> while . . . the decision in these cases, as in those in which insanity is
> pleaded, is for the jury and not for doctors, the verdict must be
> founded on evidence. . . . If the doctors' evidence is unchallenged and
> there is no other on this issue, a verdict contrary to their opinions
> would not be 'a true verdict in accordance with the evidence'.

The importance of Matheson's case for psychopathic murderers lay not in anything which the appellate court said about psychopathy, but in its declaration that if there was unchallenged medical evidence to the effect that the mental condition of the accused amounted to diminished responsibility, the jury was not entitled to find otherwise.

The case which probably benefited psychopaths more than any other, however, was that of Patrick Byrne, which is described in volume I (p. 155). The crucial part of the medical evidence, on which the prison medical officer and two specialists in psychological medicine seemed to agree, was that he was a 'sexual psychopath', suffering from violent and perverted desires which he found it difficult or impossible to control. It was fortunate for other psychopaths that the trial judge was unsympathetic to his defence, for the result was that the Court of Criminal Appeal arrived at the authoritative interpretation of diminished responsibility which made it clear that lack of self-control could now be the basis of a defence.

The subsequent case of Jennion,[39] however, emphasises that when the medical witnesses disagree a defence based on psychopathy is unlikely to convince even the appellate court. Yvonne Jennion was a twenty-three-year-old unemployed cook, who had a history of minor delinquency, promiscuity and homosexuality. She lived with her aunt, from whom one day in 1958 she tried to borrow money; but the request was refused. In the ensuing quarrel her aunt slapped her and she knocked her aunt down with an ashtray, afterwards throttling her. Her defence of diminished responsibility was unsuccessful. Called by the defence, the prison medical officer and Dr Finkelman agreed that her responsibility for her act had been substantially impaired by abnormality of mind. But whereas the prison medical officer thought that she had been suffering from simple schizophrenia in an early phase, Dr Finkelman thought that the abnormality was psychopathic personality (both doctors appear to have regarded the chief symptom as 'emotional flattening'). For the Crown, Dr Vaillant said that she had a 'psychopathic personality without psychosis'. But he was satisfied that this did not constitute such abnormality of mind as substantially to impair her mental responsibility. She was found guilty of non-capital murder. In 1961 she sought leave to appeal; but after obtaining a full transcript of the trial the Court of Criminal Appeal refused leave, holding that the jury were entitled to come to this decision on the evidence, and that there had been no misdirection by the judge. There may have been no misdirection from a lawyer's point of view, but the trial judge's remarks were most misleading from a psychiatric standpoint. At one point he explained to the jury that 'schizophrenia' meant 'a split mind', and at another he professed himself puzzled by Dr Vaillant's phrase 'psychopathic personality without psychosis'.

It is clear from these cases that while a diagnosis of psychopathy is now recognised by English courts as an acceptable basis for a defence of diminished responsibility, the psychopath's chances of succeeding in this defence are by no means high. Unless his conduct at times other than that of the killing shows signs of gross abnormality–preferably sexual abnormality–the medical witnesses for the defence may very well find themselves contradicted by a sceptical prison medical officer; and if the medical evidence is not 'all one way' the details of the psychopath's conduct are likely to render the jury antagonistic rather than sympathetic towards him. Nor will the Court of Criminal Appeal interfere with an unsympathetic verdict unless it flies in the face of unanimous medical evidence, or is preceded by a legally defective summing-up from the judge. Indeed, while it was conceded by the Court of Criminal Appeal in Byrne's case that it was for medical witnesses to say what the 'aetiology' of the accused's abnormality is, the court emphasised that it is for the jury to decide whether he was suffering from that abnormality at the time of the killing, who may take into account not only the medical evidence but also his acts or statements. Finally, the differences of theory or even terminology between medical witnesses may disguise from judges and juries the extent to which they are in agreement about the abnormality of the accused.

So much for the criminal liability of the psychopath in murder trials. But most psychopaths were charged with less serious offences, and could not avail themselves of any of the special defences. Their only hope of escaping an ordinary custodial sentence was a court order under the 1913 Act or a reception order or psychiatric probation order under the 1948 Act. When the Percy Commission reviewed the situation a few years after the Gowers Commission, and in a wider context, they were more impressed by the confusion than the unanimity of diagnostic practice. There seemed to be a group of persons whose intelligence was not seriously impaired, but whose inadequate, aggressive or sexually promiscuous behaviour called for special forms of treatment and control, and which was being variously described as 'feeble-minded', 'morally defective' or 'psychopathic'. When there was no apparent impairment of intelligence, many doctors considered it improper to certify the person under the statutory label 'feeble-mindedness' or 'moral defectiveness', and resorted to the term 'psychopathic'. Moreover, in spite of the Radnor Commission's view that 'unsoundness of mind' covered such cases, this term was still being interpreted too narrowly to do so. Consequently neither the 1913 Act procedures nor 'reception orders' could be used in such cases, although if the psychopath appeared in a criminal court he could sometimes be made the subject of a psychiatric probation order.[40]

The Royal Commission and Parliament

The Percy Commission's approach to this problem was confident, perhaps over-confident. 'We are convinced from the evidence we have received that it is not difficult for doctors to recognise these characteristics in individual patients and to make a diagnosis that is readily acceptable to an intelligent layman on the basis of his observation of the patient's general behaviour. The difficulty of describing them is a difficulty of language rather than of diagnosis.' (This was written before that highly intelligent layman, Lady Wootton, had demonstrated that a diagnosis of this kind was far from being 'readily acceptable' to the sociologically minded.[41]) In fact the Commission were putting a bold face on their inability to agree on any specific definition.[42] To clear up the terminological confusion moreover, they proposed only three statutory subdivisions of what would be generically called 'mental disorder'–'mental illness', 'severe subnormality' and 'psychopathic personality'. The last would include any type of aggressive or inadequate personality which did not amount to severe subnormality, but which was recognised medically as a pathological condition; and could thus include persons whose intelligence was not markedly limited. But when it *was* markedly limited the person could be called a 'feeble-minded psychopath'.

Whether this solution (which had not been proposed to them by any of their witnesses) would have improved matters is uncertain. In particular, 'inadequate personality' was a very wide and vague term on which to base compulsory admission to a mental hospital. Many a man, woman and child is 'inadequate' without being dangerous or even troublesome.

Nor did the Commission's solution provide for the person who was feeble-minded without being psychopathic, although they could reasonably have argued that there was no need to provide for the admission of feeble-minded people who were neither inadequate nor aggressive. However that may be, the Commission's categorisation was so unpopular with the medical profession and in many other quarters[43] that the Ministry devised a solution which not only recognised mere subnormality (i.e., feeble-mindedness in the Commission's terminology) as a ground for admission without psychopathy, but also defined psychopathy more restrictively as

a persistent disorder of personality (whether or not including subnormality of intelligence) which results in abnormally aggressive or seriously irresponsible conduct on the part of the patient and requires or is susceptible to medical treatment.

This definition improved on the Commission's in several ways. It insisted on the importance of *conduct* as evidence of a disorder of personality. Instead of 'aggressive' it said 'abnormally aggressive'. Instead of the vague term 'inadequacy' it referred to 'serious irresponsibility'. Like the Commission's definition it did not stipulate that the disorder must have been detectable at an early age; but unlike theirs it insisted that it must be persistent. It also stipulated that the disorder must 'require medical treatment', and it was not the Ministry's fault that—as we shall see in the next chapter—this was to give rise to an important misunderstanding. Finally, an important restriction (applying to all the statutory subdivisions of mental disorder) made it clear that nobody could be dealt with under these definitions 'by reason only of promiscuity or other immoral conduct'.[44]

During the Bill's passage the definition of psychopathic disorder was the first part of clause 4 to be attacked in Committee. Dr Johnson wanted to delete it altogether, so that hospitals could not be compelled to accept this troublesome group of patients: an aim which would have received stronger support today than it did then. Other members pointed out that 'abnormally aggressive' and 'seriously irresponsible' were terms which could be applied even to their colleagues. The Minister had no difficulty, however, in resisting amendments. In the Lords, a more formidable attack was led by Lady Wootton, recently the author of some trenchant criticisms of the concept which will be discussed in the next chapter. She pointed out that the Ministry's definition, which referred merely to a 'disorder of personality', would make it possible for anyone under 21 whose conduct was persistently anti-social to be compulsorily committed to hospital without the protection of trial by a criminal court; and she thought that the clause ought therefore to make 'mental abnormality' an essential part of the definition. Secondly, it ought to insist that the aggressive or irresponsible conduct should be *dangerous*. Thirdly, the words 'require or' would open the door to anti-social people who needed treatment but were not *susceptible* to it (a point which will also be discussed in the next chapter). The Lord Chancellor rejected the last two points as being too restrictive, but agreed to reconsider the phrase 'disorder of personality'. The result was a Government amendment, so that the definition in its final form read as follows:

4 . . . (4) In this Act 'psychopathic disorder' means a persistent

disorder or disability of mind (whether or not including subnormality of intelligence) which results in abnormally aggressive or seriously irresponsible conduct on the part of the patient, and requires or is susceptible to medical treatment.

The most serious defect of this definition was a rather subtle one. The four named subdivisions of mental disorder–mental illness, severe subnormality, subnormality and psychopathic disorder–were meant to be generic headings and not specific diagnoses. Mental illness, for instance, would cover a number of psychiatric labels, and so to a lesser extent would subnormality. Similarly, psychopathic disorder was intended to cover all the labels, fashionable and unfashionable, for all disorders of behaviour: 'personality neurosis', 'behaviour neurosis', 'sociopathy', 'acting out behaviour' and so on. But since many psychiatrists had adopted 'psychopathy' as a specific label, its use as a generic heading appeared to set the seal of official approval on this term, and in all probability reduced the incentive to work out better subdivisions. It seems ironical that in Scotland, where Henderson was for so long the *doyen* of psychiatry, his profession refused to have the word 'psychopathic' anywhere in the Scottish Bill, with the result that it refers simply to 'a persistent disorder which is manifested only by abnormally aggressive or seriously irresponsible conduct'.[45] Henderson's Hamlet was disguised as 'the Prince of Denmark'.

Notes

1. 'But see the Madman rage downright
   With furious looks, a ghastly sight.
   Naked in chains bound doth he lie,
   and roars amain, he knows not why.
   Observe him; for as in a glass
   Thine angry portraiture it was.
   His picture keep still in thy presence;
   Twixt him and thee there's no difference.'

2. *Observations on Man* (London, 1749).

3. *Observations on the Nature, Kinds, Causes and Prevention of Insanity* (Leicester, 1782) 2 vols.

4. Surely the forerunners of the beloved monomanias of nineteenth-century psychiatry.

5. See his preface to his second edition of 1806.

6. From *Traité medico-philosophique sur l'alienation mentale, ou la manie* (Paris, 1801). Translation by D. Davis (London, 1806).

7. From his *Treatise on Insanity and other Disorders affecting the mind* (1835).

8. See his smaller book, *The different forms of Insanity in relation to Jurisprudence* (1842) where he defines moral insanity as 'a disorder of which the symptoms are only displayed in the state of the feelings, affections, temper and in the habits and conduct of the individual, or in the exercise of the mental faculties which are termed the active and moral powers of the mind (p. 30).

9. J.C.Bucknill and D.H.Tuke, *A Manual of Psychological Medicine*
(London, 1858) 2nd ed. 1862. Elsewhere, however, in an *Explanatory Note on Moral Insanity* the authors concede that the interpretation which most doctors placed on 'moral insanity' was not that
intended by Prichard.

10. What Prichard meant has for some time been a subject of debate.
See for example D.Leigh, *The Historical Development of British
Psychiatry*, vol. 1 (Oxford, 1961); A.Walk and D.L.Walker's
article 'Gloucester and the beginnings of the R.M.P.A.', in (1961)
107, *Journal of Mental Science*, 609 ff; and F.A.Whitlock's article
'Prichard and the Concept of Moral Insanity', in (1967) 1, 2,
Australian and New Zealand Journal of Psychiatry, 72 ff.

11. We should like to acknowledge here the help of Miss Anita
Warneford, St Anne's College, who drew our attention to the
early German literature on moral imbecility.

12. He called it 'anomia', but failed to popularise the term.

13. *Die Pathologie und Therapie der psychischen Krankheiten* (Stuttgart, 1845). Translation, C.Lockhart Robertson and J.Rutherford
Mental Pathology and Therapeutics (London, 1867), 378.

14. Ignoring for our purposes their other minor subdivisions: the
'mentally infirm' (*sc.* in old age), epileptics, deaf and dumb persons
with mental defects and inebriates.

15. Sir James Crichton-Browne.

16. Section 1 of the Mental Deficiency Act, 1913.

17. See p. 10.

18. Cmd. 2561.

19. Mental Deficiency Act, 1927 s. 1.

20. See the Report of the Royal Commission on Mental Illness and
Mental Deficiency, 1954-7 (Cmnd. 169), 57.

21. *Lehrbuch der artzlichen Seelenkunde* (Vienna, 1845). Translation
by H.E.Loyd, *Principles of Medical Psychology:* revised B.E.
Babington (London, 1847).

22. We cannot find a record of any English translation.

23. See W.James, *Varieties of Religious Experience* (London, 1902).

24. See the Seventeenth Annual Report of the State Commissioners in
Lunacy for 1905 (Collected Works of Adolf Meyer (Baltimore,
1950-52), vol. 11, 144). Meyer never published any full-length
exposition of his views, and his papers make scrappy and unsatisfactory reading when one considers his enormous influence.

25. C.Burt, *The Young Delinquent*, 4th ed. (London, 1944), 595.

26. See the Prison Commissioners' Annual Report for 1956, p. 161. In
fact he was using the word in its residual sense rather than (as he
claimed) its etymological sense.

27. *Pall Mall Gazette*, 21 January 1885, p. 3, col. 2.

28. I am indebted for this information to Professor V.Kudriavtzev, of
the All-Union Institute for the Study of the Causes of Crime, etc.,
Moscow.

29. 'A study of 608 Admissions to Sing Sing Prison', in (1918) 2, *Mental Hygiene*, 85 ff.

30. A.P. Noyes, *Modern Clinical Psychiatry* (Philadelphia, 1927). The quotation first appears, however, in the 1934 edition.

31. D. Henderson, *Psychopathic States* (London, 1939).

32. J. Cox, *Practical Observations on Insanity* (London, 1804).

33. P.J. Moebius, *Die Nervosität* (Leipzig, 1882).

34. W. Healy, *The Individual Delinquent* (London, 1915).

35. D.J. West, *The Habitual Prisoner* (London, 1963).

36. E. Glover, *Searchlights on Delinquency* (New York, 1949).

37. See G. Blake (ed.) *The Trials of Patrick Carraher* (Edinburgh, 1951).

38. (1958) 42 Cr. App. R. 145.

39. (1962) 46 Cr. App. R. 212.

40. Max Grünhut's survey reported in his book *Probation and Mental Treatment* (London, 1963), found that of his sample of 414 offenders dealt with by psychiatric probation orders no less than 47 per cent were classified as psychopathic by his two psychiatric advisers (who examined the medical reports). It is possible, of course, that his psychiatrists were using 'psychopathic' in the wider sense; but a more likely explanation is that this was the only legitimate way of ensuring that psychopaths of normal intelligence received psychiatric treatment outside prison.

41. See Baroness Wootton, *Social Science and Social Pathology* (London, 1959).

42. See Mr Kenneth Robinson's disclosures during the Committee stage of the Mental Health Bill (Standing Committee E for 10 February 1959, col. 34).

43. See the remarks of the Minister of Health (Mr Walker-Smith) during the Committee stage of the Bill, which did not, however, name the 'other quarters'. He argued, with some justice, that the Percy Commission's solution would have applied the term 'psychopath' to a category of case completely outside the popular understanding of the word. In other words, what we have called the 'ethical' usage was now too firmly established.

44. A curiously prudish piece of drafting which omitted the all-important word 'sexual'.

45. See Section 23 of the Mental Health (Scotland) Act, 1960, and paras. 5-10 of the Dunlop Committee on Mental Health Legislation (HMSO, 1958), on which this Act was based. It seems to have been the intention in Scotland that abnormally aggressive or seriously irresponsible conduct should not be a ground for compulsory admission to a mental hospital unless it was associated with 'mental deficiency' or 'mental illness', although since 'mental illness' was left undefined (as in England) it cannot be said that Scottish psychiatrists have had their hands tied very tightly in this respect.

Chapter 10. **Psychopathy in the Sixties**

Having seen how an uneasy collaboration between psychiatrists and legislators produced the definition of psychopathic disorder in the 1959 Act,
we can now consider how this definition seems to work in practice.

Interpreting the Statute

Let us consider first how it has been interpreted. Although there has been
no authoritative discussion of its exact meaning in a court of law, many
psychiatrists have interpreted it in a curiously restrictive way. Reluctant
to admit patients who do not respond to treatment, they have argued that
a person whose behaviour is beyond doubt 'abnormally aggressive' (or
seriously irresponsible, as the case may be) and equally clearly arises from
'a persistent disorder of mind', may nevertheless be outside the scope of
the definition because his condition is not responsive to treatment. Even
the 1961 Working Party on the Special Hospitals[1] seemed to swallow this
interpretation when they wrote

> Secondly, medical knowledge of psychopathic disorder as such is still
> at an early stage, and there is little agreement as to what medical
> treatment is appropriate or possible. This disagreement, incidentally, is
> likely to be of importance as regards the number of people who will be
> admitted to hospital for compulsory treatment for psychopathic
> disorder, since part of the statutory definition of psychopathic
> disorder is that it should require or be susceptible to medical treatment.

This argument rests on a very superficial reading of the definition, which
says that the disorder may either be susceptible to medical treatment (i.e.,
presumably, improve under it) or merely *require* it. 'Require' must therefore mean something different from 'be susceptible to'; so that it must be
possible to 'require' medical treatment to which one is not susceptible.
This is far from nonsensical when one realises that in the terminology
of the Act 'medical treatment includes nursing, and also care and training
under medical supervision' (Section 147). It makes complete sense to say
that there are disorders which may not improve under nursing (or other
types of care) but which *require* it: there are many examples in physical
medicine, of which terminal cancer is one.

But, it might be asked, is the physically healthy and aggressive psychopath comparable to the dying cancer patient? In what sense can he be
said to *require* what is unlikely to improve him? There are two possible
answers. One is that without it he is likely not merely to remain as he is

but to become worse. It is quite plausible to argue that if the alternative to 'medical treatment' is imprisonment, during which his conduct may provoke retaliation from unenlightened custodians or fellow-prisoners, depriving him of 'medical treatment' will probably embitter him. To which the retort might be that, if so, the psychopath could be said not merely to 'require' but to be 'susceptible' to medical treatment, if only in the weakest possible sense. The other possible answer is a non-utilitarian one: that since his behaviour springs not from choice but from 'disorder of mind', and yet is such that society needs protection from him, this protection should take the non-punitive form of custody in the care of people who are trained to accept that he is not fully responsible for his actions. To argue in this way that he 'requires' medical treatment is of course a moralistic answer; but there is nothing in the statute to rule it out. Note, however, that it makes sense only when the alternative to 'medical treatment' is punishment of a more or less official kind. If the alternative is to leave him at liberty (as it may be when compulsory admission without prosecution is under consideration), it is less plausible to argue that in this sense he can be said to 'require' treatment. The utilitarian answer – that 'requires' means 'will deteriorate if not given' – is less dependent on the assumption that the alternative is a penal measure, for he might deteriorate if simply left at large. Nevertheless, enough has been said to show that 'require' can have a meaning which is distinguishable from 'be susceptible to'.

If so, however, another question arises. Could there be any forms of psychopathic disorder which did *not* at least 'require' medical treatment? For it would be fatal to the interpretation just offered if it obviously applied to all psychopaths, since the statutory definition is clearly meant to distinguish between cases which *will* and cases which *will not* require or be susceptible to medical treatment. It seems possible to answer this question too with reassurance. It is not implausible to suppose that there are psychopaths who will not deteriorate if left to themselves or to the penal system. Nor, if one prefers the non-utilitarian interpretation, is it any more implausible to say that there may be psychopaths whose responsibility is so little diminished that we need not feel obliged to excuse them altogether from punishment.

The Responsibility of Psychopaths

So much for the interpretation of the statute. As we have just seen, however, this can raise the old issue of culpability: an issue which, however infrequent the insanity defence, is still raised by the defence of diminished responsibility, and as we saw in chapter 5, may still be in the minds of sentencers when the use of a hospital order is under consideration. The question 'How culpable is this man for what he did?' is even more awkward than usual when the offender in question is diagnosed as a psychopath. For unless one adopts either the extreme form of determinism which holds nobody culpable for any of his acts or omissions, or the equally extreme and even rarer belief that everyone, however immature or insane, is culpable for all his conduct, the concept of psychopathy is an embarrassing one. If one has to make a clear-cut choice between two irreconcilable courses – in particular between punishing a man and not punishing him—and if this choice has to be made by looking to his culpability, the decision is least difficult if people can be divided unequivocally into those who can help what they are doing and those who cannot: we punish the former but not the latter. Unfortunately modern psychiatric notions, with their gradations of disorder, seem to be filling in a gap which, from the lawyer's point of view, would be better left as wide and deep as possible.

The notion of psychopathy is not, of course, the only psychiatric concept which creates difficulty by blurring the distinction between normality and abnormality. Diagnoses of 'schizoid personality', or 'mild subnormality', to name only two examples, are just as awkward. But if Lady Wootton is right there is an additional feature of the notion of psychopathy which makes it peculiarly disquieting. Whereas it is possible to assess the severity of other mental disorders (however roughly) by tests or symptoms which are independent of the offender's offences, Lady Wootton argues that this is not so in the case of the psychopath:

> ... the psychopath makes nonsense of every attempt to distinguish the sick from the healthy delinquent by the presence or absence of a psychiatric syndrome, or by symptoms of mental disorder which are independent of his objectionable behaviour. In his case no such symptoms can be diagnosed because it is just the absence of them which causes him to be classified as psychopathic. He is, in fact, the model of the circular process by which mental abnormality is inferred from anti-social behaviour while anti-social behaviour is explained by mental abnormality.

She goes on to make the point that

> Paradoxically ... if you are consistently (in old-fashioned language) wicked enough, you may hope to be excused from responsibility for your misdeeds; but if your wickedness is only moderate, or if you show occasional signs of repentance or reform, then you must expect to take the blame for what you do, and perhaps to be punished for it.[2]

In a later article[3] she carried the attack a stage further:

> Indeed the usual argument from the psychopath's history of anti-social behaviour might very well be turned upside down to provide an equally good defence of the apparently normal man of previous good character who one day commits a crime of violence. Does not the fact that such a man has acted out of character in itself create at least as great a presumption of mental aberration as does the psychopath's consistently acting in character?

The last of these three quotations need not detain us very long. It implies that it is illogical to infer mental aberration from the frequency of a man's misdeeds as well as from their infrequency. This might be so if both a high and a low frequency were taken as conclusive signs of the *same* type of disorder; but nobody is so naïve as to reason quite like this. And unless they do, I can see nothing *illogical* in the belief that exceptionally frequent offences suggest one sort of disorder, while an isolated offence by a man of good character suggests another sort, any more than it is illogical to believe that both excessively frequent and excessively infrequent bowel movements suggest different disorders of the alimentary tract.

Q

This does not, of course, dispose of Lady Wootton's second point, which is that if the mere frequency of a man's misdeeds, and his failure to respond to penal measures, is to be taken as evidence that he cannot help his conduct, the possibility of drawing a distinction between the culpable and the non-culpable offender has been virtually destroyed. But this argument assumes that mere frequency and incorrigibility are by themselves accepted by psychiatrists nowadays as sufficient evidence of abnormality, without any supporting evidence. No doubt some psychiatrists do reason in this way, and could, if they wished, defend themselves on the deterministic ground that they simply have no ambition to draw an impossible distinction between the pathological and the merely wicked. Others, however, could argue with justice that even if their only evidence for a diagnosis of psychopathy were the individual's criminal career, this cannot be reduced merely to the frequency and incorrigibility of his offences; the diagnostician also takes account of the *nature* of the offences. They could argue that the aggressive psychopath's crimes of violence differ in character from assaults by normal men; that the dishonest psychopath commits his thefts or frauds when a normal criminal would foresee inevitable detection, or against victims (such as parent, wife or girl-friend) for whom a normal thief or con-man would feel too much pity or affection.

So much for Lady Wootton's second and third paradoxes. But it is her first which has to be taken most seriously. The essence of it is twofold. First the psychopath is said to be classified as such not because of 'symptoms', but because of the absence of them. Second, this means that his 'psychopathy' is inferred from his anti-social behaviour, but is then used to explain that behaviour. This is the process of reasoning which is dismissed as 'circular'.

It would be unfair to attack this argument by pedantically questioning the distinction between 'behaviour' and 'symptoms'. The commonsense reply is that 'behaviour' is what makes people take you to a psychiatrist, and 'symptoms' are what he finds when he talks to you or examines you. But is it the case that a diagnosis of 'psychopathy' is considered only when he finds no 'symptoms' of other mental disorder? This does not seem to be borne out by the diagnoses in the Oxford Survey dossiers.

These dossiers, it will be remembered, asked hospitals to state not only the statutory classification which is all that medical witnesses need give in court but also a clinical description, subdivided into 'predominant disorder', 'any associated mental disorder' and 'any associated physical disorders or disabilities' (see Appendix D). In a substantial minority of cases the hospital left the 'predominant disorder' blank, sometimes inserting an 'associated disorder', sometimes not. Since the space for 'predominant disorder' was immediately below the statutory classification it seemed reasonable to assume that in these cases the hospital meant us to infer that the predominant disorder was sufficiently described in the statutory classification. This was especially likely when the statutory classification was 'subnormality' or 'psychopathic disorder'. It was less likely when it was 'mental illness', which is hardly an adequate clinical description; but it was reassuring to find that blanks were much less frequent in such cases.

One of the most striking features of our dossiers was that while only

TABLE 25. Statutory classifications compared with clinical diagnoses of male hospital order cases whose dossiers contained a mention of psychopathy[b]

Statutory classification	N[a]	Priority in dossier	Psychopathy[b]	Blank[c]	Subnormality	Schizophrenia	Manic-depressive psychosis	Neurosis	Epilepsy	Brain damage	Addiction	Others
Psychopathic disorder only	73	'predominant'	56	15	4	1	1	2	—	—	2	—
		'associated'	21	d	3	7	1	2	—	—	1	—
		otherwise mentioned	1	d	4	2	1	—	1	4	17	6
Subnormality only	88	'predominant'	25	23	42	1	—	1	—	—	—	—
		'associated'	51	d	16	1	—	5	1	—	1	—
		otherwise mentioned	2	d	3	—	1	—	6	5	5	10
Mental illness only	71	'predominant'	13	6	1	38	8	4	1	—	1	1
		'associated'	40	d	3	4	1	2	—	—	3	1
		otherwise mentioned	4	d	2	1	—	—	4	3	13	2
Psychopathic disorder with subnormality	14	'predominant'	6	3	6	—	—	—	—	—	—	—
		'associated'	7	d	3	—	—	1	—	—	—	—
		otherwise mentioned	1	d	2	—	—	—	2	—	1	3
Psychopathic disorder with mental illness	12	'predominant'	5	1	—	4	2	1	—	—	1	—
		'associated'	10	d	—	2	1	—	—	—	—	—
		otherwise mentioned	—	d	—	—	1	—	1	3	2	—

[a] These totals represent the 258 offender-patients. But the diagnoses sometimes total more, since two or more were occasionally coupled together.

[b] Or its equivalents: see p. 236 n. 5.

[c] When the statutory classification was 'psychopathic disorder' or 'subnormality' a blank under 'predominant disorder' probably meant that the clinical diagnosis was the same: see the text.

[d] 'Blanks' were of course to be expected under 'associated disorder', etc.

We should like to acknowledge the help which we received from Mr Philip Burgess, of Nuffield College, in compiling and interpreting tables 17, 25 and 26.

11 per cent of our male offender-patients[4] were labelled 'pyschopathic' in court, no less than 29 per cent of our males' dossiers contained some mention of psychopathy or its equivalent.[5] Moreover, as table 25 shows, even when the offender-patient had been classified as psychopathic in the first place, it was by no means uncommon to find that in the clinical description his 'predominant disorder' had become subnormality, neurosis, hysteria, addiction, or even schizophrenia or manic-depressive psychosis. Conversely, the dossiers of offender-patients who in court had been

'subnormal' or 'mentally ill' would not infrequently show 'psychopathy' or its equivalents as the predominant disorder.[6] Among the 'associated mental disorders', too, psychopathy or its equivalents would appear, usually in company with subnormality but also with a variety of mental illnesses, especially schizophrenia and drug addiction. The association between diagnoses of subnormality and psychopathy will not surprise anyone who has followed our account, in the previous chapter, of the development of the concept.

This analysis casts serious doubt on Lady Wootton's allegation that it is the absence of symptoms of other disorders which causes a person to be classified as a psychopath. To make our point more forcibly, out of 258 males whose dossiers mentioned psychopathy or its equivalents, only 25 contained no other psychiatric label, and of these 25 we do not know how many would have done so if the responsible medical officer had been more conscientious in completing the dossier. For the other 233 dossiers abounded in notes such as

'hysterical features'
'a schizoid psychopath who is able to simulate psychosis'
'schizoid episodes, perhaps due to amphetamine-like drugs'
'abnormal EEG'
'paranoid traits'
'borderline subnormal'
'schizophrenic thought disorder, especially under stress'
'clouding of consciousness' and 'transient hypoglycaemia'
'may be suffering from an early schizophrenic illness'.

Clearly, Lady Wootton's assumption that a diagnosis of psychopathy is based on an absence of 'symptoms' is not confirmed by the facts.

Psychopaths, Schizophrenics and Subnormals

Nevertheless, Lady Wootton might still defend her primary paradox by arguing that even if the psychiatrist seems willing—or even prone—to diagnose psychopathy in patients with 'symptoms', he does so not because of these symptoms but because of the patients' 'behaviour'. Indeed, the very fact that so many of our 'psychopaths' appeared to have exhibited symptoms of other disorders raises the question 'What led the psychiatrists to label them psychopathic rather than subnormal, schizophrenic and so on?' We therefore decided to compare our male[4] psychopaths with samples of the other two diagnostic groups which were sufficiently numerous for this purpose—schizophrenics and subnormals—in order to see whether the answer to this question lay in the sort of information about patients' *careers* which psychiatrists might be expected to have (and certainly did have in the case of our sample).

Since we were testing a hypothesis about which we were sceptical, but had to use data in which—as we have just shown—the distinction between 'psychopaths', 'schizophrenics' and 'subnormals' was not as clear-cut as we could have wished, it seemed fairest to maximise any possible differences by taking only those male 'psychopaths' whose dossiers showed a statutory classification of 'psychopathic disorder' which was confirmed by the clinical description—that is, had not been replaced by a diagnosis of some other predominant disorder. There were 64 such cases. It also seemed necessary to match them in respect of age at least with their schizophrenic and subnormal controls, since otherwise one or other group might, on average, have had more years of life in which to incur convictions, hospital admissions and so on.[7] Allowing a year's difference either way, we managed to match all but two of our 64 psychopaths.[8]

We also decided to match for 'predominant offence'.[9] This may or may not have been a wise decision. As we shall see, it enabled us to demonstrate more rigorously the 'career' differences between the groups, as distinct from the nature of the offences. It also demonstrated that it was possible to find schizophrenics and subnormals whose predominant offences were of much the same sort as those of our psychopaths. It might have tended, however, to obscure the differences between the frequency of, say, violent offences in each group. It was fortunate from this point of view that we ran out of matches about halfway through our psychopaths. Thus we had two groups of psychopaths, 32 who were matched each with a schizophrenic and subnormal for age and predominant offence, and 30 who were so matched only for age. Table 26 shows the current offence–that is, the

TABLE 26. Current offences of matched male psychopaths, subnormals and schizophrenics

Current offence	Matched for age and predominant offence			Matched for age only		
	Sub-normals	Schizo-phrenics	Psycho-paths	Psycho-paths	Schizo-phrenics	Sub-normals
Acquisitive	19	17	13	13	16	19
Sexual	4	4	4	5	2	7
Personal violence	3	3	7	7	2	2
Assaulting police	—	1	—	—	—	—
Malicious damage	1	3	2	1	4	—
Arson	3	—	4	—	—	2
Frequenting	—	1	—	—	—	—
Vagrancy	—	1	—	1	1	—
Taking and driving away a motor vehicle	2	2	2	—	—	—
Other	—	—	—	3	5	—
Totals	32	32	32	30	30	30

incidents which resulted in the hospital order. The most numerous category was, as usual, the acquisitive offence–theft, burglary, robbery, fraud– and this was true of all three diagnoses. Violence was commoner among the psychopaths than among the other two groups. So far as sexual offences are concerned, the differences were less marked than one would expect. In our whole sample of males it was the subnormal who was most likely and the schizophrenic who was least likely to have a sexual current offence; and the figures in table 26 are consistent with this. The sexual victims of psychopaths, like those of subnormals, tended to be young children of either sex. The only other interesting group was malicious damage. We have shown arson separately because it is usually regarded as an offence of the subnormal; but here again the psychopaths are almost as numerous, and this too is true of our whole sample. In short, the only characteristic which clearly distinguished the current offences of 'psychopaths' from those of schizophrenics and subnormals was the presence of a violent minority among the psychopaths. Even when a psychopath's current offence was not violence, he was more likely than a schizophrenic or subnormal to have a violent incident in his previous career. Otherwise, however, the offences of the three groups were not as different in their distribution as might have been expected. The careers of the three groups are best compared by concentrating on those who were matched for predominant offence as well as age, especially since certain types of offence are likely to lead to longer periods of detention in penal or medical institutions.

Here again, as table 17 in chapter 6 showed, the similarities are more striking than the differences. Moreover, some of the differences can be explained in a fairly straightforward way. Since schizophrenia, unlike psychopathy and subnormality, tends to have an 'onset'–or at least to become obvious–well after the age at which one can begin to acquire criminal convictions, it is not surprising to find that the schizophrenics had higher mean ages at first conviction and first hospital admission than the other groups, or included more first offenders. Other differences–such as the greater tendency of psychopaths to be dealt with by imprisonment –merely confirm that the schizophrenic and subnormal have a better chance, under the present system, of being dealt with non-penally. It is true that the psychopaths have been in court more often than the other two groups–more often even than the subnormals, in spite of the fact that both subnormals and psychopaths tend to begin their court appearances in the late teens. But the difference is hardly great enough to support Lady Wootton's assumption that it is the sheer frequency of anti-social acts which is the basis of a diagnosis of psychopathy.

We cannot claim that our dossiers–which were not designed for the purpose of analysing psychiatrists' diagnostic habits–provide the best possible evidence against Lady Wootton's strictures (although we do not know of any published data that provides better evidence so far as British psychiatrists are concerned). What our data do suggest very strongly, however, is that what leads to a diagnosis of psychopathy or its equivalents is not a crude counting of convictions or even a categorisation of offence, but some more complex process of diagnosis. For one thing, the diagnosing psychiatrist may well have had–and in some cases we know they had –information about non-criminal types of anti-social behaviour on the part of their offender-patients. For example, it was said of one of our psychopaths that he had 'abducted the wife of another man, fathered a child, abandoned them both, returned to them, and so on'; and 'when in this hospital he needs high security because of his nuisance value' (since he was in a Special Hospital this indicated that he must have been very awkward indeed); 'six hours after his discharge he left the hostel without permission and within a week he had breached all the conditions of his discharge'.

This case illustrates a distinction which Lady Wootton sometimes allows to slip out of sight. Her discussion of criminal responsibility is concerned with the reasoning by which we excuse certain people from the normal penalties for their breaches of the criminal law. But in the quotations we have cited she does not distinguish between these breaches of the law and 'anti-social behaviour' in general. If she did, it would become clear that, instead of reasoning in a circle as she asserts, psychiatrists may be doing something quite legitimate. Let us suppose that we are faced with two offenders whose penal careers are very similar, not merely in the frequency but also in the nature of their offences and in their tendency to be reconvicted after experiencing penal measures. It may nevertheless be the case that one of them behaves irresponsibly or callously in ways that do not constitute breaches of the law, while the other is a good family man, honouring his parents, and keeping all or most of the commandments. There is nothing logically objectionable in the inference that the psychological processes which lead to the crimes of one are very unlike those which lead to the crimes of the other, or in the proposal that measures of different kinds should be applied to the two individuals. We do not suggest that we are or should be content with reasoning on these lines; merely that by talking about 'anti-social behaviour' in general, without distinguishing between the criminal and the non-criminal varieties of it, Lady Wootton has exaggerated the circularity of the diagnostic process.

Again, the psychiatrists may have based their diagnoses on conversations with their patients which suggested that the states of mind in which their offences were committed were different from those which lead to a diagnosis of schizophrenia, depression or subnormality. Impulsiveness, and absence of appropriate remorse or anxiety about consequences are often referred to in the literature on the subject, although some writers believe that this lack of 'affect' is more apparent than real, or that the affect is unconscious. We do not find this aspect of the literature altogether convincing. It is possible to point to plenty of incompetent recidivists whose incompetence is the result of impulsiveness; and to fairly successful 'professional' criminals who are not remorseful but whom few psychiatrists would call psychopathic. To make lack of remorse a convincing criterion the offence itself must be so repulsive that we would find it hard to imagine a mentally normal person committing it without having it on his conscience. Nevertheless, this is part of the defence which psychiatrists could put up in rebuttal of Lady Wootton's indictment.

The Diagnostic Function of 'Psychopathy'

Having said this, however, we must make it plain that we have our own criticisms of the diagnosis, although these are of a different kind. In order to make them clear it is necessary to begin with the question 'What does a diagnosis of psychopathy or of any other mental disorder *tell* us?'

When a psychiatrist says 'This patient is suffering from X' he is placing him in a class. He may think of the class as one whose abnormal characteristics all have the same explanation: for example, encephalitis lethargica.

He may think of it as a class about which he can make a fairly confident prognosis: for example, Huntington's Chorea. If he is a very rigorous pragmatist, he thinks of it as the class which responds to some form of treatment; but this approach is rare. Finally he may simply think of it as the class to whose behaviour a general description can be applied: manic-depressives are an obvious instance. These four uses of diagnosis can be labelled 'explanatory', 'prognostic', 'therapeutic' (or 'pragmatic'), and 'descriptive'.

Which of these functions does the diagnosis of 'psychopathy' perform? Some authors seem to offer it as a form of explanation, as Glover does.[10] Monolithic explanations of psychopathy, however, are unfashionable in these days of electro-encephalograms, XYY chromosomes and 'conditionability'.

Can it be regarded as a pragmatic label, which tells us something about the right way to treat the patient? Only, it seems, in a negative sense. For as we have seen, the fact about which there seems to be the greatest consensus is that psychopaths rarely respond to any form of treatment.[11]

It is slightly more plausible to regard it as a prognostic label, which says in effect 'I may not be able to explain or treat this disorder, but at least I can tell you that the patient is going to go on behaving badly (unless of course he is kept in custody)'. This function, however, needs a closer examination. If the diagnostician is claiming that he can distinguish in this way between psychopaths and mentally normal criminals, the evidence seems to be against him. Dr Gibbens[12] followed up for eight years a group of imprisoned psychopaths, selected as 'particularly severe cases', and compared their subsequent criminal records with those of a control group of prisoners. Because the number of previous convictions is known to be a predictor of subsequent reconviction, his final analysis compared only the 24 psychopaths with 1-4 previous convictions with the 26 controls with similar records. As he put it:

> ... The result shows rather disconcertingly that there is little difference in the behaviour of the two groups: the difference in the proportion of psychopaths and controls who have one or no reconvictions is quite insignificant ($\chi^2 = 0.003$). Whatever the prognosis of the psychopath may be in terms of his mental state, his criminal prognosis appears to be very uncertain and not very different from that of any other man with the same number of previous convictions. ...

All that this suggests, of course, is that a diagnosis of psychopathy does not distinguish prognostically between psychopaths and ordinary recidivists. But may it not distinguish prognostically between psychopaths and other offender-*patients*? This we felt able to test ourselves, in two ways. Our analysis of the two-year follow-up enabled us to compare the subsequent careers of the main diagnostic groups, and so far as psychopaths were concerned it could be said that, *other things being equal*

(a) male psychopaths seemed slightly less likely to be rehospitalised than schizophrenics or (manic-) depressives; but the same could be said of subnormals;

(b) male psychopaths were slightly more likely to be reconvicted than schizophrenics or (manic-) depressives, but the same could be said of subnormals; the reconvictions of psychopaths and subnormals were slightly more likely to lead to detention in prison or hospital;

(c) the employment records of the male psychopaths were no worse than those of the other groups, with the possible exception of the subnormals, which seemed very slightly better;

(d) the only respect in which the female psychopaths seemed to differ from schizophrenics and (manic-) depressives was in their slightly higher probability of reconviction, but the female subnormals were just as likely to be reconvicted, and slightly *more* likely to be recommitted to hospital or imprisoned as a result.

As was pointed out, however, in chapter 8, all these relationships were rather weak. A clearer–but very similar–picture emerged from a matching operation. We were able to match 45 out of our 47 psychopathic first-year leavers with 45 schizophrenic first-year leavers, and 32 with subnormal first-year leavers. Each pair was matched in respect of sex, age, previous convictions and any known after-care. The results, summarised in table 27, were interesting. The employment record of the psychopaths was not significantly worse than those of the other two groups; and indeed when we calculated the mean numbers of months in employment of those who

TABLE 27. A comparison of matched[a] pairs of psychopaths, schizophrenics and subnormals in the two-year follow-up

	Psycho-paths	Schizo-phrenics	Psycho-paths	Sub-normals
Numbers of pairs	35 male 10 female		28 male 4 female	
Reconvicted	55·6%	35·6% ($p < 0.01$)[b]	53·1%	62·5%
% of 12 reconvicted pairs who were rehospitalised as a result	50·0%	100·0% ($p = 0.01$ approx.)[b]	50·0%	100·0% ($p = 0.01$ approx.)[b]
Rehospitalised	35·6%	62·2% ($p = 0.01$ approx.)[b]	28·1%	37·5%
Either reconvicted *or* rehospitalised	66·7%	55·6%	62·5%	62·5%
In contributory employment (males only)	65·7%	68·6%	67·9%	75·0%
Mean months of employment for males employed	12·35	9·14 ($p = <0.005$)[b]	13·88	14·14

[a] The criteria for matching were sex, age (± 1 year for those under age 30, ± 3 years for the remainder), previous convictions (0; 1–3; 4+) and whether or not the discharging hospital reported any subsequent contact that could be regarded as after-care.

[b] The significance of the differences between means was calculated by Wilcoxon's signed rank test; the other probabilities by Stuart's modification of the χ^2 test for matched pairs, using Yates' correction for small numbers (see p. 145n). Where 'p' is not given, it was greater than 0·1, and in most cases a good deal greater.

were recorded as employed for any period, however short, the psychopaths did significantly better than the schizophrenics, though not better than the subnormals. So far as reconvictions were concerned, psychopaths fared significantly worse than schizophrenics, but not worse than subnormals: indeed, the latter were slightly worse, although the difference was not significant. In contrast, schizophrenics were significantly more likely to be readmitted to hospital. The differences diminished, however, to a non-significant level when we examined the percentages of each group who were either reconvicted *or* rehospitalised *or both*.

The most striking difference that emerged was that among the reconvicted schizophrenics and subnormals every one was readmitted to hospital on or soon after reconviction, but this was true of only 50 per cent of the psychopaths. This is a prognostic difference, however, which says more about the system than about the post-discharge behaviour of the three groups. Once again, the similarities are more striking than the differences, and especially where psychopaths and subnormals are concerned.[13]

It remains to consider the possibility that the label is descriptively useful. So far as criminal behaviour is concerned, this is true only to a limited extent. There is undoubtedly a minority of psychopaths who are characterised by impulsive violence. Probably too there is an even smaller group whose offences are a mixture of violence and sexual behaviour, although the sexual offences of our sample were more often like those of subnormals. It is the remaining majority, whose offences seem to be neither violent nor sexual nor bizarre, which makes it difficult to claim that 'psychopathy' is a descriptive label. Moreover, even if we grant that 'aggressive psychopath' or 'sexual psychopath' *is* a descriptive label, it is the words 'aggressive' or 'sexual' which seem to constitute the informative half of the label. In other words, the label is hardly descriptive unless it tells us what it is that the psychopath *does*.

(The psychiatrist might reply that the word 'psychopath' is meant to tell us not what the offender does, but something about the way he does it. We have already mentioned the emphasis in psychiatric literature on impulsiveness and lack of remorse or regard for the consequences. But we have also pointed out that these do not distinguish very satisfactorily between psychopaths and some fairly numerous types of recidivist. The psychiatrist may be prepared of course to go to the length of saying that most recidivists are in some degree psychopathic; but this would reduce the value of the diagnosis to the minimum.)

A label which is carelessly applied is likely to obliterate more information than it conveys; and this is what seems to have happened to 'psychopathy'. It would be of more use to psychiatrists to tell them that this or that patient is easily provoked to violence, is prone to sexual sadism, exploits women, commits impulsive thefts or whatever it is about his conduct that arouses disapproval, than to call him a psychopath.

We have argued that as a description the diagnosis tells one nothing; that prognostically it exaggerates the difference between 'psychopaths' and ordinary recidivists on the one hand, or on the other hand schizophrenics and subnormals (especially the latter); that it cannot be an explanatory label; and that as a method of indicating suitable forms of treatment it tells us only that none have been found very profitable. What cannot be argued away, however, is the fact that psychiatrists seem to feel a need to use it. There has been no significant diminution since the 1959 Act came into operation in the percentage of hospital and guardianship orders based on a statutory classification of 'psychopathic disorder'. Indeed, in the case of women the percentage has risen in the last few years and in the case of men it might well have risen too had hospitals been more willing to take these troublesome patients.

The explanation may simply be that most psychiatrists do not philo-sophise about the functions of diagnosis,[14] or that if they do they exag-gerate the prognostic value of this particular diagnosis. It seems very likely, however, that the label is fulfilling a function which is *pseudo*-diagnostic. The final chapter of volume I emphasised the difficulty in which psychiatrists are placed by a system of trial and sentencing that asks them to distinguish in black and white terms between offenders who should be excused punishment and those who should not. This difficulty is at its most acute when the offender cannot be confidently called schizo-phrenic, subnormal, manic or depressive, but is in some way 'not as other men'. As we have seen, 90 per cent of our male psychopaths' dossiers also used some rather vague psychiatric terms, such as hysteria, paranoid traits and schizoid episodes. Sometimes the offender's behaviour, or his way of discussing it with the psychiatrist, seems to the latter to be abnormal (and for our present argument it does not matter whether one would agree with the psychiatrist or not). For historical reasons which were outlined in the previous chapter, the law has offered the psychiatrist a ready-made label which will help him to get his patient through the customs-barrier of the courts if he wants to. The psychiatrist might well prefer to write the label in his own words; but this would probably cause confusion at a critical moment, and endanger his patient's chances of ending up at what he regards as the right destination. In this situation the psychiatrist would have to be puritanically honest as well as clear-headed to refuse the label that is offered to him. Moreover, we are not even suggesting that this collusion between the customs officers and the labellers is a conscious process. If the psychiatrist is both clear-sighted and cynical he may lick the label with his tongue in his cheek. More often, probably, both parties play their part with a clear conscience, in a situation created partly by the hard-and-fast decisions demanded by the penal system, partly by the evolution of this curious concept. It is a unique example of a pseudo-diagnosis for which legislators are partly, if unwittingly, responsible.

Finally, since the points we have made could easily be misunderstood as an attempt to discredit completely the concept of 'behaviour disorders', we must make it clear that this is not our intention. What we are arguing is that to use a single label with so disreputable a history to cover behaviour of widely differing kinds, which is probably the result of several different pathological processes, is justifiable only as a draftsman's expedient, and −as the Scots seem to have shown−an unnecessary one at that. It seems highly likely that current and future research will identify subgroups of 'psychopaths' whose behaviour is attributable to completely different causes: for example cerebral pathology, grossly abnormal upbringing and perhaps 'low conditionability', to mention only three possibilities. Progress of this kind, however, is not assisted by the assumption that all 'psychopaths' have something in common – apart from the label. To categorise someone as psychopathic is all too often to exclude him from the hospitals where research is being most actively carried out; and sometimes it ensures that he is refused *any* hospital vacancy.

Notes

1. See p. 12.
2. *Social Science and Social Pathology* (London, 1959), 250 ff.
3. 'Diminished Responsibility: a layman's view', in (1960) 76, *Law Quarterly Review*, 224.
4. It seems best to exclude females from this analysis. Psychiatrists may well reason rather differently when deciding whether to label a woman 'psychopathic'.
5. E.g., 'personality disorder', 'inadequate personality', 'anti-social personality', 'dissocial personality', 'immature personality', behaviour disorder' or 'pathological lying and stealing'.
6. What the dossiers did not tell us was the nature of the observations which led the psychiatrist to supplement or replace a diagnosis of subnormality or psychosis with one of psychopathy. Was it simply that by this time he had fuller information about the offender's past misdeeds? Or was it the offender's conduct in hospital? Certainly it was clear from the reports we received on the progress of our offender-patients that some of our psychopaths had succeeded in surprising and outraging even the tolerance of their responsible medical officers.
7. This was not an entirely satisfactory procedure, since schizophrenia tends to be diagnosed, on average, at a later age and subnormality at an earlier age than psychopathy; so that it could be argued that our controls were not unbiassed samples of schizophrenics and subnormals. This criticism, however, would have had more force had we tried to include within our controls a group of disorders – such as depressive states – which are associated with a markedly different age-range from that of psychopaths. So far as *offender-patients* are concerned there is considerable overlap between the age-ranges of psychopaths, schizophrenics and subnormals (see tables 9 and 10 in chapter 6).
8. These were two fifteen-year-old boys.
9. Offences were categorised as acquisitive, sexual, violent (to the person) or involving damage or annoyance to the public and a category was regarded as predominant if it occurred more often than any other group.
10. E. Glover, *The Roots of Crime* (London, 1960).
11. We are not ignoring the somewhat more optimistic views – or the

supporting data—of psychiatrists such as Dr Michael Craft: see, for instance, his *Psychopathic Disorders* (Oxford, 1966).

12. See T. C. N. Gibbens, D. A. Pond and D. Stafford-Clark, 'A Follow-up Study of Criminal Psychopaths' in (1959) 105, *Journal of Mental Science*, 108 ff. Since the sample of psychopaths was collected long before the 1959 Act, and they were selected as 'particularly severe cases', many of them would nowadays have found their way into mental hospitals, either under hospital orders or as a result of transfer from prison.

13. In passing, it is worth noting that when we matched second-year leavers with first-year leavers (for sex, diagnosis, previous convictions and previous hospital admissions: see p. 185) and compared their rehospitalisations, reconvictions and employment records during their first year after leaving, psychopathic first-year and second-year leavers behaved with striking similarity. The only difference—for which an explanation has been suggested on p. 186 —was that the second-year leavers seemed more likely to be readmitted to hospital; and even this difference barely reached the 0·05 level of significance.

14. Although there are many studies of the different ways in which psychiatrists use labels (such as schizophrenia or psychopathy) not many of them discuss the functions of diagnosis. But after the publication of our analysis (in the Cropwood Conference Proceedings in 1968) a similar (but more elaborate) analysis was published by R. M. Silberman in 'CHAM: a classification of psychiatric states,' (1971) *Excerpta Medica Monographs*.

Chapter 11. **Conclusion**

The first volume of this book was concerned with the development of the law's traditional approach to the disordered offender, and in particular its ways of trying to answer three questions: 'Is he fit to be tried?'; 'Is he to blame for what he did?' and (if the answer to both of these was 'Yes') 'Is he nevertheless too insane to punish?'

In this second volume we have tried to show how these questions[1] have come to be more or less superseded by a fourth one: 'Is a psychiatric or penal measure more suitable?'[2] This utilitarian revolution–if so gradual a process can be given such a stirring name–took place not so much through the influence of Bentham or any other philosopher of punishment as under the pressure of circumstances, and in particular the increasing numbers of disordered offenders who were indiscriminately pumped into the prison system since the middle of the nineteenth century by that more or less new creation, the magistrates' court.

An optimistic utilitarian might well concede that this important change has been dictated by expediency rather than enlightenment, and yet claim that it had given us a more rational system. Instead of muddled attempts to assess the culpability of a schizophrenic, subnormal or a depressive offender, sentencers and medical officers are allowed to engage in sensible discussions about his or her suitability for psychiatric treatment.

Yet it does not seem to work as simply as that. As we have hinted in the sub-title and demonstrated in the text, new solutions have entailed new problems. The question 'Is a psychiatric measure more suitable than a penal one?' is itself ambiguous: what does 'suitable' mean in this context? Sentencers, appellate courts and Mental Health Review Tribunals have interpreted the statutes in curious ways. Hospitals have refused to accept offenders whom medical witnesses considered in need of treatment. Substantial numbers of offender-patients abscond, including some whom medical witnesses and courts considered dangerous enough to place under restriction orders. Others are being discharged by medical officers who do not always have sufficient information about their behaviour at large. The rate of recidivism is depressing and the only encouraging results which emerged from our follow-up were those which suggested that high-risk groups could be identified by very simple scoring systems, and would respond to after-care.

It is of course the weak points of any system which are bound to assume prominence in any operational study, and we are very conscious that we have had less to say about the beneficial aspects of the Act than about its defects. It must be emphasised that it has made it easier–though not obligatory–for sentencers to reason in a non-retributive way, and even to follow a policy of well-intentioned 'occasionalism' (see p. 101). Where dangerous offenders are concerned the indefinite restriction order is often the solution for a sentencer who would otherwise have to choose between two unsatisfactory alternatives: a long determinate sentence and 'life'. As a result it has diverted a substantial annual quota of offenders to a milieu which is at best more therapeutic and at worst more tolerant than the prisons to which most of them would have gone, and in doing so has incidentally relieved the prisons of a responsibility which they were not adequately equipped to shoulder.

Moreover, the utilitarian could argue that some at least of the problems we have described are due to nothing more than minor mistakes in the design of the 1959 Act. He could point out that the Act has been in operation for a whole decade during which it has not been found necessary to make any important amendment to it[3]: a sharp contrast to the suspended sentence provision of the 1967 Act, which had to be amended within a few years. For this the Percy Commission and the civil servants who transformed its proposals into workable legislation must take some of the credit. So too, however, must clerks of courts, prison medical officers, psychiatrists and hospital administrators. One of the factors which make it possible to postpone the overhaul of such systems is the capacity of those who have to operate them to make them work by hook or by crook. The result is that defects are almost unconsciously concealed. For this reason some of those we have noticed may be dismissed as unimportant, although to us they do not seem so.

Important or not, some of the malfunctioning to which we have drawn attention could undoubtedly be avoided or reduced by improvements in the statutory provisions. For example, the deliberately ambiguous phrase 'the most *suitable* method of disposing of the case' could surely nowadays be reworded so as to exclude retributive reasoning. There are avoidable differences of opinion as to whether dependence on drugs or alcohol can of itself be regarded as a disorder that justifies compulsory admission (pp. 83-5). Again, we have suggested that instead of misusing the power to make a hospital order without conviction, summary courts should be allowed to find that an offender is unfit for trial (p. 107). Fourthly, we have drawn attention (on p. 109) to the need for a power, on the lines of s. 54 of the Scottish Act, to remand the accused compulsorily to a psychiatric hospital, instead of relying on the illogical expedient of remand on bail with an undertaking that he will become an informal in-patient. We have argued that hospital orders should not be confined to imprisonable offences (p. 103). As for restriction orders, we have pointed out the irrationality of allowing courts to specify a time-limit for them (p. 91), and we endorse the view of the Court of Appeal (Criminal Division) that if an offender is dangerous enough to be sent to a Special Hospital he should invariably be subject to a restriction order, so that he cannot secure his discharge by persuading a Mental Health Review Tribunal. At the same time, we have suggested that the advisory function of the tribunals in restriction order cases should be taken over by the Parole Board (p. 201).

Some of our suggestions, however, would involve more than mere amendment of the statute. The results of our follow-up, especially where conditionally discharged restriction order cases were concerned, emphasised the importance of after-care in keeping the stage-army out of further trouble with the law. It is true that by no means all offender-patients would co-operate with efforts to arrange after-care for them; but our impression is that a great deal more could be done by the ordinary hospital in this direction. Moreover we have suggested a simple method of selecting high-risk groups for specially intensive efforts.

We have also drawn attention to the paucity of information which hospitals have in their case-histories about the precise nature of the offender-patient's anti-social behaviour. Examples were given in chapters 5, 6 and 7 of cases in which the discharge of the patient could be excused only on the assumption that the hospital staff were not fully informed of the offence which led to the hospital order.

Indeed we must reiterate that even the current offence is by no means always a reliable indicator of the offender's dangerousness, and in our view a hospital should always ask the police for at least the official record of an offender's antecedents, of the kind which is made available to sentencers and probation officers. Moreover, since an entry recording 'indecent assault' or 'actual bodily harm' may refer to a serious or trivial incident, hospitals would be well advised to ask for more details of such incidents.

(Conversely, we must also mention again the remarkable fact that the Mental Health Enquiry index is not used by police, courts, probation officers or even psychiatrists to check whether an individual has previously been a psychiatric patient. As has been said, there has been a policy decision that the index is to be used only for statistical and research purposes; and the justifications for such strict confidentiality are obvious. At the same time, it *could* be used in such a way as to prevent courts from sentencing an offender to prison in complete ignorance of his psychiatric history, in the same way as the Central Criminal Records are used to ensure that an offender's penal record is known to the sentencer. Clearly, safeguards would be required against unnecessary use of the index, or disclosures that would harm the ex-patient; but that is not an argument for the *status quo*.)

To return, however, to the subject of the dangerous patient: the problem is not solely one of ensuring the availability of information–it is also one of security. It is clear that at present ordinary hospitals are reluctantly accepting patients whom they would prefer to see being admitted to Special Hospitals, and that the locked wards of 'open-door' hospitals are not always as secure as they sound (see, for example, pp. 162-3). No doubt the building of the fourth Special Hospital will ease the accommodation problems which compel the existing three to refuse a substantial number of patients each year.[4] It is also possible that in the seventies Regional Hospital Boards will at last begin to provide medium security units of the kind recommended by the 1961 Working Party (see pp. 13-14).

As this book was being completed, however, another major reform of the mental health service was announced by the Department of Health and Social Security, although at the same time it was made clear that it would take some years to carry out. The objective is to be the establishment of a department for the mentally ill in each district general hospital or group of hospitals, 'with the ultimate aim of replacing the large mental hospitals'.[5] Many of the implications of this have still to be made plain, and may not become so for some time to come. In particular, the method of looking after patients requiring security of something less than maximum degree is said to be 'under review'.

Nevertheless, the policy is still apparently to be one of minimum restraint:

41. Some patients are a risk to themselves or to others. In extreme cases the risk may be so serious that admission to a special hospital with maximum security is necessary. In other cases patients may present disorders of behaviour necessitating lesser degrees of security for varying periods. The services needed for such patients are under review. The degree of control needed may vary from continuous supervision while in hospital to regular contact at an out-patient clinic. Security does not necessarily entail keeping a patient in a locked room or a locked ward, but involves a variety of factors including staff observation and staff/patient relationships. Where a nurse develops a therapeutic relationship with a patient the degree of physical security required may be less. Observation and constant attention may be more essential than locked doors or other restraints. The degree of supervision can only be decided on the merits of each individual case. Many patients who are at first thought to present security problems may later prove manageable on open wards. In all cases it is essential that the degree of risk should be known to the staff concerned, not only to doctors and nurses but occupational therapists and all others who at times may be responsible for the care and supervision of the patient. Those who present security problems should be kept fully occupied. All appropriate treatment should be available including groups for occupational therapy or other social or recreational activities. A gradual extension of freedom rather than a sudden change to full independence is usually good clinical practice.[5]

What seems to be suggested in this cautiously drafted paragraph is that the degree of security required for patients who do not qualify for a place in a Special Hospital will seldom call for a locked ward or room, and is therefore compatible with the absorption of the large hospital for the mentally ill into the general district hospital.

Anyone who expressed an equally cautious concern about the implications of this paragraph would be regarded as a deviationist from the ideology of minimum restraint. This is an ideology, however, which deserves a little examination. The cases we have described earlier in this book show that it entails a small but regrettable annual quota of harm done by offender-patients who abscond or are discharged by doctors or tribunals from ordinary hospitals. If instead these had been prisoners who had escaped or been paroled the criticism in Parliament and the Press

R

would have been loud and sharp. Yet only one of these cases, to our knowledge, became the subject of comment in the national Press and that only briefly.[6] Paradoxically, paroled or escaped prisoners are in all probability less likely to do serious harm than offender-patients who abscond or are discharged.[7] The plain fact is that our outlook allows—perhaps it would be fairer to say 'constrains'—psychiatrists to take bigger risks than prison administrators. No doubt it can be argued that the prison service (and Parole Board) might well be encouraged to be bolder, although to do them justice they have been moving circumspectly in this direction. The question which interests us, however, is 'Will the absorption of hospitals for the mentally ill involve psychiatrists in more risk-taking or less?'

A problem which must be distinguished from the dangerous patient is the unco-operative one. One of the anomalies of the system is that an offender who has been made subject to a psychiatric probation order can be brought back to court and sentenced for his offence if he breaks off treatment without his psychiatrist's approval, but that a hospital order patient cannot be brought back to court to be dealt with differently, however unco-operative he is, or even if it is later decided that he was feigning disorder, as happened in one of our cases. Indeed, as we have seen, he can often secure his legal freedom by absconding. It is true that even breaches of psychiatric probation orders seldom result in a fresh appearance in court; but this is usually because the hospital fails to inform the probation officer of the breach, or because the probationer has disappeared. It is also true that many psychiatrists prefer to treat even offender-patients with the minimum of compulsion or sanction; and no doubt this is the ideal. But some patients—as Mrs Woodside[8] has so vividly emphasised—cease to be co-operative once the process of remand, trial and sentence is past. Such patients benefit little, if at all, from therapy or the tolerant milieu of hospital, and indeed they sometimes interfere with the treatment of others who are more amenable. The temptation to let them abscond and so be rid of them must be a strong one; and we have described at least one case (on p. 169) in which even a Mental Health Review Tribunal got rid of an untreatable offender by directing his discharge. There is of course no easy solution; but we suggest that it might help if ordinary hospitals[9] were enabled to bring such offender-patients back to court in much the same way as probationers can be. In some cases this would operate as a sanction (for it is a fallacy to suppose that all hospital order cases are so disordered that they cannot control their behaviour at any time). Its main point, however, would be that the psychiatrist who had, perhaps reluctantly, accepted an unco-operative patient would have a more honest way out than merely letting him loose. He would be enabled —though not obliged—to tell the court that the patient could not be treated satisfactorily *in his hospital at least*. If another hospital (including a Special Hospital) were willing to accept him, the court would have power to make another hospital order. If not, it would have to decide whether the offender-patient's conduct was so objectionable that a custodial sentence was called for. It is not that we want to see these unco-operative offender-patients imprisoned, but that only in this way will courts and administrators be compelled to face the fact that hospital orders are being used for some disordered offenders whom it is in nobody's interest to send to ordinary hospitals. This problem will be accentuated rather than eased by the absorption of mental hospitals into the general hospital system. Whether the best solution is the extension of psychiatric prison units or the creation of hospital units which specialise in unco-operative but not dangerous offenders is a debatable question. The point which we are making, however, at the moment is that an unpalatable but important fact about our would-be utilitarian system is being brushed under the carpet.

This is that the utilitarian revolution has to a considerable extent outstripped the technical capacity of the system to live up to utilitarian ideals. In more concrete terms, the penal system is now unloading onto the health service offenders whom the latter cannot 'treat' with any real success. The unco-operative patient is only the most obvious example of this. There are also patients who are well-behaved in hospital but soon relapse outside.

The fact that this unloading operation can take place only with the connivance of the customs officer–that is, the psychiatrist–merely increases the complexity of the problem. The psychiatrist's connivance is by no means always the result of over-optimism. He is often extremely realistic in his estimate of the improbability of successful treatment. Yet he not only agrees to accept the offender-patient as his responsibility: he has even devised, for use in court, a pseudo-diagnosis called 'psychopathic disorder', which allows him to admit to hospital offenders who are not deluded, hallucinated, elated, depressed, imbecilic, epileptic or brain-damaged.[10]

Can this be reconciled with a utilitarian approach? It is no answer to this question to admit that some psychiatrists still reason in a moralistic way, when they argue that if an offender is disordered he should be exempt from ordinary penal measures, because he could not help doing what he did. The question is not so much what motivates psychiatrists as whether their practice can be justified on utilitarian grounds.

The justification might take one of three forms. The most ambitious of these would be that it is more *effective* to unload disordered offenders onto the psychiatric hospitals than to deal with them within the penal system. In this context effectiveness must be measured in terms of further convictions,[11] and it must be remembered that these can be reduced either by successfully treating and discharging an offender or by keeping him in prolonged custody. One might even be more ambitious, and compare *cost*-effectiveness, by relating reconviction-rates to the comparative costs of psychiatric and penal methods of disposal. At present, however, we do not have the necessary data on which to base a comparison of effectiveness, let alone cost-effectiveness. A sound comparison of this sort would involve a deliberate decision to leave to the penal system a random selection of offenders who would otherwise have been handed over to psychiatric hospitals.

It is tempting to say that scarce and expensive types of trained manpower such as psychiatrists, psychiatric social workers and mental nurses are probably at their most effective when dealing with co-operative non-offenders; but though this is our belief we are not in a position to demonstrate it with figures. In short, cost-effectiveness as a justification has still to be proved.

A less ambitious justification would be that whether or not unloading these offenders onto hospitals is more cost-effective in terms of *their* relapse-rates and the resources devoted to *them*, this practice enables the penal system to deal better with *other* offenders. Prisons, as we have seen, find it very difficult to cope with this group (just as do probation officers and psychiatrists). But this argument is a dangerous one. Granted that the prison and probation services may find it *easier* to function without them, this is a justification only if it means that other prisoners or probationers are dealt with more *effectively* or more *humanely*. Not only is there no evidence that this is so; some would even argue that the probability is in the opposite direction. For, they might suggest, one thing which makes prisons at least more humane is a psychiatric approach; and a prison which gets rid of its disordered prisoners can forget about psychiatry. They might also argue—though with less factual support—that the psychiatric approach to offenders in general is likely to increase the effectiveness as well as the humanity of the penal system. Without taking such optimistic arguments for granted, we are simply pointing out that the attempt to justify large-scale hospitalisation of offenders on the grounds that this makes the *rest* of the penal system more effective is likely to misfire.

If so, the utilitarian must, it seems fall back on the argument that it is more *humane* towards the disordered offender to put him in hospital. But this too needs examination. If 'more humane' means 'less objectionable to the offender himself', this cannot always be taken for granted. Some mildly disordered offenders prefer a short term of imprisonment in the company of prisoners whom they regard as normal and congenial to compulsory commitment to a hospital, with the resulting stigma, the uncertainty of the date of discharge and the enforced association with more severely disordered patients. It is true that the more sophisticated members of the stage-army know that they have a good chance of discharge within a few months, and that if hospital becomes intolerable before then they can abscond; but even the sophisticated are afraid of transfer to a Special Hospital. This raises the awkward question 'Should the offender's consent to a hospital order be required (as it is to a probation order)?' Some utilitarians might dodge this issue by saying that 'being more humane' has nothing to do with the offender's own preferences, but means something like 'being less destructive of the valuable attributes of a human being'.

The assumption that a psychiatric hospital's regime is less destructive of these attributes than a prison would be challenged by some, but we would hesitate to make too much of that line of argument. What we would ask is 'If the utilitarian's case rests on nothing but humanity, can he show why the disordered offender has a stronger claim to humanity than other offenders?'. The utilitarian might well feel driven to reply 'because he deserves better treatment': which is very close to the traditional exculpatory reasoning of the law. If he wants to avoid this answer, he can only say that the disordered offender has enough of a burden to bear without punishment: an argument which Modestinus expressed very neatly a long time ago—*satis furore ipso punitur*.[12]

Notes

1. For even the issue of fitness for trial can be glossed over nowadays in summary courts, as we have shown on p. 107.
2. We have taken the word 'suitable' from s. 60 of the 1959 Act: in s. 4 of the 1948 Act the word is 'expedient'.
3. The Criminal Procedure (Insanity) Act of 1964 affected it only to the extent that as a result the disposal of offenders subject to special verdicts was assimilated more closely to the disposal of restriction order cases.
4. In the five years 1967–71 there were 2,395 applications for places in Special Hospitals, some on behalf of offender-patients, some on behalf of patients compulsorily admitted under Part IV of the Act. Of these 25 per cent were at first refused, although 5 per cent were accepted on a later application.
5. The quotations are from the Department's memorandum of December, 1971, entitled *Hospital Services for the Mentally Ill*.
6. The case of Michael Johnson: see pp. 153-4).
7. Unfortunately there are no figures for prisoners with which we can compare the 22 out of our 1,160 offender-patients who committed serious personal violence, sexual offences or arson (see p. 194); but it is most unlikely that any comparable cohort of prisoners would yield a figure of this order.
8. Loc. cit. *supra* (ch. 4, n. 11).
9. We do not think that Special Hospitals need have or would want such a power.
10. Or at least do not exhibit any of these characteristics to a marked degree; for, as we saw on pp. 227-8 they may creep in as subsidiary features of the diagnosis.
11. Since re-admission to hospital without conviction is something which the penal system could hardly be expected to prevent.
12. 'His madness is punishment enough': see volume I, p. 27.

Table of Statutes

Date	Regnal year and chapter	Title and page reference
1853	16 & 17 Vict., c. 97	An Act to consolidate and amend the Laws for the Provision and Regulation of Lunatic Asylums . . ., *p.* 15n1
1860	23 & 24 Vict., c. 75	An Act to make better Provision for the Custody and Care of Criminal Lunatics, *p.* 15n1
1864	27 & 28 Vict., c. 29	The Insane Prisoners (Amendment) Act, *pp.* 22, 36n9
1877	40 & 41 Vict., c. 21	The Prison Act, *p.* 41
1879	42 & 43 Vict., c. 49	The Summary Jurisdiction Act, *p.* 59
1884	47 & 48 Vict., c. 64	The Criminal Lunatics Act, *pp.* 22, 36n10, 141
1885	48 & 49 Vict., c. 52	An Act to Amend the Law relating to Lunatics, *pp.* 255, 262n14
1886	49 & 50 Vict., c. 25	The Idiots Act, *p.* 23
1889	52 & 53 Vict., c. 41	The Lunacy Acts Amendment Act, *pp.* 52, 57n15
1890	53 & 54 Vict., c. 5	The Lunacy Act, *pp.* 23, 57n15, 63, 65, 165, 178n16, 256, 262n13
1898	61 & 62 Vict., c. 60	The Inebriates Act, *pp.* 60-1
1907	7 Edw. VII, c. 17	The Probation of Offenders Act, *pp.* 59, 60, 64
1908	8 Edw. VII, c. 59	The Prevention of Crime Act, *p.* 61
1908	8 Edw. VII, c. 67	The Children Act, *pp.* 62, 80n4
1913	3 & 4 Geo. V, c. 28	The Mental Deficiency Act, *pp.* 10, 12, 23, 24, 36n12, 42, 59-64, 65, 72, 73-4, 79-80, 105, 106, 211-12, 218, 221n16, 255
1927	17 & 18 Geo. V, c. 33	The Mental Deficiency Act, *pp.* 24, 62, 105, 211-12, 221n19
1930	20 & 21 Geo. V, c. 23	The Mental Treatment Act, *pp.* 64-5
1946	9 & 10 Geo. VI, c. 81	The National Health Service Act, *p.* 254
1948	11 & 12 Geo. VI, c. 58	The Criminal Justice Act, *pp.* 11, 12, 15n1, 31, 51, 52-3, 56n11, 57n17, 63-7, 73, 74, 79-80, 86, 157, 218, 245n2
1952	15 & 16 Geo. VI & 1 Eliz. II, c. 55	The Magistrates Courts Act, *pp.* 57n17, 64, 74-5
1957	5 & 6 Eliz. II, c. 11	The Homicide Act, *p.* 216
1959	7 & 8 Eliz. II, c. 72	The Mental Health Act s.3, *pp.* 167-9, 178n19 s.4, *pp.* XV, 12, 25, 29, 68-70, 79, 82-5, 110n9, 169, 219-20, 223-4, 239 s.5, *pp.* 55, 163 s.25, *pp.* 54, 70, 82, 85, 102, 103, 109, 118, 141, 163 s.26, *pp.* 30, 54, 70, 82, 85, 103, 109, 118, 141, 163 s.28, *p.* 82 s.29, *pp.* 70, 85, 118 s.30, *pp.* 164, 178n9 s.33, *p.* 115

Table of Cases

Corrections and Additions to Volume 1

p. 19   Miss Naomi Hurnard, in her subsequently published book
The King's Pardon for Homicide before 1307 (Oxford University Press,
1970) corrects this interpretation of Richard of Cheddestan's case.

p. 41   Mr Glazebrook, in (1969) *Criminal Law Review*, p. 164, has
pointed out that the ignorance of the infant and the madman were
spoken of in the same breath at a much earlier date, and cites the
Year Books of Henry VII (3 H. 7, plea 4). But ignorance of what?
Of the nature or of the wrongness of the act? In the case he cites
the reason given for excusing children and madmen was lack of
'discretion'; and earlier in volume I (p. 28) it was argued that when
children under 14 were held excusable it was for lack of knowledge
of 'what was what', not of moral wrongness. It is highly relevant that
the child in Mr Glazebrook's case was aged 9.

p. 43   Bethlem served London as a public madhouse from 1375, not
1377.

p. 44   Mr Glazebrook (ibid., p. 163) has pointed out that in Hale's day
the word 'trespass' could refer to misdemeanours, which *were*
indictable.

p. 144   The reference to a statutory *definition of* murder should of
course have been to a statutory *penalty for*.

p. 224   Dr D. Nicholson, in (1877) *Journal of Mental Science*, says that
John Frith *was* eventually tried (and found insane) two years later;
and while the source of this information is not cited the author must
have had good grounds for this circumstantial statement.

pp. 236, 237   The references to Lord Goddard should of course be
references to Lord Parker, who had recently succeeded Lord
Goddard as Lord Chief Justice.

p. 258   The page reference to R. v. Frith should include pp. 223-4.

p. 281   Fitzherbert's 'Newe Booke of Justices of Peas' was not a
translation of *La Nouvelle Natura Brevium*.

Appendix A. **By-passing the Law**

This appendix is concerned with a minor but interesting area on the borderline between psychiatry and law enforcement. Mentally disordered men and women sometimes behave in ways which clearly threaten harm to others. They may brandish weapons, light fires in dangerous places, take their clothes off or shout at strangers. Yet it may be difficult to invoke the law to deal with them. It is not always easy to say whether they are committing an offence; and even when it is this may seem a cumbersome or inhumane procedure when no actual harm has been done. On the other hand, it may not be easy to find a doctor to examine them; nor would it be at all easy to examine some of them until they have calmed down.

Traditional custom – and to some extent law – has looked to the relatives of madmen and idiots to keep them under control, if not in their homes then in private madhouses or, later, asylums. Friends and relatives, however, could not always be found; indeed, as was pointed out in volume I, chapter 2, there was an era in which they must often have done their best to rid themselves of this burden, thus adding to the numbers of lunatics who were vagrants by choice.

The solution until comparatively recent times was that administrative maid-of-all-work, the justice of the peace. This was literally a task of peace-keeping. Long before the justices were given express statutory powers to deal with lunatics under vagrancy legislation they were expected to dispose summarily of those who were a public nuisance. In those days summary disposal often did not involve anything that we would call a trial, as can be seen from Sir Thomas More's account of how he dealt with a wandering Bedlamite in the sixteenth century (volume I, p. 45); and we have already recounted (on p. 2) how Charles I's Privy Council instructed the justices of Westminster to send 'King Robert', 'Doctor Owen' and 'Mistris Vaughan' to Bedlam.

When it was the sovereign's own safety or privacy that was threatened, it seems that lunatics could be put away without even recourse to the justices. According to two authorities, Sheppard[1] and O'Donoghue,[2] they could be committed by the Board of Green Cloth, 'a board or court of justice held in the counting house of the King's household for the taking cognisance of all matters of government and justice within the King's court-royal and for correcting all the servants that shall offend'.[3] Unfortunately, although Sheppard recounts a number of incidents in the eighteenth and nineteenth centuries in which lunatics forced their way into the royal presence and were put away as a result, the only case in which he specifically says that this was done by the Board of Green Cloth was that of Margaret Nicholson, and she, as we saw in volume I (p. 185), was in fact sent to Bethlem by order of the Home Secretary after she had appeared before the Privy Council. What is certainly the case is that her upkeep at Bethlem was *paid for* by the Board of Green Cloth, as was that of several other Bethlem inmates in the eighteenth and nineteenth centuries. One of these, for example, was a mad cobbler called Bannister Truelock, whose *folie à deux* with Hadfield was revealed at the latter's trial,[4] and who seems to have been committed between the shooting and the trial, perhaps as part of a 'round-up' of dangerous characters.

However that may be, there was evidently a feeling at the time of Hadfield's trial that the procedure for dealing with such cases needed regularising. A final section was therefore included in the Act of 1800 to deal with insane persons who 'endeavoured to gain admittance to His Majesty's presence by intrusion on His Majesty's palaces . . . and otherwise', thus endangering him. It allowed the Privy Council or one of the principal Secretaries of State (who would usually no doubt be the Home Secretary) to have these people brought before them, and committed to a 'place of safety', after which their sanity would be pronounced upon by a jury.

As a result, a small trickle of such cases found their way into Bethlem during the first half of the nineteenth century. They were not 'criminal lunatics' (see pp. 15-16) but were cared for in the ordinary wings for 'curable' or 'incurable' patients, although listed in a special 'Quarterly Report of the Patients admitted at the Recommendation of the Secretary of State . . .'[5] Most of the patients on this list had created a scene of some kind involving the sovereign or a royal palace: an example was John Shocklidge, who is mentioned in volume I, pp. 186 and 193. Another was Charles Mann, whose admission in 1841 was the ironical result of his excessive concern for the *safety* of the Royal Family. In one or two cases, however, the incidents seemed to have nothing to do with the sovereign or his palaces. Marie Girardier, a Swiss woman who had been governess to Sir Robert Peel's family and had made a nuisance of herself in some ill-defined way, was sent to Bethlem (in 1842) not by the Home Secretary but by the Lord Mayor of London.[6]

At all events, this procedure seems to have fallen into disuse early in Victoria's reign: the last admission of this kind recorded in Bethlem's records was in 1843. Eighty years later, in 1963, the Criminal Law Revision Committee called it 'elaborate and archaic', and what was more to the point 'obsolete and unnecessary'. On their recommendation this last remnant of the 1800 Act was repealed by the Criminal Procedure (Insanity) Act, 1964.

So much for the protection of royalty from minor nuisances. But even lunatics who had done or threatened serious harm could be disposed of with remarkable informality. In the eighteenth century the private madhouse, subject to no official control or inspection until 1774 (and not much thereafter), provided well-to-do families with an excellent means of disposing of their less normal members, to say nothing of those who were committed merely in order to gain undisputed possession of their property. Some of the people received by the mad-houses had committed crimes for which they could well have been prosecuted. The Old Bailey Sessions Papers for 1730 record a curious case in which one, John Draper, who seems to have attacked and wounded the Mayor of Bury St Edmunds, was simply packed off to a private mad-house without prosecution. He was fetched from his lodgings by two keepers, who told him that 'he had better be in a mad-house than in Newgate'. They were evidently experienced in handling lunatics, and would not let him have his garters for fear he hanged himself with them. He later prosecuted them for robbing him,[7] but they called Dr Monro of Bethlem to testify that he was disordered, and were acquitted.

Even homicide could on occasion be dealt with in this unofficial way, as the story of Charles Lamb's sister Mary illustrates. She had always been regarded as of weak mind, and by 1795 was said to be worn out with years of day-and-night attendance on her invalid mother, as well as by her needlework, in which she had recently obtained the help of a young apprentice. According to her biographer Mrs Gilchrist, her family observed symptoms of insanity in her a few days before the tragedy, and had tried unsuccessfully to get a doctor for her. One afternoon she snatched a knife from the table and pursued the young apprentice round the room. Her mother called out to stop her and was fatally stabbed. Charles reached the scene too late, and was able to do no more than snatch the knife from his sister. She was taken to a private mad-house, and a coroner's jury found that she had killed her mother while temporarily insane. Strictly speaking she should have been brought to trial, and when she seemed well enough to leave the mad-house the 'authorities of the parish'[8] seem to have felt that a prosecution should be instituted, especially since no medical assurance could be given that she would not become dangerous again. Charles, however, seems to have been able to satisfy them that he would take her under his care for the rest of her life (she was 33 at the time, and he only 21). She left the mad-house without prosecution, and at first lived in lodgings near Charles and his father, later with Charles himself.[9]

In the nineteenth century the newly created police forces, like their predecessors the constables and Bow Street Runners, had to deal with the disturbances and nuisances caused by lunatics. Henry Goddard, who had been a Bow Street Runner before being appointed Chief Constable of Northamptonshire, relates in his memoirs[10] how he had dealt with Sir Francis Mackenzie, who appeared at the Northampton cattle-fair in 1841 in full highland dress, complete with dirk, and proceeded to make outrageous bids for whole herds of cattle. Goddard, who had a great reverence for the gentry, handled him with Machiavellian tact, giving him lunch at the George Hotel. Although Goddard had subordinates, he seems to have handled the whole affair personally, devoting nearly three days to accompanying Mackenzie on his impulsive jaunts, until with his family's help he was tricked into entering a private mad-house in St Johns' Wood, where—again with Goddard's personal help—he was disarmed, overpowered and put in a strait-jacket. Goddard had probably forgotten that he was no longer a Bow Street Runner, who could be hired by the rich to act as detective or bodyguard, for he accepted 'a very handsome present' from Mackenzie's brother.

Such incidents, however, really belong (like Goddard himself) to a more informal era of law enforcement. The legislation of 1800 provided not only for the safe custody of lunatics who were acquitted or found unfit for trial after committing treason or felony, but also persons

> . . . discovered and apprehended under circumstances that denote a derangement of mind, and a purpose of committing some crime for which, if committed such a person would be liable to be indicted. . . .

Mackenzie ought to have been dealt with under this section, which was expressly 'for the better prevention of crimes being committed by persons insane'. It allowed such people to be brought before any justice of the peace, who would 'commit' them by warrant. An important stipulation was included: that they were not to be bailed except by two justices, one of whom should be the author of the original warrant (or by certain superior judicial authorities).

To modern eyes there were oddities in the drafting. The section simply provided for 'commitment' without saying whither he was to be committed. At that date there were so few places outside London which were willing to receive a probably penniless lunatic that to specify his destination would have been difficult, to say the least. Nor did the section require the justices to take medical opinion. As we saw in volume I (chapters 3 and 4) doctors did occasionally testify at trials on the issue of a person's sanity, but verdicts were—and in theory can still be—reached by juries without medical evidence. By the beginning of Victoria's reign, however, the situation had changed considerably. There were more county asylums and licensed houses which were able to receive these lunatics, and the advisability of obtaining medical advice was recognised. A little Act of 1838[11] indicated that county asylums, public hospitals or licensed houses could be used to look after these people. As regards those who recovered, relatives could be allowed to take them into their care, on giving recognisances for their 'peaceable behaviour or custody'.

On the subject of medical advice, however, the Act offered a realistic compromise. The justices could 'call to their assistance a Physician, Surgeon or Apothecary', but to oblige them to do so would have created obvious difficulties, especially in rural areas where the only physicians, surgeons or apothecaries with any experience of insanity were probably in the asylum or licensed house to which the lunatic would have to be sent. Why not therefore let him be properly examined when he had arrived there?

The section remained in force for more than a century, although we have been unable to find any clear examples, to say nothing of statistics, to show how or whether it was used. It was clearly obsolete in 1946, when it was repealed—along with a few other minor enactments affecting lunatics —by the National Health Service Act (9 and 10 Geo. VI. c. 81). What almost certainly led to its obsolescence was the rough and ready way in which lunatics who were a nuisance could be dealt with under the Poor Laws.

Even in the second half of the nineteenth century many thousands were still in the workhouses and not in the county asylums as they should have been.[12] Provided that they were not 'dangerous' it was not absolutely certain that this was illegal. In theory the parish relieving officer was supposed to take any insane pauper before a magistrate, who ought to have him examined by a medical man and then, if he were certified, have him committed to a county asylum. In fact the numbers involved would have placed an intolerable burden on the asylums, and magistrates in many areas were more or less declining to operate this system. Instead, the relieving officers were being compelled to send these lunatics to workhouses as paupers. The Select Committee of the House of Commons which heard evidence on this subject from Shaftesbury and others in 1859[13] merely said that nobody should be kept in a workhouse as a lunatic without a medical certificate, renewable quarterly.

The rather belated result was a little Act in 1885[14] which, with minor amendments, was preserved in the important Lunacy Act of 1890 (53 & 54 Vict., c. 5). This applied to any 'alleged lunatic' who seemed to need 'care and control' for 'the public safety' or his own welfare. In such cases a relieving officer, parish overseer or–and this is important–a constable could put the alleged lunatic not into an asylum (that required doctors and a justice) but into a workhouse. An important safeguard was included, however: the alleged lunatic could not be kept in the workhouse for more than three days, during which the constable (or relieving officer or overseer, as the case might be) was to take the necessary steps to have him certified by doctors and committed by a justice to an asylum, failing which he was a free man again. The 1913 Act (s. 15) provided a similar procedure for dealing with mental defectives who were found neglected, abandoned, without visible support or being cruelly treated, but allowed them to be taken to any 'place of safety', a term which had been used without definition in the 1800 Act (Section IV) and was now so widely defined as to include not only hospitals, institutions, surgeries and workhouses, but also police stations, places of detention and indeed 'any suitable place the occupier of which is willing to receive (them) temporarily'.

Although the procedure was intended for emergencies rather than everyday use, it had the advantage that the lunatic could be removed right away, without the necessity for medical and magisterial co-operation. Its popularity was such that in the London County Council area at least it became more or less the standard way of arranging compulsory admissions to 'observation wards', which were often called 'police admissions'.[15]

The Percy Commission (in para. 412 of its report) agreed that the police should continue to have power to remove a person direct from a public place to a hospital if he seemed mentally disordered and in need of care and control, but thought that they should be able to do so only if the person consented or if his behaviour was such that he was liable to arrest under normal police powers. This was one of the points, however, on which the Mental Health Bill did not follow the Commission's recommendations. Instead, it merely brought up to date the fairly wide powers given to the constable by the 1885 Act. If a constable found in a public place a person who appeared to him to be mentally disordered and to be in immediate need of care or control, and if the constable considered it necessary in that person's interests or for the protection of others to remove him to a place of safety, he could do so. 'Place of safety' was almost as widely defined as before, the only obvious omission being work-houses, which had by now disappeared. There he could be kept for not more than 72 hours in order that he could be examined by a doctor and interviewed by a mental welfare officer, and if necessary, arrangements made for voluntary or compulsory treatment or care. The only important change was that henceforward only police were to have this power: the local authorities' mental welfare officers were not. It was confined to the police because of their responsibility for public order.[16] Although it could perhaps be argued that if removal to a place of safety was—as the clause envisaged—something which could on occasion be in the patient's own interests, and was thus something which could in such cases be left to a mental welfare officer, it must be admitted that so far as public places are concerned the police are much more likely to arrive on the spot before a mental welfare officer can be got hold of.

With the help of the then Ministry of Health we were able to obtain statistics showing the extent to which this power was used in 1964 (the nearest calendar year to that of our cohort for which they could be pro-vided). The results are summarised in table 28.

These figures have several interesting features. One, which is not ap-parent from the table itself, is that they include very few subnormals: only three were admitted under Sections 135[17] or 136 in 1964. No doubt the reason is that the behaviour of subnormal people is seldom bizarre enough to persuade the police to take them straight to hospital without the safe-guard of a medical opinion.[18] Another feature is the sex-ratio, which resembles neither that of compulsory admissions under Part IV of the Act nor that of hospital order cases. Amongst the former, women exceed men; amongst the latter men exceed women by about 4:1. But amongst Section 136 cases, the ratio seems to be about $1\frac{1}{2}:1$.[19] It is not easy to formulate a tidy or confident explanation of this difference. A speculative suggestion, however, is this. Mental disorder apart, men are much more likely than women to behave publicly in ways which alarm or affront others sufficiently to lead to police intervention. On the other hand, behaviour of this sort is often due to certain types of mental disorder (usually schizophrenia or senile cerebral conditions) to which women seem if anything more sus-ceptible than men. The sex-ratio for situations leading to the use of Section 136 could thus be a hybrid, as it were, of the sex-ratios for these types of mental disorder and for what might loosely be called 'breaches of the peace'.

Thirdly, the regional variation in the use of Section 136 is striking. No less than 88 per cent of the cases in table 28 occurred in one of the London regions. In contrast, none occurred in Liverpool, and we have been told by a Liverpool psychiatrist that the use of the section is unheard of there. Only one case occurred in the Leeds Region, and one or two other regions were remarkably under-represented. The explanation probably lies in the use made of the Lunacy Act powers which were described earlier

TABLE 28. Removal to hospital of persons found disordered in public places in 1964

	Males	Females
Newcastle[a]	6	1
Leeds	1	—
Sheffield	1	3
East Anglia	14	7
Oxford	1	1
South Western	5	4
Wales	12	8
Birmingham[a]	19	3
Manchester[a]	2	6
Liverpool	—	—
Wessex	—	3
North West ⎫	151 ⎫	75 ⎫
North East ⎪ Metropolitan	40 ⎬ 452	29 ⎬ 296
South East[a] ⎪	79	63
South West ⎭	182 ⎭	129 ⎭
All regions	513	332

[a] The figures for each of these regions include 1 case of unknown sex which was
dealt with under s. 135 and not s. 136. Section 135 is that which allows a
justice of the peace to authorise a constable to remove to 'a place of safety'
from any specified premises 'a person believed to be suffering from mental
disorder' who is suspected with reasonable cause to be neglected, ill-treated or
kept otherwise than under proper control, or to be living there alone and unable
to care for himself. It is occasionally invoked to arrange the removal to hospital of
senile people who barricade themselves in their homes and will not admit
visiting social workers or doctors.

in this appendix. As we have seen, the practice of admitting to observation
wards patients who had been brought without medical certification by
the police or the welfare authority became extremely popular in London,
while in other areas it may well have been used—as it was intended—for
situations in which the more regular procedure would have been too slow.
Certainly the Metropolitan police will often take a disordered person whom
they have found in a public place to a police station and then, having rung
up a hospital, to that hospital; whereas other forces often prefer to keep
the person at the police station until a doctor and mental welfare officer
can be brought there to deal with him. In both cases the statutory authority
is Section 136, but whereas the police are still acting under that section if
they take the person to hospital before he has been medically examined,
once the examination has taken place any admission to hospital must
either be informal or covered by one of the sections of Part IV of the Act
(see pp. 69-70).[20] Thus emergency admissions which begin with the
picking up of a disordered person in a public place by the police may be
recorded either as Section 136 admissions or as Part IV admissions, depending
on the stage at which the patient was seen by a doctor.[21]

Procedural differences, however, cannot explain all the variations in
regional distribution. Even within the Metropolitan Regions, the South
West Region is strikingly over-represented, as it was in our cohort of

s

hospital order cases (see pp. 159-61). Nor can *this* over-representation be accounted for by the presence of busy magistrates' courts (for these cases do not go through the courts) or of the largest remand prison. When studied together with our other regional figures (loc. cit. *supra*) these strongly suggest that there is something about the catchment areas of this region's hospitals which either attracts the mentally ill or generates them: and in this case mental illness usually means schizophrenia.

The formal procedure of Section 136 is not, of course, the only way in which a disordered offender may be dealt with. Many compulsory patients, and even some informal ones, are admitted after incidents which could have brought them into the criminal courts, had their relatives, neighbours or the police so wished.[22]

It is equally true that not all cases in which it seems necessary to a policeman to remove a disordered person from a public place 'in his own interest' or 'for the protection of other persons' are cases in which a criminal offence has or is likely to be committed. The individual concerned may be endangering nothing but his own person. Nevertheless, it is true that almost any behaviour of a markedly abnormal kind in a public place can be made the basis of some sort of charge, if only 'conduct likely to provoke a breach of the peace'.[23] Consequently, Section 136 must be regarded as only one of the procedures open to the police for dealing with threats to public order.

Several illustrations were provided by a small survey which we carried out over a six-month period in 1963, the year of our main cohort, in order to form an impression of the circumstances in which police forces would refrain from carrying proceedings to the length of prosecution. With the help of the Home Office, twelve provincial police forces and two divisions of the Metropolitan Police were asked to complete a questionnaire on any case occurring during this period in which a person 'would probably have been dealt with by a criminal court if they had not been found to be suffering from some form of mental disorder'. The harvest (consisting of 53 cases, a few of which occurred outside the six-month period) was rather small, and in any case could not be regarded as a sample from which to make reliable estimates of the frequency with which different types of situation occurred. Nevertheless it provided us with some illuminating examples of what can happen, even if we could not be sure that every kind of situation was represented in it.

The most obvious feature of this small collection—for it can hardly be called a 'sample'—was that it contained very few cases in which the person involved had not already been a patient at a psychiatric hospital, and usually recently. Some were absconders, who were simply taken back to hospital. Others were on leave, for the day or longer. Others were outpatients. One of the incidents actually occurred *in* a mental hospital. This was a theft of money from a nurse's jacket, by a psychopathic patient who was detected in the act and then absconded: after being questioned by the police he was returned to the hospital.

One of the apparent exceptions also happened to be a case in which Section 136 was invoked. A man had entered a railway station, but had been stopped at the barrier because he had no ticket. He refused to leave, and 'was not rational when spoken to', said the police report. He was taken to the police station, where it was decided that he was in need of immediate mental treatment; and he was removed to hospital. He may or may not have had a history of recognised disorder: but the police do not appear to have discovered anything about him, and were probably right to leave this to the hospital.

In most cases, however, the person concerned was known or discovered by the police to be a patient or ex-patient. Sometimes he or she was already familiar to them. Sometimes a member of the patient's family told them of his or her history. In one case—an elderly woman who was detected in shoplifting—they might not have known about it if a solicitor who had been engaged on her behalf had not told them. As we have emphasised earlier in this book, there is no routine way in which even psychiatric hospitals, let alone police, can check whether a person has a psychiatric record.

At first it was a little surprising that a substantial number[24] of our cases were or had been informal patients. This was not really remarkable, however, for one of the important features of the British psychiatric hospital system is the informal status of the vast majority of its patients. This was so even before the 1959 Act: in the early nineteen-fifties 75 per cent of all admissions to designated mental hospitals were said to be voluntary. The current percentage is over 80 per cent. Both informal and compulsory admissions include unknown numbers of patients who

(a) have committed offences which have not been traced to them;
(b) are known by relatives, victims or doctors to have committed
    offences which have not been reported to the police; or
(c) are known or suspected by the police to have committed offences,
    but have not been prosecuted.

The high percentage of voluntary admissions, coupled with the considerable discretion allowed to the police in deciding whether to prosecute for a wide range of offences, makes it probable that these groups are relatively larger in this country than in others where both informal admission and police discretion are more restricted.

This must mean, for example, that hospital psychiatrists in this country are quite often faced with patients whom they know or believe to have committed offences which have not been traced to them by the police. It is worth emphasising that although psychiatrists—like all physicians—can be compelled to testify in criminal courts, nowadays we leave it to the psychiatrist's conscience to decide whether he should report what he knows to the police. In theory, a doctor who did not report an offence which was a felony used to risk prosecution for misprision of felony, but in practice such prosecutions were unknown, and even that theoretical risk has now been abolished by the Criminal Law Act, 1967.[25] Consequently psychiatrists in England have long regarded the decision whether to report a crime by a patient as a matter for their private conscience or professional code. No doubt the decision in each case depends on the seriousness of the offence in the eyes of the individual doctor; and the number of doctors who would report serious violence or sexual molestation by a patient must be greater than the number who would disclose mere shoplifting. This is a subject on which more information would be interesting, but is most unlikely to be obtainable.

An even more difficult question to answer is 'To what extent are offenders themselves manipulating the system of voluntary admission in order to avoid prosecution?' We are referring not to the occasional attempt to feign mental disorder, but to the genuine patient whose voluntary returns to hospital tend to follow the commission of offences which are likely to be traced to him. Examples of such cases were given by witnesses to the Royal Commission of 1954–7. Certainly the offenders themselves often believe that the police are less likely to prosecute in-patients of mental hospitals, and our impression is that this is true of many police forces.

An instance of this was a sixty-three-year-old man in our cohort of hospital order cases. He had a history of drunkenness, varied with thefts and forgeries, and would go in and out of hospital as a voluntary patient. When he got into trouble he would often succeed in being taken back to hospital without prosecution by claiming the status of voluntary patient.

(Some people can even manage to avoid both prosecution and treatment. A striking example of what is sometimes called 'manipulative behaviour' was a woman in her sixties who had been a mental patient for an unknown period *fifteen years* before, and was well known to the local police because of her habit of following them on their patrols and 'interfering'. She was known to have stolen money or goods on many occasions from her lodgings or her employers, but whenever she was questioned about the thefts would shout, scream, kick furniture and throw loose objects at anyone in the room. Although she had three convictions in her fifties for being drunk and disorderly she had managed to escape any more serious charges. As the police report said, 'due to her hysterics no conclusion has ever been reached . . .' Moreover, she did not even have to resort to re-entering a mental hospital!)

It is worth noting that even the statutory provisions for the disposal of offenders makes use of the practice of informal admission. A probation order may be accompanied by a *requirement* that the probationer undergo psychiatric treatment, either as an in-patient or an out-patient for not more than twelve months. A probation order cannot be made without the offender's consent, and his status is that of an informal patient. If he walks out of the hospital, or breaks off treatment, he cannot be forced to return. All that can be done is to bring him back to court for a breach of the requirements of the order; and the most that the court can then do is to impose an ordinary penalty for his offence. Even this cannot be done if he can satisfy the court that his refusal to undergo 'surgical, electrical or other treatment' was reasonable in the circumstance.

Had this provision—which belongs to the Criminal Justice Act of 1948—been drafted more recently, it is conceivable that Parliament would have agreed that the status of the probationer under in-patient treatment should or could be that of a compulsory patient, although no doubt a number of probation officers and psychiatrists would still argue that this would be likely to impede treatment.

The kinds of misbehaviour in even our small collection ranged from the trivial to the extremely dangerous. One ex-patient, a chronic schizophrenic, stabbed her husband in the back with a knife, fortunately not fatally. Another, a paranoid schizophrenic mother on leave from hospital, set fire to the room where her four-year-old son was asleep. Another, a depressed woman in her forties, tried to kill both herself and her invalid mother.

The usual course taken by the police was to return the patient to his or her hospital. In several cases, however, a caution was administered–in at least one case to a man who was so subnormal that the police had found it almost impossible to communicate with him. Usually the decision not to carry proceedings any further was taken by the police themselves, but occasionally their hands were forced by the refusal of the victim to testify in cases where his or her evidence would have been essential. One firm refused to prosecute because the man concerned was a good worker and they wanted to continue employing him. One hospital insisted that to prosecute the patient would have an adverse effect on his mental state. Yet in another case when the same hospital was sufficiently judicious to say that prosecution would probably not do any harm, the same police force decided against prosecution. One police force said that it was 'impossible' to prosecute a man because he was already a compulsory patient, although they probably did not mean this literally.

All that we have been able to do in this short appendix is to cite enough incidents, from the sixteenth century onward, to show that the practice of dealing unofficially with known offenders–even when they are obviously dangerous–is by no means a recent innovation; and to illustrate the sort of circumstances in which it is likely to happen nowadays. Our information does not enable us to estimate the overall frequency of different sorts of situation. One final point, however, can be made. It would be very difficult to argue that there is any rational and objective distinction between offences by disordered persons which lead to disposal by a court and those which are dealt with in one of the unofficial ways that have just been described. At extremes, if the offence is very trivial and the perpetrator is found to be a present or former psychiatric patient, it is less likely to lead to prosecution than if it is very serious and the perpetrator's mental condition has not yet been officially diagnosed. But given that the perpetrator has acquired the official status of patient or ex-patient, quite serious incidents may be handled unofficially, just as–on the evidence of chapter 6–quite trivial ones may lead to hospital orders.

Notes

1. The Rev. J. J. Edgar Sheppard, *Memorials of St James's Palace* (London, 1894), vol. I. Unfortunately, Sheppard does not name the source of his anecdotes.
2. E. G. O'Donoghue, *The Story of Bethlehem Hospital from its Foundation in 1247* (London, 1914).
3. See Samuel Johnson's Dictionary of the English Language (London, 1747) s.v. 'Greencloth'.
4. See State Trials (Howell's edition) vol. XXVII, cols. 1342-3, 1348,

1501. Truelock came to Bethlem several months after the trial (in late December) with a letter from an Under-Secretary of State to say that he had been arrested in May for aiding and abetting Hadfield, but since it appeared that he was deranged, the Duke of Portland judged it proper to send him to Bethlem.

5.   For this, as for so much of our other information about Bethlem in this appendix and chapter 15, we are indebted to its archivist, Miss Patricia Allderidge.

6.   To do Bethlem justice, they did query the authority for Marie Girardier's committal, and the Lord Mayor got Mackmurdo [sic] presumably the Newgate surgeon of that name, to sign a certificate. The Lord Mayor may have thought that he was acting as a justice of the peace under Section 111 of the 1800 Act (see text, infra); but if so, what indictable crime had she seemed likely to commit? The lack of references to specific powers in the letters accompanying these cases would horrify modern lawyers.

7.   See the Old Bailey Sessions Papers for 28 August–1 September 1730.

8.   According to Talfourd, the editor of Lamb's letters, who seems to have got his information from Lamb's friend Lloyd. See also Mrs Anne Gilchrist's Mary Lamb (London, 1837), and the Morning Chronicle for September 26, 1796. Charles Lamb was on friendly terms with several influential lawyers, who may have advised or helped him.

9.   We are indebted to Dr Alexander Walk for drawing our attention to Mary Lamb's case.

10.   Henry Goddard, Memoirs of a Bow Street Runner (London, 1956), 194 ff.

11.   1 & 2 Vict. c. 14.

12.   Some 13,000 in 1859, for example. Many workhouses had special wards for them; but the standard of care was often miserable.

13.   See the Report of, and Minutes of Evidence before, the Select Committee on Lunatics, published in 1859 and 1860, especially the answers to questions 683 ff and 1734 ff. We are indebted to Dr Alexander Walk for helping us to trace the origins of s. 20 of the 1890 Act, and the way in which it was later used.

14.   An Act to Amend the Law relating to Lunatics (48 & 49 Vict. c. 52).

15.   See M. D. Eilenberg and P. B. Whatmore 'Police Admissions to a Mental Observation Ward', in (1962) Medicine, Science and the Law, 96.

16.   This explanation was given to us in a personal letter from the Home Office. 'Constable' can, however, be interpreted as including railway policemen, according to the legal advisers of the Department of Health and Social Security.

17.   For an explanation of Section 135, see pp. 69-70 and the note to table 28.

18. Although there were subnormal patients in our hospital order cohort who might well have been dealt with thus: an example is the subnormal girl who scandalised her fellow-travellers on a London bus (see p. 147).

19. So far as can be judged from the Ministry of Health's *Statistical Report Series, No. 4*, the ratio was not very different in 1965 and 1966.

20. This has been confirmed by legal advice given to hospitals by the Department of Health and Social Security in a letter of 29th November 1968. The same letter, however, confirms that there seems to be no objection to removing a person who is apparently covered by Section 136 first to a police station as a 'place of safety' and thence to a hospital as another 'place of safety' so long as a psychiatric examination has not intervened.

21. There were signs, however, that provincial forces were gradually increasing their use of s. 136 during the sixties. In 1964 they accounted for only 11·7 per cent of the cases in which this power was used; but this percentage increased over the next four years, as follows: 1964 11·7 per cent; 1965 12·9 per cent; 1966 16·5 per cent; 1967 15·8 per cent; 1968 18·9 per cent. Admittedly the figures on which these percentages are based (which are taken from the Ministry of Health's *Statistical Report Series*) include cases in which the section used was s. 135 and not s. 136; but such cases, which are defined on p. 70, are negligible in number. The increase in the provincial percentage is particularly striking when it is appreciated that the use of s. 136 in the Metropolitan regions was also increasing.

22. See Dr H. R. Rollin's fascinating chapter on unprosecuted offenders in *The Mentally Abnormal Offender and the Law* (Oxford, 1969).

23. Transvestites, for example, are sometimes charged with this, if they cannot be accused of soliciting or any other specific offence. This happened to one man in our sample.

24. Precise percentages are purposely avoided, since they would be quite misleading, in view of the nature of the 'sample'.

25. The decision of the House of Lords in the case of Sykes v. the Director of Public Prosecutions ([1962] A.C. 528; [1961] 3 All E.R. 33) confirmed that it was a common law misdemeanour, called 'misprision of felony' to omit to report a felony to the police. Lord Denning suggested that there might be a case in which such an omission by a lawyer, doctor or clergyman might be justified or excusable. However this may be, the Criminal Law Act, 1967 (which abolished the distinction between felonies and mis-demeanours) replaces misprision with the more narrowly defined offence of agreeing to accept a consideration for refraining from disclosing information about the commission of an arrestable offence –an offence of which a physician is even less likely to be accused.

Appendix B. **The Analysis of the Follow-up**

A standard computing programme (ASCOP, written by Mr B.E. Cooper of the Atlas Computer Laboratory) was used to calculate partial regression coefficients (β coefficients) for nine criteria, all relating to the two-year follow-up of 'first-year leavers':

(*a*) whether the ex-patient was recorded by the then Ministry of Health as having been readmitted to a mental hospital during the period of the two-year follow-up, either as a result of reconviction or otherwise: a binary criterion referred to as 'rehospitalisation';

(*b*) whether he or she was recorded by the central Criminal Records Office as having been reconvicted during the same period: a binary criterion referred to as 'reconviction';

(*c*) whether he or she had either been rehospitalised or reconvicted (a binary criterion which in the event did not appear to improve on rehospitalisation and reconviction when studied separately, and is therefore not tabulated);

(*d*) whether he or she had been reconvicted and as a result received a custodial sentence or been rehospitalised: it was assumed that such reconvictions would have involved a rather more serious set of offences than reconvictions not leading to custody or rehospitalisation, and this binary criterion is therefore referred to as 'serious reconviction';

(*e*) whether he or she was recorded by the then Ministry of Social Security as having had contributory employment at any time during the follow-up period: (a binary criterion referred to as 'employment') (in the event it was decided to tabulate not this but a modification defined under (*f*) below);

(*f*) whether he or she had been 'employed' (in the sense defined in (*e*)) for more than 1 month: a binary criterion referred to as 'substantial employment';

(*g*) whether he or she had been 'employed' (for any length of time) without reconviction or rehospitalisation: a binary criterion referred to as 'employment without relapse';

(*h*) *if* he or she had been employed, the number of months for which employment had lasted (not necessarily continuously): a multi-valued criterion referred to as 'duration of employment'. Since only 32 of the women were employed, this criterion has been tabulated for men only;

(i) whether he or she was known to have been rehospitalised, reconvicted or employed, or was the subject of no official information: a binary criterion referred to as 'no information'.

The analysis was designed to study the relationship between these criteria and our recorded information regarding two groups of 'variables':

i. those which were, in theory at least, ascertainable at the time of the hospital order: sex, age, nationality, living conditions, employment history, mental hospital history, criminal record, type of current offence;

ii. those which were, by their nature, ascertainable only after admission to hospital under the hospital order: current diagnosis, abscondings, length of time spent in hospital, whether any after-care was envisaged after discharge.

Many of these could be treated as binary variables. There is no theoretical objection to this when the variable is a person's sex, which allows of only two categories; nor when a diagnosis is involved (since every case in which the responsible medical officer has recorded his diagnosis can be categorised as 'schizophrenic or not' and so on. Indeed, since it is impossible to assign values on a single scale to schizophrenia, subnormality and so on, this is the most straightforward solution; and the same is true of offence types. Other variables, however, could be and were treated as multi-valued: for example, numbers of previous convictions, or time between any previous hospital stay and the current one.

The statistic used in the ready-made programme which we adopted was the beta-coefficient. This is the amount by which the criterion changes (expressed as a fraction of its standard deviation) if the independent variable changes by one standard deviation, when all the other variables are held constant.* For example, where women ex-patients were concerned, reconviction was linked to time spent in previous penal custody by a beta-coefficient of 0·27, which meant that an increase or decrease of one standard deviation in time spent in previous custody would be accompanied by an increase or decrease in the numbers reconvicted to the extent of about one quarter of the standard deviation. By expressing the relationship in terms of standard deviations the coefficient is intended to overcome the difficulty which arises when (as in our case) the values involved have widely different ranges, including binary values.

Table 29 therefore shows the beta-coefficients which describe the relationship between the variables and those criteria which seemed worth tabulating. To make interpretation easier, however, it shows the beta-coefficient only when this reaches the 0·1 level of significance and the

*It was obtained from fitting a linear additive model of the form

$$y = \beta_1 x_1 + \beta_2 x_2 + \beta_3 x_3 \ldots,$$

where $x_1, x_2, x_3 \ldots$ are the standardised prediction variables and $\beta_1, \beta_2, \beta_3 \ldots$ are the corresponding beta-coefficients and y is the standardised criterion. This model makes certain assumptions about the relationships between the variables. Since we have not investigated these we cannot say how adequate it is. It is justifiable, however, to use the beta-coefficients from this model as approximations to partial correlation coefficients.

TABLE 29. Beta-coefficients for variables used in the analysis of the two-year follow-up of first-year discharges[c]

	Rehospitalised		Reconvicted	
Criteria				
	M	F	M	F
Variables	$\beta(t^2)$	$\beta(t^2)$	$\beta(t^2)$	$\beta(t^2)$
at time of hospital order				
Age				
British?[a]				
Living at home?			−0·09(3·12)	
Previous convictions	0·11(2·72)		0·12(3·64)	0·20(3·08)
Total time spent in previous penal custody[b]			0·17(7·60)	0·27(6·80)
Current offence ⎰violent? sexual? acquisitive? disorderly?⎱	0·12(3·35)		−0·12(4·37)	
Previous hospital admissions	0·11(3·50)	0·30(7·92)		
Time since last hospital stay		−0·19(3·48)		
Employed at time of offence		−0·20(3·85)		
Previous jobs held for under one year				
In hospital or after				
Any absconding?				
Left by absconding?			0·15(7·59)	
Time in hospital				
Any after care?			−0·11(4·57)	
Diagnosis				
schizophrenia?			−0·22(4·14)	
paranoid schizophrenia?			−0·25(8·20)	
affective disorder?		−0·25(2·80)	−0·13(2·72)	
psychopathy?				
subnormality?				
R^2 (see note *d*)	0·13	0·30	0·26	0·45
N	351	105	351	105

[a] A question mark indicates a binary variable.

[b] Including borstal, detention centre, approved school.

[c] The significance of the β co-efficients can be assessed from the t^2 values (in brackets) by using the following table:

t^2	2·69	3·84	5·43	6·66	9·55	10·82
p	0·1	0·05	0·02	0·01	0·002	0·001

[d] R^2 is the fraction of the criterion's variance which is accounted for by all the variables listed in the table.

ommitted by court to prison or hospital		Any contributory employment for more than one month		Any contributory employment without rehospitalisation or reconviction		Time in contributory employment (for those in such employment)
M	F	M	F	M	F	M
$\beta(t^2)$	$\beta(t^2)$	$\beta(t^2)$	$\beta(t^2)$	$\beta(t^2)$	$\beta(t^2)$	(βt^2)
		−47(13·72)		−0·37(7·46)		
10(2·98)	0·21(2·94)	−0·12(3·84)		0·11(2·71)		
9(9·91)						
	−0·24(3·92)			0·20(10·53)		
15(5·43)		−0·30(5·77)			−0·24(3·24)	
	−0·19(3·67)					
			0·24(6·22)		0·22(4·47)	0·24(11·77)
			0·22(4·31)		0·21(3·22)	
			−0·21(4·28)			−0·12(2·74)
12(4·91)		−0·09(2·60)				−0·13(3·30)
10(3·18)	−0·29(7·45)	0·12(5·16)				
14(6·70)		0·22(16·62)		0·16(8·02)		
		−0·21(3·28)				
0·26	0·34	0·21	0·38	0·17	0·31	0·26
351	105	351	105	351	105	214

t^2 value is then indicated in brackets (e.g., $t^2 = 3.65$). We are well aware that a beta-coefficient with a p value of only 0.1 or even 0.05 cannot by itself be regarded as reaching an acceptable level of significance, especially in a table containing 210 beta-coefficients. Roughly 1 in 10 coefficients with a p value of 0.1, for example, is likely to be due to nothing more than sampling error. But in many such cases the relationship seems to hold good for women as well as men, or for two or more criteria, or is consistent with other relationships. Nevertheless, as has been pointed out in chapter 8, the most striking feature of the table is the rather low level of all the coefficients.

This brings us to an important point. In order to show what fraction of the total variance in the criterion is accounted for by all the variables in the linear model, the R^2 value is shown at the foot of each column. As can be seen, the R^2 values are for the most part low, never rising above 0.26 for men. They are higher for women, the highest value being 0.45 for women's reconvictions.

The use of beta-coefficients, however, as approximations to partial correlation co-efficients is a rather crude approach to the analysis of data in search of causal relationships. Ideally, one would merely use this table for the construction of one or more speculative models of the causal relationships, on which more refined analyses would be based; and no doubt in this way the R^2 values could be increased, although by how much is of course uncertain. (In fact at an earlier stage we had arranged with a statistician that he would work out and apply a programme suited to the particular nature of our data and needs; and it was only after considerable delay in this project that we resorted to the ASCOP programme. It is therefore conceivable that further relationships of an interesting kind will be elicited from our data; and if so they will be reported. On the whole, however, we do not expect this.)

One criterion which needs special mention is 'no information'. Taken at its face value this meant that the ex-patient had neither been reconvicted nor been readmitted to a mental hospital, but had not been in contributory employment at any time during the two-year period. He or she might, of course, have been detected in an offence which was so trivial that it did not lead to prosecution, or–if prosecuted–was not reported to the Criminal Records Office. On the other hand, he or she might have been under psychiatric treatment as an out-patient without being recorded in the Department of Health and Social Security's central register. Again, he or she might have a job of sorts without being recorded as in contributory employment. Our problem was whether to regard 'no news as good news' or the reverse.

We had hoped to form some opinion on this question by seeing whether 'no information' was more closely associated with variables which were predictive of success or variables predictive of failure. Unfortunately, the R^2 value for men was very low indeed (only 0.07) and no beta-coefficient reached even the 0.1 level of significance. For women, on the other hand, R^2 was more substantial (0.38), and three variables seemed significantly related to 'no information'. One was age: the older the woman the less likely we were to have any recorded follow-up information ($\beta = 0.138$

$(t^2 = 8\cdot70))$. Since age was similarly related to absence of employment, the explanation is in all probability simple: that we had 'no information' because the older the woman the less likely she is to get employment, at least where ex-patients are concerned. Again, the fewer previous jobs she had held for less than a year, the less likely we were to have any follow-up information about her $(\beta = 0\cdot26 \ (t^2 = 5\cdot49))$: and table 29 shows that previous jobs of this kind are positively associated with subsequent employment so far as women are concerned. Thirdly, the longer the gap between any previous hospital stay and the current one the more likely she was to appear in the 'no information' group $(\beta = 0\cdot18 \ (t^2 = 3\cdot47))$. Although this association was not impressive, it coincided with a similar association between the same variable and non-rehospitalisation, as can be seen from table 29. In other words, as far as women were concerned there were some grounds for regarding 'no news as good news'. But the same could not be said of the men, whose appearance in the 'no information' group appeared to be much more random, at least as far as our variables were concerned.

Appendix C. **The Follow-up Procedures**

Our follow-up of our offender-patients consisted of seven operations:

1. Six months after the patient's admission to hospital we sent his 'responsible medical officer' a questionnaire, of which a copy will be found in Appendix D. We shall call this 'the six-month questionnaire'.

2. Unless the six-month questionnaire indicated that he had left the hospital, we sent his responsible medical officer a second questionnaire twelve months after his admission (see Appendix D). We shall call this 'the twelve-month questionnaire'.

3. Unless the twelve-month questionnaire told us that he had left the hospital, we ascertained after two years whether he had left the hospital during the second year. Because we felt obliged to promise that the twelve-month questionnaire would be the last, we obtained this information from the Ministry of Health's Mental Health Enquiry index at Blackpool; so that we have no information about the circumstances in which offender-patients left hospital during their second year: for example, whether they absconded or were properly discharged.

4. We followed up those who left hospital within a year of admission (by whatever means) for two years after their departure, by
    1. asking the Criminal Records Office for information about any subsequent convictions which had been centrally recorded;
    2. asking the Ministry of Health for information about subsequent readmissions to mental hospitals;
    3. asking the Newcastle office of the Ministry of Social Security (as it then was) for information about the ex-patients' National Insurance contributions, in order to see what their employment records were like.

5. We followed up, by the same means, those who left hospital more than twelve months but less than 24 months after admission, but only for one year in the first place.

6. Since the great majority of restriction order cases were not discharged within the first two years, we followed up all restriction order cases until the middle of 1970, with the help of the index kept by the Home Office's Statistical Division.

7. In the first half of 1971 we asked the receiving hospitals for the dates of discharge of all offender-patients not known to have left hospital in the first two years. (We chose this method in preference to consulting the Mental Health Enquiry index because we thought it likely to be

both quicker and more accurate; and certainly the response of the receiving hospitals was both swift and helpful.) This we called 'the 1971 review', and it succeeded in accounting for all but 18 of the 1,160 men and women in our cohort.

Inevitably, the information collected in these different ways did not always tally. For example, the 1971 review showed that the numbers of offender-patients discharged in their second year was larger than the Mental Health Enquiry index had reported. On the whole, however, the discrepancies were few.

Appendix D. **Questionnaires**
relating to individual hospital order cases

1. The Police-Hospital Dossier. See pp. 114 ff.

2. The Six-month Questionnaire. (See Appendix C.)

3. The Twelve-month Questionnaire. (See Appendix C.)

T

1. *The Police-Hospital Dossier*

MENTAL HEALTH ACT, 1959

Survey of offenders dealt with under Part V

---

1. Under this Act, which came into operation in November, 1960, a higher or lower court may deal with certain mentally disturbed offenders by authorising them to be detained in a specified hospital (by means of a hospital order) or by placing them under the guardianship of a local health authority (by means of a guardianship order). Such orders are made under s.60 of the Act; under s.61 the court may deal in a similar way with children found to be in need of care, protection or control.

2. In addition, a court of Assize or Quarter Sessions which has made a hospital order may make an order imposing special restrictions on the discharge of the offender from hospital: such orders, known as 'restriction orders' are made under s.65 and may specify a period for the duration of the restrictions, or may be without a time limit. A magistrates Court cannot make a restriction order, but can, under s.67, commit an offender to Quarter Sessions with a view to the making of a hospital order, although Quarter Sessions is not then bound to deal with him in this way.

3. More information about these offenders is needed, and with the approval of the Home Office and the Ministry of Health the Reader in Criminology at Oxford University is making a study of them. This form has been devised so as to collect the information in such a way as to minimise the number of later enquiries addressed to police forces and hospitals, and to meet, as far as practicable, the requirements both of research and of normal administration. The Home Office and Ministry of Health will be grateful for the full co-operation of police forces and hospitals in the completion of the form in all relevant cases and in operating the procedure set out below.

POLICE FORCES

    (see Home Office letter of 18th March, 1963).

4. Police Forces are asked to complete the Police Section of this form in the case of any person dealt with under s.60, s.61 or s.65 by any court, and to send it to the Home Office Statistical Branch, Kingston By-Pass Road, Surbiton, Surrey (Telephone Emberbrook 5541), to whom all enquiries should be addressed. All forms should be despatched *under separate cover* as follows:

> (a) If the order is made by a magistrates' court
>   *immediately* after the proceedings are completed
>
> or
>
> (b) if the order is made by a higher court,
>   *immediately* after the close of the sessions or Assizes.

HOSPITALS

    (See Ministry of Health letter of 20th March, 1963)

5. The Home Office will send the form to the Secretary of the Hospital Management Committee for transmission to the responsible medical officer who is asked to complete it (or arrange for its completion under his direction). The entire form should be returned intact (within fourteen days if possible) to the Home Office Statistical Branch, Kingston-By-Pass Road, Surbiton, Surrey (Telephone Emberbrook 5541). Any further enquiries will be sent direct to the responsible medical officer who is asked to sign the form.

    The central Ethical Committee of the British Medical Association has no objection to the disclosure of clinical information for this purpose.

It is clearly of importance that the information recorded should be as complete and accurate as possible. Where the answer to a question is not known (and not obtainable) please write 'Not known' (or N.K.) and do not leave the space blank. The information in this form is recorded in confidence and will be so treated.

POLICE SECTION

Surname ....   Forename(s) ....

                            Sex ....

Police Force and code no. ....

Name of court making order ....

Date of order ....

Type of order (i.e. under s.60 or s.61,
with or without restriction under s.65) ....

If under s.65, what was the period
of restriction? ....

Name and address of hospital ....
(if accused* was committed to hospital;
if the order was a guardianship order
give name and address of guardian)

* This form is also intended for the few cases dealt with under s.61 in which the child or young
person is not 'accused' of any offence.

Remand or committal

Before the court made the order
had the accused been remanded

    for medical examination (e.g.
    under s.26 of the Magistrates
    Courts Act, 1952)?   ....

    If so, for how long?   ....

    for other reasons (e.g. under
    s.14 or S.28 of the M.C.A., 1952)?   ....

    If so, for how long?   ....

    Was he remanded on bail?   ....

    If not, where was he kept
    in custody?   ....

If the court making the order was a court of
Quarter Sessions, had the accused been committed by a magistrates' court under s.67 of
the Mental Health Act, 1959, *with a view to
the making of a restriction order?* (see p.1,
para.2).   ....

The offender

Other names by which the offender may
have been known (e.g. married woman's
maiden name, aliases etc.)   ....

Date of birth ....

Marital status (unmarried, married,
separated, divorced,. widowed,
cohabiting) ....

Number of children (state whether
legitimate or illegitimate) ....

The offender's employment

Present employment

a) nature of employment (e.g.
   building, farming, etc.)   ....

b) position (foreman, clerk,
   labourer, etc.)   ....

c) not employed because:
     i) unemployed   ....
     ii) retired   ....
     iii) housekeeping   ....
     iv) at school or other
       educational institution   ....
     v) maintained in hospital
       or other institution   ....

History of previous employment   (indicate nature of work and status of job)

Any other information   (e.g. about the behaviour, associates or relatives of the offender).

The Offence

Date of offence ....   **Classification code number** ....

Full description of offence and attendant circumstances (examples of information which
would be helpful are - age and sex of victim (if any), his or her relationship to the
accused, place of offence (e.g. park, street etc.), whether committed in the presence of
others, details of the offence itself (e.g. whether it was planned, whether the offender
tried to escape detection, etc.)

Other offences

How many offences did the court take into consideration?

        of a similar kind   ....

        of a different kind ....

        (please specify)

                ....

In what offences had the accused previously been detected?

How dealt with*	Court	Date	Type of offence
....	....	....	....
....	....	....	....

This should include, where possible, police cautions, action under any juvenile liaison scheme, recognisance, probation etc.

END OF POLICE SECTION

APPENDIX D

HOSPITAL SECTION

This part of the form should be completed by, or under the direction of, the responsible medical officer.

Surname .... Forename(s) ....

Hospital reference* ....

Type of order (i.e. s.60 or s.61 with or without s.65) ....

Names and designations of the two medical practitioners on whose evidence the order was made

....
....
....
....

* In order to enable Oxford University to follow up the subsequent history of each patient, a form of enquiry will be sent to the hospital at intervals. This reference, should, therefore, be that which will enable the patient's records to be most easily identified.

Statutory classification of disorder

(please tick the appropriate space)

The form(s) of mental disorder specified in the court order were:

Mental illness only ....

Mental illness and psychopathic disorder ....

Mental illness and subnormality ....

Mental illness and severe subnormality ....

Psychopathic disorder only ....

Subnormality only ....

Severe subnormality ....

Subnormality and psychopathic disorder ....

If any other form of disorder was specified in the court order, please specify it here ....

Clinical description of the disorder

(i) predominant disorder
(e.g. endogenous depression) ....

(ii) any associated mental disorder
(including personality disorders) ....

(iii) any associated physical disorders
or disabilities (e.g. cerebral damage) ....

(iv) any contributory environmental factors
(e.g. bereavement) ....

Other disorders

Was the patient, on admission,
suffering from any physical
disorder?   ....

Was the patient, on admission,
addicted to alcohol?   ....

If so, in what form?   ....

Was the patient, on admission,
addicted to drugs?   ....

If so, what drug?   ....

Previous medical history of patient

Has the patient previously been under
treatment or care for mental disorder,
whether as a result of committing an
offence or not?   ....

Period (with dates, if possible)   **Name of hospital or doctor**

....

....

....

Is there information about any other anti-
social or abnormal behaviour which has not
been the subject of criminal proceedings?   ....

Patient's freedom

What restrictions on the freedom of the
patient are considered neccessary at the
moment? (e.g., locked ward, nursing   ....
observation, free within hospital grounds,
under no restriction etc. Please be as   ....
specific as possible.)   ....

If the patient has already been discharged,
please give date and describe the circum-
stances.   ....

....

Social background of patient

Nationality and colour   ....
Place of birth   ....
Place of upbringing   ....
Religion   ....

At the time of the offence was the patient
living

                    with parents   ....
            with a brother or sister   ....
                    with a spouse   ....
              with children of own   ....
          with someone else (specify)   ....

If living with none of these,
was the patient living

                    in lodgings   ....
              in an institution   ....
                  (specify type)
              elsewhere (describe)   ....

Had the patient any siblings, if so how many?

        Older ....brothers ....sisters
        Younger .... brothers ....sisters

Has the patient any children, living or deceased, if so how many? ....

                Legitimate   Ages   Illegitimate   Ages
Sons   ....
Daughters   ....

Type of school attended ....

Educational level (e.g.
age at leaving school)   ....

Had the patient any training for
employment? (please specify)   ....

Has the patient ever served in the
Army, Navy or Air Force or a police ....
force?

If so, which?   ....

Is there any other information about the patient, the background or the offence which might be
of interest?

Date ....   Signature of responsible medical officer ....

                    END OF HOSPITAL SECTION

9736.264269.37880.2/63.S(P&D)L.

2. *The Six-month Questionnaire*

                                                      Room 325
                                                      New Bodleian Library
To the responsible medical officer   Oxford

Dear Doctor

                        Patients admitted under Part V
                        of Mental Health Act, 1959

As you know, a sample of offenders dealt with under Part V of the Mental Health Act, 1959 is being studied by the Reader in Criminology at Oxford; and we are advising him from the clinical psychiatric point of view. You were kind enough to let us have certain information about the patient named on the reverse side of this letter when he was first admitted to your hospital; and we are now writing to ask for your help in the process of follow-up, which is essential if the survey is to achieve its full purpose.

We would be very grateful if you would let us have the information asked for on the reverse side of this letter. It will, of course, be treated as confidential, and will on no account be used in such a way that it can be linked with an identifiable individual. (The forms returned by hospitals are kept in a locked room in the New Bodleian Library which is used only for criminological research.)

If the patient is still in, or on the books of, your hospital, a similar enquiry will be sent to you in six months' time. You will not be troubled in this way for an indefinite period: our sample is limited to patients admitted under Part V during a single year, and although we shall have to follow each of these up for some time afterwards, we shall not be asking you to go on reporting to us on subsequent admissions. We know that these enquiries add to the burden of your work, but the information which you can give us will be a valuable contribution to an important piece of research, and we should greatly appreciate your help.

                        Yours sincerely,

                        Patrick McGrath

                        Ian Skottowe

Code No.   Hospital Reference No.

Patient's surname   Patient's forename(s)

1. Please give, if possible, patient's national insurance No. ....

2. Is he still a patient in your hospital? ....

3. Has he (a) absconded? ....
            (b) been reclassified as a voluntary patient? ....
            (c) discharged himself? ....
            (d) been discharged on medical advice? ....
            (e) been given leave of absence (if so, for how long)? ....
            (f) been transferred to another hospital (if so, why)? ....
            (g) been taken into custody by the police for a further offence? ....
            (h) died? ....
            (i) ceased to be an in-patient in any other way? ....
    Please give dates, if possible, in whichever of these instances applies.

4. If he has ceased to be a patient, has the hospital had any subsequent contact with, or
    information about him? If so, what?

5. During his stay, is he known, or suspected to have committed any further criminal
    offence? If so, of what nature?

6. Has his conduct given rise to any other trouble, either in the hospital or in the locality?
    Has he fitted in with patients admitted in the normal ways, and with hospital arrange-
    ments generally?

7. Has there been any change in the restrictions which it has been found necessary to place
    on his freedom? (In the form which you sent us after his admission you said

8. What forms of treatment has he received? (If applied successively, in what order?)

9. If you are prepared to give an assessment of his response to treatment and any
    prognosis, this would be helpful:

10. If the patient has been discharged, to what address? (This is required simply to help in
    identifying the ex-patient subsequently in official records.)

3. *The Twelve-month Questionnaire*

Room 325
New Bodleian Library
Oxford

To the responsible medical officer

Dear Doctor

<u>Patients admitted under Part V
of the Mental Health Act, 1959</u>

As you know, a sample of offenders admitted to mental hospitals under Part V of the Mental Health Act, 1959 is being studied by the Reader in Criminology at Oxford, and we are advising him from the clinical point of view. You have already been kind enough to let us have information about the patient named overleaf, when he was admitted to your hospital and when we wrote to you six months after his admission.

We are now asking for information about those patients who had not left hospital at the time of the 'six-month' follow-up. This will be the last routine follow-up of the <u>hospital</u>* careers of this sample, although it may be necessary to clear up a few points of doubt in the occasional case. In spite of the extra work which these enquiries must cause, we have had a high degree of co-operation from hospital staffs in the course of this survey, and we hope that it will be possible for you to help us to complete this stage of the survey, by giving us the information asked for overleaf.

As usual, the information given will be treated as confidential, and will not be used in such a way that it can be linked with an identifiable individual. The forms returned by hospitals are kept in a locked room in the New Bodleian Library, which is used solely for criminological research.

Yours sincerely,

Patrick McGrath

Ian Skottowe

* Although for a period we shall try to trace any subsequent re-appearance of patients in central records of convictions or hospital admissions.

Code No.   Hospital Reference No.

Patient's surname   Patient's forename(s)

---

1. Please give, if possible, patient's national insurance No. ....

2. Is he still a patient in your hospital? ....

3. Has he (a) absconded? .... date? ....
       (b) been reclassified as a voluntary patient? .... date? ....
       (c) discharged himself? .... date? ....
       (d) been discharged on medical advice? .... date? ....
       (e) been given leave of absence (if so, for how long)? .... date? ....
       (f) been transferred to another hospital (if so, why)? .... date? ....
       (g) been taken into custody by the police for a further offence? ....
       (h) died? .... date? ....
       (i) ceased to be an in-patient in any other way .... date? ....
   Please give dates, if possible, in whichever of these instances applies.

4. If he has ceased to be a patient, has the hospital had any subsequent contact with, or information about him? If so, what?

5. During his stay, is he known, or suspected to have committed any further criminal offence? If so, of what nature? Please give dates, approximate if necessary.

6. Has his conduct given rise to any other trouble, either in the hospital, or in the locality? Has he fitted in with patients admitted in the normal ways, and with hospital arrangements generally?

7. Has there been any change in the restrictions which it has been found necessary to place on his freedom? (In your earlier report to us you said

8. What forms of treatment has he received? (If applied successively, in what order?)

9. If you are prepared to give an assessment of his response to treatment and any prognosis, this would be helpful. Is the likelihood of his being discharged in the near future substantial or negligible?

10. If the patient has been discharged, to what address? (This is required simply to help in identifying the ex-patient subsequently in official records.)

Bibliography

Dates are those of first editions unless otherwise indicated. Reports of committees and commissions will be found under the names of their chairmen; but readers who do not know the chairman's name can look up the committee in the index, where the chairman's name is given.

ADVISORY COUNCIL ON THE TREATMENT OF OFFENDERS,
  Report to the Home Secretary (1950) I, *Lancet*, 1120
ANONYMOUS *Sketches in Bedlam*, London, 1823
ANTEBI, R. 'Some Characteristics of Mental Hospital Absconders', in
  (1967) 113, *British Journal of Psychiatry*, 1087
ARNOLD, THOMAS *Observations on the Nature, Kinds, Causes and
  Prevention of Insanity* (2nd edition London, 1806), Leicester, 1782

BETHLEM ARCHIVES. The most important of these consist of
  Bethlem Sub-committee Books, 1709–1948. A series of bound
  volumes, containing the minutes of the Bethlem Sub-committee,
  whose main function was the weekly admission and discharge of
  patients. Lists of petitions read and patients admitted and discharged
  form the bulk of the entries, but the day-to-day administration of the
  hospital came to be dealt with here rather than in the Court of
  Governors (whose responsibility was for both Bridewell and
  Bethlem); so that by the nineteenth century any matters relating to
  internal management or to individual patients may be expected to be
  recorded here.
  Criminal Lunatic Books, 1810–1885. These volumes record every
  transaction of the Court or Committee relating to criminal patients,
  official correspondence, and quarterly returns to the Home
  Secretary. The latter are lists containing the name, date of admission,
  details of crime and sentence, and a note on the present state of
  health of every patient in the Criminal Department at each quarter
  from 1816–64, together with accounts for their maintenance.
  (A separate series of *Criminal Lunatic Sub-committee Minutes* was
  kept from 1816–25 (2 vols.), but these merely duplicate matters
  relating to the criminal patients already entered in the Bethlem
  Sub-committee Books.)
  Case Books and *Admission Papers* (chiefly warrants) were also kept
  separately for the criminal patients.

286 BIBLIOGRAPHY

BINNEY, J.: see Mayhew

BLAKE, G. (ed.) *The Trials of Patrick Carraher*, Edinburgh, 1951

BOTTOMS, A.E. 'Delinquency among Immigrants', in (1967) VIII, 4, *Race*, 357

BUCKNILL, J.C. and TUKE, D.H. *A Manual of Psychological Medicine*, London, 1858

BURT, Sir CYRIL *The Young Delinquent* (references are to the 4th edition of 1944) London, 1925

BURTON, ROBERT *The Anatomy of Melancholy*, Oxford, 1621

Cambridge Survey of Sexual Offenders: see Radzinowicz

CARR-HILL, R. A. 'Victims of our Typologies', in *The Violent Offender – Reality or Illusion?* Oxford Penal Research Unit Occasional Paper No. 1, Oxford, 1970

CARR-HILL, R. A. and CARR-HILL, G. A. 'Reconviction as a Process', in (1972) 12, *British Journal of Criminology*, 35

CHAYEN, E.: see Hammond

CHRISTENSON, C.V.: see Gebhard

CIBA FOUNDATION: see De Reuck

COCHRAN, W. G. 'Some Methods for strengthening the common χ^2 tests', in 10, *Biometrics*, 417.

COMMITTEES – see House of Commons, *Parliamentary Papers*, Dove-Wilson, Dunlop, Harris, Mountbatten, Priestley, Sellers, Streatfeild Walpole

COX, J. *Practical Observations on Insanity*, London, 1804

CRAFT, M. 'The moral responsibility for Welsh psychopaths', in *The Mentally Abnormal Offender* (edd. A.V.S. de Reuck and R. Porter) London, 1968

idem, 'The Balderton Psychopathic Unit'; 'The Causation of Psychopathic Disorder'; 'The Meanings of the Term "Psychopath"', in *Psychopathic Disorders* (ed. M. Craft) Oxford, 1966

Criminal Law Revision Committee: see Sellers

Criminal Statistics: see vol. 1 Bibliography s.v. *Judicial Statistics*

Cropwood Conference Proceedings: see West

DEPARTMENT OF HEALTH AND SOCIAL SECURITY *Hospital Services for the Mentally Ill* (obtainable from the Department) December 1971. *See also* Ministry of Health

DE REUCK, A.V.S. and PORTER, R. (edd.) *The Mentally Abnormal Offender, a symposium*, London, 1968

DOVE-WILSON, Sir JOHN (Chairman) *Report of the Departmental Committee on Persistent Offenders*, Cmd. 4090, HMSO, London, 1932

DUNLOP, JOHN (Chairman) *Mental Health Legislation: report by a committee appointed by the Scottish Health Services Council*, HMSO, London, 1958

EAST, W. NORWOOD and HUBERT, W.H. de B. *Report on the Psychological Treatment of Crime*, HMSO, London, 1939

EILENBERG, M.D. and WHATMORE, P.B. 'Police Admissions to a Mental Observation Ward', in (1962), *Medicine, Science and the Law*, 96

EMERY, D. (Chairman) *Report of the Working Party on Special Hospitals*, Ministry of Health, HMSO, London, 1961

Estimates Committee of the House of Commons: The Special Hospitals and the State Hospital (second Report 1967–8) HMSO, London, 1968

FENTON, G.: *see* Gunn

FENTON, NORMAN *Explorations in the use of group counseling in the county correctional program* (published for the Institute for the Study of Crime and Delinquency), Palo Alto, Cal., 1962

FERRERO, G.: *see* Lombroso

FEUCHTERSLEBEN, ERNST VON *Lehrbuch der artzlichen Seelenkunde*, Vienna, 1845 (tr. H.E. Lloyd and revised by B.E. Babington as *Principles of Medical Psychology*, London, 1847)

GAGNON, J.H.: *see* Gebhard

GEBHARD, P.H., GAGNON.J.H., POMEROY, W.B. and CHRISTENSON, C.V. *Sex Offenders: an analysis of types*, London, 1965

GENERAL REGISTER OFFICE *Census, 1961* (various volumes published from 1962) HMSO, London

GIBBENS, T.C.N., POND, D.A. and STAFFORD-CLARK, D. 'A Follow-up Study of Criminal Psychopaths', in (1959) 105, *Journal of Mental Science*, 108

GILCHRIST, ANNE *Mary Lamb*, London, 1837

GLADSTONE, HERBERT (Chairman) *Report from the Departmental Committee on Prisons*, C.7702, HMSO, London, 1895

GLOVER, EDWARD *The Roots of Crime*, London, 1960

idem, Searchlights on Delinquency, New York, 1949

GLUECK, BERNARD 'A Study of 608 Admissions to Sing Sing Prison', in (1918) 2, *Mental Hygiene*, 85

GODDARD, HENRY *Memoirs of a Bow Street Runner*, London, 1956

GOWERS, Sir ERNEST (Chairman) *Report of the Royal Commission on Capital Punishment 1943–53* (Minutes of evidence separately published at various dates from 1945 to 1953) Cmd. 8932, HMSO, London, 1953

GREENLAND, C. *Mental Illness and Civil Liberty: a study of Mental Health Review Tribunals in England and Wales*, Occasional Papers in Social Administration No. 38, London, 1970

GRIESINGER, W. *Die Pathologie und Therapie der psychischen Krankheiten*, Stuttgart, 1845 (tr. C.L. Robertson and J. Rutherford as *Mental Pathology and Therapeutics*, London, 1867)

GRIFFITHS, A. *Memorials of Millbank*, London, 1875

GRÜNHUT, MAX *Probation and Mental Treatment*, London, 1963

GUDMUNDSSON 'Epilepsy in Iceland: A Clinical and Epidemiological Investigation', in (1966) 43, *Acta Neurologica Scandinavica*, Supplement 25

GUNN, J.C. 'Epilepsy, Automatism and Crime', in (1971) 1, *Lancet*, 1173

idem, 'The Prevalence of Epilepsy among Prisoners', in (1969) 62, *Proceedings of the Royal Society of Medicine*, 60

GUNN, J.C. and FENTON, G. 'Epilepsy in Prisons: A Diagnostic Survey', in (1969) 4, *British Medical Journal*, 326

HAMMOND, W.H. and CHAYEN, E. *Persistent Criminals*, HMSO, London, 1963

idem, *see also* Walker, N.D.

Hansard's Parliamentary Debates, London, 1804–

HARRIS, S.W. (Chairman) *Report of the Departmental Committee on the Social Services in Courts of Summary Jurisdiction*, Cmd. 5122, HMSO, London, 1936

HARTLEY, DAVID *Observations on Man*, London, 1749

HEALY, W. *The Individual Delinquent*, London, 1915

HEINROTH, J.C.F.A. *Lehrbuch der Störungen des Seelebens*, Leipzig, 1818

HEMSI, L.K. 'Psychiatry Morbidity of West Indian Immigrants', in (1967) 2, *Social Psychiatry*, 95

HENDERSON, Sir DAVID *Psychopathic States*, London, 1939

HOBBES, THOMAS *Leviathan*, London, 1651

HOME OFFICE *People in Prison, England and Wales*, Cmnd. 4214, HMSO, London, 1969

HOOD, W.CHARLES *Suggestions for the Future Provision for Criminal Lunatics*, London, 1854

House of Commons Committee Report on the State of Madhouses in England with Minutes of Evidence 1815 (1814–15) *Parliamentary Papers* IV

House of Commons Official Reports: Standing Committees, Session 1958–9, Vol. IV *Mental Health Bill: Street Offence Bill*

HOWARD, JOHN *The State of the Prisons in England and Wales*, Warrington, 1777

HOWELL, T.B.: *see* Vol. I Bibliography s.v. *State Trials*

HUBERT, W.H.de B.: *see* East

JAMES, WILLIAM *Varieties of Religious Experience*, London, 1902

JOHNSON, SAMUEL *A Dictionary of the English Language*, London, 1747

JONES, KATHLEEN *Mental Health and Social Policy 1845–1959*, London, 1960

Judicial Statistics (England and Wales): see Vol. I Bibliography

JUUL-JENSEN, PALLE 'Epilepsy', in (1964) 40, *Acta Neurologica Scandinavica*

KIEV, A. 'Psychiatric Morbidity in West Indian Immigrants in Urban Group Practice', in (1965) 3, *British Journal of Psychiatry*, 51

KOCH, LUDWIG *Die Psychopathischen Minderwertigkeiten*, Ravensberg, 1891

KRAEPELIN, EMIL *Psychiatrie: Ein Lehrbuch für Studierende und Aerzte*, (8th edition 1909–13, 3 vols.) Leipzig, 1896
KRAFFT-EBING *Psychopathia Sexualis*, Stuttgart, 1886 (7th ed. tr. G.C. Chaddock, Philadelphia, 1892)

LAMB, CHARLES: *see* Talfourd
LEIGH, DENIS *The Historical Development of British Psychiatry*, Vol. I, 18th and 19th century, Oxford, 1961
LOMBROSO, CESARE and FERRERO, G. *The Female Offender*, London, 1895

MACMILLAN, H.P. (Chairman) *Report of the Royal Commission on Lunacy and Mental Disorder*, Cmd. 2700, HMSO, London, 1926
MAUDSLEY, HENRY *Responsibility in Mental Disease*, London, 1872
MAYHEW, H. and BINNEY, J. *The Criminal Prisons of London and Scenes of Prison Life*, London, 1862
MEYER, ADOLF, *Collected works of* (gen. ed. E.E. Winters) 4 vols., Baltimore, 1950–2
MINISTRY OF HEALTH
Memorandum on Parts I, IV–VI and IX of the Mental Health Act, HMSO, London, 1960
Mental Health (Hospital and Guardianship) Regulations 1960 (S.I. 1960 no. 1241) HMSO, London
Mental Health Review Tribunal Rules 1960 (S.I. 1960 no. 1139) HMSO, London
Statistical Report Series,
    No. 4: Psychiatric Hospitals and Units in England and Wales: in-patient statistics from the Mental Health Enquiry for the years 1964, 1965, 1966 (pub. 1969):
    No. 11 ditto for the year 1968 (pub. 1970):
    No. 12 ditto for the year 1969 (pub. 1971); HMSO, London
MOEBIUS, P.J. *Die Nervosität*, Leipzig, 1882
MORE, Sir THOMAS *The apologye of syr T. More, Knyght*, London, 1533
MOREL, BENEDICT AUGUSTIN *Traité des dégénérescences physiques, intellectuelles et morales de l'espèce humaine, et des causes qui produisent ces variétés maladives*, Paris, 1857
MORRIS, PAULINE *Put Away: A Sociological Study of Institutions for the Mentally Retarded*, London, 1969
MOUNTBATTEN Earl (Chairman), *Report of the Inquiry into Prison Escapes and Security*, Cmnd. 3175, HMSO, London, 1966
MULLINS, CLAUD *Crime and Psychology*, London, 1943

NICOLSON, D. 'A Chapter in the History of Criminal Lunacy in England', in (1877) 23, *Journal of Mental Science*, 165
NOYES, A.P. *Modern Clinical Psychiatry*, (references are to the 1934 edition) Philadelphia, 1927

ØDEGAARD, Ø. 'Emigration and Insanity', in (1932), *Acta Psychiatrica et Neurologica*, Supplement 4, Copenhagen

U

O'DONOGHUE, E.G. *The Story of Bethlehem Hospital from its Foundation in 1247*, London, 1914
Old Bailey Sessions Papers: see Vol. 1 Bibliography

PAILTHORPE, GRACE W. *Studies in the Psychology of Delinquency* (Medical Research Council Special Report Series 170) London, 1932
idem, What we put in Prison and in Preventive and Rescue Homes, London, 1932
Parliamentary Papers
  Report of the Inspectors appointed under the provisions of the Act 5 & 6 Will. IV c.38 to visit the different prisons of Great Britain (1836) *Parliamentary Papers* XXXV
  Report of the Penal Servitude Commissioners (1878–9) *Parliamentary Papers* XXXVII–XXXVIII
  Return of 2 addresses of the Honourable the House of Commons, 5 July 1836 and 12 May 1837 *Parliamentary Papers* XLIV
  see also: Estimates Committee, House of Commons Committee, Walpole
PARTRIDGE, RALPH *Broadmoor: A History of Criminal Lunacy and its Problems*, London, 1953
PERCY, Lord (Chairman) *Report of the Royal Commission on the Law relating to Mental Illness and Mental Deficiency 1954–7*, Cmnd. 169, HMSO, London, 1957
PINEL, PHILIPPE *Traité medico-philosophique sur l'alienation mentale, ou la manie*, Paris, 1801 (tr. D. David as *A Treatise on Insanity*, London, 1806)
PINSENT, R.J.F.H. 'Morbidity in an Immigrant Population', in (1963) 1, *Lancet*, 437
POMEROY, W.B.: *see* Gebhard
POND, D.A.: *see* Gibbens
PORTER, R.: *see* De Reuck
PRICHARD, JAMES COWLES *The Different Forms of Insanity in relation to Jurisprudence*, London, 1842
idem, Treatise on Insanity and other Disorders affecting the Mind, London, 1835
PRIESTLEY, J.C. (Chairman) *Report of the Departmental Committee on Sexual Offences against Young Persons*, Cmd. 2561, HMSO, London, 1925
Prison Commission (from 1963 the PRISON DEPARTMENT OF THE HOME OFFICE) *Annual Reports*, HMSO, London
  Medical Inspector's Report for 1889–90 in the Annual Report of the Prison Commissioners and Directors of Convict Prisons
PRIVY COUNCIL, *Acts of: see* Vol. 1 Bibliography s.v. *Nicholas*
PSYCHIATRIC REHABILITATION ASSOCIATION *The Mental Health of East London* (cyclostyled 1968), London, 1966

RADNOR, Lord (Chairman) *Report of the Royal Commission on Care and Control of the Feeble Minded 1904–1908*, HMSO, London, 1908
RADZINOWICZ, Sir LEON (ed.) *Sexual Offences*, London, 1957

RAPOPORT, R.N. *Community as Doctor*, London, 1960

Reports: see Dove-Wilson, Dunlop, Emery, Gladstone, Gowers, Harris, Macmillan, Percy, Priestley, Radnor, Sellers, Streatfeild, Walpole: *see also: House of Commons Committee, Parliamentary Papers* and *Prison Commission*

ROGERS, P.G. *The Battle of Bossenden Wood: the strange Story of Sir William Courtenay*, Oxford, 1961

ROLLIN, H.R. *The Mentally Abnormal Offender and the Law*, Oxford, 1969

Royal Commissions: see Gowers, Macmillan, Percy, Radnor

Select Committees on Lunatics: see Walpole

SELLERS, Sir FREDERICK (Chairman) *Criminal Procedure (Insanity)*, (Third Report of the Criminal Law Revision Committee) Cmnd. 2149, HMSO, London, 1963

SHEPPARD, EDGAR *Memorials of St. James's Palace*, 2 vols., London, 1894

SILBERMAN, R.M. 'CHAM: a classification of psychiatric states', in (1971) *Excerpta Medica Monographs*

SIMON, FRANCES H. *Prediction Methods in Criminology* (a Home Office Research Unit Report) HMSO, London, 1971

SMITH, M. HAMBLIN *The Psychology of the Criminal*, London, 1922

SPARKS, RICHARD F. 'The Decision to Remand for Mental Examination', in (1966) 6, *British Journal of Criminology*, 6

STAFFORD-CLARK, D.: *see* Gibbens

State Trials: see Vol. I Bibliography

STEER, D.J.: *see* Walker, N.D.

STREATFEILD, Sir GEOFFREY (Chairman) *Report of the Interdepartmental Committee on the Business of the Criminal Courts*, Cmnd. 1289, HMSO, London, 1961

STUART, ALAN 'The Comparison of Frequencies in Matched Samples', in (1957) X, 1, *British Journal of Statistical Psychology*, 29

TALFOURD, THOMAS NOON *The Letters of Charles Lamb, with a sketch of his life*, London, 1837

TAYLOR, F.H. 'The Henderson Therapeutic Community', in *Psychopathic Disorders* (ed. M. Craft) Oxford, 1966

THOMAS, D.A. 'Comment on R. v. Molyneaux', [1968] *Criminal Law Review*, 229

idem, 'Sentencing the Mentally Disturbed Offender', in [1965] *Criminal Law Review*, 685

TUKE, D.H.: *see* Bucknill

WALK, A. and WALKER, D.L. 'Gloucester and the beginnings of the R.M.P.A.', in (1961) 107, *Journal of Mental Science*, 603

WALKER, NIGEL DAVID 'A Century of Causal Theory', in *Frontiers of Criminology* (edd. H.J. Klare and D. Haxby) Oxford, 1967

idem, *A Short History of Psychotherapy*, London, 1957

idem, *Crimes, Courts and Figures*, London, 1971

U*

WALKER, N.D., HAMMOND, W.H. and STEER, D.J. 'Repeated Violence', [1967] *Criminal Law Review*, 465

WALPOLE,S.H. (Chairman) *Reports from the Select Committees on Lunatics*, 11th April, 1859 (Minutes of evidence only) (1859) *Parliamentary Papers* 111; 27th July, 1860 (Report and further minutes of evidence) (1860) *Parliamentary Papers* XXII

WEBB, SIDNEY and BEATRICE *English Prisons under Local Government*, London, 1922

WEST, CHARLES *Lectures on the Diseases of Infancy and Childhood*, London, 1848

WEST, DONALD J. *The Habitual Prisoner*, London, 1963

idem (ed.) Psychopathic Offenders (Papers presented to the Cropwood Round-Table Conference) Cambridge, 1968

WHATMORE, P.B.: *see* Eilenberg

WHITLOCK, F.A. 'Prichard and the Concept of Moral Insanity', (1967) 1, 2, *Australian and New Zealand Journal of Psychiatry*, 72

WINSLOW, FORBES *Recollections of Forty Years,* London, 1910

WODDIS,G. 'Depression and Crime', in (1957) 8, *British Journal of Delinquency*, 81

WOODSIDE, MOYA 'Probation and Psychiatric Treatment in Edinburgh', in (1971) 118, *British Journal of Psychiatry*, 561

WOOLF, P. GRAHAME 'The Back Door: Discharge by Operation of the Law after 28 Days' Absence', in (1966) 6, *British Journal of Criminology*, 59

WOOTTON, Baroness 'Diminished Responsibility–A Layman's View', in (1960) 76, *Law Quarterly Review*, 224

idem, Social Science and Social Pathology, London, 1959

Working Party on Special Hospitals: see Emery

Index

Cases and statutes (including important sections of the Mental Health Act, 1959) will be found in the tables of cases and statutes respectively. Place-names are included in this index only if they are of importance (e.g. Grendon but not Whitstable Bay). Commissions, Committees and similar bodies are indexed as such (e.g. 'Royal Commission on Lunacy and Mental Disorder') with a reference to the chairman's name so that they can be found in the bibliography (referred to as 'bib.'). Appendixes are referrred to by letter: e.g. 'A'. For references to volume I the index to that volume should be consulted.

---

abnormality
  anti-social behaviour and mental, 225
  applied to homosexuality, 83
  belief in congenital origin of, 209
  blurring of distinction between normality and, 225
  degrees of, 205-6
  suggested use of 'mental abnormality' in 1959 Act, 219
absconding, absconders
  absence of hue and cry after, 165
  by dangerous offenders, 238
  by restriction order patients, 195, 196-8
  by schizophrenics, 26, 27, 176
  by subnormals, 176
  criminal sophistication and, 33
  defined, 165
  diagnosis and, 37
  euphemisms for, 165
  for the necessary period, 26, 164, 165
  from borstal, 166
  from ordinary hospitals, 33, 95, 166-7
  from prison, 166
  from special hospitals, 166
  harm done by, 241-2
  previous convictions and, 37
  psychopaths, 176, 258
  rates, 160, 176, 184-5
  reconviction and, 31, 196-8

  subsequent emergency admission and, 258
  successful, 31
  temporary, 184-5
  transferred prisoners and, 27, 33
  see also discharge by operation of the law
acquisitive offences
  by female offenders, 128
  by male offenders, 127
  connection with disorder, 126-9
  current offence and diagnosis, 127, 128
  defined, 126
  diagnostic groups and, 127, 128, 144, 229
  in Oxford survey, 126-9
  reasons for, 152
  with violence, 132
acquittal by reason of insanity, 2, 3, 19
addiction, *see* alcoholism, drug abuse
Adler, Alfred, 56, 64
administrative pressures influencing legislation, 58-9, 238
admissions to hospital
  compulsory: conditions governing, 83, 86; female, 147; for observation, 70, 82, 85, 109; for treatment, 70, 82, 85; judicial orders not required, 68; of informal patients, 163

Date		Issued to
		JACK SCARRA
NOV 27 1995		